I AIN'T MARCHING ANYMORE

Dissenters, Deserters, and Objectors
to America's Wars

CHRIS LOMBARDI

NEW YORK
LONDON

Requests for permission to reproduce selections from this book should be made through our website: https://thenewpress.com/contact.

Published in the United States by The New Press, New York, 2020
Distributed by Two Rivers Distribution

ISBN 978-1-62097-317-2 (hc)
ISBN 978-1-62097-318-9 (ebook)
CIP data is available

The index for this book is available at http://aintmarching.net/index

The New Press publishes books that promote and enrich public discussion and understanding of the issues vital to our democracy and to a more equitable world. These books are made possible by the enthusiasm of our readers; the support of a committed group of donors, large and small; the collaboration of our many partners in the independent media and the not-for-profit sector; booksellers, who often hand-sell New Press books; librarians; and above all by our authors.

www.thenewpress.com

Book design and composition by Bookbright Media
This book was set in Adobe Garamond and Electra

Printed in the United States of America

10 9 8 7 6 5 4 3 2 1

To Ben Lombardi, who learned in the U.S. Navy that books open up the world. Wish you had lived to see this one in print.

CONTENTS

CHAPTER ONE

1754 to 1803

By the time Jacob Ritter's unit marched, one could smell the blood as far as Brandywine Creek.

Chadds Ford, Pennsylvania, was beautiful on September 11, 1777. Its succession of wooded hills made for a steep climb, both for the British and for the insurgent Continental Army. In between hills, level ground allowed for fierce fighting. "I mentioned, that the Enemy were advancing and had began a Canonade," George Washington wrote to Congress mid-battle. "I would now beg leave to inform you that they have kept up a brisk fire from their Artillery ever since."[1]

Jacob Ritter, a young member of the Pennsylvania militia, watched as the active-duty "standing troops" took casualties. "The bombshells and shot fell round me like hail, cutting down my comrades on every side, and tearing off the limbs of the trees like a whirlwind. The very rocks quaked, and the hills that surrounded us seemed to tremble with the roar of the cannon."[2] Ritter's unit stood ready, sweating somewhat in the summer heat.

By nightfall, hundreds were dead on both sides. The Army's newest officer, the Marquis de Lafayette, was shot in the leg as his platoon withdrew. It was then that the Pennsylvania militia units were "ordered to march forward to the charge. Our way was over the dead and dying, and I saw many bodies crushed to pieces beneath the wagons, and we were bespattered with blood."

The troops all carried muskets, and some of Ritter's platoon-mates fired into the distance. Ritter did not fire his; he had already decided, without telling anyone, that to do so would be wrong.

Raised Lutheran, Ritter knew that there were people who did not believe in war. As a child, he had sneaked into a Quaker meeting house. Now a member of the Pennsylvania militia, he had been seized just that morning by the un-Lutheran conviction that "it was contrary to the Divine Will for a Christian to fight." As he stood completely still amid mortars at Chadds Ford, "I supplemented [*sic*] the Almighty that if he would be pleased to deliver me from shedding the blood of my fellow-creatures that day, I would never fight again."[3] As the fighting subsided, "no orders were given to use our small arms; and thus, I was enabled to rejoice, that though I was provided with sixty cartridges, I did not discharge my musket once that day." The rest of Jacob Ritter's life was shaped by that moment of conscientious objection, a term invented by the Quakers a century before.

Ritter's vivid descriptions of the Battle of Brandywine have long been quoted by historians, most of whom see Ritter's battlefield pacifism as yet another casualty. Lafayette biographer Sarah Vowell writes, "It says something about the ugliness of September 11, 1777 that this boy woke up a Lutheran and went to bed a Quaker."[4] It also says a lot about the country that was busy being born, with young Ritter no one's subject, but a citizen.

At every touchstone in the American Revolution, soldiers claimed the newish role of *citizen* by exercising their right to dissent. In doing so, these new Americans were also defining what that role meant, and for whom. They were drawing on the new republic's soup of ruling ideals—a mix of Calvinist stubbornness, Quaker slow-moving radicalism, Enlightenment liberalism, and the insistent pressures of commerce. Chief among those civic covenants was the concept of "volitional allegiance," drawn from John Locke's theory of government by contract.[5] Locke's books were bestsellers in the colonies, with excerpts reprinted as pamphlets and filling newspaper pages.[6]

Colonists also devoured Thomas Paine's *Common Sense* and the endlessly published work of Benjamin Franklin, believing along with the latter that "in free governments, the rulers are the servants and the people their superiors and sovereigns."[7] Rather than being a subject by birth, as in Europe, each member of a community was seen as a citizen, a person who voluntarily acceded to government power in exchange for the protection of certain rights. That "social contract" felt like a birthright to most ordinary people, including those in the new country's armed forces. Then, as now, most soldiers came from working-class families, and both officers and enlisted took seriously the "all men are created equal" assertion of the Declaration of Independence. They prized the "inalienable rights" listed therein.

Jacob Ritter found most crucial an individual right of conscience not confined to any one religion, and spent most of the rest of his life elaborating on that 1777 moment. Captain Daniel Shays, appointed as such by General Washington after the Boston Massacre, joined other veterans a decade later for a famous Massachusetts rebellion, asserting his right to seek redress against postwar economic inequality. Colonel Matthew Lyon, who as one of Vermont's famed "Green Mountain Boys" had been part of the colonial Army's first victories, prized his freedom of speech as both a member of Congress and a newspaper publisher, even facing imprisonment for insulting the president in one of his papers.

While in uniform, these new citizens formed committees, petitioned their officers, and took their grievances to local elected officials. Others were insubordinate to officers, refused direct orders, or spent day after day on sick call; in the most drastic step, some deserted their commands entirely. (Desertion does not always equal dissent, but it usually signals something deeply wrong.) Still others, members of pacifist religious sects, when conscripted refused to follow orders or to arm themselves, often enduring imprisonment and even torture.

As early as 1754, Continental militias were unafraid to dissent when called up to assist the British Army in the local front of the Seven Years' War (called the French and Indian War in North America). In New England, where civic activities like speaking at meetings and filing petitions were part of daily life, colonial soldiers formed committees, in addition to those petitions, and occasionally went on strike.[8] These soldiers' democratic actions extended to the way units were structured, including the right to serve only under their chosen commander. One company presented a letter in 1756, explaining why provincial soldiers would refuse to be commanded by British officers: "the Privates Universally hold it as one part of the Terms on which they Enlisted that they were to be Commanded by their own Officers and this is a Principle so strongly Imbib'd that it is not in the Power of Man to remove it."[9]

By calling their government employer an "Executor in Trust," charged with fulfilling mutually agreed upon contracts, these young men were helping to determine the nature of citizenship in the new country. They had already claimed the word "citizen" for themselves; for the rest of the eighteenth century, soldier-dissenters would define what that title included.

Like most new Americans, soldiers were immigrants, many of whom had gotten their start as indentured servants. Matthew Lyon was fourteen years old when he arrived from Ireland in 1758, one of many "redemptioners" agreeing to a term of service in exchange for passage. After his three-year term was up, Lyon apprenticed with numerous merchants and later moved to the unincorporated New Hampshire Grants (now called Vermont). He scraped together enough money to buy some acreage there and married the niece of local militia leader Ethan Allen.

In 1774, eight years past his time as an indentured servant, Lyon chose another form of service and formed a militia when "British encroachment on our rights was raising the spirit of resistance."[10] His neighborhood "hired an old veteran to teach us discipline, and we each of us took the command in turn, so that every one should know the duty of every station."

That Vermont crew was too small to engage Britain directly. The ambitious Lyon then approached his father-in-law, a well-known maverick recently freed from a British jail, about joining Allen's Green Mountain Boys. In 1775, Lyon and Allen helped wrest a prized New York State garrison from the British in the Battle of Ticonderoga, the war's first clear victory. "Eighty-five of us took from one hundred and forty British veterans the fort Ticonderoga, [seizing] the artillery and warlike stores."[11] The capture took less than a day, but the Green Mountain Boys knew the main struggle was in Boston. They quickly funneled to the Massachusetts militiamen most of the 78 cannons and 115 flintlock muskets they had seized, joining the fight against the British occupation. Those munitions, Lyon exulted, "drove the British from Boston" at the Battle of Bunker Hill.

As Lyon's Vermont troops left Fort Ticonderoga, newly minted Massachusetts Lieutenant Daniel Shays arrived at the recently conquered fort to stand guard. Like Lyon, Shays was of Irish ancestry, though it was his father, Patrick, who had first arrived as an indentured farmhand. Daniel, the second of eight children, was born just outside Boston in 1747.

The prospects offered by fast-expanding Western Massachusetts were well known, the sparsely populated region now rich with a new wave of non-slaveholding "yeomen" farmers. In 1772, after years as an itinerant laborer, Shays married and bought sixty-eight acres in Pelham, in the state's northwest. He soon joined the local militia, known as the Committee of Safety, and was already a sergeant in 1775, when the Boston Massacre prompted the formation of the Continental Army. At Bunker Hill, Shays' regiment of the Army's 25th Infantry held off a British advance long enough for civilians to leave the war zone.

Shays, described by New York colonel James Lyman as "not only a patriot and soldier, but an upright and honorable man of upright character," would go on to fight in other storied battles of the war. In the fall of 1777, soon after Jacob Ritter's epiphany at Brandywine, Shays' bravery at the Battle of Saratoga would earn him a ceremonial sword from the Marquis de Lafayette. Shays would later sell that sword when his paltry soldier's wages made it hard to support his growing family. The inadequate pay made soldiers like Shays and Lyon suspect that those in power, from state legislators to General Washington, saw them as somehow disposable. Dissent seemed their only recourse.

Dissent was in the air when Matthew Lyon woke up on July 4, 1776, in Jericho, part of "Upper Canada" (now northern Vermont). That morning, encamped with his unit, Lyon heard shouts from outside his tent: "Turn out! Turn out!" The twenty-seven-year-old Lyon opened his eyes and reached for his weapon. What he saw when he opened the door of his hut is what he had feared most: not the red coats of the British, nor the five hundred armed Native Americans reportedly massing at the next hill. Just the uniformed backs of his own men, still in formation as they deserted their positions and left the camp.

Lyon could hardly blame them. This was not the mission that he had promised his men when he got them to reenlist to fight the British. He had not recruited them to guard land owned by some rich men they did not know. As Lyon told Congress years later, the powerful General Horatio Gates had ordered his platoon sent to Jericho to guard land held by absentee landlords. Unlike the farmers Lyon's own Ethan Allen had once planted in this same territory, these landlords were speculators who hoped to make a killing, not a living. "The soldiers considered themselves sacrificed to the interest of those persons who had bought the crops for a trifle, and wanted to get our party to eat them for a trifle."[12]

Neither Lyon nor his soldiers could afford to buy corn at the owners' war-inflated prices. The young soldiers, personally recruited by Lyon, might or might not have even heard of the local rich men found among this land's absentee owners, such as William Bingham or John Cleves Symmes, perhaps instead recognizing their company names, like the Connecticut Company or the Symmes Purchase.[13] When the platoon learned that five hundred Algonquin and Iroquois warriors were preparing to attack those same lands, their sense of being used in a commodities gamble was at least as strong as their fear of being scalped. Why, they asked, should they risk dying for speculators' profit?[14] Nonetheless, they had orders.

Lyon told his men that he would rather suffer death than the dishonor of court-martial, but "all entreaties were ineffectual. As they were going to take the canoe to the other side, they insisted on [the officers] going [with them], and threatened violence if we refused."

All, including Lyon, were then court-martialed in Ticonderoga and cashiered to service elsewhere; Lyon, though humiliated, managed to wrangle a promotion, becoming paymaster for the regiment that had led the capture of Ticonderoga. In Vermont, the Green Mountain Boys ignored the court-martial and welcomed Captain Lyon home. His father-in-law even secured back pay for Lyon's Jericho service, which by then was sorely needed.

Lyon, Ritter, and Shays were typical members of the new country's armed forces, and as members of immigrant families were far from Thomas Jefferson's republican ideal of a force of wealthy yeomen farmers. For most soldiers, the far starker economic realities were clear in the way their Army was constructed and managed.

Designed by Congress for a total strength of twenty thousand, the Continental Army was about half that size in January 1776. The state militias, where service was theoretically mandatory, still needed new recruits to supplement junior officers, for whom militia service was more a social and political club. But many who had been excited to sign up in 1775 now preferred to find and pay someone to serve in their place; John Adams declined militia service over and over, citing his sickly constitution.

A now-familiar phenomenon emerged, where the likes of Adams hired the lower class to take risks in their place. Recruiters offered bounties (which ballooned as the war dragged on, from $1 in 1775 to $16 in 1778).[15] Sometimes a wavering recruit's stray mark was the signature on an enlistment contract.[16] Such recruiting swept up a diverse set of skills: the Pennsylvania Line, whose 17,000 men and 143 infantry companies made up one-fifth of the entire American fighting force, listed in one of its regiments twenty-three shoemakers, nineteen weavers, twelve carpenters, ninety-three farmers, and forty-two other trades, some simply marked as "laborer."[17]

In addition to brand-new immigrants like Matthew Lyon, recruiters zeroed in on hungry teenagers, indentured servants, and former slaves.[18] Congress tried to prevent what we know now as human trafficking: the *New-York Reader* and *Weekly Mercury* on January 17, 1776, published the requirement "that the Recruiting Officers be Careful to Enlist [sic] only sound, able-bodied men of at least 16 years of age . . . the soldiers will be Paid ten Shillings per. . . . No bought indentured servants be employed on board the Fleet or in the Army of the Colonies, without the consent of their Masters." As it turns out, such unpropertied young men were even more keen to uphold their democratic rights than were their officers.

If former indentured servants were hot prospects, a larger pool of potential recruits was the far bigger population of enslaved African Americans. Recruiters were competing with the British for Black recruits, especially after the royal governor of Virginia promised immediate manumission to all who crossed over to the loyalists.[19] Washington aide John Laurens fruitlessly pleaded with his father, Henry, a South Carolina delegate to the Continental Congress, to release his "able bodied men Slaves, instead of leaving me a fortune." Laurens dreamed of his own Black regiment, wherein "I am sure of rendering essential Service to my Country." Though Henry Laurens refused his son's request, many governors on both sides were willing to free slaves in exchange for service.[20]

Both Rhode Island and Connecticut raised entire regiments of African American soldiers, promising them equal payment with white soldiers in addition to their freedom. A 1778 strength report of the entire Army showed 755 "Negroes" in fifteen different infantry brigades.[21] In the earliest stages of the war, many commanders recruited members of the local indigenous population, employing Native Americans as scouts, interpreters, and medics.

The word "citizenship" is not included in mentions of the latter troops, but it is unlikely to have been forgotten by those who enlisted. One Pennsylvania captain said of New England battalions, "Among them there is the strangest mixture of Negroes, Indians, and Whites, with old men and mere children, which together with a nasty, lousy appearance makes a most shocking spectacle."[22]

Mingled quietly among the regulars were a fair number of women. Earning an Army pension was the nurse Mary Ludwig Hays, usually called "Molly Pitcher," and Margaret Corbin, who after her husband's death wielded his cannon in the battle to defend Fort Tryon in Washington Heights. Scores of other women fought in male uniforms, their presence unnoticed.[23] As with African American and Native recruits, their very presence in the war constituted a form of dissent, a demand for citizenship not yet offered by their government.[24]

The right to dissent was taken for granted by both militia and army enlistees, who kept close their belief in the sacred rights of the common man. They saw the enlistment contracts signed by free men as near-sacred documents with obligations on both sides. And they acted quickly when colonial governments failed to live up to their side of the bargain, either by attempting to retain soldiers past their commitment or by failing to feed, clothe, and equip them as promised. In those early days, they often signed to serve under a specific officer: when then-Lieutenant Daniel Shays recruited twenty men from Western Massachusetts for the Continental Army in 1775, their enlistment was explicitly "conditioned upon [Shays] being appointed captain."[25]

George Washington, the troops' Virginia-born commander-in-chief, was no fan of this sense of agency among eighteenth-century grunts, their sense of themselves as full citizens and their chosen officers as "Executors in Trust." Washington famously called the New England militias "a nasty lot." He acted to curb that sense of agency after the Continental Army started to lose battles, following those early successes at Fort Ticonderoga and Princeton.

After bruising losses at Manhattan's Kip's Bay and Monmouth, New Jersey, commanders of the fourteen Continental brigades and their allied militias could only content themselves with how many British had died. Washington blamed the nasty lot he had inherited from the militias, where desertion rates were between 20 and 50 percent. Washington brought in former Hessian generals to train his troops and stiffened the Laws of War: newly increased penalties for insubordination included a threat of execution for desertion and mutiny. Judge Advocate General Henry Tudor declared, "When a man assumes the soldier he lays aside the citizen, and must be content to submit to a temporary relinquishment of some of his civil rights."[26]

Among the rights being relinquished, the most problematic was that of individual conscience, as young Jacob Ritter was soon to discover. After enlisting when his Lutheran pastor spoke of "the propriety and necessity of coming to the defense of our country against her enemies," Ritter joined the militia and spent two days with his platoon building a battery against the British assault. No other choice was available: he was not a Quaker or a Mennonite or in one of the other "peace churches" opposed to all wars.

The peace churches were already familiar to General Washington. According to a 1760 narrative compiled by the Society of Friends, when Washington was still a colonel in the British Army, he saw quiet determination, rather than fear, in the eyes of Quakers watching an execution who knew that they could be next. The man who would soon command the new nation's army remarked with respect, "All he asked of them in return was that if ever he should fall as much into their power as they had been in his, they would treat him with equal kindness."[27]

By 1775, the civilian laws guiding command behavior toward such men formed a diverse colonial patchwork. Records kept by the peace churches contain the names of scores of conscientious objectors (the term itself coined in 1650) who were beaten, imprisoned, and had their usually minimal property seized by local militia and Continental Army commanders alike.

Rhode Island's charter guaranteed that none "shall be persuaded in his, their conscience or consciences . . . that he nor they cannot nor ought not to train, to learn to fight, nor to war, nor kill any person or persons." Ritter's Pennsylvania, whose founder meant specifically to create a haven for oppressed sects like the Quakers, was the most explicit in declaring members of such churches exempt from militia service.

By 1777, when Jacob Ritter showed up for muster, the peace churches mostly handled the conscription issue by paying fines to the states, enough to hire a substitute for the objector's service. Some had to fight to be excused from service regardless: one young Quaker conscript had his claim dismissed by his "presiding officer," who told him that "you have not the cootermants" (meaning accoutrements, the extreme plain dress of many Friends). Upon seeing written documentation, "the officer now called for a shears that he might trim him: and so he cut off his capes and his lapels and sich a hair tail he had behind, and them said to him, 'now you may go, now you look more like a Quaker.'"[28]

Then as now, military authorities struggled with these strange people, tending not to believe testimonies like that of Jacob Ritter, dictated by no official church doctrine. To those watching him hold onto his never-fired musket, Ritter's principled stillness may have looked like cowardice, but Ritter, who as a Lutheran had not even had the choice to hire someone, felt he had no recourse on September 11, 1777.

Ritter had always been intrigued by what he knew of Quakers, and knew on that fateful day at Brandywine that conscientious objectors existed. The day after the battle, Ritter woke up overwhelmed, still thinking in religious terms: "A sense of my forlorn condition covered my mind. I knew I had sinned in entering into the war, and no man going to execution could have felt more remorse." Then, Ritter behaved as many objectors have since: he fled the camp and took refuge in the nearest village, only to be captured by the enemy and taken to prison in Philadelphia.

Being captured by British soldiers terrified Ritter, a native Dutch-German speaker who did not understand English when spoken quickly. Ritter remembered the prison well. "During the first five days of our confinement, most of us had nothing to eat, and many died from want." The prison, on Walnut Street near Washington Square, was being managed by the "infamously cruel Commissioner Cunningham," described as "such a wretch" by local scribe Joseph Fanning: "Numbers of them died of hunger and cold, and were daily carried out and interred in Potters' Field."[29] Ritter was also having flashbacks of the day of the battle at Brandywine, and "feeling myself as a poor worm of the dust." He spent a lot of time crying and praying.

Despite the ill treatment, Ritter was a twenty-year-old with all four limbs, and thus the provost-captain "sought to entice me into English service, and for that end offered me a whole handful of English guineas." Ritter responded the way he had on September 11—with dissent. "I firmly refused, and then they beat me most cruelly until I was much bruised." Finally, Ritter's family reached out to a loyalist judge who had been born Quaker; a week later, a set of trusted local Quakers came to help him return home. Afterward, Ritter fell ill with fever and near-debilitating weakness, signs of the "ague" (malaria) he had contracted in prison.

It would take a full recovery and another few years before another of Ritter's pacifist visions compelled him to "find the Bank meeting." That meeting was held in a hundred-year-old Quaker meeting house on Front Street; Ritter remembered that "opening the door, [I] found a number of people assembled and sitting in solemn stillness . . . it seemed as if a window had been opened in a dark room, and let in the bright sunshine." After a few more visits in which "sweet peace covered my Spirit, and I felt as if I could have sat there till night," Ritter began to separate from the Lutheran church. After the war he would be known as a high-profile Friend, who traveled the region sharing his story.

The rights of soldiers like Ritter would continue to vex Washington's army. But their numbers were few, compared to those dissenting because they were underfed and under-clothed. Neither Congress nor the states wanted to admit the war would last long by budgeting for it. Troop-created civic action was near-inevitable as the war continued, rendering the new nation's currency worthless and enriching merchants, who appeared to play with food supplies. The combination demeaned soldiers' paltry wages further. In 1779, the 1st Artillery of Philadelphia confronted the moneymakers head on during the Fort Wilson Riot, after Congress ignored six months of quieter civic action.

These soldiers had been recruited to fight the British, or at least to protect their own communities. Their sense of citizenship sprang from ideas that dated back to at least the seventeenth century, when British Whig thinker Algernon Sidney exalted a citizenship based on labor and personal valor. Both militiamen and Continental Army troops were well schooled in republican tracts (such as Thomas Paine's *Common Sense*) and were serious about their rights. They also took seriously the "all men are created equal" section of the Declaration of Independence. The new citizens were also, sadly, enthusiastic participants in what has come to be called "settler colonialism," claiming Native land as their birthright.[30]

The tide of the war was turning in 1779, with colonial victories in Philadelphia and at Stony Point, a town north of New York City. But suppliers could still create and exacerbate food shortages. With crops burned, shipping damaged, and state currencies subject to intense inflationary pressure, many farmers and craftsmen found themselves in deep debt or worse. Rather than release the grain for flour, shipping magnate and congressman Robert Morris left grain stores in their ships at the harbor to keep prices high.

The shortages enraged those who had fought at Brandywine, Princeton, and on the Indian front, who resented the wealthy families able to buy their way out of militia service. The 1st Artillery formed a Committee of Privates, which wrote the State Assembly on May 12, "Many of us are at a loss to this day what Course or Station of Life to adopt to Support ourselves and Families," they began, adding that "the Midling and the Poor will still bear the Burden, and either be ruined by heavy Fines, or Risque the starving of their Families, whilst themselves are fighting the Battles of Those who are Avariciously working to Amass Wealth with the Destruction of their Community."

As their plea for price controls went unheard, the Germantown and Philadelphia committees met repeatedly. On October 4, Captain Ephraim Faulkner urged "All Militiamen" to march with him toward the home of the wealthy Congressman James Wilson. The next day, scores poured into the city, gave three cheers at the City Tavern on Second Street, and marched toward the fifty-year-old Mercantile Exchange. Local police arrested twenty-seven militiamen; townspeople—called mobs by loyalist newspapers—then surrounded the jail and courthouse.

The militiamen spent only a night in jail. Afterward, citing the "apprehensions of great distress among poor house-keepers in this city, from the high price of Flour," Pennsylvania governor Joseph Reed asked the assembly to order the distribution of one hundred barrels, with a preference being given "to such Families as have performed Militia duty." Similar revolts followed.

As 1779 ended, Daniel Shays broke down and sold—for about $200 in today's dollars—the ceremonial sword that the Marquis de Lafayette had given to him after the Battle of Saratoga. Newspapers noticed the sale and lambasted Shays, though he was hardly the only colonial soldier to sell off his medals and other precious metals when bills came due. With bills unpaid for most of the war and six children to feed, Shays and his Massachusetts farm were deeply in debt. Shays' wife, Abigail, sometimes took out a loan from Shays' creditors to pay household expenses.[31]

Shays resigned his commission after he was injured in early 1780 (how is unclear). As he arrived at home in Pelham, the town was abuzz about the state constitution just finalized by the state legislature. Many were outraged by provisions limiting political participation for those without substantial property; people like Shays and his peers were now ineligible for nomination in state elections. The concept of government by and of the people may have seemed like just talk, as faint as the concept of citizenship.

While Ritter, Lyon, and Shays were starting their postwar lives, the war was far from over, and was being fought by enlisted personnel whose contracts lasted "for three years or the duration of the war." The Pennsylvania Line, one of the largest, spent 1780 at Morristown, New Jersey, its soldiers' wives and children in separate tents. Many had not been paid in over a year. Their "Mutiny in January" started on New Year's Day 1781, after "a day of customary felicity."[32]

At first, the rebellion may have seemed spontaneous: Benjamin Franklin's *Pennsylvania Packet* noted that "an extra proportion of rum was served out to the soldiers" for New Year's Eve, and shots fired just before midnight left one mutineer dead and an officer injured. Before the day was over, the platoon had seized all four of the line's cannons and begun to march toward Philadelphia.

By then, the mutineers had formed a Committee of Sergeants, which went to Princeton to tell their superiors what they wanted. Defecting to the British, they told General Anthony Wayne, "was not their intention, and that they would hang any man who would attempt it."[33] The sergeants' demands were simple and specific: a year's back pay, adequate clothing, and discharges for those whose enlistments had exceeded three years. When British spies made an offer to the mutineers, the sergeants instead took the spies prisoner, prompting the *Packet* to call the men heroes and not traitors.

General Washington offered to join Wayne at Princeton, but then thought better of it, instead writing a "Circular Letter" to Congress warning that there might be more desertions if they kept ignoring his pleas for more funds. In Princeton, Wayne made a deal with the committee: discharges for three-year enlistees, amnesty from prosecution for the rest, and agreed-upon compensation, including 160 acres of land.[34] After those mutinies, Washington cracked down, starting with one led by New Jersey troops. The following spring, when elements of the Pennsylvania Line rebelled again, Washington agreed with Wayne's orders to have two deserters shot, including the rebellion's leader, "Macaroni Jack."

That summer, the British would surrender at Yorktown. But the battles within the new nation's military would continue.

On June 17, 1783, hundreds of soldiers amassed in Philadelphia, where independence had been proudly declared only seven years earlier. They surrounded meetings of both Congress and the state legislature, demanding compensation. Washington had already tried to warn against sending a million unpaid troops home to raise trouble: "I fix it as an indispensable [sic] Measure, that previous to the Disbanding of the Army, all their accounts, should be compleately [sic] liquidated and settled, and that every person shall be ascertained of the Ballance due to him; and it is equally essential, in my opinion, that this Settlement should be effected, with the Army in its collected Body, without any dispersion of the different Lines to their respective States."[35] Where the funds would come from was not clear. The War for Independence had enriched some and impoverished others.

By 1786, the new republic was struggling with its finances (a fact now popularly known due to recent interest in Treasury Secretary Alexander Hamilton). Now that the fight against the British was over, large landowners in the South and banking families up North felt empowered to demand payment for states' official war debt and the considerable personal debt accumulated by soldiers' families. This situation was hard on both former loyalists, who now had to contend with the new order (and pay for its war), and those who had done most of the fighting. "From South Carolina to the District of Maine, farmers banded together to fight the official machinery for the collection of taxes and debts."[36] Veteran-farmers resisted foreclosure of property, broke up sheriffs' sales of delinquent estates, and rescued neighbors from debtors' prison.

If authorities persisted in their duties, they courted harassment. In Washington County, Pennsylvania, an angry crowd "cut off one half of [the] hair" of a luckless tax collector and "cued the other half on one side of his Head," voicing revenge on the wolf who normally fleeced the sheep. Through such collective action, militants aspired to shape public policy.

In Pennsylvania, dissenting farmers were "Angry Yankees." In Maine, they called themselves "White Indians," a reference to the region's now-dispossessed Iroquois.[37] In Massachusetts, where Daniel Shays returned after eight years of war, the already-brewing insurgent movement took on the name first used by an older colonial-farmers' rebellion: the Regulators.[38]

Shays' formerly prosperous home state of Massachusetts was now in depression, its crops burned and shipping revenue eliminated. Taxes averaged far more than most farmers earned in a year: $50 a year for every man, woman, and child, upwards of $200 for every family. During the war, many farmers and manufacturers had suffered losses due to their inability to sell their goods to the British, which forced them to go into debt to meet consumer demand. Their cost of living jumped further when Massachusetts imposed new taxes to pay the war debt. By the mid-1800s, hundreds of the state's craftsmen and small farmers, increasingly unable to pay their debts, found themselves in debtors' prisons.

Shays' 251-acre farm was among those in distress. He was sued twice by creditors between 1780, when he returned from the war, and 1786, when debts forced him to sell half of the farm. While he never went to debtors' prison, such incarceration was an everyday reality in Worcester County. Ninety-four citizens out of 104 brought to court in 1785 for debt were incarcerated, as were eighty the following year. Luke Day, one of Shays' Springfield militia colleagues, was incarcerated for much of 1785 due to mortgage debt. In the fall of 1785, Shays and Day went to a meeting in Hatfield, where vets and non-vets alike agreed that it was time to assert their right to "regulate" the local economy.

Shays and Day served on the Committee of Seventeen, under whose aegis the Regulators repeatedly marched on courthouses and broke up debt courts. The Regulators practiced with drills at Day's and Shays' farms. "I earnestly stepped forth in defense of this country, and liberty is still the object I have in view," one soldier wrote to the *Connecticut Mercury*, just before the Regulators attempted to storm the region's armory in Springfield.

Finally, Governor James Bowdoin ordered the committee's capture and arrest, asking President Washington for help. As 1787 began, four thousand state militia troops were called up by the governor and Secretary of War Benjamin Lincoln. Most of the latter troops hailed from coastal towns far from the Regulators' western farms, and were too young to have served in the war against Britain.[39]

Before the final confrontation, Luke Day wrote the Regulators' last communique, published in the *Hampshire Gazette*. He demanded that the militiamen withdraw on behalf of the "body of the people assembled in arms, adhering to the first principles in natural self-preservation." Shays then led a platoon of veterans, moving slowly with their guns down, but General Lincoln ordered the state militia forward, driving the badly outnumbered Regulators to disperse. Shays fled to Vermont, a state so new that it had no extradition treaty.

These rebellions were precursors to the 1787 Constitutional Convention. Shays' Rebellion revived long-simmering debates about revision of the Articles of Confederation, the document governing the way the country was put together; President Washington had discussed the farmer rebellions with many signers of the Declaration of Independence, who joined him in Philadelphia that September to create a new constitution. Many came with ideas: James Madison had drafted a "Virginia Plan," whose bill of rights spelled out what was contained in "life, liberty and the pursuit of happiness."

By the end of 1787, Daniel Shays had built a fortified village in Vermont for himself, and was asking Governor John Hancock for a pardon. Jacob Ritter was a busy shoemaker/preacher, converting others to the Society of Friends while traveling to sell his shoes to southern Quakers. And Matthew Lyon was a Vermont legislator and Federalist publisher. All three would have followed the convention as it was reported in the newspapers—including Lyon's own *Fair Haven Gazette*.

Lyon likely noticed, if too politic to mention, how few of the fifty-five delegates had themselves seen military service, including his soon-to-be-enemy John Adams, with his well-known medical militia waivers. Yes, there were storied generals, between Commander-in-chief Washington, Pennsylvania's John Armstrong Sr. and Jr., and Pierce Butler, who had mobilized southern patriots to retake Charleston from the British. But to find any of lower ranks, one must dig into the fine print of delegates' biographies, such as Connecticut's Thomas Mifflin, Army Quartermaster General until 1780. The convention was a gathering of politicians and intellectuals, from Alexander Hamilton to Benjamin Franklin. Delegates were bankers, landowners, owners of small factories; some were slave owners. These were elite citizens, meeting to define how their government would interact with the non-elite.

Among the delegates' few truly shared beliefs was that they did not want to put soldiers in charge. Very few topics consumed the convention more than that of how to simultaneously defend the new nation and avoid oppressive standing armies like those of the British Empire. Lyon and Shays likely nodded at the Second Amendment's mention of a "well-regulated militia," though Shays may have also remembered with pain the militia ordered against his men in Springfield.

Jacob Ritter would have been more interested in the rest of the amendment, which set guidelines for those militias' future. Where in that scheme were the likes of Ritter, or other doves in uniform, like the Quakers admired by the young Colonel Washington? "This was called the land of liberty, and yet we are going to make a respectable class of citizens pay for a right to a free exercise of their religious principles?" asked Aedanus Burke, a South Carolina delegate who had been deeply affected by his own militia service.

The writers of the Constitution listened, at least at first. James Madison's first draft of the Second Amendment contained explicit language to protect the rights of conscience: "The right of the people to keep and bear arms shall not be infringed, a well-armed and well-regulated militia being the best security of a free country; but no person religiously scrupulous of bearing arms shall be compelled to render military service in person." This "conscience clause" survived weeks of negotiations before it was jettisoned, its implied national jurisdiction over state militias unacceptable to Southern legislators already angered by the Quakers' explicit antislavery position. Even Burke, the pacifists' unlikely ally, said of the Friends' antislavery petitions: "It gives particular umbrage that the Quakers should be so busy in this business. That they will raise up a great storm against themselves appears . . . very certain." The centuries to come would not contradict him.

Quakers' interest in the Constitution's final draft was matched by other constituencies, all of whom showed up at the state ratifying conventions that followed. Their sessions were notoriously brutal, from Vermont to Virginia. Lyon covered the proceedings of his home state in his newspaper. Daniel Shays was still a fugitive in Vermont, living in the fortified village he had built for his family, but some of his fellow Regulators were aggressive participants at the Massachusetts convention. On February 3, 1788, Madison wrote to Washington, "We have in the Convention 18 or 20 who were in Shay's army [sic]," many of whom opposed the draft as written.[40]

Then John Hancock, recently elected governor of Massachusetts, brokered the "Massachusetts Compromise," in which the bill of rights drafted by Madison was added to the published Constitution. Hancock was also in the process of negotiating a pardon for Daniel Shays, which became final in 1788.[41] No explicit mention was made, in either the compromise or the pardon, of Shays' role in jump-starting the nation's Constitution.

While Shays was free to go back home and congratulate his peers on their victory, Matthew Lyon was soon to test that Constitution's boundaries, even if it was from a jail cell. The issue was one that the Constitution's authors thought they had just settled: who determines when the nation goes to war.

By 1798, Lyon was midway through his first term as Vermont's representative to the U.S. Congress, which he had begun by boycotting Congress' annual trip to the White House for the State of the Union. Lyon's Federalist news sheets included the *Fair Haven Gazette* and the *Scourge of Aristocracy and Repository of Important Political Truths*, the latter full of scorn toward the new president, John Adams. Such over-the-top rhetoric was common in eighteenth-century newspapers, but Lyon was known sometimes as "the asp." His rhetoric only escalated with the naval duel with France known as the Quasi-War (1798–1800). Meanwhile, Quaker physician/militiaman George Logan tried to prevent the ongoing naval sorties from becoming all-out war.

Logan did so by going to France unasked by the president or secretary of state, leading to Logan's arrest when he returned from Paris with a peace offer. The result was the eponymous Logan Act, which banned such freelance diplomacy—part of the administration's effort to tamp down dissent against Adams' undeclared war. The president was especially hoping to crack down on the famously aggressive press, such as Lyon's anti-Adams *Scourge*.

The Alien and Sedition Acts, of which the Logan Act was an amendment, made it a crime to criticize the president. Fines of up to $2,000 were set for any person convicted of uttering, writing, or printing any "false, scandalous and malicious statement against the Government of the United States; or either House of the Congress of the United States, with intent to defame . . . or to bring them . . . into contempt or disrepute." The Logan Act called Logan's freelance diplomacy traitorous. Despite the latter, George Logan was not the first war hero jailed for sedition. That distinction belonged to Col. Matthew Lyon.

Lyon's October 1798 arrest on Sedition Act charges was for an editorial in the *Scourge* that accused Adams of "ridiculous pomp, foolish adulation, and selfish avarice." Lyon served a year in jail in Vergennes, Vermont, during which time he was re-elected to Congress from his sixteen-by-twelve-foot cell. By the time of his release at the end of 1799, the Quasi-War was over, with a new treaty signed by the two countries early in the New Year.

Soon enough, Lyon could act out against the man who had put him in prison. When the Electoral College deadlocked in 1800 between Adams' chosen successor, Aaron Burr, and Thomas Jefferson, Lyon's vote helped break the tie and put Jefferson in the White House.

By 1800, Daniel Shays was living quietly in upstate New York, and Jacob Ritter was as well known in Quaker circles as Shays and Lyon were in politics. All three would soon participate in the fledgling veterans' pension system, having helped start the debate about how to best compensate soldiers and veterans.

Shays' pension was $20 a month. As for Ritter, whose application was made after his death, his funds were awarded to his mother, Barbara Ritter (his wife having died a few years prior). Matthew Lyon's pension, also $20, was awarded in Kentucky, the state he would next represent in Congress. By then, Lyon had already been compensated for his service with one of those land grants so often promised to members of the Continental Army. By accepting it, Lyon became an active participant in America's foundational injustice, the theft of land from indigenous peoples.

Just as he had eagerly claimed citizenship with all its inalienable rights, Lyon accepted his government's proffer of "empty" land as further evidence of that citizenship. That bargain's terms are made clear in his pension certificate, awarded in 1819. Inserted by hand above its notation of Lyon's prior residence as Vermont, careful handwritten script adds "He Was with Ethan Allen at the Surprise at Ticonderoga in May 1775." This award, recorded in Kentucky's Revolutionary War records, does not mention that his land in western Kentucky had once been part of Lower Shawnee Town, the capital of a multi-tribal confederacy that pre-revolutionary French ambassadors called Le Republique.[42] When Lyon chose it in 1800, on the advice of fellow Revolutionary veteran Andrew Jackson, Le Republique had long since been dissolved by disease and war. But for several decades, the land Lyon chose had been prime Shawnee hunting grounds.

From Lyon's perspective, according to the criteria set by none other than Thomas Jefferson about excess land, his new home was on land that was not being well used. They failed to acknowledge that this land was hunting grounds shared for generations. Jefferson's policy had long treated Indians like wayward children in need of discipline, finding some tribes more "civilized" than others. Military necessity had often made that discipline harsh, as in 1779, when General John Sullivan's forces cut a swath through the Northeast, with commanders and soldiers referring only to "those damn Indians." Along the way, America lost Simon Girty, who deserted his western Pennsylvania militia.

Simon Girty, a "half-breed" raised by Seneca Indians after his home was burned in 1750, rejoined white society twenty years later, becoming a scout and interpreter at Fort Pitt, in Pittsburgh. As an adult, he was known as a "white Indian," someone who never shunned native dress or the language of his childhood.[43]

In 1778, Girty began to doubt his homecoming after being ordered to march with five hundred militiamen deep into the Cuyahoga River Valley, part of the notorious "Squaw Campaign" under General Edward Hand. The Pennsylvania militiamen, after they failed in their assignment to find British munitions, took their frustration out on the nearest villages. Hand reported that one camp attacked by the troops held "four women and a boy . . . of whom [only] one woman was saved."[44] After seeing how his peers regarded all Indians, Girty ended his scattered Army career, fought on the side of loyalists, and died decades later in Canada.[45] He would be the first of numerous Native soldiers to question their own involvement in U.S. forces.

A few years later, now-President Jefferson accelerated the country's expansion with the 1803 Louisiana Purchase, when he agreed to help Emperor Napoleon Bonaparte pay off some of France's war debt in exchange for lands that nearly doubled the new nation's size. What Jefferson had secured was the right to wrest those lands from their current inhabitants.

It was now the job of every American serviceman to help settlers expand America, sometimes joining in, as Lyon had. When Congress began debating another war with England, most knew that it would be fought on Indian land. Some knew that they would recruit on their side some former slaves and Indians. Some even recognized that it would be unjust not to extend to the latter the rights for which they had fought.

During the first war for independence, soldiers asserted their own citizenship; during the next, they would start to test how far that citizenship extended, and to whom. As the nineteenth century proceeded, soldier-dissenters would keep pushing those limits, until the words war, peace, and dissent acquired entirely new meanings.

CHAPTER TWO

1803 to 1844

AFTER TWO GENIAL SOLDIERS OFFERED William Apess another drink, he stopped asking why.

In the spring of 1813, fifteen-year-old Apess had spent most of the previous two months running. He was done with being an indentured servant, done with being tormented by a Connecticut farmer who thought he could batter an African-Pequot boy at will. But his Bronx boarding house was not much better, he told the recruiters. "By then I had acquired many bad practices. . . . I took some more liquor and some money, had a cockade fastened to my hat, and went off in fine spirits." Not that Apess was particularly interested in the new war: "I could not think why I should risk my life, my limbs, in fighting for the white man, who had cheated my people out of their land."[1] Still, William Apess signed and reported to basic training that very day. Before he knew it, he was on Governor's Island, watching as a captured deserter was executed before his eyes.

William Apess was one of the first soldiers whose dissent can be traced to America's foundational injustice, a racism enacted variously in chattel slavery and in the destruction of the country's first inhabitants.

Apess was recruited in 1813, a year after Congress declared the War of 1812, often called America's second War of Independence. Apess' initial enthusiasm about enlisting in the Army of white America fit the expansionist aims of a war that, for all its geopolitical context and diplomatic spittle, ended only with the United States' agreement to stop abusing Native Americans.

U.S. Indian policy had become more nuanced since the brutal settlement wars that had killed Apess' ancestors. In a conflict that was especially bloody, even for that era, Connecticut Puritans had fought a dozen tribes, which all fought under the charismatic Metacom (also known as King Philip). That struggle climaxed in a 1676 massacre at Mystic, Connecticut, in which the Puritans lost only one thousand men while killing more than three times that number. "The Englishman's fight" disgusted even the Puritans' Indian allies, the Narragansett, who called their tactics "too furious, and slays too many men."[2]

A hundred years later, King Philip's War was a legend in the life of young William Apess. Born to a Pequot father and a "Negro" mother near the Pequot reservation in Massachusetts, at age six Apess was rescued by town officials from his abusive grandparents and "bound out" as a pauper eligible for indenture. At nine, he would sneak away for Sunday worship at a Hartford Methodist church, joining Connecticut Mohegans long since "Christianized" by missionaries. By the time the two recruiters from Fort Columbus found him in May 1813, he had fled Connecticut, gained passage on a ship headed for Philadelphia, and was struggling to pay rent at a boardinghouse in the Bronx.

Apess did not record anything said by those Army recruiters regarding his skin color. But the recruiters were likely aware of the potential of soldiers of color, given the all-Black "Canadian Corps" that had helped the British at Niagara, and the "motley set [of] blacks, Soldiers and boys" still on Lake Erie with Admiral Perry. In any case, even if he was near-homeless, Apess was in good health and could read and write. "They thought that I would answer their purpose, but how to get me was the thing."[3]

They chose a simple solution, Apess remembered: demon rum. "They treated me to some liquor, and when that began to operate, they told me what a fine thing it was to be a soldier." Apess had no idea that "my enlistment was against the law," doubly as both a minor and an indentured servant. He had misgivings even as he signed the contract, but he went as instructed to Fort Columbus, where "I engaged in many bad practices" and "took comfort in beating on an old drum."

Soon after arrival, Apess was chastened/traumatized by the execution of

Patrick Byrne, who had been found guilty of "highly mutinous conduct," including desertion.[4] "I cannot tell how I felt when I saw the soldiers parade and the condemned clothed in white, with bibles in their hands, come forward," Apess wrote. "An officer then advanced and raised his handkerchief as a signal for the platoon to prepare to fire—he then made another for them to aim at the wretch who had been left kneeling on his coffin; at a third signal the platoon fired, and the mortal essence of the offender in an instant was in spirit-land."[5]

Byrne's public humiliation and execution had a specific educational purpose: to discourage such behavior once the troops were deployed in Canada. Insubordination had characterized prior invasions, despite Thomas Jefferson's previous assurances that the whole thing would be "just a matter of marching."[6] During General William Hull's infamous first attempt from Detroit, on July 12, 1812, two full brigades of Ohio militiamen refused to cross the river, their reasons equal parts "We're not allowed" and "We're not obligated." One platoon, commanded by Major Thomas van Horne, "retreated in disorder by squads."[7] *Disorder* appears to have been a synonym for insubordination, given that it was conducted squad by squad. Faced with a combined force of British troops and Shawnee warriors, Hull surrendered at Detroit.

Even when the war's tide began to turn, with a series of naval victories over the British and triumph by disciplined Ohio troops, some soldiers refused to be part of the invasion. In May 1813, the Vermont militia only reported for duty at Plattsburgh "at the point of a bayonet." Half of the soldiers under General Henry Dearborn's command refused to advance north from Lake Champlain. At Sackett's Harbor, near Lake Ontario, newly recruited troops—described by General Jacob Brown as "raw troops unaccustomed to subordination"[8]—fired quickly and then ran away when the enemy attacked.[9]

Apess had already gone AWOL once by the time his 46th Infantry arrived in Plattsburgh. Transferred to the infantry from the fife-and-drum corps, he reread his contract: "As I had only enlisted for a drummer, I thought that this change by the officer was contrary to law, and that the bond thus broken, liberty granted me." He left camp to search for his father, but was soon forced back to join the march to Canada. "During this dreary march, the officers tormented me by telling me that it was their intention to make a fire in the woods, stick my skin full of pine splinters and after having an Indian pow-wow over me, burn me to death."

After the 46th moved north, its spring 1814 assault on Montreal had little glory. Fifteen hundred Vermont militiamen refused to cross the border, and Apess saw his peers sliced by cannon:[10]

> We had not time to remove the dead as they fell. The horribly dis-figured bodies of the dead—the piercing groans of the wounded and the dying—the cries of help and succor from those who could not help themselves—were most appalling. I can never forget it.[11]

Despite his command's racist harassment, Apess' narrative of the succes-sive invasions reflects the sensibility of a hardened soldier. He even mocked his own general, who had ordered a retreat: "Thus were many a poor fellow's hopes of conquest and glory blasted by the timidity of one man."

When the troops returned to Plattsburgh, they learned that the British had also burned much of Washington, D.C., brushing aside the mix of Army regulars and militia at Bladensburg, Maryland, the latter having "run most disgracefully."[12] The Maryland defeat came courtesy of the Colonial Marines, an all-Black battalion recruited by a pair of British admirals who had adver-tised widely and welcomed hundreds of enslaved men to their training camp on the Chesapeake.

Apess' command found a potential positive aspect in the Washington fire: instant re-enlistment. "'Now,' says the orderly sergeant, 'the British have burnt up all the papers at Washington, and our enlistment for the war among them, we had better give in our names as having enlisted for five years.'" Apess never did so, having more in common with the deserting Maryland militia, or even the Colonial Marines, than with the sergeants presuming his obedience.

By then, dissent on the part of ground troops had moved from gossip to center stage, mostly because of the war's Southern endgame—including troops who defied the charismatic Andrew Jackson.

Jackson, a Tennessee landowner, was major-general and the commander of Tennessee's forces. In this capacity, it was Jackson's job to enact the country's Indian policy, whether he liked it or not.

When one captain in the militia of neighboring South Carolina raised an armed party aimed at finding Choctaw villages "over our boundary" and "breaking them up," Jackson did not bring his own troops into that fight, instead requesting the captain's court-martial.[13] He ordered the troops under his direct command to set a better example: "For an officer thus to violate the law and hazard the peace of our country . . . must require a speedy corrective." As the years went on, however, Jackson became more interested in eliminating hostile native populations than in protecting their treaty rights.

After 1810, when Shawnee leader Tecumseh gathered more than fifteen tribal representatives at Tippecanoe (now northern Michigan), Jackson feared there would be increasingly vicious "Indian wars," with Britain and Spain both aiding Indians in their battle against the upstart new nation. U.S. Indian agents described Tecumseh's 1811 trip south to his mother's Creek nation, including Tecumseh's now-infamous invocation: "Burn their new dwellings! Destroy their stock! This is our land, and they must not be allowed to enjoy it!" The Creeks then split into two factions, with "Red Creeks" attacking both white settlers and their assimilationist "White Creek" brethren.

In May 1812, after a Red Creek raid near his home county, Jackson demanded "the perpetrators, at the point of the Bayonet, and—if refused— that we lay their Towns in ashes."[14] Two months later, his militia gave a whoop of enthusiasm when he asked, "Are you ready to follow your general to the heart of the Creek nation?" The opportunity to do so was magnified by a new war with England, declared in response to British naval insults, which promised to increase his army's size too.

But the war against the Creeks was costly. More than a quarter of Jackson's 2,500 troops died in the war against the Creeks, even in victory at the Creek stronghold of Talladega. Morale plummeted at Fort Strother, the fort built on the bones of Talladega; Jackson watched the desertion of two brigades, both the one-year volunteers and his beloved militia. "There is grate talk about the 10th of December," one wrote. "I do not think that Genl Jackson intends to discharge us that day but I still think we shall go home."[15]

By the end of 1813, Jackson counted "two hundred and ninety-nine dead on the field of the thousands he had commanded. Nearly as many had deserted. "I was compelled [to stop] by a double cause—the want of supplies and the want of cooperation from the East Tennessee troops," he wrote. In an oft-recounted episode, Jackson stood shakily on his weapon. "If two men will remain with me, I will never abandon this post," he said, eventually convincing 109 men to stay. Though he released the rest, the final battles of that campaign included far harsher penalties for insubordination. When young recruit John Woods left his post and talked back to an officer, Jackson ordered his troops to watch as Woods was shot by his fellow soldiers with seventy-caliber rifles, just as William Apess had witnessed in New York a year earlier.

Mutinies soon ended at Jackson's fort. What remained was a hardened, disciplined group that followed orders—right up to the climactic battle of Horseshoe Bend, which killed three thousand Creek and sent the rest fleeing to the south. By then, the war against Britain was two years old, and Jackson was well on his way to making official Jefferson's threat "to shut our hand [and] crush them."

Jackson's victory lap in New Orleans demonstrated both the general's bigotry and his canny ability to ignore it for military necessity. After seeking New Orleans' support by warning that British were bringing "black assassins," Jackson turned around and placed ads in Black newspapers, promising freemen that if they joined his militia as "Sons of Freedom," they would receive the same cash and (Indian) land that white troops received. In January 1815, while a peace treaty for the war was being finalized in Ghent (in present-day Belgium), Jackson faced the British and their Cherokee allies with "a ragtag force of Creoles, Baratarian pirates, free blacks, Indians, and assorted militia from Louisiana and neighboring states."[16] Those forces were not immune to dissent; four hundred Kentucky volunteers deserted mid-battle, leaving the left flank of the city unprotected.

Those volunteers could have had left because they had heard peace had been declared, but it was more likely a mix of hunger, confusion, and the fear of being mutilated.

Navy Secretary Daniel Patterson's report on the battle was the lead story in February's *National Intelligencer*, in an issue that could have been subtitled "Desertion Special." On page two, the paper reported the exoneration by a court of enquiry of Brigadier General William H. Winder for his failure at Washington the previous summer. The military court instead blamed Winder's hastily convened troops, most of whom "were unknown to General Winder, and but a small number of them had any military training or experience." These new recruits had thus entered the battle "much fatigued" even before the mass desertions.

Two pages of the sixteen-page daily were taken up entirely with lists of deserters from Andrew Jackson's southern campaign. Those lists compete for space with the commonplace evidence of the country's racial hierarchy: advertisements offering rewards for the return of escaped slaves.

The Treaty of Ghent, the 1815 agreement that ended the war, addressed (albeit weakly) the country's foundational injustices. Agreeing that "the Traffic in Slaves is irreconcilable with the principles of humanity and Justice" and that they would work to end overseas import of Black human beings as chattel, the United States pledged to end "hostilities with all the tribes or nations of Indians with whom they may be at war at the time of such ratification; and forthwith to restore to such tribes or nations, respectively, all the possessions, rights, and privileges which they may have enjoyed or been entitled to" before the war. The latter promise, though a beloved cause of New Englanders, was not a priority in a Washington, whose hero was Andrew Jackson.

By war's end, twenty thousand American soldiers had died, with thousands more injured. For those who remained in uniform, peace with England did not mean their jobs were done. There was still two-thirds of the continent claimed by its original inhabitants, with settlers depending on soldiers to help defend against incursions, despite the treaty signed at Ghent. There was talk in Washington of conscripting still more men, despite New England legislator Daniel Webster's question, "Where is it written in the Constitution, in what article or section is it contained, that you may take children from their parents, and parents from their children, and compel them to fight the battles of any war, in which the folly or the wickedness of government may engage it?"[17]

As America's first war of choice ended, its peace treaty with Britain contained a promise to stop fighting the country's Natives—a promise broken most memorably by the war-hero-turned-politician Andrew Jackson. As commander-in-chief, Jackson would spark the removal of Indian tribes to points far west. Meanwhile, slavery was growing more entrenched, as America's other original sin provoked dissent and awaited its own war.

Uniformed dissent did not end after 1815. In private journals and public campaigns, both officers and ordinary soldiers raised questions about expansion, the federalization of the armed forces, and the sometimes brutal conduct seen during the war. Questions of compensation abounded, including at the Army's new military academy at West Point, whose students were as prepared by its Ivy League–style education to debate policy and question authority as to assume it.

One West Point graduate, Ethan Allen Hitchcock, spent his half-century military career agonizing over the policies he was ordered to implement. William Apess, last seen at the 1813 invasion of Montreal, resurfaced as a Methodist "Indian preacher" who dissented via storytelling as he fought for the rights of Native Americans in the still-new nation. Meanwhile, Reverend Noah Worcester, whose New Hampshire militia had fought beside Matthew Lyon in the Battle of Bennington, began preaching against war in 1812, and in 1815 started the American Peace Society.

Worcester, descended from New Hampshire Congregationalist ministers, had heard debates over war and peace since he was a child, including what he later called "the Quaker opinion" that all war was immoral. None of this interfered with his youthful "delight with military exercises and parade," including being "chosen captain of a company of boys." In 1774, Worcester joined his father in the local militia, despite a self-admitted soft side—"I was easily moved to tears by any affecting objects or circumstances."

In the Battle of Bennington, young Worcester misunderstood an order to retreat and ran toward the bewildered but well-armed redcoats, almost suffering capture by the British before he turned sixteen (just as Andrew Jackson had).[18] He witnessed hand-to-hand fighting with British, Hessian, and Iroquois forces: "The bayonet, the butt of the rifle, the sabre, the pike were in full play; and men fell, as they rarely fall in modern war. . . . The enemy retreated on every side, leaving their dead, and many of their wounded on the field."[19] After the war, Worcester followed his father into ministry, and found he had moved closer to "the Quaker opinion."

In 1812, Rev. Worcester angered the Salisbury, Massachusetts, town elders by opposing the new war. "On the day appointed by [President James] Madison for national fasting, I delivered a discourse on the pacific conduct of Abraham and Lot to avoid hostilities between their herdsmen. The President had called on ministers of the gospel to pray for the success of our arms. This I could not do." Soon he was on his way to Boston, hired by *The Christian Disciple*, a magazine of the new Unitarian faith.

His new position gave Worcester more time to reflect on his time as a soldier. After Bennington, he wrote, something inside him was different: "The first funeral I attended at home after having been in the army, I was shocked to find myself changed . . . [which] I could not observe without alarm." Worcester felt free to weigh in on the imputed cause of the war. Impressment claims had been exaggerated, he wrote. The war was instead born of "our own party contests, and the indulgence of vile passions;—and, on the whole, as unnecessary and unjust."

Worcester's landmark essay, "A Solemn Review of the Custom of War, Showing That War is the Effect of a Popular Delusion and Proposing a Remedy," laid the foundation for the nation's very first organization aimed at ending war. Such words were legal to publish, but nearly illegal to distribute. Anyone that might "flatter or menace" a member of the militia could be fined, or worse, by state officials from Vermont to Florida and as far west as Ohio.

By then Congress had increased the Army's size, to an eventual 35,000, attracting to its new regiments significant numbers of immigrants and recently indentured servants, alongside the printers' and shoemakers' sons who dreamed of class mobility through the promised grants of Indian land. These recruits had no tradition of electing their officers, but they still scanned their enlistment documents like sacred compacts. They had been taught that they were citizens and that gave them rights—a conviction that for William Apess translated into a cry: "Many say that we should enjoy our rights and privileges as they do. If so, I would ask, why are we not protected in our persons and property throughout the Union?"[20]

For Worcester, writing as "Philo Pacificus," the central question was different: how could man "abolish so barbarous a custom, and render wars unnecessary and avoidable?" In Massachusetts, Worcester had perhaps the most receptive audience for anti-war views in the nation. New England legislators had blocked a proposed national conscription law in 1814, and in the summer of 1815 held a convention in Hartford that came close to threatening secession.

The first Peace Society had just been founded in the United Kingdom. In June 1816, British Quaker William Allen convened "a meeting to consider a new society to spread tracts, and against war." That sentence's order may be striking to experienced campaigners of any kind: these activists knew that tracts were their first tools to achieve their goal. Noah Worcester took up both halves of that mission.

As with nearly all such groups prior to the internet, the Peace Society measured its success in piles of paper. The group's first anniversary report celebrated the distribution of 4,230 copies of their publications. "The principles of peace are rapidly gaining ground in different parts of the country," Worcester exulted, praising the blooming of reform societies, whether temperance groups, abolitionists, or communal utopian experiments.

The Friend of Peace, published by Worcester's Massachusetts Peace Society, questioned even the prized state militias: "The nation that has not virtue enough to execute its laws by the help of the constable's staff and the sheriff's wand, but must call in a military force, will soon have a 'military chieftain' for its ruler," Worcester wrote. No wonder militia officers spoke of "the noxious influence of peace men."[21]

Worcester was also deeply cognizant of America's founding injustice, writing that the Creek war was "a foul reproach on our national character." Meanwhile, Tennessee Major General Andrew Jackson was preparing his next sweep into Florida, commanding, among others, "a son of the late Honorable Samuel Hitchcock, formerly one of the Judges of the United States Circuit Court, and grandson of the late General Ethan Allen." In some ways, Ethan Allen Hitchcock seemed born to the job: Ethan Allen had recruited Iroquois warriors to help fight the British, and Hitchcock's uncle, the husband of Ethan Allen's granddaughter, Lorraine, had fought with Jackson at Talladega.

In 1814, after young Ethan graduated high school with few prospects, Lorraine asked her husband, Major George Peters, to help her cousin enter into the family trade: "Brother Ethan would make a very pretty little officer,— one that we should be quite proud of."[22] Peters, an early graduate of West Point, soon wrote to the governor of Vermont requesting that he nominate the sixteen-year-old: "[He is] well bred, extremely correct in his moral habits, [and] possesses strict ideas of honor and integrity." Peters knew the latter were sorely needed in the Army, both in and out of West Point.

At the close of the War of 1812, the United States had 38,000 men under arms, comprising 25,000 regulars as well as state militia and one-year volunteers. The number of regulars soon dropped to 10,000. Most of the officer corps was in deep disarray; even Thomas Jefferson's beloved military academy at West Point had only managed to graduate eighty-two full officers. West Point was now more of an officer's club of the worst kind, Hitchcock wrote. "The war with England in 1812 brought into the army a body of newly appointed officers of all grades who had scarcely been selected at all. . . . Most of the officers were dissipated in the worst sense of that word: profane, indecent, and licentious, and very many of them drunkards." As promised, "Brother Ethan" distinguished himself at the academy and graduated on schedule in 1817. After a few years as an Army recruiter in New York, Hitchcock went back to West Point as an artillery instructor. By then, the academy had a new superintendent, Sylvanus Thayer, who had already faced down a mutiny and set firm limits on cadets' right to dissent.

Thayer, often called the "Father of West Point" for his firm hand, arrived just after Hitchcock's graduation. He was brought in to clear the school of those "idle dependents upon respectable connections" that Hitchcock had noticed. Thayer abolished summer vacations, made student advancement dependent on a complex system of merits and demerits, and appointed Captain John Bliss as commandant of cadets. Capt. Bliss was known for either his "fiery temper" or his "horrible abuse," depending on who was talking.

Bliss reportedly kept the cadet corps disciplined using a manner that was more drill sergeant than team-building platoon leader. Cadets sometimes responded with defiance. Matters came to a head on November 22, 1818, when Bliss moved into the ranks after seeing a cadet move slowly and deliberately out of step. Bliss then "shook, jerked and publicly damn'd" the young man.[23]

Afterward, a ninety-strong Committee of Cadets brought to Thayer's door an extensive list of alleged misconduct by Bliss and other failings at the academy. Finding such group action distinctly unmilitary, Thayer ordered the entire corps to "desist" and asked the chief of engineers for an official inquiry. He feared that these young men would claim dissent as their birthright.

> The radical cause of the disturbance to which the Mil. Acadamy [sic] is liable is the erroneous and unmilitary impressions of the Cadets that they have rights to defend. So long as these impressions shall remain the Academy will be liable to combinations &

convulsions & the reputation of the institution & of the officers connected with it will be put in jeopardy.[24]

Were the cadets soldiers or citizens? Was there a difference? In Washington, Secretary of War John C. Calhoun pronounced himself "surprized" at the question, adding "no young man who would submit to be struck should be permitted to go into the Army."[25] Nonetheless, Attorney General William Wirt ruled that "the corps at West Point form a part of the land forces of the United States, and have been constitutionally subjected by Congress to the rules and articles of war, and to trial by court-martial."[26] They were already soldiers and had fewer rights. Enforcing discipline among them soon fell to Ethan Allen Hitchcock, who rose under Thayer to become the new commandant of cadets in 1829.

When Hitchcock assumed leadership of West Point's cadets (which would include Edgar Allan Poe,[27] Robert E. Lee, and Ulysses S. Grant), Andrew Jackson had just become president. Jackson, the "Old Hickory" militia general who had carved new states out of "Spanish" soil, had even created a new political party, the Democrats, to help him finally defeat establishment favorite John Quincy Adams. Jackson was no fan of West Point, either, a fact cheered by some rebellious cadets, who celebrated his election by planting a hickory pole on the academy's parade grounds. Some cadets got their families to direct their complaints, over Hitchcock's head, to the commander-in-chief. At one point in 1832, Jackson's blue eyes blazed as he denounced Thayer: "Why, the autocrat of the Russias couldn't exercise more power!" Soon afterward, Thayer and the loyal Hitchcock left West Point.

By then, Matthew Lyon, a Revolutionary peer of both Jackson and Hitchcock's great-grandfather, was in Arkansas, working with the Cherokee Nation on a mountaintop trading post. Lyon would die on that mountain, a decade before the Cherokee were driven from Arkansas by the "Indian removal" accomplished by his old friend Andrew Jackson. Hitchcock would bear witness to the roots of that removal.

Hitchcock's differences with Jackson over West Point regulations were precursors to decades of opposition over graver matters, especially the president's plans for the country's indigenous inhabitants. After leaving West Point, Hitchcock returned to active service. He knew that his next mission was likely to take him either south or farther west. His fellow officers called this obsessive diarist the "Pen of the Army" because Hitchcock carried with him his voluminous notes of each campaign and traveled with books of ethics and philosophy, including both Kant and Spinoza. His later-published diary is one long dissent.

In 1830, Thomas Jefferson's speculations about relocating the tribes "somewhere else" became explicit policy with the passage of H.R. 102: "An act to provide for an exchange of lands with the Indians residing in any of the States or Territories, and for their removal West of the river Mississippi." Commonly known as the Indian Removal Act, the legislation made the "exchange" mandatory and ordered a forced relocation of all tribes mentioned, producing long journeys to points west—to a territory named "Indiana," and then to the Oklahoma hunting grounds of the Osage, christened "Indian Territory" by the Bureau of Indian Affairs. Jackson's stated reasons for the act echoed Jefferson's principles: to preserve and enhance the "America" unified after two wars.

Dissenters thus found themselves reacting to Jackson and his policies. The oldest dissenting veteran, Noah Worcester, denounced the First Seminole War in *The Friend of Peace*'s first issue in 1815, and kept at it until he retired in 1828. Afterward, Worcester's family carried that legacy; his nephew Samuel went south to volunteer with the Cherokees, refused to leave, and was subsequently arrested, leading to the 1831 Supreme Court decision upholding Indian sovereignty, *Worcester v. Georgia*. By then, Jackson's Indian policy had blossomed into official policy passed by Congress, and William Apess had found a voice, denouncing the Indian Removal Act along with others (including the better-known Davy Crockett).[28]

Apess' 1829 book, *A Son of the Forest: The Experience of William Apes, A Native of the Forest, Comprising a Notice of the Pequod Tribe of Indians, Written by Himself,* gave the world a glimpse of his demand for full citizenship for Native Americans. Apess cited his own military service: "I could never think that the government acted right toward the 'Natives,' not only in refusing to pay us, but in claiming our services in times of perilous emergency, and still deny us the right of citizenship."

After the Army, Apess had spent four years in Canada deepening his Methodist faith; when he returned to Massachusetts, his father told him that he had a "calling" to preach the gospel. Soon, Apess was a popular circuit rider, often finding "a great concourse of people who had come out to hear the Indian preach."

Apess was one of the first soldier-dissenters to do so via storytelling. Both his sermons and books, which combined commentary with citizen journalism, bore a revolutionary message of full racial equality, including both "savages" and former slaves.[29] His next monograph, *The Experiences of Five Christian Indians of the Pequod Tribe, or An Indian's Looking-Glass for the White Man* (1833), satirized Western stereotypes about Indians as shiftless drunks, before assailing what might have ruined his people:

> Can you charge the Indians of robbing a nation almost of their whole continent, and murdering their women and children, and then depriving the remainder of their lawful rights, that nature and God require them to have? And to cap the climax, rob another nation to till their grounds and welter out their days under the lash with hunger and fatigue under the scorching rays of a burning sun?

Apess' last home was in Boston, a hotbed of anti-removal activism. In 1832, William Lloyd Garrison's abolitionist newspaper *The Liberator*, whose masthead included a symbol of broken treaties, noted, "A short interview with [Apess] has given us a very favorable opinion of his talents and piety." Garrison was also a key supporter when, the following year, Apess was arrested in what the newspapers called the Mashpee riot.

On a visit to the Groton Pequot reservation soon after he met with Garrison, Apess was told by his father that if he truly wanted to help Indians, Apess had to go north and minister to the Mashpee. A tiny, 329-strong nation, the Mashpee had tried without success to disrupt their absentee overseers, but were blocked by an assigned, Harvard-paid, white Congregationalist missionary. When Apess arrived, the Mashpee adopted him so that he could advocate for them. He either wrote or heavily influenced the petition with an accompanying four-point autonomy plan that the tribe presented to Governor Josiah Quincy. The petition mentioned Mashpee warriors who had died while in the Continental Army.

Apess was certainly at the Mashpee plantation when four white lumbermen showed up and began to cut wood from the tribal forest, only to be informed by some large, armed Indians that they had better stop and leave. Governor Quincy, reportedly fearing a Nat Turner–style rebellion, sent in the state militia and ordered the "rioters" arrested, including the "Indian preacher."

For the next six months, Apess became famous and/or notorious in the now classic role of civil-rights-organizer-as-outside-agitator. One issue of *The Liberator* swooned over Apess' statement before the state House of Representatives. "He illustrated the manner in which extortions were made from the poor Indians, and plainly declared that they wanted their rights as men and as freemen," Garrison wrote. The following year, with support from "Garrisonian" legislators, a far-reaching law gave the Mashpee more autonomy over their lands.[30]

Such limited victories were hardly the kind of justice for which Apess was riding around the country. His final work was the passionate *Eulogy for King Philip*, referring to Metacom, the seventeenth-century Wampanoag leader who had fought the Puritans. "Does it not appear that the cause of all wars was and is: That the whites have always been the aggressors, and the wars, cruelties and blood shed, is a job of their own making, and not the Indians?"[31]

When Apess died in 1836, the East Coast "Indian removal" was still ongoing: the Chickasaw had followed Choctaws and Creeks to Arkansas and Indiana, to be followed by the well-known Cherokee "Trail of Tears" to Oklahoma. Carrying out the removals were a combined seven thousand militia, regular Army, and volunteers, led by General Winfield Scott. Major Ethan Allen Hitchcock joined in when, in 1837, he was "ordered to Wisconsin to remove the Winnebagoe [*sic*]" before heading to his next duty station.

As he wound his way to Fort Crawford in Mississippi, Hitchcock shared his misgivings with his diary: "The presence of the whites is a blight upon the Indian character. . . . This service is harder on me than on most others, for I know the cruel wrongs to which the enemy has been subjected." The Second Seminole War was beginning; it would last nearly a half-century and take lives from Tallahassee to the Florida Keys.

Hitchcock had looked carefully at the history of the 1832 Treaty of Payne's Landing, in which the Seminoles supposedly agreed to give up their Florida territory and move west, a treaty signed by none of the tribe's leaders. "The government is in the wrong, and this is the chief cause of the persevering opposition of the Indians, who have nobly defended their country against our attempt to enforce a fraudulent treaty. The natives used every means to avoid a war, but were forced into it by the tyranny of our government."

Describing the end of the campaign, Hitchcock's agonies are as clear as his facts. "They are right in defending their homes and we ought to let them alone. . . . The army has done all that it could. It has marched all over the upper part of Florida. It has burned all the towns and destroyed all the planted fields."

Toward the end of the war, Hitchcock tried fruitlessly to leave the Seminole with some autonomy and some land. By 1842, most Seminole had been burned out of their homes, those left alive chased west. The Second Seminole War had left 1,500 troops dead—a low uniformed toll, considering that the war involved more than 10,000 regular Army soldiers and about 30,000 militia. Also dead: an intentionally uncounted number of Seminole.

Meanwhile, even the more "peaceable" of the Indian removals were rife with fraud and bloodshed. Alexis De Tocqueville witnessed the removal of the Choctaws: "In the whole scene there was an air of ruin and destruction, something which betrayed a final and irrevocable adieu; one couldn't watch without feeling one's heart wrung."[32]

In 1841, Hitchcock was put in charge of an army investigation that alleged fraud by the Bureau of Indian Affairs against the Cherokee Nation. Thus began one of the first Army investigations to be suppressed before Congress or the press could hear about it.

After nearly a year of crossing the country and talking to tribal leaders, Hitchcock assembled a long report with over one hundred exhibits documenting that "bribery, perjury, and forgery, short weights, issues of spoiled meat and grain, and every conceivable subterfuge, was employed by designing white men on ignorant Indians." But the new secretary of war, Jackson's old friend John Bell, refused Congress' request to review the material, which was subsequently destroyed. Hitchcock never got the congressional hearings and newspaper coverage he expected. Soon, he would find himself in Mexico under the same generals who had overseen the destructive removal.

As the antebellum era took hold, the middle-of-the-road American Peace Society found itself displaced by less staid rivals, most of whom had far less support from veterans. In particular, abolitionist William Lloyd Garrison was gaining followers for his deep pacifism, which he called "non-resistance" for declining to pick up a weapon. Garrison's hatred of militarism extended to the veterans leading the old peace societies, dismissing one Peace Society president as "a good-natured man, but somewhat superficial."[33] The old soldiers were skeptical in return, especially since Garrison had not really practiced "non-resistance" when the Boston militia called upon him in 1829. Instead, Garrison boasted in *The Liberator*, "I pleaded near-sightedness and non-residence, and consequently refused to meet the extortion. . . . What is the design of militia musters? To make men skilful murderers. I cannot consent to become a pupil in this sanguinary school."[34] Garrison's mix of pacifism and abolitionism thus split the movement in half.

But that soldier-citizen spirit was not through diagnosing and trying to address the republic's ills. In the next war, with Mexico, outrage from Transcendentalists and Garrisonian pacifists at home would be well matched by soldier-dissenters, of whom Ethan Allen Hitchcock was only the first.

CHAPTER THREE

1845 to 1861

IN JANUARY 1846, HUNDREDS OF soldiers crowded the train platform in New Castle, New Hampshire, just outside Portsmouth. The 10 a.m. train on the brand-new Portsmouth line was usually a place for happy hellos and good-byes. That was not the case now.

The three-hundred-strong 7th Infantry, from Fort Constitution, wore the smart long coat of the regular Army, its wool providing only partial relief from the winter. "Many of them had families who resided near the Fort," noted local minister Silas Ilsley.[1] With war brewing, "the countenances of the soldiers were all sad." After Boston, the regiment was bound for Louisiana, and then to the Gulf of Mexico.

None knew whether the soldiers would be in combat or support roles, but they had prepared for both. Despite the snow, some were also dreading the weather down south; Reverend Ilsley noticed in their bearing "the suffering and hardships which came of exposure and climate" from "the Florida war" against the Seminoles. They were all pretty sure that war was coming; Boston preacher William Lloyd Garrison had been saying for at least a decade, "We are speedily to be involved in a war with Mexico."[2]

Garrison, editor of the anti-slavery newspaper *The Liberator*, was a celebrity in New Hampshire, which like all of New England was a hotbed of anti-slavery sentiment. Garrison wrote that war with Mexico would be "ostensibly to redress injuries, but really to extend slavery and the slave trade."[3] (Sadly, that anti-slavery sentiment did not extend to having compassion for Native Americans, such as the Seminoles those soldiers had faced in Florida.) Portsmouth was also half a day away from abolitionist Springfield, Massachusetts, which boasted both a Free Church, founded by free African Americans, and an Anti-Slavery Association dominated by a talkative wool broker named John Brown.

Reverend Ilsley's account of that day in New Castle appeared in *The Advocate of Peace and Universal Brotherhood*, the newsletter of the American Peace Society. The society was led by prominent local abolitionist Charles Sumner, who had inveighed against the new war the prior Fourth of July: "The precious blood of millions unjustly shed in War, crying from the ground, demands it; the heart of the good man demands it; the conscience, even of the soldier, whispers 'Peace.'"[4] Those whispers were apparently unheard by President James Polk.

By the time of Sumner's speech, Polk had welcomed the Republic of Texas into the United States and ordered troops to establish the new southern border. The 7th Infantry was joining this campaign. Ilsley described its soldiers sadly boarding the train, kept from deserting by their oath and the bonds of brothers in arms. "Never did we feel so sensibly the terribleness of war."[5]

In early 1846, war and slaveholding were equally repugnant to American dissenters, both in and out of uniform. William Lloyd Garrison's New England Anti-Slavery Society, along with other abolitionist groups, such as the Oneida County Anti-Slavery Association and the Pennsylvania Immediatists, had been inspired by the well-organized networks and newspapers of free African Americans. All challenged the Quaker idea that the "peculiar institution" would naturally wither away, perhaps aided by "colonization" (in other words, returning African Americans to Africa). Garrison's newspaper, *The Liberator*, demanded slavery's immediate end, which he preached could be achieved through constant and persuasive "moral suasion," if enough white men confronted what anti-slavery forces called "the Slave Power."[6] This phrase, popularized by thinkers such as *New York Tribune* founder Horace Greeley, had become common among abolitionists, including Garrison and former President John Quincy Adams.[7] All excoriated the South's near-stranglehold on both the United States' economy and its government.

Garrison's pacifism had not prevented him from defending violence by enslaved people, including the 1831 rebellion led by the brilliant/infamous young South Carolina slave, Nat Turner. This revolt, in which formerly enslaved people left fifty-five white Virginians dead, spurred Garrison to respond to charges that his newspaper was to blame: "Ye accuse the pacific friends of emancipation of instigating the slaves to revolt. Take back the charge as a foul slander. The slaves need no incentives at our hands. They will find them in their stripes—in their emaciated bodies."

Most anti-war campaigns were paired with anti-slavery activism. Throughout the Northeast, an "Anti-Slavery Hymn Book" circulated in churches like Reverend Ilsley's, and annual "Anti-Slavery Pic Nic" gatherings marked the 1834 end of slavery in the Caribbean. In 1844, Frederick Douglass starred in at least one of these picnics in Massachusetts, a tenth-anniversary event in which Garrison himself held the banner, praising the British immediatists who had secured the 1834 emancipation: "SHALL A REPUBLIC, WHICH COULD NOT BEAR THE BONDS OF A KING, CRADLE A BONDAGE WHICH A KING HAS ABOLISHED?"[8] *The Liberator*, which reported on three such picnics that year, makes no mention of whether Douglass and Garrison had brought along their families, allowing ten-year-old George Thompson Garrison and six-year-old Lewis Henry Douglass to share the fun. Also unmentioned was the local abolitionist family of Amasa Soule, whose eldest son was named after Garrison. *The Liberator* taught the Soule children hatred of slavery and of the war against Indian nations. Years later, both Soule sons would join George Garrison and Lewis Douglass in choosing to fight slavery as soldiers, extending that fight when needed to protect the rights of Native Americans.

In 1845, as the first U.S. troops were ordered to the Mexican border, the American Peace Society kept up a drumbeat of anti-war editorials. New England writer Henry David Thoreau went to prison, having refused to pay the tax established to fund the war. Thoreau declared upon his arrest that July, "I cannot for an instant recognize . . . as my government [that] which is the slaves' government also." Afterward, he elaborated on that sentiment in his influential "On Civil Disobedience," dismissing Peace Society types: "The soldier is applauded who refuses to serve in an unjust war by those who do not refuse to sustain the unjust government which makes the war."[9] In 1846,

Frederick Douglass, abroad on a speaking tour, told an Irish newspaper that the United States was "stretching their long, bony fingers into Mexico, and appropriating her territory to themselves in order to make it a hot bed of negro [*sic*] slavery."[10]

While civilian peace activists thought about how to confront war and the Slave Power, members of the military faced war's realities. Colonel Ethan Allen Hitchcock raged at the news from Washington: "Our people have provoked the war with Mexico and are prosecuting it not for 'liberty' but for land, and I feel averse to be an instrument for these purposes." Hitchcock had begun that year on recruiting duty in New York State; he had not wanted to return to Florida to serve under General Zachary Taylor, a Kentucky slave owner and one of the Seminole Wars' most notorious/celebrated "Indian killers." Taylor had spent the intervening time acquiring Western real estate. His friend Sam Houston, a former Tennessee senator and Andrew Jackson stalwart, had gotten a head start a decade earlier when he founded the now nine-year-old Republic of Texas, first shedding Mexican blood in Texas' own independence battle.[11]

Hitchcock knew that Houston and Taylor were planning for another slave state. "The acquisition of Texas by the United States was a darling object with certain politicians of the South, and [I was told] that Jackson himself had originally advised Houston to emigrate to [what became the Republic of] Texas having in view a possible rupture with Mexico and the final annexation of Texas to the United States." Houston and his cronies, now wealthy plantation owners in Mexico's northeast, had fought for Texas' independence only after 1839, when the Republic of Mexico granted Blacks full Mexican citizenship. When Texas was admitted to the Union, it would be a slave state.[12] Hitchcock added in 1845, "I not only think this Mexican war unnecessary and unjust about Mexico, but I also think it a step and a great step towards a dissolution of our Union [which will] bring on wars between the separated parts."

Not long after writing this, Hitchcock was ordered to Taylor's forces as they occupied Corpus Christi, on the newly declared southern boundary of the Rio Grande, formerly one of Mexico's interior rivers. By June, Ethan Allen Hitchcock was commanding the Army's 3rd Infantry: "My heart is not in this business. It looks as if the government sent a small force on purpose to bring on a war, to have a pretext for taking California and as much of this country as it chooses."

One of Hitchcock's former students, Ulysses Grant, later described the war in the same terms: "The occupation, separation and annexation were, from the inception of the movement to its final consummation, a conspiracy to acquire territory out of which slave states might be formed for the American Union." But as the war began, neither Grant nor his mentor saw a way out. "As a military man," Hitchcock wrote, "I am bound to execute orders."

Another former Hitchcock cadet, Ephraim Franklin Kirby Smith, now a captain with the 5th Infantry, would similarly bewail the war, though not at first. "I wish you could look at us," he wrote to his wife in October 1845. "On the right are the Second Dragoons, on the left a corps of artillery volunteers from New Orleans . . . and when the residue of the troops ordered here have arrived [it] will be the largest body of regulars, it is said, which has been assembled since the Revolution."[13] It was a trial, Smith added, to drill "volunteers from different commands, sneaks and invalids of all the regular companies who were left behind at this place. Nevertheless, by rigid discipline and close watching I succeeded in controlling them." From that moment of pride, Kirby Smith's letters to his wife chart a journey of doubt—from whether his side was engaged in the disciplined pursuit of victory, to whether such victory was moral. Active-duty dissent in this war would come mostly from enlisted soldiers, who did not feel bound by Smith and Hitchcock's West Point code of honor.

In 1846, the full force fighting in Mexico consisted of two new Army regiments, 26,992 strong, bolstered by 73,000-plus state-based "volunteers." With the war unpopular in the North (and lacking any support for conscription), generals like Hitchcock and Taylor had to supervise volunteer regiments composed of political appointees, West Point dropouts, and retirees anxious for some new adventure. Men volunteered for the free land, to get off the farm, and in the case of Southern volunteers, to preserve their "way of life" from the abolitionists. Hitchcock concentrated on drills to turn them into soldiers.

Further north, the 1st New York Regiment, based at Harlem's Fort Hamilton, filled up quickly with "about eight hundred rank and file, three hundred Americans, the balance Dutch, Irish, French, English, Polish, Swedes,

Chinese, Indian. . . . For officers we had barbers, tailors, bar-tenders, and a few gentlemen." A few even came from Five Points, the city's notorious downtown slum. Nearly all had been wooed in advance by promised signing bonuses of three months' pay. "Many enlisted for the sake of their families, having no employment . . . and were promised that they could leave part of their pay for their families to draw in their absence," wrote one such recruit, adding that "they, poor duped men, but with patriotic and noble feelings toward their wives and children, sacrificed everything for the sole purpose of their support. Thus, it will be seen that the non-commissioned officers and privates have been cheated, swindled, and their families left destitute, by rascally promises and deception!"[14]

"A few days previous to our departure to the land of death and slaughter," the soldiers went on strike. "The men became more and more dissatisfied. Mothers, wives, and suffering children—crying for money to buy bread." Their rebellion was short-lived, and little record survives of that particular regiment. They sailed to Veracruz, where Winfield Scott led more than thirty thousand into the country's heartland.[15]

Once on Mexican soil, both volunteers and regular Army soldiers were in unfamiliar territory; some did not feel they belonged. The 1st Massachusetts Volunteers refused to march in the uniforms issued by the Army, demanding their right as a militia to wear their own uniforms.[16] By then Winfield Scott had bombed Veracruz for five days, killing 1,150, nearly half civilians.

Those newest to the uniform most often expressed their dissent by deserting, with between 9,000 and 10,300 making such a statement.[17] Officers like Hitchcock or Kirby Smith criticized the war on paper while fighting it, until another former Hitchcock student, Nicholas Trist, defied the commander-in-chief and brought home a peace treaty.

By January 1847, Kirby Smith saw needless devastation in his first "real" war. In small Los Muertes, he wrote, "The people were all gone, not one left, driven off by the volunteers, the houses in ruins, the shade trees girdled or cut down, and the ground strewed by the carcasses of dead horses and mules."

Kirby Smith was not the only one to blame the volunteers for questionable practices. One Army artillery officer decried the Louisiana Volunteers as a "lawless drunken rabble," adding that during the 1846 invasion of Matamoros, they had "driven away the inhabitants, taken possession of their houses and were emulating each other in making beasts of themselves." A year later, as platoons of Texas riflemen powered the invasion of Mexico City, "many were perfectly frantic with the lust of blood and plunder." Troops stripped churches, humiliated priests, and moved into the homes that families had fled. In 1848, after one of those riflemen was killed, random revenge shootings resulted in "eighty bodies in the morgue left unclaimed by friends or relatives."[18]

The widely reported carnage energized the war's opponents. Frederick Douglass inveighed regularly against the war in *Frederick Douglass' Monthly*, assailing "the puny opposition arrayed against [President Polk]. None seem willing to take their stand for peace at all risks." His final call to non-violent arms suggested mass action via tracts: "Let the press, the pulpit, the church, the people at large, unite at once; and let petitions flood the halls of Congress by the million, asking for the instant recall of our forces from Mexico. This may not save us, but it is our only hope."[19]

Neither Douglass nor the Garrisonians were suggesting desertion, but they hardly needed to; levels of functional dissent via desertion were endemic. A soldier who deserted could melt into the scenery; deserters who fled to Galveston, a Boston newspaper reported, "easily found employment, one as a school-master at $60 a month" (approximately $1,850 in 2018 dollars).

Some stayed in Mexico, such as the Saint Patrick's Battalion. John Riley, a British-trained Irish immigrant who had left Scott's command in April 1846 without firing a shot, assembled the battalion from Catholic soldiers discomfited by the nativism and anti-Catholicism of the American troops. Recruited and welcomed by the understaffed, under-trained, and under-equipped Mexican Army, they fought against Zachary Taylor's troops in Monterrey, helping Mexico hold the city for a time, and in 1847 they became an official foreign legion of the Mexican Army, the 1st and 2nd Militia Infantry Companies of San Patricio.

For much of the war, American deserters claimed to be San Patricios, and thus were guaranteed food and shelter from Mexican families. After the battalion's defeat at Chiarabusco in September 1847, fourteen San Patricios, including Riley, were flogged and branded with two-inch D's on both sides of their faces. The rest were tried and some were executed, whether or not they had fought against the United States.

Meanwhile, as Winfield Scott approached Mexico City, two regiments deserted *en masse* before the Americans even reached the capital. By then, Ephraim Kirby Smith had begun to sour on the war. With an ill wife back at home, he decided to submit his resignation, convinced that Polk's war was no longer worth the sacrifice. He also knew from Hitchcock about the lives they had ruined: "I passed an exceedingly interesting hour this morning with Colonel Hitchcock in listening to the translations of many letters from a large mail coming from the [i.e., Mexico's] Capital . . . all in a tone of utter heartbroken despondency."[20]

Pressure for the United States to end the war was fierce, with Americans divided only by how much land should be their prize. Peace negotiations between the Mexican government and Washington were stalled by political jockeying: both Polk and his tremendously popular political rival Scott wanted to set the terms, as did Mexico's assorted factions. The person to break that logjam was the personally awkward, politically muddled, super-studious Nicholas P. Trist.

Trist, a Virginian whose grandmother had been close to Thomas Jefferson, had been at West Point during the aborted cadet rebellion of 1819, but left soon afterward to marry Jefferson's granddaughter and become the third president's aide. Trist had learned Spanish during his ten years as consul-general of Cuba, where he had navigated competing interests and endured unpopularity at home, whether from abolitionists claiming that he was aiding the illegal slave trade or seamen charging him with favoring Cuban shipping interests. So, in 1847, Secretary of State James Buchanan was counting on the multilingual Trist to broker a treaty among the diverse Mexican factions.

Thrilled to be plucked from obscurity, Trist was anxious to honor the words of his long-dead grandmother. Elizabeth Trist had been happy to see Nicholas quit West Point: "Those who wage war for subjugating nations to their will," she had written to him, "are guilty of a heinous crime."

During the summer of 1847, Trist stayed in the former bishop's hacienda at Tacubaya, beside Hitchcock and Winfield Scott. Initially distrustful of someone sent by his political enemies, Scott relented and even helped Trist secure a bribe to ease negotiations. Nothing seemed to work. Trist wrote home that he was considering quitting.[21] "Mr. Trist came home last evening evidently

dispirited and unusually fatigued, and his appearance is a kind of thermometer to us," Hitchcock wrote in his diary of September 3. A few weeks later,
the Mexicans elected a new legislature and then a new peace committee, and
Trist delivered Washington's proposed terms into their hands.

Soon after, on November 16, Trist was recalled to Washington by a letter from Polk, who was under pressure from the "All Mexico Movement" to
demand all of Mexico as part of the United States.[22] Trist did not respond,
taking the advice of a New Orleans journalist and old friend: "Make the
treaty, Sir! . . . I know your country. I know all classes of people there. They
want peace, Sir. They pant for it. . . . Instructions or no instructions, you are
bound to do it."[23]

His convictions affirmed, Trist wrote to his wife that he planned to ignore
Polk's order. "Knowing it to be the very last chance, and impressed with the
dreadful consequences to our country which cannot fail to attend the loss
of that chance."[24] The sixty-page explanation that Trist sent to Polk did not
persuade the president, who wrote in his diary that Trist "is destitute of honor
or principle and he has proved himself to be a very base man."[25] As negotiations dragged on, Ephraim Kirby Smith agreed with Polk. "How many times
must [the U.S. negotiators] be gullied and deceived before they learn to treat
all Mexican promises with scorn? . . . I am much afraid that peace cannot
be made, but this satisfaction remains to us, that the world must see that,
though always victorious, we have extended the olive branch, always ready
to sheathe the sword."[26] Kirby Smith died soon after writing those words,
mortally wounded while following the commander-in-chief's orders to keep
fighting.

In January 1848, Trist went into hiding at Guadalupe-Hidalgo with the
three Mexican commissioners, and refused to leave without a peace treaty.
On February 3, all parties signed an agreement that gave one-third of Mexico's territory—including Texas and California—to the United States. Trist
agreed with Hitchcock that the treaty fell short of what Mexico deserved,
but the boundaries had already largely been drawn by generals. This, he
thought, was the only chance to end the war. As it turned out, most of his
country agreed. The treaty was praised by newspapers from Boston to New
Orleans.

After the war, Trist and his family went to Philadelphia, and Hitchcock to

St. Louis. Hitchcock was "vigorously besieged by the participants in the Mexican War, entreating him to write a history of that contest," but he declined and awaited his next set of orders.[27]

The Mexican-American War's unintended result was that despite their anti-war speeches, the conflict helped persuade many of those who opposed war on moral grounds to support a war against slavery. Even William Lloyd Garrison, who had long boasted that "Every anti-slavery man is also a peace man," publicly hoped for a Mexican victory in the war.

Afterward, *The Liberator* ran articles by many who proposed enslaved African Americans take arms against their masters; *The Advocate of Peace* praised the not-exactly-bloodless 1848 independence movements that surged from Italy to France to Germany. Pacifist anti-slavery leaders were saying things like, "We are compelled to choose between two evils, and all that we can do is take the least, and baptize *liberty in blood*, if it must be so."[28] Meanwhile, most anti-slavery groups had gone beyond speeches and pamphlets to direct action, such as organizing and funding the Underground Railroad.

For a generation that had grown up hating the Slave Power, the concept of a "just war" was beginning to gain traction; most visible among them was Garrison's good friend Frederick Douglass, who had always been skeptical of "non-resistance."

In 1847, after his return from Europe, Douglass had moved to upstate New York. His Rochester home was a well-known station on the Underground Railroad, an operation that spanned from the Deep South to Canada. He had heard about John Brown, the rangy wool broker from eastern Ohio. Brown famously used his travel up and down the Mississippi River as cover to help Black communities sneak enslaved families north: "Escaping slaves would be handed off from conductors in Jefferson County to Hagerstown, Maryland, on to conductors in Chambersburg, Harrisburg, and Philadelphia, PA, and from there to New York and Canada."[29] Brown now lived in Springfield, Massachusetts, and when Douglass spoke there in July 1847, Brown sought him out.

Douglass listened closely as Brown shared his vision of a holy war against slaveholders. "From this night spent with John Brown in Springfield, Mass. in 1847 while I continued to write and speak against slavery, I became all the same less hopeful for its peaceful abolition. My utterances became more and more tinged by the color of this man's strong impressions."[30]

The admiration was mutual. By 1849, Brown had, like Douglass, moved to one of the thriving African American communities near Rochester, New York. That year also marked the arrival in Philadelphia of twenty-seven-year-old escaped slave Harriet Tubman. Congress was then debating a strengthened Fugitive Slave Act, which would turn a 1793 constitutional provision into a criminalization of the Underground Railroad, giving more power to authorities to seize the formerly enslaved and drag them across state lines.

The stronger Fugitive Slave Act passed in 1850. It served to unite the fractious anti-slavery movement, which saw the legislation as a virtual declaration of war. John Brown went back to Springfield to organize the Gileadites, a self-defense league that waged armed struggle on behalf of former slaves and successfully prevented the recapture of a single slave from Springfield. Money poured into cities' "vigilance committees." Tubman led Philadelphia's committee, while Garrison promoted Boston's New England Freedom Association, which delivered scores of formerly enslaved people to Canada.

The new act was part of legislation that added California as a free state, but allowed popular sovereignty (local votes) to determine whether Utah and New Mexico were slave states. The 1854 Kansas-Nebraska Act opened the possibility of additional new slave states' being created the same way, sparking the formation of emigrant aid groups in the Northeast, which sought to help seed new anti-slavery communities out west. Amasa Soule founded one such group, and brought his family to Kansas in December 1854. Fourteen-year-old Silas arrived the following summer. The next five years became known as "Bleeding [or Bloody] Kansas."

As free state majorities wrung the state from pro-slavery forces, new Kansans were pitted against one another. Missouri-based armed bands launched raids against free state communities like Lawrence, Kansas (named after abolitionist Amos Lawrence). The city, about eight miles from where the Soules had built their homestead, saw its newspapers and churches sacked repeatedly. As far as either side was concerned, this was war, and there would be casualties. In 1857, Silas Soule joined the Immortal Ten, which specialized in cross-border raids and helping enslaved people sneak into free Kansas.[31] Describing that time years later to a Kansas City newspaper, Silas' sister Julia made sure to mention her family's role: "Our house was on the 'Underground Railway,'" she said. "John Brown was often there."[32]

Brown began to feel that these efforts would never beat the Slave Power without a wider war. In 1856, he invoked the struggle's recent past and probable future: "They never intend to relinquish the machinery of this government into the hands of the opponents of slavery. It has taken them more than half a century to get it, and they know its significance too well to give it up. If the republican party [*sic*] elects its president next year, there will be war."[33] That interview, with a New York attorney, was aimed at the East Coast abolitionists from whom Brown raised money.

Bleeding Kansas, with New Englanders among its casualties, made antislavery activists far more willing to consider violence. Charles Sumner, former president of the American Peace Society, told William Lloyd Garrison: "I trust, also, that the people of Kansas will stand firm, and, if need be, that they will know how to die for freedom . . . for there is to be fought the great battle between freedom and slavery—by the ballot-box, I trust, but I do not forget that all who destroy the ballot-box madly invoke the cartridge-box."[34] Sumner and Garrison were becoming some of John Brown's most important backers, hosting Brown, Douglass, and Harriet Tubman at fundraising events, chiefly in Boston.

Brown's well of support was not confined to the Northeast. He stayed in touch with friends from Ohio like Lucius Bierce, former Akron mayor, district attorney, and major-general of its militia. Bierce—a raging abolitionist like Brown, ever since witnessing a slave auction in South Carolina—had given Brown a going-away gift when he moved to Kansas: "a wagonload of arms and ammunition somewhat questionably appropriated from a disbanded militia store in Tallmadge."

Included in the haul were the broadswords carried by Lucius and his men in the Windsor campaign, the same broadswords that Brown and his henchmen would use to butcher a cluster of pro-slavery settlers on the banks of Pottawatomie Creek, Kansas, a few months hence. If Lucius felt any complicity in the crime, he never let it bother him.[35]

Brown spent years developing his plan for war, in which a vanguard based in western Pennsylvania would spark hundreds of African Americans, both enslaved and free, to revolt against slaveholders. As a crew of Kansas veterans ran a boot camp in Iowa, Brown traveled to Rochester to recruit Frederick Douglass, who then introduced him to Harriet Tubman. While she, like Douglass, was skeptical that Brown's plan would work, Tubman became one of its chief strategists, drawing on the experience she had gained on repeated crossings down South.

In August 1859, Brown's attack at Harper's Ferry, West Virginia, failed. Despite ample funds and "General" Tubman's Underground Railroad experience in moving people and materiel, Brown was captured by Army troops under the command of Colonel Robert E. Lee. Silas Soule, who had never left Kansas, offered to come East to help Brown escape, but Brown refused, preferring to become a martyr instead of a fugitive. Certainly he was treated as such in the elegies of abolitionists from Douglass to Henry David Thoreau.

Lucius Bierce got Akron, Ohio, to stop all public proceedings, and gave his own requiem to Brown at a mass meeting. William Lloyd Garrison saw Brown's death as a call to action: "God forbid that we should any longer continue the accomplices of thieves and robbers, of men-stealers and women-whippers! We must join in the name of freedom."

That call to action, and others like it, helped spark a new generation of dissenters who would become soldiers in Brown's cause, including Garrison's own son, George; Frederick Douglass' two sons; and Lucius Bierce's rogue nephew, Ambrose. For this new generation, dissent was in their lifeblood, as was determination to confront the Slave Power. When the country broke in half a few years later, they would go beyond asserting their citizenship, or even extending such to others. They would seek to heal the breach by creating an entirely new country, even if they died doing it.

CHAPTER FOUR
1859 to 1880

FORT WARREN WAS A TWENTY-EIGHT-ACRE pentagon of granite and stone that took up nearly all of Georges Island, located at the entrance of Boston Harbor. On May 12, 1861, it was so full of soldiers that the parade ground showed more blue than green. Veteran militiamen of the 1st and 2nd Massachusetts Artillery were joined by two new regiments, the 11th and 12th, all now officially part of the Union Army—a national army created because of the newly declared Confederate States of America, which in April 1861 had fired on Fort Sumter, South Carolina. The state's adjutant general wrote about the surge in volunteers after Sumter:

> It is impossible to overstate the excitement which pervaded the entire community. . . . The railroad depots were surrounded with crowds of people; and the companies, as they arrived, were received with cheer of grateful welcome. . . . Men and boys carried miniature flags in their hands or on their hats. The horse-cars and express-wagons were decked with similar devices; and young misses adorned their persons with rosettes and ribbons, in which were blended the national red, white, and blue.[1]

Soldiers and civilians alike cheered as a U.S. flag was raised above their heads. The flag's upper-left corner held thirty-four stars, the latest added in January for Kansas, while retaining those representing the states that had seceded from the United States. It was that act of treason that the assembled soldiers planned to make right.

After the flag was aloft, the soldiers started singing.

The tune came from the folk song "Say, oh, brothers, will you meet us?" Now the song's first words were, "John Brown's body lies a-mouldering in the grave," and its chorus was "His soul goes marching on." The song included pledges to "hang [enemies] from a sour apple tree," ending with, "Three cheers for the Union!"[2]

Unlike the New England soldiers considered in the previous chapter, these young men had a specific sense of why they were going to war. They were about to confront the long-hated Slave Power in a war against a status quo they had long resisted.

The young men at Fort Warren had grown up learning about that "Power," the Southern planters who controlled half the national economy and much of its government.[3] They had read newspapers and novels describing how those planters terrorized their enslaved workers. They had heard John Brown's name since Bleeding Kansas, during which Brown had helped free state militias battle bands of pro-slavery Missourians over the future of the now newest state. They knew the Slave Power had hanged Brown two years ago, after he had tried to jump-start a war against slavery. Some even knew Brown's 1856 prediction: "If the republican party [sic] elects its president next year, there will be war." The next presidential election had brought the nation President Abraham Lincoln, the secession of most Southern states, and the assault on Fort Sumter. The soldiers' choice of "John Brown's Body" was hardly a surprise.

These members of the Union Army, called up by the official government, were dissenters; they acted against a status quo that had long since become intolerable. Like many a group of young revolutionaries, they felt they were creating something entirely new and were willing to die for it.

Their ranks included Ambrose Bierce, whose enlistment with the 9th Indiana honored an uncle who had broken laws to supply John Brown with weapons; Quaker Jesse Macy, whose insistence on serving as a battlefield medic created a new form of conscientious objection, and Harriet Tubman, a Union spy soldiering when women could not; she was often disguised as a male field hand. Tubman was not waiting for the president to recruit Black soldiers. But when that happened, Frederick Douglass' sons would be among the very first African Americans in the U.S. Army.

Each of these dissenters defied society's expectations for their lives, for the sake of the future they wanted. Until President Lincoln declared two years later that the end of slavery was the war's goal, few Quakers joined the fight. Most of those who answered the new president's call in 1861 for one hundred volunteer regiments came from abolitionist families who had cheered the election and inauguration of their anti-slavery president.[4]

Ambrose Bierce immediately joined Indiana's 9th Infantry Division. Blond and slender, with an incongruous mustache on his otherwise seraphic face, the nineteen-year-old Bierce had been working a series of odd jobs after his exit from the Kentucky Military Institute. When Bierce went off to Indianapolis, he had no idea that he would "engage in a four years' battle fighting for [freedom]."[5] But he was glad to join what he later called the truest of citizen soldiers:

> Not professional life-long fighters, the product of European militarism—just plain, ordinary American, volunteer soldiers, who loved their country and fought for it with never a thought of grabbing it for themselves; that is a trick which the survivors were taught later by gentlemen desiring their votes.[6]

Also enlisting in 1861 was Silas Soule, who had years of combat experience under John Brown. Soule and his brother were in Colorado, managing *not* to strike it rich in the burgeoning Pike's Peak Gold Rush. Soule joined the war Brown had helped spark in a new Denver-based Union Army regiment, the 1st Colorado Infantry. Soule's unit was full of Kansas-based abolitionists; Bierce's 9th Indiana was loyal to the state's abolitionist governor, Oliver Morton; and the New England Anti-Slavery Society had poured its sons into Boston's Fort Warren forces. All over the country, Union troops trained, attracted new officers, and prepared to confront the 100,000 men called up by the new Provisional Confederate Armed Service, led by Robert E. Lee and

Braxton Bragg. These two men were both West Point graduates and former students of Ethan Allen Hitchcock.

By 1861, Hitchcock had returned to Vermont after semi-retirement in Missouri, anxious "to get out of the secession fever which now agitates this city [St. Louis] and State." The "Pen of the Army" wrote that he was being urged to come out of retirement for the war, but "I cannot think of it . . . when did fighting make friends?" On February 9, 1862, Hitchcock was appointed major-general of volunteers, supplanting his ex-student, Ulysses Grant, for an attack on Fort Donelson in Tennessee.

"Before [the order] reaches me I have written to the Secretary of War declining it," Hitchcock noted. "My health will not allow me to accept it."[7] If he had not turned away from this call to active service, Hitchcock would have been leading troops into the maelstrom of Shiloh, of which Ambrose Bierce later wrote, "To what monstrous inharmony of death was it the visible prelude?"[8]

Hitchcock's call-up was a sign of near desperation; the war for the Union against rebel slavers was going badly. Neither forty new regiments of state volunteers, nor ten new Union Army regiments, nor 18,000 new Navy and Marine Corps recruits, nor General Winfield Scott's prized Anaconda naval blockade had prevented Confederate victories at Manassas, Winchester, and Wilson's Creek, Missouri. Only slightly better news came from farther west, when the Confederates were stymied by an assortment of regiments from Santa Fe and Fort Union, including Silas Soule's 1st Colorado Volunteers. On March 12, Soule wrote in a letter to one of his New England friends, a poet and volunteer nurse named Walt Whitman, that the journey was far from fruitless: "We have travelled through mountains and plains and seen many musing things."[9]

In March 1862, Soule's brigade was marching the hundreds of miles to New Mexico from Denver. "Men, women and children and thousands of head of stock arrive here daily . . . and they are all glad to see the soldiers. Three or four companies of the 5th infantry will march with us to Santa Fe."[10] That letter drops off quickly as if of exhaustion. The taxing journey became more so when they reached Glorieta Pass, a canyon to the south that required Soule and his platoon to rappel to the bottom while the Texas artillery pounded. There, they attacked Confederate supply trains and seized the Texans' ammunition, though without reducing Confederate strength.

Most engagements ended in similar standoffs, with few clear victories. Ambrose Bierce would learn that the following month, when his 9th Indiana would join what would turn out to be the bloodiest battle of the spring campaign.

The rocky terrain of east Tennessee was unfamiliar to both the Indianans and the Louisianans they opposed. Bierce's unit had been sent to hold and expand recent Union gains. "As there is a deep and impassable ravine for artillery or cavalry, and very difficult for infantry, at this point, no troops were stationed here, except the necessary artillerists and a small infantry force for their support," General Grant later wrote in his summary report to Lincoln.[11] To Bierce, the unfamiliar terrain was exquisitely beautiful, as emerges in bits and pieces of his later essay, "What I Saw of Shiloh." His descriptions make almost bearable the account they contain:

> The ground was tolerably level here, the forest less dense, mostly clear of undergrowth, and occasionally opening out into small natural meadows. Here and there were small pools—mere discs of rainwater with a tinge of blood. Riven and torn with cannon-shot, the trunks of the trees protruded bunches of splinters like hands, the fingers above the wound interlacing with those below. . . . Very often we struck our feet against the dead; more frequently against those who still had spirit enough to resent it with a moan.[12]

In a corner nicknamed the Hornet's Nest, Union troops took advantage of deep woods behind a sunken road. One of those Louisianans wrote, "The enemy reserved their fire untill [sic] we were within about twenty yards of them and then the whole line simultaneously with their battery loaded with grape opened on us again mowing us down at every volley."[13] A Michigan volunteer added: "It was the first battle I have seen, and I hope it will be the last one. [. . .] It almost makes me shudder to think of it, although at the time I did not think more of seeing a man shot down by my side than you would think of seeing a young beast killed."

Grant reported Shiloh as a victory, though it was not enough of one for President Lincoln, who was waiting for an unambiguous victory before he declared the South's slaves free; only after such a declaration would some young abolitionists be willing to join the fight. To them, Lincoln's careful politicking about "preserving the Union" was a craven distraction from the issue upon which he had won election, and made his war not worth dying for.

In Grinnell, Iowa, Quaker Jesse Macy "was two months shy of nineteen years, and in perfect health." Macy's lifetime membership in the Society of Friends did not diminish his interest in the war. "We as Friends, were fundamentally opposed to war, but I might join the army as a noncombatant if the administration took a position I could conscientiously endorse."[14] But Macy's news bibles—*New York Tribune* and *The Principia*—told him Lincoln had taken no such position: the war was officially about bringing the South back into the Union. "This war was in no sense for the liberation of the slave. I could not support it." Macy's sentiment was shared by many young abolitionists, including William Lloyd Garrison's son, George.

William Lloyd Garrison's revulsion to taking up arms remained, even though the pacifist side of his work had shattered along with the bones of John Brown.[15] Most of his sons followed his example, including future *The Nation* editor Wendell Phillips Garrison. But in 1862, as Lincoln waited to unleash his proclamation, Garrison told a fellow pacifist, "George is inclined to think he shall go, if drafted, as he does not claim to be a non-resistant." Garrison did make a last-ditch effort to persuade George to take a stand as a conscientious objector, writing also in the words of a fearful parent, "Personally, as my son, you will incur some risks at the hands of the rebels that others will not." Also waiting were Frederick Douglass' sons, who had helped their father set type for many columns urging Lincoln to bring the freedmen into the fight. "Fighting A War With One Hand Tied Behind Our Backs," Douglass wrote in *The North Star.*

One of Silas Soule's fellow Kansans, James Montgomery, had enlisted and was stirring up trouble in South Carolina, in an unofficial regiment aided by Harriet Tubman, in defiance of Union general George McClellan.[16] Montgomery drilled freedmen, freed slaves, and turned them into soldiers. While Tubman was already an active participant, Lewis and Charles Douglass would wait for the words that would inspire them to enlist, which came in

September, after the "charnel-house of a battle known as Antietam." Antietam, the bloodiest day in American military history, was a sort of Pyrrhic standoff in which Grant's forces failed to invade Virginia and Lee's failed to reach Washington, D.C. That "charnel-house" phrase comes from a great-grandson of John Adams: "It seemed as if we were doomed—so deafening was the discharge of artillery on either side."[17]

Also at Antietam was Private "Frank Thompson" of the 1st Michigan Artillery, a soldier-dissenter in multiple ways. Thompson was female; her real name Sarah Emma Edmonds. Edmonds was often tapped for spying missions south of the border, alternately disguised as a Southern belle or an enslaved boy. After she deserted rather than risk exposure while still in uniform, Edmonds published the memoir *Nurse and Spy in the Union Army*, dedicated to "The Sick and Wounded Soldiers of The Army of the Potomac."[18]

Edmonds was among eight women passing as male on the battlefield that day—the others one Confederate soldier and six in the Union Army. One of the latter, Mary Galloway, was found out by forty-one-year-old schoolteacher Clara Barton, whose gender-dissent lay in her creation of a formerly inconceivable all-female battlefield nursing corps. Barton expressed little surprise when she discovered that Private Galloway, a "soft boy" shot in the neck and back, was the brave young woman Mary Galloway; she persuaded the injured soldier to leave the fight and rejoin her family up North.

By the end of the war, hundreds of women had passed as male in both armies, including Confederate soldier S.M. Blaylock, whose official records give "being a woman" as the reason for discharge.[19] Their dissent lay in their claiming full citizenship, most by fighting slavery. Years later, those whose names we know would make that citizen-soldier claim public, as they asked Congress for veterans' compensation.

Female soldiers served side by side with civilian women, who provided support in non-combat roles. In addition to nurses like Barton, women wrote letters for soldiers, cleaned guns, and ran "contraband camps" that sheltered escaped slaves.

"General" Harriet Tubman ran one such camp. In January 1863, Tubman, upon hearing about the Emancipation Proclamation, barely paused in her multiple roles as nurse, cook, laundress, and strategist, saying, "I had my jubilee three years ago." However, like other female stealth soldiers, Tubman could now activate herself as a spy, joining James Montgomery's operation. On January 7, 1863, Tubman received one hundred dollars in "secret service money" from the Union Army, commissioned to collect information from slaves still living in Confederate-controlled territory and recruit new soldiers.[20]

On March 6, the secretary of war was informed that seven hundred and fifty Black men "had been rescued from slavery under the leadership of Harriet Ross Tubman" and were waiting for an opportunity to join the Union Army. Soon, units were organized to receive them—perhaps most famously the all-Black 54th and 55th Massachusetts Regiments, led by white officers, including George Garrison. Lewis H. Douglass was a member of the 54th; his father, Frederick, had seemingly recruited the rest. As the Massachusetts 54th paraded in Boston, Frederick Douglass said proudly that the Army would "by striking down the foes which oppose it, strike also the last shackle which binds the limbs of bondmen in the Rebel States."[21]

Twenty-three-year-old Lewis Douglass soon became sergeant-major, a top administrative and command position. Most of his letters to his father from training are brief (and ask for money to supplement the paltry wage). For Lewis, who had grown up in mostly white Rochester and attended its desegregated schools, the Massachusetts 54th marked the first time he had lived surrounded by other Black men. When the 54th deployed to South Carolina and joined a battle to reclaim Fort Wagner, Lewis' letter to his fiancée, Amelia Logan, doubled as a report from the field: "I have been in two fights, and am unhurt. I am about to go in another I believe to-night. Our men fought well on both occasions."

Logan may have gasped as Douglass added, "[We] were repulsed with a loss of 300 killed and wounded. I escaped unhurt from amidst that perfect hail of shot and shell . . . it was a trying time. Men fell all around me." Douglass was also being a good son: "This regiment has established its reputation as a fighting regiment not a man flinched. . . . Remember if I die I die in a worthy cause. I wish we had a hundred thousand colored troops we would put an end to this war."[22] The Douglass family soon had more support for the latter goal from Harriet Tubman, who in June led a now famous raid on South Carolina's Combahee River.

Described in the Union Army's own report as "the only military command in American history wherein a woman, black or white, led the raid," Tubman's operation was reported by both the Confederate *Charleston Mercury* and the pro-Union *Commonwealth* without mentioning Tubman by name: "Colonel Montgomery and his gallant bank of 300 black soldiers under the guidance of a black woman, dashed into the enemy's country, struck a bold and effective blow, [freeing] nearly 800 slaves."[23]

A few months after the Combahee raid, William Lloyd Garrison's son George joined Tubman at Port Royal with the Massachusetts 55th. In a letter, his father was gracious. "I have nothing but praise to give you that you have been faithful to your highest convictions, and taking your life in your hands, are willing to lay it down . . . for the suppression of slavery and the rebellion," William Lloyd wrote. Unable to resist one last effort, he continued, "I could have wished you could ascend to what I believe a higher plane of moral heroism and a nobler method of self-sacrifice; but as you are true to yourself, I am glad of your fidelity, and proud of your willingness to run any risk in a cause that is undeniably just and good."

When the 55th Massachusetts arrived in South Carolina that fall, George Garrison led the troops through Charleston in a rousing chorus of "John Brown's Body." Then it was off to their base on Folly Island, where Harriet Tubman had been headquartered for two years cooking and caring for troops. "[Tubman] no sooner saw me than she recognized me at once, and instantly threw her arms around me, and gave me quite an affectionate embrace," George wrote in his diary. "She wants to go North, but says Gen. Gilmore will not let her go . . . he thinks her services are too valuable to lose."[24] Tubman and Garrison would both serve the Union Army for the next two years, Tubman moving to Virginia's Fort Monroe, while Garrison's 55th saw combat up and down the coast.

Promoted to captain, Garrison soon befriended some of the Black NCOs (non-commissioned officers), and was often their conduit to the colonel as they fought for equal pay. Unlike the somewhat older, more educated, and more well-off African Americans in the 54th, the 55th was a younger group, far more likely to push their grievances with their commands. During a year-long wage dispute over the Army's refusal to give Black soldiers equal wages, some in the 55th deserted rather than work without pay.

A few even chose execution rather than return to duty, as in the October

1863 hanging of "John Smith, aged 21," who had been a shoemaker before enlistment.[25] Black newspapers published letters from 55th enlistees regarding their lesser pay; one stated, "We do not wish to go home, but we came out here for our rights, and for [the] promise given us is not made good."[26] If our earliest dissenting soldiers asserted citizenship and counted the costs of war, these Black troops were replicating that struggle, but in less than a third of the time.

While newly free Black citizens fought for equal treatment in the country built on their backs, the Quakers fought in their own way. The Society of Friends had negotiated an agreement with the Lincoln administration, hoping to settle the issue of Quaker participation in the struggle. Quaker families could hire a substitute for their sons, at a sum even not-wealthy parents could scrape together: $300 (about $7,500 in 2020). But other Quakers saw the payment of a substitute as too much participation in a sin, including Cyrus Pringle, a Vermonter drafted right after Gettysburg.

In 1863, Pringle was among a group of Quakers struggling with induction. "I go tomorrow where the din/Of war is in the sulphurous air. I go the Prince of Peace to serve/His cross of suffering to bear." Before that summer was over, Pringle was subject to an ad hoc trial and punishment. "Two sergeants soon called for me, and taking me a little aside, bid me lie down on my back, and stretching my limbs apart tied cords to my wrists and ankles and these to four stakes driven in the ground somewhat in the form of an X."[27]

Eventually, the U.S. surgeon general intervened to allow non-resistants to serve instead in a local hospital, in line with already established guidelines allowing religious objectors who did not or could not pay a substitute to choose "hospital service or work among the Freedmen."[28] The work there "would be quite free from objection, being for the direct relief of the sick; and that there we would release none for active service in the field, as the nurses were hired civilians." That solution was again too moderate for Pringle, who chose deployment so that he could continue to refuse to carry a weapon. But it suited a number of the others in his group, and prefigured what became known in the twentieth century as alternative service.

As the military sorted out what to do with Quakers, both sides faced desertion rates that at times reached 45 percent.[29] No wave of abolitionists moved to enlist by the Proclamation could compensate for the losses incurred by the fierce desertion and draft resistance of white men unwilling to fight a war against slavery.

Of the 776,829 men called up in the four national drafts between July 1863 and April 1865, only 46,347 ultimately served in the Union Army. While many men received exemptions or hired substitutes, "20.8 percent of all individuals called to serve—161,244 men—refused to report to their draft boards."[30] Not all of the latter are on record for refusing to fight against slavery, but the boards with the highest rate of non-reporters were in the bracelet of states just above the Mason-Dixon line and from high-immigration states like Pennsylvania and New York, the latter's resistance made obvious in the July 1963 draft riots.[31]

If they did not want to resist the draft, men who were against the war could desert. One soldier from Pennsylvania's Clearfield County wrote to General John Patton in late 1862: "You should keep in mind that the army is all democratic, and awfully down on the Niggers and Abolitionists, for we begin to feel that we are fighting to liberate a people that are too indolent to raise a hand to liberate themselves."[32] Clearfield County, a densely wooded region in west-central Pennsylvania, became known as deserter country because of how many of the 197,000 Union Army deserters managed to hide there (some on their way to Canada). Walt Whitman wrote, "The north has been & is yet honeycombed with semi-secesh [secessionist] sympathisers."[33] Underground "Peace Democrats," also known as Copperheads, named erosion of the Union Army in their mission statement.[34]

A mirror pro-Union network threaded the South, based in the strong local groups that had opposed secession. Members knew each other by a dizzying set of handshakes, including "a constitutional peace grip," and elaborate pass-phrases like "I dreamt the boys are all coming home."[35] Many of these groups bore the name "Peace Society," though peace was less their goal than reunification. In Alabama, whose pro-Union north had voted against secession, the state's Peace Society dominated a number of local elections, as well as the Board of Surgeons at Talladega, which allowed draftees to be released due to "ailments." If an Alabaman soldier-prisoner murmured the word "Washington" four times, a fellow member might secure his release.[36]

On July 28, 1863, Confederate General Gideon Pillow reported between eight thousand and ten thousand "deserters and tory conscripts in the mountains of [North] Alabama, many of whom have deserted the second, third, and (some of them) the fourth time."[37] At the Battle of Vicksburg, in late 1863, one Union general found that the spaces between the headquarters' tents were full of deserters anxious to switch sides: "They would during the night crawl over a big tree which had fallen across the creek, and then surrender to our pickets."

There was a "winged word" among the poor people of the South, which strikingly portrayed the situation, as they conceived it to be, in a single sentence: "It is the rich man's war and the poor man's fight." Many of them saw nothing dishonorable or criminal in desertion or voluntary surrender.[38]

A soldier's "longing for home" proved a powerful trigger of desertion: half of all Confederate deserters left shortly after receiving a letter from home.[39] Others deserted due to food shortages and the still-pitiful pay. In Galveston in 1863, soldiers "took their meagre rations into the street and burned them," Ella Lonn writes in her iconic *Disloyalty in the Confederacy*. "Sometimes there were as many as fifty or sixty deserters a day." Again, these workaday triggers don't detract from the act of dissent, from the decision not to be part of a war.

Some desertions were less than voluntary, as combat trauma's name shifted from "nostalgia" to "soldiers' heart." Military hospitals both North and South were filled with patients like Michigan volunteer David Kells, who had wandered off, "sick and exhausted," after fighting in the costly battles of Chancellorsville and Gettysburg.[40] The federal *Manual of Instructions for Enlisting and Discharging Soldiers* named "nostalgia" as grounds for discharge, fearing suicide resulting from the "extreme mental depression and the unconquerable longing for home [coupled with] loss of appetite, derangement of the assimilative functions, and, finally, disease of the abdominal viscera." By the end of the war, the Union Army's official records of noninfectious diseases from May 1861 to June 30, 1866, cited 5,213 cases and 58 deaths attributed to nostalgia among white troops, with 334 and 16 deaths among "colored troops."[41]

These are aggregate numbers, not broken down for various stages of the war. But both kinds of desertion increased dramatically in 1864, after General Grant shifted to what has since been described variously as attrition and total war. Silas Soule's friend Walt Whitman, a volunteer at New York hospitals, wrote to his mother, "Grant is determined to bend everything to take

Richmond and break up the banditti of scoundrels that have stuck themselves up there as a 'government.' He is in earnest about it; his whole soul and
all his thoughts night and day are upon it."[42]

Grant told General William Tecumseh Sherman, now charged with the
Union Army's Western campaign (i.e., west of the Mississippi), to "create hav-
oc and destruction of all resources that would be beneficial to the enemy."[43]
This directive envisioned neither the big, discrete battles of Chancellorsville
and Gettysburg, where volunteers fought and then took a day or two to bury
and tend to the casualties, nor still-discrete-if-shorter battles like the three-
day Battle of Chickamauga in September 1863, later described by Ambrose
Bierce as "a fight for possession of a road." Instead, there would be daily,
relentless killing as at Vicksburg, which had required a temporary ceasefire
when the Confederates found themselves unable to travel, blocked by all the
dead and wounded.

Combat continued throughout 1864 at Vicksburg and at Morris Island,
where Lewis Douglass reported that the 54th was "still hammering away at
Fort Sumter." That summer of slaughter included battles like the Wilderness
and Spotsylvania. Those who found the carnage too much to bear were subject to mid-battle courts-martial as suspected "malingerers."

After Ambrose Bierce was shot by a sniper during Sherman's Atlanta campaign, he was taken to a military hospital in Chattanooga. There is no record
that he ever saw a clinician for soldier's heart, or that the Tennessee field hospital that treated him could contend with wounds that were not of the body.

Bierce's injury meant that he was not part of Sherman's March to the
Sea. He had no chance to meet the thousands of new combatants on that
campaign—including, finally, one pesky Quaker.

In September 1864, Jesse Macy received a draft notice he could answer. "A
draft was ordered for the State of Iowa, and my name was drawn," he writes.
"My parents would still have held me back from what seemed to me my
duty. . . . We were profoundly opposed to war at any and every seeming need."

Many of Macy's classmates did what Macy's parents expected of him: "For
three hundred dollars, I could secure a substitute in the army and be free . . .
I left for Grinnell with the money in my hand." Macy's memoir does not
note how his parents responded when he decided to instead report for duty,
determined to serve without carrying a weapon. "I would enter the govern-

ment service as a noncombatant, and so informed the enrolling officers at Grinnell." The officer in charge at Camp McClellan, his first duty station, said of Macy's special status: "I recognize no such law." Macy knew that some Quakers were allowed to serve in hospitals: why not tend soldiers at the battlefield? Such duty was untested ground for conscientious objectors, but Macy meant to change that.

In the ensuing six-month drama, Macy—in that quiet Quaker way that has confused authorities from Flushing in 1664 to Selma in 1965—repeatedly refused any orders that would keep him from his chosen role. He stood still when told, "You *will* carry a weapon." He refused offers to leave the Army, to become the regiment's cook, or to carry weapons handed to him "temporarily" by others. When asked why, he answered, "I am a drafted Quaker."[44]

From Ohio to Tennessee, Macy stayed firm against pressure from a man he calls Captain Smith, who once "flew into a rage and swore that I should be *compelled* to carry a gun." As Macy sat aside, waiting for such compulsion, "one of the most popular members of the company" approached him, saying, "Macy, don't you draw a gun. Stand by your principles."[45] These standoffs appear to have continued for months.

Eventually, though not officially reassigned, Macy found his way into a medical unit, carrying one soldier's backpack to Chattanooga and making himself useful all the way to Resaca, Georgia. Sometimes, he wrote later, a march of fifteen miles seemed to go by in seconds.

Meanwhile, Bierce was still in a Chattanooga hospital, and Lewis Douglass was at Fort Sumter. More active combat awaited Silas Soule, now a Colorado cavalryman, and George Garrison, whose "colored regiment" was a hotbed for dissent. Each would remember November 29 and 30, 1864, whose battles would soon explode around them.

Soule's commander, John Chivington, promoted him to captain just as his company was officially charged with handling "Indian affairs." On November 29, 1864, Capt. Silas Soule refused the orders of his colonel to move against Indians on the plain outside their reservation, during an incident now known as the Sand Creek Massacre.

Soule was hardly the first to question the extreme (and genocidal) aspects of the government's Indian policy. Throughout the later stages of "the conquest of the West," numerous officers—some, like Edward Steptoe, later acclaimed

"Indian fighters"—were quietly horrified by some of what they were ordered to do. In 1861, renowned California explorer Kit Carson stood up to the homicidal James Carleton: "You have been sent to punish [the Mescaleros] for their treachery and their crimes, you have no power to make peace; that you are there to kill them wherever you can find them."[46]

In the fall of 1864, Soule witnessed a conference in which Cheyenne and Arapaho chiefs agreed to concede their land claims and stop fighting the U.S. troops. While they waited for affirmation of the new boundaries from Washington, Arapaho chief Black Kettle flew the Stars and Stripes as a signal of peace. But Chivington's intent was different. He and the lower-ranking enlistees were hungry and desperate. That November, Soule wrote to a Kansas friend, Chivington decided to leave no Indian alive.

"I told him I would not take part in their intended murder," Soule wrote, "but if they were going after the Sioux, Kiowas or any fighting Indians, I would go as far as any of them. We arrived at Black Kettle's and Left Hand's camp at daylight. . . . [Chivington] made a circle to the rear and formed a line 200 yds from the village, and opened fire."

When questioned in January 1865 about the massacre by Army investigators, Soule's answers were laconic, perfectly in sync with military discipline. "Were the women and children attempting to escape?" "They were." But in the personal letter mentioned above, Soule's emotions flooded out. "You would think it impossible for white men to butcher and mutilate human beings as they did," he wrote. "I tell you Ned it was hard to see little children on their knees have their brains beat out by men professing to be civilized. One squaw was wounded, and a fellow took a hatchet to finish her." Soule would go on to testify at Chivington's court-martial about the Sand Creek Massacre.[47]

The day after Sand Creek, George Garrison's regiment would wage a battle much closer to the front. The Battle of Honey Hill was something like a last stand for the Massachusetts 54th and 55th Regiments recruited by Frederick Douglass.

It was supposed to be an adjunct to Sherman's March: an assortment of units would sail to Hilton Head, South Carolina, and interrupt the Savannah–Charleston railroad, thus enabling Sherman's forces to take the island sooner. The reality for the 55th, at least, was quite different: "After Marching a few miles and encountering slight opposition from the enemy, we came upon them, heavily entrenched behind an earthwork, and a battery of field pieces," Colonel Hartwell T. Burge wrote in his official report. "The leading brigade had been driven back, when I was ordered in with a portion of my brigade; and I was also knocked out."

The companies of the 55th Regiment marched repeatedly into that artillery, losing one-third of their enlisted soldiers and one-half of their officers, the highest toll in that battle. The Army found the regiment to have "performed well" amid the loss, although the "generalship displayed was not equal to the soldierly qualities of the troops engaged," Captain Charles Carroll Soule (no known relation to the Maine/Kansas Soules) wrote later in the *Philadelphia Weekly Tribune.*

In his "Federal account" published by one of the Northeast's top Black newspapers, Charles Soule lamented the "bad judgment which ordered [or allowed] single regiments to charge successively by a narrow road upon a strongly fortified position, defended by artillery and infantry."[48] Perhaps, he suggested, a different strategy might not have cost so many lives.

Soule's editorial ran in a paper that had, like most Black newspapers, closely followed the 55th's struggle for a decent wage, and cast Honey Hill as another sign of disrespect for Black soldiers. Many were still not receiving promised pay increases; battlefield losses kept delaying an official petition started by Garrison and other white officers on their troops' behalf. Garrison would continue to write letters in support of his former soldiers for years afterward, as they submitted requests for pensions and other compensation.[49]

Capt. Garrison did this from the Garrison family home in Newton, Massachusetts, having declined to participate in Reconstruction, the flood of Northern efforts to help repair and remake the South in partnership with free Blacks. Ambrose Bierce accepted a job with the Treasury Department in Alabama, while Jesse Macy used all his connections to ensure that the freedmen in his hospital were not abandoned without care or homes. Lewis Douglass was appointed one of the first Black members of the short-lived Legislative Council of the District of Columbia.

Within a few years, Douglass found himself boycotting the united veterans' organization, the Grand Army of the Republic. Black soldiers originally made up more than half of the GAR's membership; after it was reorganized into chapters separated by race,[50] Southern posts became all-white or melted away.[51] Decades later, when asked by a GAR president to come to one of the national encampments, as they called their meetings, Douglass declined in words as crisp as his handwriting was impeccable: "The indications are that ex-Confederate soldiers are more kindly received [than colored heroes]. There may be 'fraternity in the G.A.R.,' [but] I fail to perceive it."[52]

George Garrison attended those same encampments, despite the color bar; by then, there were not many other events where he could be with others who had survived Honey Hill or marched through Richmond after victory. In the years after, Garrison married and tried repeatedly to start new businesses, none of which prospered. This author is tempted to attribute this pattern to combat trauma, though it is impossible to know; Garrison was never treated for "soldiers' heart," and, unlike his father and brothers, did not reflect on paper about his experiences.

Ambrose Bierce, by contrast, would go on to become one of the best-known stewards of American war literature, with reflections that suggest trauma that was never considered by doctors, but that created a cottage industry of scholarship about the man one historian called "the most notable example of PTSD in American letters." The Civil War is where the emotional damage of war became an area of medicine, providing the first generation of writers for whom that damage yielded dissent: Bierce, Merchant Marine veteran Herman Melville, and Army nurse Walt Whitman.

Such damage was often cited when Union vets appealed to their member of Congress for pensions. As the century ended, "General" Harriet Tubman was finally awarded her own, thanks to her congressman, Sereno Payne: "She was employed as nurse, cook in the Hospital, and spy during nearly the whole period of the war," Payne wrote to the House Committee on Invalid Pensions. "I know her personally, and she is a most interesting old colored woman." Interesting indeed: Tubman was also in active correspondence with Susan B. Anthony about the rights of women, though she never mentioned her generation of stealth soldiers.

As the century ended, there was still plenty of work to do in terms of asserting citizenship and the rights of all Americans, as Douglass and Tubman did; standing up against war crimes, as Soule did; and continuing to explore the role of non-violence. The next wars would need these, as the next generation was explicitly invited to pursue an empire.

CHAPTER FIVE

1880 to 1902

DURING THE LAST DECADES OF the 19th century, Lewis Douglass typeset stories chronicling horrors wrought by the former Slave Power long after the Civil War ended. "The Riots and Murder at Meridian, Mississippi" was followed by "Mixed Schools Allas Social Equality," "Ku-Klux Raid in Rutherford County," and "The Assailants of the Civil Rights Bill."[1] He had also lived some of those stories as the long, slow arm of Jim Crow descended: he had helped write that civil rights bill, organized among freedmen working to gain the franchise in Colorado, and been blocked from membership in the Washington, D.C. typesetters' union on the basis of race. After Frederick Douglass died, so did their paper, *The New National Era*. But Lewis Douglass still needed to speak out.

Thirty-five years after serving in the Massachusetts 54th, Lewis watched a new war unfold. Young Black men who were likely not even born when Douglass stormed Fort Wagner were enlisted in a war against Spain. One, 9th Infantry chaplain George Prioleau, wondered in *The Cleveland Gazette*: "Is America Any Better Than Spain? Has she not subjects in her midst who are murdered daily without trial, judge, or jury? Has she not subjects in her own borders whose children are half-fed and half-clothed, because their father's skin was black?"[2]

In May 1899, Douglass wrote his own commentary, a direct challenge to the commander-in-chief: did the Union his brothers had died for deserve to expand beyond its shores? Coming a year after the war began, the editorial was a firecracker tossed at his father's biographer, Booker T. Washington, a proud booster of Black enlistment. "When the United States learns that justice should be blind as to race and color, then may it undertake to, with some show of propriety, expand," he wrote. "Now its expansion means extension of race hate and cruelty, barbarous lynchings and gross injustice to dark people."[3]

Douglass was hardly the first soldier to object to the new war, but his analysis cut close to its heart, and to the task uniformed dissenters had set for themselves.

The Spanish-American War and the Philippine War, while establishing Washington as a force in global politics, intersected with the country's post–Civil War turmoil, both creating and magnifying racist tropes and realities. Some of those charged with enforcing the new American powers were enthusiastic participants in empire-building, but others responded with dissent, their voices audible all the way to the U.S. Senate. Civil War vets like Douglass were joined by younger officers questioning authority, along with an assortment of enlisted men who spoke truth to power.

If the Revolution's soldier-dissenters were asserting their citizenship, and the Civil War's fought to extend that citizenship to all, these fin-de-siècle soldiers and veterans were taking a hard look at the nation's foundational injustices: slavery and the eradication of Native Americans.

This war's dissenters included those who had gone to war to end slavery and now battled the siege against Reconstruction, and who questioned the "conquest" of the West at the expense of the lives and lifestyles of its indigenous inhabitants. Storytelling remained an important tool of dissent, often probing the depths of the new "soldier's heart," later known as post-traumatic stress disorder. As this mental side effect of war raised ever-more-complex questions of compensation and war's costs, new battlefields bred new war crimes. Alliances between soldiers and pacifists brought such crimes to light, giving muscle to efforts to stop them.

By the time Douglass wrote his 1899 commentary, the national zeitgeist was less martial than mournful. Many now saw the Civil War as a wound that needed healing. The U.S. government had spent thirty years exhuming and reburying Union and Confederate soldiers. Military cemeteries and Civil War memorials dotted the nation.[4] Printing presses were churning out thousand-page memoirs from Ulysses Grant, William T. Sherman, and thousands of other veterans. Civil War veterans were at the top of most political tickets, most soft-pedaling the war's origins.

The Supreme Court, in *Plessy v. Ferguson* (1895), affirmed the countless state laws collectively known as Jim Crow, which reincarnated the former Slave Power's control over Black citizens. Dissent against this new consensus seemed rare. On May 31, 1897, as a sculpture was unveiled in Boston honoring the Massachusetts 54th, pacifist William James knelt by the memorial with his 54th-veteran brother Willkie. Booker T. Washington intoned, "The greater monument is slowly and silently builded among the lowest in the South [i.e., former slaves]."[5] Few spoke about the fate of the former "Negro soldiers" after their war, or the situation of the current Black soldiers enrolled in the continuing fight for Native land.

In the 1880s, Black soldiers were welcomed into the 9th and 10th Cavalry Divisions and the 24th and 25th Infantry Divisions. The resulting four all-Black regiments (commanded by white officers) were nicknamed Buffalo Soldiers. The recruits "were mostly homeless men, the backwash of war and civil upheaval. Because of their composition, these colored regiments served almost continuously on the frontier, and because most of the Negro soldiers had been homeless men, the percentage of reenlistments was very high."[6] Sent to keep order on a "disorderly frontier," these soldiers might build a fort in one state or break up an unauthorized encampment in another, keeping indigenous families on the reservations that constituted their only remaining homelands. And when the Buffalo Soldiers met resistance, they engaged: "Depending on which of three overlapping listings of combat engagements you choose, in the years between 1866 and 1897, they fought in between 135 and 163 of 939 to 1,282 battles and skirmishes." They also were less apt to desert when things got tough, enlisted personnel's usual means of functional dissent.

Back in 1867, General George Armstrong Custer had faced the desertion of half his all-white cavalry, left with 168 of the original 300.[7] After thirteen of those escaped by horseback, "Custer impulsively ordered the deserters seized dead or alive and ordered some shot without a trial . . . [a] rash action he always justified as essential to the preservation of unity and authority in the face of desertions during an Indian campaign."[8] Few deserters left signs that they disagreed with Custer or Indian policy. That was left to a handful of officers, many of whom echoed the late Ethan Allen Hitchcock in their quiet dissent.

Most dissenting officers retained the cultural prejudices of the time, while trying to face the dilemma of the liberal occupier. Ninth Infantry commander Benjamin Grierson stood up against the abuse of Indians, "whatever the consequences may be," just as he had for his own beleaguered troops.[9] Before Fort Sumter, Grierson had been a musician and bandleader from Maine, terrified of horses; as a cavalryman, Grierson had led a daring raid during the Vicksburg campaign. Most of his subsequent thirty-year army career was spent as commander of one of the "colored" regiments established in 1866.

By refusing to join in as concepts of race hardened after Reconstruction, Grierson was called a Quaker, the ultimate insult to a military man, and ostracized by his white peers. Grierson insisted that his unit be addressed as the 10th Cavalry, not the "Colored Cavalry," although his fellow white officers did not follow that lead. He risked court-martial when the 3rd Infantry's Colonel William Hoffman tried to order the 10th off the parade grounds. "General Grierson immediately took up for the supposed right of his darkies, and he and General Hoffman seemed to have it pretty hot for a while."[10] Grierson was equally willing to challenge authority in New Mexico in 1870, when he noticed that the Comanche and the Kiowa were being denied the provisions promised by treaty, and then being shot at for leaving their reservations. "What is required to settle the 'Indian question,'" he wrote his brother, is "strict fulfillment of all government observations."[11] Rather than fire the hero of Vicksburg, the army appointed a general to outrank him.[12] "I too must be considered too much of a Quaker or a peace man to be left here in charge of military affairs on this Reservation," Grierson mused. "If I had launched out and killed a few Indians—on the principle of . . . 'wherever he saw a head to hit it'—I would no doubt be considered *successful*."

Union Army service had brought Clay MacCauley to the Battle of Chancellorsville: "Rather large drafts were made on our moral forces, [with] mutilation and death at our very feet." MacCauley's moral forces would become a voice of dissent that crossed continents. By 1880, MacCauley was a forty-something Presbyterian minister, pastor of the First Unitarian Church of Washington, D.C. The Smithsonian Institution's Bureau of American Ethnology hired him for a different sort of Indian mission: to study the remaining Cherokee of North Carolina and Seminole of Florida. Tired of the burdens of church administration, MacCauley was glad to accept the offer.

Forty years after Andrew Jackson's wars, there were only 208 Seminole in eighty-seven families living in twenty-two encampments from Key West to the Miami River. MacCauley's language skills improved out of necessity. "The knowledge of the Seminole language which I gradually acquired enabled me, in my intercourse with other Indians, to verify and increase the information I had received." His conclusion was angry, if ethnocentric, describing "people our Government has never been able to conciliate or to conquer . . . the Seminole have always lived within our borders as aliens." MacCauley moved to St. Paul, Minnesota, and tried for seven years to build a multiracial community there; he finally applied to the Unitarian Church's new Foreign Service, and in 1889 became its first representative in Tokyo, Japan. MacCauley kept in touch with the homeland, writing a series of columns for the *Boston Evening Transcript*—including several from the newest political hot spot, the Philippines.

But before either MacCauley or Lewis Douglass wrote about the new war, Ambrose Bierce was making journalistic history and signaling, in his own acerbic fashion, the latest signs of the country's twin founding injustices.

By 1898, Bierce was on his tenth or eleventh life. After having drifted West shortly after the Civil War and resigning from the army a brevet major, Bierce had become a San Francisco voice known for his misanthropic language and take-no-prisoners attitude.[13] After years as a columnist at his own *San Francisco News-Letter* and *The Wasp*, Bierce was hired as a senior staffer by the much younger William Randolph Hearst. Bierce became a pioneer of American war literature, one who questioned every verity while bearing witness to his own trauma.

Bierce published his first stories based on his war experiences in Hearst's *San Francisco Examiner*: both essay-reportage like "What I Saw of Shiloh" (quoted extensively in the previous chapter) and gothic fiction like "An Occurrence at Owl's Creek Bridge," told from inside the mind of a deserter being executed. In the latter piece, Bierce used war's surreal comedy as a way to keep sane. But when these tales were published in book form in 1891, sales were poor; there was no room, in those years of building memorials, for such astringent memories.

Bierce had avoided the syndromes that affected many of his fellow Civil War veterans. He had not ended up in jail for alcohol, unlike the thousands in America's penitentiaries after the war who had "come to us with constitutions shattered by wounds, disease or intemperance."[14] Nor had Bierce looked for treatment or compensation, unlike the 5,700 the Union Army had discharged for "nostalgia" (or the 2,700 chaptered for "insanity").[15] But his stories bore witness to both the trauma of war and the complex self-defense reaction now called PTSD.[16]

In this new war against Spain, Hearst demanded long-distance military commentary. "Horrid War!—[between the] United States and Spain has already broken out like a red rash in the newspapers," Bierce wrote.[17] All of them, including Hearst's, seemed to support U.S. interference in Spain's decades-long occupation of Cuba and the Philippines. Cuba's successive wars for independence had begun, the horrified *New-York Times* pointed out, with freed slaves.[18] To Americans after the Civil War, every war was a possible race war. As more acceptable (white) revolutionaries joined the fight against Spain, the newspapers' interest morphed into cheers for the liberty of the Cuban people. One "Wealthy Cuban Now in This City" told the *Times* in 1895, "I know of scores of educated men—doctors, dentists, and lawyers—who have joined the insurgent ranks. . . . They all want to free their native island from the tyranny of the Spanish Government or die in the attempt."[19] Hearst saw the opportunity and jumped in: with his *New York Herald-Journal* in a pitched battle for circulation against Joseph Pulitzer's *New York World,*[20] he sent dozens of correspondents to Cuba, whose stories bore lurid headlines: "SPANIARDS AUCTION OFF CUBAN GIRLS."[21]

On February 15, 1898, an explosion in Havana Harbor destroyed the U.S. battleship *Maine.* It's still unclear why, but Hearst and the charismatic young secretary of the Navy, Theodore Roosevelt, blamed Spain. Soon thirty thousand troops were headed for deployment, including thirteen thousand hastily recruited volunteers. One career officer, who had fought at Ambrose Bierce's side at Chickamauga in 1864, was ambivalent about his mission's rousing reception. "I am glad the question of 'war or peace' was not left unto me," he wrote his family, adding that as his unit's train wound its way from Fort Leavenworth to Georgia, revenge was cheered: "All along our route from Fort L. we were greeted at every station by crowds of people (women and girls predominated) waving flags and cheering. . . . A soldier wrote with chalk in large letters on the side of one car, *Remember the Maine shall be our battle cry.* I do not admire this. Revenge is not an ennobling pursuit."[22]

Similar thoughts crossed the mind of Charles Erskine Scott Wood of Portland, Oregon. Wood had moved there fifteen years earlier, as his army service ended, becoming one of the city's most famous attorneys, representing celebrities such as Emma Goldman. After the *Maine,* Wood volunteered for reserve duty in Cuba; although he was not sure of the war, he wrote, "the country once involved, my duty seemed clear." When both the governor of Oregon and the secretary of war refused his offer,[23] Wood was glad, in view of the rhetoric coming from the likes of Senator Albert Beveridge: "We acted toward the Indians as though we feared them, loved them, hated them—a mingling of foolish sentiment, inaccurate thought, and paralytic purpose. . . . Mr. President, that must not be our plan. This war is like all other wars. It needs to be finished before it is stopped."[24]

As Wood's radicalism began to evolve, he knew the last thing he wanted was to ally himself with such talk. Neither did Lewis Douglass, who had to contend with allies who hoped to change such rhetoric by bringing in more Black combatants. Booker T. Washington promised the secretary of the Navy that the call for war would be answered by "at least ten thousand loyal, brave, strong black men in the south who crave an opportunity to show their loyalty to our land and would gladly take this method of showing their gratitude for the lives laid down and the sacrifices made that Blacks might have their freedom and rights."[25]

Fifteen Black sailors had died in the *Maine* explosion. That week, the "Faith Cadets," a division of the 9th U.S. Infantry, spontaneously reported for duty, assembled at their old headquarters in New Orleans, elected officers, and offered their services in a body to go to Cuba. They did so despite countless insults against black soldiers, as seen at New Orleans' Jackson Barracks in 1895, when raging "mobs of [white] river-laborers"[26] attacked "colored crewsmen and longshoremen [who threw] their tools into the Mississippi river." When four Black regiments sailed for Manila in July 1898, the *Colored*

American exulted: "We have secured honorable stations in military life. . . . We are better represented upon the official roll than would have been probable in two decades of peace." But the day-to-day reality was often different, as troops saw on their trip South before sailing.

Under the "Black Codes" adopted by Southern state legislatures, many of the Black soldiers bound for Cuba could not cross the same streets as white soldiers; some were attacked, belittled, and excluded even from the Army commissary. "Why sir, the Negro of [America] is a freeman and yet a slave," 9th Infantry Chaplain George Prioleau wrote in the *Cleveland Gazette* in July. "Talk about fighting and freeing poor Cuba, and Spain's brutality."[27]

Prioleau's piece appeared around the same time as Bierce's "Horrid War!" column in the *Examiner*. Bierce wrote other pieces expressing skepticism of the war—"Letter from a Dead Sailor," "The Seamy Side of This War," "A Word of Warning."[28] Then the publisher corralled his stateside war correspondent into a column with the neutral title of "War Topics," which would over the next ten years range from battle tactics to corruption to a proposal to introduce a permanent standing army. Bierce would wait nearly twenty years before even making an indirect critique of Roosevelt's famous mission in Cuba with the 1st U.S. Volunteers, known as the Rough Riders. See Bierce's eventual *Devil's Dictionary*: "Indeed, a certain class of persons who probably traveled faster than others came to be called 'rough riders,' and for their sufferings were compensated by appointment to the most lucrative offices in the gift of the sovereign."[29]

In 1898, Bierce refrained from such critique, but his anger was clear: "The passion for territory once roused rages like a lion; successive conquests only strengthen it. That is the fever that is now burning in the American blood."[30] A month prior, Bierce had gotten Hearst to reprint what may be his most eloquent anti-war statement, the memory piece "What I Saw of Shiloh." He did the same on December 4, 1898, instead of his popular "Prattle" column, ending the year by declaring: "I will willingly surrender an other life than the one that I should have thrown away at Shiloh."[31]

That same week, a treaty was signed, ceding not just Cuba[32] but all of Spain's island possessions, including the Philippines, to the United States.[33] A few weeks later, as the treaty was debated in Congress, an American living in Tokyo accepted an invitation to visit the United States' new supreme commander of the Philippines.

By the time Reverend Clay MacCauley stepped off the ship from Hong
Kong, he was no longer the lean, dark-haired man who had fought at Chancellorsville in 1863 or even the trim forty-something who had learned Seminole. The additional years had added to his frame a plump strength, a stark
white mustache softening his otherwise severe face. Between the girth and his
six-foot height, the reverend struck an imposing figure.

The mix of Malay and Spanish architecture and polyglot of languages
did not faze the scholar: "Against the eastern horizon, stretched in sombre,
irregular outline the roofs, towers and battlements of the famed capital of
the Oriental tropics, named three hundred years ago." His elegiac *A Day in
Manila, The Noble City* sets the scene:

> There appeared on the sea-side . . . a stately mansion approached
> by a driveway that encloses a beautiful fountain and is enclosed
> by masses of flowering plants and large-foliaged tropical trees.
> Not far from the club is a Red Cross Hospital, large, open and
> clean. Then, we drove by some barracks crowded with soldiers of
> the United States regular army. . . . [Soon] I was carried through
> a generous gateway, along a gravelled [*sic*] path to the steps of the
> side entrance of the house that my American friends had made
> for themselves.[34]

"The blazing hot noon of the tropics had come," MacCauley wrote, "and I
was glad to rest for a while from the bewildering hours spent on Manila's
streets." During those "bewildering hours" MacCauley had spoken to Filipino soldiers, and to a few of the American enlisted men. Now, in a mini-
mansion "with enough space [to dance] a good-sized Virginia reel," he was set
to dine with the elite—including, most significantly, the islands' new military governor.

The day before MacCauley's visit, the news had been ablaze with the U.S.
response to Emilio Aguinaldo's imprecations. Aguinaldo, who had spent his
life fighting Spanish rule, had been returned to the islands from exile by
U.S. troops, who then relied on him to lead Philippine forces until Spain's
surrender. On New Year's Day 1899 (a few days before MacCauley's arrival),
Aguinaldo had been elected president of the newborn Philippine Republic by
a constitutional convention whose founding document was clearly modeled

after that of the United States. Even the named Cabinet of Republica Filipina echoed Washington's, with ministries of Finance, War, and Interior.

In his letter of December 1898, Aguinaldo had called on the United States to live up to its own advertising and allow Philippine independence: "The Filipino people have learned to love liberty, order, justice, and civil life. . . . I and my leaders know how to admire and are ready to imitate the disinterestedness, the abnegation, and the patriotism of the grand men of America, among whom stands preeminent the immortal George Washington."[35] The reply from General Elwell Otis, "Military Governor of the Philippines," had been to send readiness orders to the U.S. Army troops.

MacCauley was both critical of and sympathetic to his fellow officer: "I still think that General Otis, conscientious, faithful administrator and brave soldier that he is, was not as tactful as one should have been in his dealings with Aguinaldo and his followers. . . . Yet now it seems clear to me that General Otis did his work, in the main, in literal obedience to his superiors in America," who assumed "what the Filipinos themselves might wish need not be taken into the account in formulating plans for their government."[36]

Both Otis and Commodore George Dewey, architect of the United States' naval victories against Spain, joined MacCauley at that same Manila dinner table: "'Yes,' said the general, 'Manila is an interesting city, and the Philippine Islands may be very valuable, but, I tell you, it would be an act of supreme folly for the United States to incorporate them into its own territory, or to enter into intimate political and social relations with the Philippines people.' We took the general's judgment for our text. Our talk was in large part but comment upon it. . . . *The situation if properly understood in the United States—so we believed—would soon stop the growing movement there for annexation of the islands*" (emphasis added).

In his essay about that day, MacCauley is blunt, more ethnographer than soldier or theologian. "Most white men instinctively feel themselves to be the superiors of men of colour, and their demeanor ordinarily shows it," writes the man who had failed to integrate his Minnesota church. "The Anglo-Saxon never fully coalesces with people of any other race. The fact is never successfully concealed. . . . The two can not be brought together as equals and as companions in the same political household."

After the preceding was published in the *Boston Evening Transcript*, it created a furor among pro-annexation newspapers and politicians. It was also included in a box of mail bound directly for the Philippines—thanks to an unlikely group that called itself the Anti-Imperialist League.

The Anti-Imperialist League was founded in Boston in the spring of 1898 with Committees of Correspondence, named for their precursors in the American Revolution. Wendell Phillips Garrison and other abolitionist pacifists joined reformers like Josephine Shaw Lowell, sister of Lewis Douglass' commander, Robert Gould Shaw.

During the Civil War, Lowell had been a volunteer nurse, serving long after her brother's death in 1862; after the war, she worked ceaselessly on behalf of low-income families, becoming the first female commissioner of the New York State Board of Charities. Her views on the Philippine war were deeply tied to her Civil War experiences. Lowell told a New York audience, "What can be said of a war in which the nation makes no sacrifice, does not even feel the weight of added taxation, goes about its own selfish business and its own selfish pleasures exactly as if not in any sense responsible for the war? Great moral evil must ensue."[37]

The League's national newsletter, *The Anti-Imperialist*, blasted President William McKinley and Vice President Theodore Roosevelt, though its foreign affairs criticism was muddied with arguments over monetary policy between "Silver Republicans" and "Gold Democrats." By December, the League's ever-expanding roster of vice presidents included both Andrew Carnegie and Grover Cleveland, though not hard-working women like Lowell, who built an auxiliary organization that out-published and out-donated (per capita) its male counterparts.[38] Women also helped bring in allied organizations, including (briefly) the increasingly powerful Women's Christian Temperance Union (perhaps at the urging of Lowell, a longtime member).[39]

The Anti-Imperialist League included former Confederates like Donelson Caffery, whose riflemen had fought against Ambrose Bierce's Union Army at Shiloh. The League notably did *not* include either Bierce, whose skepticism of the new wars seared his columns, or Douglass, for whom the presence of those Confederates was likely a deal-breaker. And while few of their words and acts seem to have changed policy, they opened space for the active-duty soldiers who might.

By January, the League was influencing the public debate over the treaty with Spain, including on the Senate floor. Caffery, now a Louisiana senator, invoked Shiloh along with Presidents George Washington and Thomas Jefferson: "When Washington besought his countrymen to avoid all foreign complications and entanglements was he a 'little American?'" Caffery, whose opposition was ethnocentric (he declared the Filipinos "ungovernable"), would soon be hailed by the *New York Times* as a "A Rational Anti-Imperialist," being a Southern landowner not associated with the League's Boston types.

Though Lewis Douglass never openly allied with the League, he was likely aware of the efforts of its one Black vice president, Reverend William H. Scott, to recruit more Black supporters to the cause. He may not have heard about the proposed Colored Auxiliary to the League, or the July 1899 creation of a separate-but-not-equal Colored National Anti-Imperialistic League, followed by the Democratic Party–themed National Negro Anti-Expansion, Anti-Imperialist, Anti-Trust, Anti-Lynching League. The Black press ignored it all, preferring to print letters from Black soldiers.

Such letters kept coming as the conflict became a shooting war. Instead of taking the advice of MacCauley and his Manila colleagues, the United States had spent January sending *more* brigades and ships, Filipino troops no longer Spain-fighting allies but "insurgents." As they chased Aguinaldo's government from Malolos to San Isidro and emptied the historic Santa Cruz "rebel stronghold," the war escalated quickly, with both Otis and hawkish members of Congress asserting that 100,000 troops were now necessary.

Spring and summer headlines announced "amnesty" for "immediate surrender." In addition to its eternal love–hate relationship with counterinsurgency doctrine,[40] the press gleefully reported politicians claiming the islands on behalf of American "manhood" and ran spreads featuring those "manly" Colorado, California, and Oregon volunteers, both in Manila and being welcomed home.[41] Some in the Anti-Imperialist League saw cause for desperate action—or, at least, desperate pamphleteering—and discussed using Donelson Caffery's quasi-racist Senate speech, a letter from Aguinaldo, and Mac-Cauley's report from Manila. To modern eyes, these pamphlets are hardly the stuff of revolutionary agitation—for example, *The Cost of a National Crime*, with pages of numbers on debt and tropical diseases. Some speculated that the League plotted to distribute them to U.S. troops stationed in Asia; upon hearing the accusation, Massachusetts activist Edward Atkinson decided it was a great idea.

Without the group's blessing, in May Atkinson sent test samples of *The Cost of a National Crime*, *The Hell of War and Its Penalties*, and *Criminal Aggression: By Whom Committed?* in packs addressed to Dewey and Otis in Manila. The postmaster general stopped the potentially subversive tracts before they were loaded on ships, declaring at his visit to the White House that perhaps post–Civil War laws against "giving aid and comfort to the enemy" applied.

The League's board immediately distanced itself from Atkinson's mailer, then proceeded to publish two other sets of military voices against the war: Clay MacCauley's op-ed explainer, "A Straightforward Tale," and a book, *Soldiers' Letters*. MacCauley's tale is vivid, and the excerpts from those letters more so, with stories as diverse as the thirty-thousand-strong fighting force. Some simply described the battle in front of them: "When you can realize four hundred or five hundred persons living within the confines of five or six blocks, and then an order calling out all of the women and children, and then setting fire to houses and shooting down any niggers attempting to escape from the flames, you have an idea of Filipino warfare," wrote Colorado Sergeant Will A. Rule. Fred D. Sweet, of the Utah Light Battery, wrote of the battle of Santa Cruz, "The scene reminded me of the shooting of jack-rabbits in Utah, only the rabbits sometimes got away, but the insurgents did not."

Others described atrocities. "I don't know how many men, women, and children the Tennessee boys did kill. They would not take any prisoners," wrote Arkansas volunteer Leonard F. Adams. "One company of the Tennessee boys was sent to headquarters with thirty prisoners, and got there with about a hundred chickens and no prisoners."

One Kansas regiment captain wrote somberly that in Maypaja, once boasting five thousand residents, "now not one stone remains upon top of another. You can only faintly imagine this terrible scene of desolation. War is worse than hell." More than half the letters were explicitly anti-war. "I am not afraid, and always ready to do my duty, but I would like some one to tell me what we're fighting for," wrote Nebraska sergeant Arthur Vickers.

One soldier's matter-of-fact delivery would not have surprised Ambrose Bierce:

> That twenty million dollars that they paid bought only Manila. Most all the men who think in the Army Corps are opposed, and have been from the start, to holding these islands. Well, I hope we may never get another weak-kneed politician in the presidential chair at a critical time like this. Herbert Cooper Thompson, Co. C, Second Oregon Regiment.

The League was busy organizing its first national conference, for October in Chicago.[42] The speakers' list featured assorted clerics, congressmen from Philadelphia and New York, and the seventy-something Carl Schurz, his voice honed by fifty years of service as interior secretary, senator from Missouri, newspaperman, and officer in two radical wars—Lincoln's and the 1848 German revolution.

The factions had an agreed-upon platform statement, including: "A self-governing state cannot accept sovereignty over an unwilling people. The United States cannot act upon the ancient heresy that might makes right." With McKinley running for re-election the following year, they hoped to build momentum for his defeat, both in the election itself and the policies in question. However, two days before the conference, the president himself arrived in Chicago for a gathering with the pre-Orwellian name of "The Peace Jubilee."[43] As twelve thousand stood for hours to see McKinley,[44] the *Chicago Tribune* applauded his promise that the Filipinos, under American rule, would "not be governed as vassals or serfs or slaves" but would "have a government under liberty and law." But the Jubilee's *coup de grace* was its closing speaker: none other than Booker T. Washington, busy earning W.E.B. Du Bois' later name for him, "The Great Accommodator."

Calling the U.S. victory over Spain "magnificent," the vigorous forty-two-year-old Washington went on to caution that there remained "one other victory for Americans to win," invoking the spirit of the 10th Infantry soldiers who had died fighting with Roosevelt the previous year. "The trenches that we built around Santiago shall be the eternal burial ground of all that separates us in our business and civil relations."[45]

While the *New York Times* and the *Chicago Tribune* wrote rapturously of Washington's and McKinley's speeches, Lewis Douglass responded with a different perspective, reflecting the daily reality of many Black soldiers, which was discussed every day in Black newspapers across America. The latter had been evenly divided on the question of war with Spain, with the half following Washington given a slap by anti-lynching activist Ida B. Wells.[46]

The debate was lively enough for some soldiers who did go to Asia to evince skepticism on arrival, according to the *Army and Navy Journal*.[47] If the *New York Times* had feared a race war in Cuba, it had helped breed one in the Philippines. Theodore Roosevelt, the hero of San Juan Hill who had long denounced Blacks as "a perfectly stupid race" that was as "kept down by lack of intellectual development as by anything else," found it easier to rouse his troops against the "dark" Filipinos.

The ensuing war encouraged many to take up that call. "When we capture a suspicious nigger, we generally loose him in the swamps, that is he is lost and he isn't lost but he never shows up any more," wrote one sergeant from Luzon. "Turn about is fair play. They do it to us and we do it to them, they killed three of our fellows without mercy but we have taken a very sweet revenge and a very clear revenge to them too."[48]

Nearly as soon as four Black regiments joined the 29,000 troops on the island, letters from Black soldiers to their local newspapers described an atmosphere of xenophobia crossed with racism. Sgt. John Galloway, of the 24th Infantry, reported, "The whites have begun to establish their diabolical race hatred in all its home rancor in Manila, even endeavoring to propagate the phobia among the Spaniards and Filipinos so as to be sure of the foundation of their supremacy when the civil rule is established."[49] Another stated sarcastically, "We're here to take up the White Man's Burden!" On November 17, 1899, the Kansas City *American Citizen* featured Lewis Douglass' retort to Washington's theory of Black-power-via-war:

President McKinley knows that brave, loyal, black American soldiers, who fight and die for their country, are hated, despised, and cruelly treated in that section of the country from which this administration accepts dictation and to the tastes of which the President, undoubtedly, caters. . . . It is a sorry, though true, fact that whatever this government controls, injustice to dark races prevails. The people of Cuba, Porto Rico [*sic*], Hawaii and Manila know it well as do the wronged Indian and outraged black man in the United States.

There's no record that Douglass ever attempted to share this statement with the Anti-Imperialist League he had refused to join.

Most Black soldiers and vets appear to have ignored both. Knowing all this, and perhaps remembering the San Patricios a half-century earlier, Emilio Aguinaldo's *insurrectos* wrote to the same newspapers, offering commissions to deserters. Perhaps due to the tight unit cohesion of their regiments, Black soldiers had a much lower desertion rate—only nine deserters out of four regiments[50]—than white units, whose rate by mid-1900 was more than 10 percent (3,993 of 29,026 total).[51]

The few who did take the offer gained notoriety. David Fagen of Erie, Pennsylvania, was on his second enlistment with the 24th Infantry in 1899, after the regiment's Cuba tour had left it "reduced by bullets and yellow fever to fewer than 400 men."[52] Since no correspondence from Fagen survives, we do not know what stories he told about that tour, but six months after his February re-enlistment, the 24th was plunged into a massive three-part struggle for the island of Luzon, near the Mount Arayat *insurrecto* headquarters. On November 17, the same day that Lewis Douglass' anti-war editorial was published, Fagen jumped on a horse helpfully supplied by an *insurrecto* officer and melted into the jungle. Fighting beside General Jose Alejandrino, Fagen was promoted to captain in the Philippine Army and became the U.S. Army's Public Enemy Number Two (after Aguinaldo).

The following year, Ambrose Bierce passed judgment in one of his "War Topics" pieces for the *Examiner*, using his most sardonic voice while "teaching" militarism to Americans:

Observe, now, how Providence overrules the intentions of the truly good for their advantage. We went to war with Mexico for peace, humanity and honor, yet emerged from the contest with an extension of territory beyond the dreams of political avarice. We went to war with Spain for the relief of an oppressed people, and at the close found ourselves in possession of vast and rich insular dependencies and with a pretty tight grasp upon the country for relief of whose oppressed people we took up arms. We could hardly have profited more had "territorial aggrandizement" been the spirit of our purpose and the heart of our hope.[53]

By 1902, when Aguinaldo was captured, the war had taken the dark turn warned of by its opponents, with officers court-martialed for war crimes and the president seeking a way out. Warnings from soldier-storytellers marked the new century—not just Bierce, but also Portland dandy C.E.S. Wood and Samuel Clemens, who had returned from Europe to become the nation's most public anti-imperialist.

Charles Erskine Scott Wood had long conducted a successful law practice while he wrote poems and stories about his time in the northwest's Nez Perce War, an "outrageous tale of the strong over the weak."[54] He had become a Democratic Party activist, and in April 1899, just as the war began, was the keynote speaker at the party's annual Jefferson Dinner.

Wood spoke of Manila's occupying troops: "I was in the army myself, and I tell you the idea of discipline and loyalty to orders is the one dominant idea. I claim to be an educated man. I was born a democrat, and yet when I was in the army I would have executed any order whatever; I might have questioned, but I would not have disobeyed. That is a spirit dangerous to the Republic. It is obedience, not love for the job, that keeps our soldiers in the Philippines."[55]

Wood also saw his position as an election strategy for presidential candidate William Jennings Bryan. Over the next few years, the League would diverge into two main streams—one focused increasingly on electoral politics and Bryan's campaign (serving as an easy spur for newspaper editorials decrying "Bryanite" perfidy), the other bringing the voices of those who had witnessed atrocity to the attention of the public.

A singular effort to unmask war crimes as they occurred, the 1902 Senate Investigation of Activities in the Philippines featured testimony not only by Otis and other generals, but also by young former volunteers. The League's Massachusetts chapter had done something unprecedented: its founder had sat down with these young men and prepared them to speak to a roomful of senators and generals.[56] From January to June of 1902, the Senate (and the nation, via ubiquitous newspaper coverage) first heard charges that American occupiers took few prisoners and burned towns to the ground. They also learned that their forces had invented something called the "water cure," known in the twenty-first century as waterboarding. In April, Charles S. Riley of Northampton, Massachusetts, formerly a sergeant in Company M, 26th Volunteer Infantry, was among those who testified:

> [Riley] said he had witnessed the "water cure" at Igbaras, in the Province of Iloilo, on Nov. 27, 1900. . . . [One prisoner] was then thrown under a water tank which held about 100 gallons of water, and his mouth placed directly under the faucet and held open so as to compel him to swallow the water which was allowed to escape from the tank. Over him stood an interpreter repeating one word, which the witness said he did not understand, but which he believed to be the native equivalent of "confess."[57]

Massachusetts native Riley had been subpoenaed for his testimony after he wrote about the "cure" in a letter to the *Northampton Daily Herald*.[58] A few days later, a former sergeant in Company M, 26th Volunteer Infantry, confirmed Riley's testimony regarding Igbaras—a small city, he told the committee, that he had seen burnt to the ground. "[Igbaras] contained about 10,000 people but no business places. All except about fifteen houses were destroyed, and men, women, and children were forced out indiscriminately. The witness also said that a neighboring town containing about 12,000 people had been burned."[59]

When the testimony was published, partisan fireworks ensued. General Nelson A. Miles, asked by the Senate to investigate all the reports of atrocities, issued a damning report in late 1902: "I found that with certain officers the impression prevailed that such acts were justifiable . . . an erroneous and dangerous impression." The Miles Report documented "fifty-seven verifiable instances . . . [of] murder of prisoners; 6 murders of civilians; 18 rapes; administration of the 'water cure,' and other forms of torture of prisoners and civilians. In addition, sixty cases of aggravated assault may be identified which in their features of calculated cruelty closely approximate the category and definition of torture."[60] After their testimony, Riley and Davis disappeared from public view, the ranks of dissenting vets growing ever-thinner.

By 1902, C.E.S. Wood was no longer in the process of commenting on the Philippine War: after campaigning fiercely for Bryan, he had moved on to arguing (without success) before the Supreme Court and discoursing on "philosophical anarchism." But there were a few still in the fight—including one whose Confederate service had consisted only of two weeks in a self-organized regiment after Sumter, but whose name would be better known than anyone else in this chapter—or this book.

Samuel Clemens, better known as Mark Twain, returned to the United States in 1900, after more than five years in Europe working to pay off his debts. Before the year was out, he said at Manhattan's posh Lotos Club, "We started out to set those poor Filipinos free too, and why, why, why that most righteous purpose of ours has apparently miscarried I suppose I never shall know." Twain had initially favored the Spanish-American War, but then, he told the *New World*: "I have thought some more, since then, and I have read carefully the treaty of Paris, and I have seen that we do not intend to free, but to subjugate the people of the Philippines."[61] Twain would go on to say much more about the war, about now-President Theodore Roosevelt ("the worst president"), and even about "the United States of Lynched." He would dine with Woodrow Wilson in 1908, years before Wilson shepherded millions into uniform for what everyone called "The World War." Those millions would include a new crop of dissenters, as passionate as their predecessors and even more diverse.

CHAPTER SIX
1912 to 1919

THE SUMMER OF 1915, NEW York City smelled of war. Evan Thomas could not wait to leave.

On every corner newsstand, newspaper headlines screamed of battles in Europe. Thomas, a lean young man with a narrow face and alert eyes, hated that he was still in New York working at the American Parish, an immigrant settlement house in Harlem, under the direction of his brother Norman. The house's residents looked at the newspapers with anxiety: they did not need English to count the battle zones, from Amiens to Gallipoli. America was officially neutral in Europe's conflict, less so New York City. In a May attack on the British ship *Lusitania*, a German submarine killed 1,198 people, of whom forty-three were Americans.[1] Both tabloid and broadsheet newspapers called Germans murderers and demanded vengeance. City officials called for preparedness, as if it were possible to be prepared for hell.

Union Theological Seminary, where Thomas was pursuing a divinity degree, offered little respite. It clustered next to Columbia University, whose flagpole banners urged students to honor "the flag of peace and prosperity." Thomas' classmates discussed ad infinitum what "preparedness" might require of them.

On Memorial Day of 1915, tens of thousands crammed onto Riverside Drive to see the veterans of five conflicts march uptown to the Soldiers and

Sailors Memorial. At the memorial, a marble stand of Corinthian columns, the United Spanish War Veterans saluted General Leonard Wood and retired Rear Admiral Charles D. Sigsbee, who had commanded the *U.S.S. Maine* when it exploded in 1898. Thomas didn't go across town to watch the spectacle. He could almost smell its martial spirit from miles off, its smoke, firework sparks, and heavy sweat.

A few weeks later, a similar scent suffused Princeton, New Jersey, when Thomas went down for his brother Ralph's graduation. Princeton University's castle-like buildings stood proud, not unfamiliar with war. The site of both a 1777 battle and the 1781 Mutiny in January,[2] his alma mater had whole rooms honoring alumni on both sides of the Civil War. At graduation, its president told the graduating class of the dangers of peace. If they avoid war, he said, they might lose the chance to become real men. Present in the crowd's thoughts was the university's former president, Woodrow Wilson, who now sat in the White House. No one mentioned the recent words of William Edward Burghardt (known as W.E.B.) Du Bois, editor of the NAACP magazine *The Crisis*: "We may blunder into murder and shame. . . . But it will not be war. It will be a crime."[3]

Later, Thomas and some fellow alumni, self-named "The Crusaders," huddled to discuss what they should do. The group's founder, also a Union minister, said the choice was clear: Jesus did his best to stop violence, after all.[4] Evan Thomas squinted in the blinding sunlight.

Back in New York, far downtown from the American Parish, W.E.B. Du Bois feared the probable new war. Author and college professor, editor of *The Crisis*, and the voice of the National Association for the Advancement of Colored People (NAACP), Du Bois had a well-known anti-war tilt; he had written the "It will be a crime" editorial a year earlier. Back then, the international peace movement had been growing, partly due to the Allies' massive losses on the war's Western Front. NAACP co-founder Lillian Wald chaired a local Anti-Militarism Committee, soon to be renamed the American Union Against Militarism (AUAM).

Just before the *Lusitania* disaster, the *Atlantic Monthly* had published Du Bois' fullest statement about war yet, "The African Roots of War."[5] In that essay, he cast himself as a passionate anti-militarist, asking at a "meeting of peace societies in St. Louis," "should you not discuss racial prejudice as a prime cause of war?" only to be told it was too controversial. "We have extended gradually our conception of democracy beyond our social class to all social classes in our nation. . . . We must [now] extend the democratic ideal to the yellow, brown, and black peoples." Acknowledging how "unreasonable" that sounded to many in 1915, Du Bois nonetheless found it essential to acknowledge his country's founding injustice: "We have to choose between this unspeakably inhuman outrage on decency and intelligence that is the World War" and capitalism's interest in exploiting people of color as property, labor, or leverage. "We shall not drive war from this world," he wrote, "[without] a world-democracy," with participation by all. For the rest of his life, Du Bois would continue to explore and expose these links between militarism and racism.

After the *Lusitania* sank, Du Bois' response in *The Crisis'* June issue quoted the *Atlantic* piece, connecting the war to European colonialism: "The last horror of a horrible war is come! . . . [Western civilization's] failure did not come with this war but with this war it has been made manifest."[6] Du Bois then contrasted the sorrow over the maritime tragedy with the much higher body counts "when Negroes were enslaved, or the natives of Congo raped and mutilated, or the Indians of the Amazon robbed, or the natives of the South Seas murdered, or 2,732 American citizens lynched." That last was a pointed jab at President Wilson, who had taken no action in the face of widespread, routine extrajudicial killings of Black citizens.

The NAACP board's pacifist faction had supported Du Bois as he questioned whether the military was a force for positive change for the Black community. But now, with the United States' entry into the war more likely, Du Bois and the NAACP decided to regroup, knowing that any such war would include Black soldiers. As an organization founded to assert Black Americans' full citizenship, NAACP owed it to those soldiers to ensure their equal treatment.

Thus, the cover of *The Crisis'* September 1915 issue featured one of the stars of that year's Memorial Day parade: Charles Young, a Black National Guard colonel whose "Fighting Eighth" Army regiment had fought beside Theodore Roosevelt in Cuba. Celebrating Black military success followed the thread started by Frederick Douglass a half-century earlier about the value of Black soldiers. Such a military cover might anger the more pacifist members of NAACP's board, including *New York Post* publisher Oswald Garrison Villard. But Du Bois was thinking about an audience of one: President Woodrow Wilson, who was about to make decisions affecting hundreds of thousands of people of color.

Evan Thomas booked passage on a ship to Scotland; he would continue his studies in Edinburgh and observe a country at war first-hand. He was not the only American inspired to do so, many choosing France. One Harvard professor was in Paris, setting up the American Ambulance Field Service, a chain of volunteer ambulance drivers that would soon include Ernest Hemingway.[7] Paris' American expatriates included Maryland nurse Ellen La Motte, described by her friend Gertrude Stein as "still gun shy but she did want to nurse at the front."[8] LaMotte would soon be in Belgium, in her free time writing a book that would be censored in three countries.

Thomas' choice of Edinburgh was strategic: it was the hotbed of Britain's anti-war movement, including a "No-Conscription Fellowship," which was trying to prevent a draft. Back in the States, such efforts were broached by Thomas' older brother Norman, the Harlem pastor, who had co-founded the American Union Against Militarism (AUAM). The war's most famous public opponents were millionaires who feared losing German clients; Henry Ford sent his cruise ship *Oscar II* on a heavily publicized "Peace Expedition" to Europe, where he was welcomed in Stockholm by the Women's International Peace League.[9]

The press laughed openly at Ford's "folly," and mostly ignored earnest peace efforts like those of AUAM or the Women's Peace Party. President Wilson did meet with representatives of the AUAM, largely because Evan Thomas' brother Norman was a close friend and Princeton classmate. But Wilson had reason to believe the movement would buckle: he had already wooed the Civil War veterans, securing praise from Grinnell College president Jesse Macy, once a Quaker medic on Sherman's March, and Reverend Clay MacCauley from the American Peace Society and the Anti-Imperialist League. In January 1916, as the last of the passengers from Ford's expedition came ashore in New York, the president addressed Congress about the need for a bigger Army and Navy.

"Of course Wilson became less of a liberal, and began to feel that the country would have to go to war," reflected Frances Witherspoon, a founder of the Women's International League for Peace and Freedom.[10] Witherspoon's recently deceased father, a Mississippi senator and fierce peace advocate, had

taught her to shun "that sham patriotism which finds expression in the doctrines of force" and "the propaganda of jingoism masquerading under the
guise of preparedness."[11] In early 1917, in her father's honor, Witherspoon
began organizing to stop the war, not knowing that before it was over, her
name would be written on barracks and prison walls.

Before *Lusitania* was sunk, America's peace movement had been optimis-
tic, its message a mixture of Progressive do-gooder energy and the experience
of wise old soldiers like Mark Twain. Celebrity allies included Thomas Edi-
son, Albert Einstein, and Helen Keller, along with suffragist Carrie Chapman
Catt. Combining anti-war with women's suffrage had been potent ever since
Jane Addams' Women's Peace Party led a women's march in late 1914. Horror at Europe's carnage was near mainstream in the United States: William
Jennings Bryan, the Anti-Imperialist League's presidential candidate, was
Wilson's secretary of state.

The German submarine attack that sank the luxury liner on May 7 frac-
tured the peace movement. Secretary of State Bryan resigned from the administration to concentrate on anti-war work. *The Advocate of Peace* ran articles
about "peace through strength." Clay MacCauley, now president of the Peace
Society's Japan chapter, wrote in a letter reprinted in the annual report of the
Carnegie Endowment for International Peace: "Here is our answer. Longing
for international peace, as I do most earnestly, I can see the way to its conclusion only through victory for America and her allies."

After *Lusitania*, American publishers who had been begging for descriptions of the war's horrors turned queasy. That included *The Atlantic Monthly*,
which, in addition to Du Bois' work, had been running a series of dispatches
from Nurse Ellen La Motte, asking, "Was it not all a dead-end occupation,
nursing back to health men to be patched up and returned to the trenches, or
a man to be patched up, court-martialed and shot?"[12]

In her reporting, La Motte described soldiers' anguish, including suicide
attempts, and noted this war's other combat victims, as "soldier's heart"
became "shell shock." In a later piece, LaMotte gently poked fun at the volunteer ambulance drivers:

> *"Sales strangers!"* [the patient] screamed. "What are *you* here for?
> To see me, with my bowels running on the ground? Did you

come for me ten hours ago, when I needed you? My head in mud,
my blood warm under me? Ah, not you! There was danger then—
you only come for me when it is safe!"

Following that series, a major New York publisher issued a collection of
LaMotte's sketches, entitled *The Backwash of War*. The book was almost
immediately banned in both England and France, as a detriment to morale.[13]
It sold well in the United States, and sometimes women active in the Women's
Peace Party smuggled copies abroad. But the more likely U.S. entry into the
war seemed, the fewer works were published that questioned military glory.

Evan Thomas wrote home from Scotland often, mostly about how it felt to
study theology in a nation where war was everywhere. St. George's, the Edinburgh church where he was associate pastor, was across town from Craiglock-
heart, the convalescent home where Wilfred Owen and Siegfried Sassoon
were treated after horrific service on the Western Front. Talking to his peers
in the "No Conscription Fellowship," Thomas closely followed news reports
as men were being drafted throughout the United Kingdom, some jailed for
refusing to enter the military. Those conscientious objectors were mocked in
British newspapers and attracted angry mobs at jails, but he thought of them
as role models.

He had learned a lot about the military, Thomas wrote, from the soldiers
he met, and from counseling German prisoners of war. "The minute a man
enlists his mouth is closed for any public utterance. He cannot discuss peace
publicly. Nothing is his own, least of all his conscience. Now it is one thing
to fight fairly, another to practice all sorts of atrocities. The minute an army
starts atrocities, however, the other side feels called upon to do the same.
Therefore, any decent man, let alone a [Christian], is called upon often to do
things he abhors."

Every sentence seemed to come back to the question his group of "Crusaders"
had asked that sunny day in Princeton: what was the moral thing to do now?

Evan soon announced that he was quitting his ministry studies and would
accept a draft notice should conscription come to the United States. He would
refuse military training and declare himself a conscientious objector. "This
is not the decision of a moment but of some pretty hard study and thought."
Norman supported his brother's philosophy, but he could not understand

Evan's decision to end his training. His letters to Evan, full of brotherly worry, contain warmth and news of their mother, Emma.

"Only when some people have made a start," Evan wrote, "by refusing to fight and going the limit, will the nations begin to take practical steps toward stopping war."

To his family in New York, those "practical steps" felt far away. Citizens' Preparedness Marches filled cities, and President Wilson spent much of the year campaigning for spending to support the National Defense and Naval Expansion Acts, which might create a military equal to those it would face in Europe. Wilson's pitch for the coming election was simple: re-elect him, and "Keep the Country Out of War" (his campaign slogan) by keeping America strong. That promise garnered endorsements, but not from everyone who had supported him in 1912.

W.E.B. Du Bois was one disgruntled former supporter. It was a long way from 1913 and Wilson's first inaugural, when Du Bois had exulted in *The Crisis* that Wilson could heal the nation of its racist past: "While a Southerner in birth and tradition, you have escaped the provincial training of the South and you have not had burned into your soul desperate hatred and despising of your darker fellow men." Three years later, Du Bois could only ask why Wilson's request for ramped-up defense spending did not include defending the thousands of African Americans killed by mob violence. "Is there any 'preparedness' for Christianity, for human culture, for peace or even for war, that is more pressing than the abolition of lynching in the United States?"

The NAACP's anti-lynching campaign issued a report with stark numbers: lynch mobs had taken more than two thousand African American lives since 1890, seventy-four in 1915 alone.[14] In the May 1916 *The Crisis*, a section entitled GHETTO noted each new lynching, along with other indignities: "J. J. Beale and Frank Guinn, election officials of Blaine County, Okla. . . . have been given a full and complete pardon by President Wilson" despite having been convicted of "intimidating Negroes and preventing them from voting." The juxtaposition was deliberate, as Jim Crow laws constituted another, slower war on Black Americans.

The need for such a section, the piles of letters asking for help, underlined Du Bois' loss of patience with the twenty-eighth president. "We need scarcely to say that you have grievously disappointed us," began *The Crisis'* fall 1916 editorial, listing a few of the ways in which Wilson had failed to keep his promise to voters of color. In the name of "racial harmony," Jim Crow laws had been strengthened, and the number of Black federal employees, from the post office to Congress, had declined. Then there was the White House endorsement of D.W. Griffith's *Birth of a Nation*, which portrayed African Americans as savages and the Ku Klux Klan as national heroes. *The Crisis* endorsed neither candidate in 1916, but that did not prevent the Democratic president from squeezing out a win, although without the Northeast vote.

A month after his re-election, Wilson first faced pressure for his first, but not last, military action as commander-in-chief, sending U.S. troops into Mexico to fight the forces of Francisco "Pancho" Villa. U.S. troops had been shadowing the Mexican revolution since 1906, including a 1914 Veracruz landing bemoaned by Du Bois in *The Crisis*. Wilson launched the "Punitive Expedition" in March 1916, after Villa's forces attacked a base in Tampico, Arizona, and sent 14,000 regular Army troops into Mexico under General John Pershing. Those troops included a Black battalion commanded by one of Du Bois' best friends, Major Charles Young, who had been only the third African American to attend West Point.

Sensing a possible quagmire, the AUAM organized to stop the expedition from becoming a full-on occupation. The group seized on testimony from Army Captain Lewis More about a bloody ambush in Carrizal and placed advertisements urging Wilson to refrain from all-out war.[15] A few months later, Wilson agreed and stopped the invasion, but it was hardly a victory for peace. U.S. entry into the European war was already in motion.

In April 1917, Wilson signed Congress' declaration of war, and military recruiting spiked nationwide. A full-size wooden battleship, "U.S.S. Recruit," was built in New York's Union Square Park, home base for Navy and Coast Guard personnel. The ship soon became a popular space for public events, including debutante balls. "[During] the exciting period when troops were parading down Fifth Avenue," wrote one socialite, "every available church basement, social hall and YMCA had been converted to a Red Cross center, a relief office or a canteen. The city was seething with men in uniform."[16]

At the NAACP's offices on Fifth Avenue, Du Bois wrote a ten-point list of demands for Black recruits, from "The right of our best men to lead their own troops in battle" to the abolition of Jim Crow and equal civil rights. The latter demand had already been denied to NAACP leaders meeting with the secretary of war, but the conversations would continue. Point #3, "the immediate stopping of lynching," felt less rhetorical after July riots in East St. Louis, in which hundreds of Black homes and businesses had burned, displacing six thousand and killing up to two hundred African Americans.

Du Bois described "white soldiers killing Black Americans" in St. Louis and reported accusations that the Missouri National Guard had joined in the massacre. The violence, he wrote, was a direct result of Wilson's failure to enact anti-lynching laws years earlier. As summer ended, Du Bois joined the NAACP-organized "Silent March" down New York's Fifth Avenue. Hundreds of anti-lynching activists, all dressed in white, seemed to hush the avenue that had hosted so many "Marches for Preparedness."

None of which slowed the preparedness train. That same summer, Congress passed the Selective Service Act, authorizing the formation of draft boards and the building of new facilities for recruits, and Secretary of Defense Newton Baker began to realize his plan for turning conscripts into soldiers. To spur anti-war dissent, Norman Thomas co-founded the U.S. No-Conscription League to support draft resisters, and he agreed to head the new U.S. branch of the international Fellowship of Reconciliation. Meanwhile, Wilson signed legislation that effectively banned dissent: the new Espionage Act prohibited not only the leakage of government information, but also any actions or statements showing the "intent to interfere with the operation or success of the military or naval forces of the United States."

The Espionage Act, especially after its expansion the following year with an additional, more punishing Sedition Act, enabled the administration to shut down much explicit anti-war ferment and to imprison leaders of the movement's constituent groups, from Eugene Debs' Socialist Party to the Fellowship of Reconciliation and the Women's Peace Party.

Publishers acted immediately. Even paid advertisements for Ellen LaMotte's explicitly non-political *The Backwash of War* could not be carried legally by the U.S. Postal Service; neither could socialist newspapers like *The Masses* or the Fellowship of Reconciliation's *The World Tomorrow*, edited by Norman Thomas.

Such censorship was educational for Norman Thomas and his fellow peace activists. When they started to recruit lawyers on behalf of conscientious objectors, they kept the correspondence of their infant National Civil Liberties Bureau as private as possible. It was important to be ready for the millions of drafted young men being ordered to the nation's new training camps.

Security was tight from Georgia to Oklahoma, at Camp Custer in Battle Creek, Michigan; Camp Evens in Ayer, Massachusetts; Camp Frémont in Menlo Park, California; Camp Funston in Fort Riley, Kansas; and dozens of others. The camps were still segregated, despite efforts by Du Bois and the NAACP, who kept talking to Defense Secretary Baker about the training and treatment of conscripted African Americans. Du Bois advocated, along with some of the less-pacifist NAACP board members, for the training of enough Black officers to lead these men, while Major Charles Young was being forcibly retired because of protests from white officers from Mississippi.

Du Bois adopted Wilson's rhetoric, about a war against injustice, and conflated those promises into a new vision, despite his traditional anti-militarism. "Let us enter into this war for Liberty with clean hands," he proposed in the September 1917 issue of *The Crisis*. "We black men have fought for your freedom and honor. Wherever the American flag floats today, black hands have helped to plant it." Du Bois identified the NAACP with national defense, Oswald Garrison Villard notwithstanding; this reframing almost led to Du Bois' own commission as a military intelligence officer a year later.

Getting white troops to respect their officers was hard enough. Just as white junior officers' complaints forced Charles Young away from command, Mississippi troops deploying in New Jersey were unwilling to salute Black officers on the base. Du Bois was soon hearing that matters were far more dire for the 370,000 enlisted Black men, most of whom were in menial positions with the quartermaster and engineer corp and overseen by white officers for whom Jim Crow was second nature. "[White] MPs regularly threw black soldiers into the guardhouse, where their jailers indiscriminately beat them, put them to work, or let them go."[17]

Black units clashed with military police in California at Camp Funston, in Georgia at Camp Gordon, and overseas, charging unfair treatment. The NAACP, the Black press, and Army inspectors were kept busy reporting abuses, including the summary execution, without a trial, of at least five Black soldiers in Texas.[18] The results of many of those investigations would emerge only after the war.

In the interim, such racism was enabled in the ranks, as seen in the June

1918 court-martial of Captain Eugene C. Rowan of the 102nd Infantry Brigade, "charged with having refused to obey an order issued by the brigade commander calling for a troop formation because both black and white [units] were included in the formation." As the Georgia captain's lawyer explained, "They are all Southerners and it would have been a direct violation of the customs they had abided by all during their lives." While Rowan was dismissed from the Army despite twenty-five years of service, his brigadier general quietly acted to prevent such a formation from ever again being ordered.

As the NAACP communicated regularly with Secretary Baker, so did advocates for conscientious objectors. The newborn Civil Liberties Bureau, with Norman Thomas on its board, had started as a project of the American Union Against Militarism; divided about Wilson's war, the AUAM had come to a consensus that whatever they thought of the war, they had to support the conscripts seeking help. These young men wanted to be declared "conscientious objectors" by the military, without having to go through the trials of Cyrus Pringle during the Revolution or the Civil War's Jesse Macy.

President Wilson and Secretary Baker were already aware of, and somewhat sympathetic to, venerable peace churches such as the Quakers, Mennonites, Hutterites, and Seventh Day Adventists. The Selective Service Act acknowledged the members of "any well recognized religious sect or organization present organized and existing and whose existing creed or principles forbid its members to participate in war in any form," were nonetheless declared subject to "service in any capacity that the President shall declare to be noncombatant." Between May 1917 and November 1918, nearly 57,000 of the ten million men receiving letters from their draft boards sought and gained official conscientious objector status.

One objector, Oklahoman Henry Becker, came from a German immigrant family that belonged to the Mennonite Church. "We didn't think Wilson would go to war," Becker said of the president elected in 1916 on an anti-war platform. When the reverse happened, Becker obeyed government orders and showed up at Camp Travis. Unlike many of his fellow Mennonites, Becker put on the uniform when ordered; he did not blink when the drill sergeant howled, "Now we'll separate the sheep from the goats!" As a member of the pacifist Church of the Brethren, Becker soon joined hundreds of COs scattered across the training camps and military prisons of America.

Many, like Becker, were put to work building the camps. Others, the "absolutists," refused to do even that, not wanting to serve as enablers for the military machine; 3,989 men spontaneously declared themselves to be conscientious objectors when they reached the camps, with only 1,300 choosing noncombatant service. Nearly 1,200 other objectors spent at least some of the war on their own land, on "farm furloughs," which allowed objectors to count some portion of work toward their required military service.

As the War Department began to include those men in their plans, Evan Thomas was "ready to take the out and out nonresistant basis so far as war is concerned." Thomas was one of a smaller but significant group of "absolutist" COs. When he arrived in January 1918 at his training camp, Long Island's Camp Upton, Thomas was in high spirits: "My day has come!" He asked Norman to reassure their mother about his welfare: "I just don't see why she doesn't understand."

At first, he was drawn to the place's camaraderie. It was a struggle to continue declaring his opposition when the adrenalin was urging toward violating his own convictions: "To give up the being part of the fun and hardship of all this, yes of fighting and perhaps dying along with your fellows in all sides of this terrible tragedy makes my stand seem so terribly aloof and terribly nonhuman." Thomas felt "more sympathy for those who changed in this war," but stood his ground: "I will see it through." Thomas' self-identified martyrdom for his personal definition of anti-militarism would try his family's patience and last nearly as long as the war.

The next two years were difficult for objectors and those trying to determine their fate. Commands hated having to contend with the issue while they drilled others. The Pentagon and White House issued a succession of decrees "clarifying" what was meant by "noncombatant," trying for service alternatives that they considered taxing enough and that would be accepted by the objectors (including an option for soldiers whose objections arose after time in service, such as Jacob Ritter in 1777, standing still amid the Battle of Brandywine).

As in all eras, troops with fewer options often chose the simple functional dissent of desertion, now punished more harshly. Reflecting a belief that Civil War desertion had increased because its troops had escaped with few penalties, those now charged with desertion and insubordination faced possible execution. But even with tightly locked camps and the threat of the death penalty, over ten thousand soldiers fled; most, as reported at the time by the *Chicago Tribune*, were recaptured and frog-marched onto troop ships to Europe.

While cracking down on insubordinate troops, the Wilson administration took a similar approach to journalists, labor organizers, and other civilian dissenters. In its crosshairs were the more radical labor unions: in September 1917, the Industrial Workers of the World (IWW) was raided coast to coast, with more than 150 officers, members, and sympathizers arrested. Of that group, 110 were put on trial in April 1918. A few months later, Socialist Party leader Eugene Debs was arrested for "an attempt to cause insubordination in the army and obstruct recruiting."[19]

The latter charge was a living threat to newspaper editors like W.E.B. Du Bois. The U.S. Postal Service refused to mail "disloyal" publications, such as the *Milwaukee Leader*, edited by socialist congressman Victor L. Berger, and the Black newspaper *The Messenger*, the home of union organizer A. Philip Randolph.[20]

Du Bois was determined to be a respected figure with whom governments must contend. After being warned by the wartime Committee on Public Information that *The Crisis'* mail privileges were in jeopardy, he toned down his rhetoric and wrote the controversial "CLOSE RANKS" editorial, urging Blacks to support the war and to believe in Wilson. The column's words echoed those of Booker T. Washington twenty years earlier: "Out of this conflict you need expect nothing less than the enjoyment of full citizenship rights," Du Bois wrote, "the same as are enjoyed by every other citizen."

Du Bois was also acting to ensure that Black participation in the military had some dignity. He agreed to promote a short-lived initiative by NAACP's Joel Springarn to strengthen African American communities through military sponsorship—an initiative whose only lasting result was a training camp for Black soldiers. At the initiative's apex, and with Secretary Baker's approval, Du Bois was offered a commission as a military intelligence officer, one that would have let him stay stateside in his NAACP position. Although he accepted, the offer was rescinded almost immediately, caught between the objections of Southern officials and those of the NAACP's anti-militarists. Neither Du Bois' involvement in the initiative nor the editorial kept Du Bois

off the list of potentially disloyal "persons of interest," but it may have protected *The Crisis* from censorship under the Sedition Act.

Norman Thomas' *The World Tomorrow* had no such protection, but that
was not his most pressing issue. He had to divide his time between his brother
Evan and the fate of hundreds of other recruits begging the Civil Liberties
Bureau for help. A range of reports was flooding into both Thomas' shop
and Frances Witherspoon's Bureau of Legal Advice about harsh tactics being
implemented by eager sergeants and lieutenants anxious to show how tough
they were. Some abuse was indirect and used as racist propaganda: Fort Riley
objectors were forced to watch as thirteen Black soldiers, charged with a range
of offenses, were executed by hanging, as a lesson to all malcontents. Other
commands were not nearly as subtle.

Affidavits by the hundreds pleaded with servicemembers' congressional
representatives. Attorney Theo H. Lunde described forty cases to Congress,[21]
such as a captain at Fort Oglethorpe who "ordered soldiers to put C.O. waist
deep in feces of latrine pit" and a "Polish drafted deserter" whose captain
"grabbed and beat him viciously" until he was "too sick to work. . . . leaning
against wall for support as jabbed 4 times with bayonet until exhausted he
passed out." Only after describing these horrors did Lunde mention his own
brother, Erling, and Evan Thomas, by then the most famous of the absolutists.

While Thomas had become a cause célèbre, plenty of absolutists were suffering at Leavenworth, including David and Julius Eichel, German-Jewish
immigrants and fervent socialists. Julius Eichel had refused to submit to an
induction physical at Camp Devens in Massachusetts. The brothers, both
court-martialed, were now serving their sentence of twenty years of hard
labor at Leavenworth.

After refusing to work during basic training, Thomas had led a hunger strike at Fort Riley (Kansas), until Norman Thomas and their mother,
Emma, arrived.[22] After much negotiation and pleading, Emma wrote with
satisfaction, "When I left Evan this evening, he was eating supper." But then
came Evan's arrest a month later, his conviction at court-martial, and his
transfer to the U.S. Military Disciplinary Barracks at Fort Leavenworth on
October 19, 1918.

Though initially provided with a desk job at the prison, in keeping with the
improved conditions Norman and Emma had negotiated, Evan announced

on November 2 that from that moment on, he would refuse to work. He felt self-conscious about being treated decently as other COs imprisoned at Leavenworth were mistreated—like the members of the Russian Molokan sect who were dragged by the hair and starved by guards.

In his last statement to his family before going into solitary confinement, Thomas said he was "protesting against the entire prison system as well as the fact that conscientious objectors are not distinguished from ordinary criminals and against the mistreatment of individual conscientious objectors." Of Thomas, one advocate wrote, "His sufferings in Solitary were much accentuated due to his height which compelled a stooping position when chained to the base of the double-decked Solitary cell."

Advocates kept pressing for all the COs in the facility to be released: "Whatever the particular charges on which they were sentenced," the Civil Liberties Bureau wrote to Wilson and Baker, "they are imprisoned for one reason only and that is their steadfast refusal on religious or other conscientious grounds to accept any form of conscript service under military authority."[23] Why not honor their religious freedom?

While waiting for an answer from Washington, advocates pored over the prisoners' military records, looking for any other reason to release them. A military attorney, hired to review Thomas' Fort Riley court-martial, found slipshod practices and inadequate evidence of guilt. Thomas was back in New York by Christmas, though under protest and determined to keep fighting for the release of the other COs.

The armistice was signed in November 1918, ending the war the resisters had sworn against, although their fighting was far from over. Open rebellions continued against military authorities, like the one fomented by the conglomeration of deserters, COs, and malcontents that filled the U.S. Disciplinary Barracks in January 1919.

Two months after the armistice, Fort Leavenworth's prison was full. Workers at the seventy-five-year-old sandstone fortress, located on twelve acres surrounded by a forty-foot concrete wall, had built more barracks in 1917 so that it could hold 1,500 more men—soldiers convicted of theft, murder, or desertion, in addition to conscientious objectors like Thomas. But the war had brought the total number of prisoners to 2,272, with many of the new arrivals dumped by other military installations that could not handle them.

Colonel Sedgwick Rice, the prison's commandant, was trying to contend with these challenges when the prisoners went on strike.[24]

The rebellion began with a melee after a card game between Black and white soldiers, several weeks after the release of Evan Thomas and 112 other objectors. Rice could deal with that. Then prisoners refused to work: no one was cooking, cleaning the toilets, or painting the new training grounds across the way. On the morning of January 29, Rice made his way down to the boiler room to see the strike organizers. "Who here thinks he has a grievance?" A slender young man with cheeks flushed by cold rose to his feet.[25]

H. Austin Simons remained still for the Colonel's inspection. A poet and sometime journalist, he was not surprised when the older man asked, "Are you with the I.W.W. [International Workers of the World]?"

Simons could barely make himself heard over the steam pipes. "No, sir. I never belonged to that organization."

Rice also asked if Simons was a "constitutional objector—one who objects to all forms of government and order."

"No, sir, I do not."

"Well, most Socialists do," said Rice.

Others in the group approached with complaints ranging from their individual sentences to the "rotten" meat served the prisoners. "The war is over," cried W. Oral James, a small-bodied man shivering in his thick raincoat. "The government has already released 113 of our fellows. Has it had time to investigate the justice of other claims?"

On February 1, the various "strike committees" assembled after three days of negotiation. Holding a telegram from the capital in his hand, Rice read aloud a statement from Secretary of State Dean Baker, which promised that each of their cases would be reviewed. "I fully appreciate that the cessation of hostilities and the return of conditions approximating those of peace," Rice intoned on Baker's behalf, "render it just and proper that clemency should now be exercised."

Pentagon sources quoted in contemporary accounts of the disturbances at Leavenworth consistently blamed the International Workers of the World, right up until they started blaming "the Bolsheviks." And thus began, perhaps, a complex love–hate romance between rebellious GIs and the sectarian left, one that has lasted ever since.

The Survey tells of the strikers' "last soviet [council]" with Simons, who said that one worker could be moved "but together, we are immovable." After the war, Simons would join his friend and fellow poet Wallace Stevens in writing for *The Masses* and *The Liberator*, while Norman Thomas would be hailed in 1918 as "Comrade Thomas" by the Socialist Party, having joined just as his brother, Evan, was released from prison.

The January strike was only the first. The last ended in July 1919, after most of the conscientious objectors had been released and the remaining prisoners were demanding full-fledged amnesty. Appropriate to the period, they had nicknamed their barracks *Lenine, Anarchia,* and *Internationale,* according to contemporary newspaper accounts.

Those Russian names for military cells may have felt like misplaced nostalgia to those in command. Back in 1916, Evan Thomas' letters from Scotland had quoted newspapers talking about "the coming alliance to fight Russia." Just as Thomas' ordeal ended, rebellion flared among two regiments of American soldiers stationed in the frozen waters of North Russia.

The Army's North Russia Expeditionary Force was based at the White Sea archipelago Arkhangelsk Oblast, or "Archangel Island." Its mission, one perhaps familiar to modern ears, was to "encourage" the remaining anti-Bolshevik armies to stop the Communists from assuming power. Regular Army troops were already based in Siberia, supplemented by National Guard forces farther north; the September 1918 Archangel mission was supposed to be quick.

There were five thousand so-called Polar Bear troops in Archangel, mostly from the Midwest, part of an international coalition composed of most of the Allies. Wilson had first sent over a few brigades to "protect supply lines" from Bolshevik attacks, but as the months went by, the mission grew less and less clear to the soldiers on the front lines. "No one has been able to tell the troops why they are fighting in Russia," one Detroit soldier told the *Chicago Daily Tribune.*

Despite censorship, guardsmen wrote home and even to the president, complaining of conditions and questioning their presence: "Believe me, when the main issue ended in France, with it ended our reason for being here," said one letter quoted by the *New York Times.* "Why should we interfere with the political interests of Russia? Let them settle their affairs themselves."

The Civil Liberties Bureau appealed to Wilson and Baker about censorship, but did not complain about the lack of a clear mission: those sentiments are instead in an unpublished essay by Rodger Sherman Clark, a Michigan National Guardsman still stuck in Russia. He titled it, "What Ails the [American North Russia Expeditionary Force] ANREF?"

> Censorship sits grinning in the safety-valve and the steam pressure is heavier than you might surmise. Meanwhile the fog of official vagueness and deceipt [sic] looks like a normal exhaust and doubtless people at home would throw up their hands at the thought of mutiny among the Soldiers of Democracy.[26]

Clark may have underestimated the "folks at home." In response to their sons' misery, more than two hundred Michiganders signed a petition in March 1919, demanding the "immediate withdrawl [sic] of the American Soldiers from the entire country of North Russia." The petition, addressed to Secretary Baker and to Michigan's congressional delegation, asserted that "now the war is practically if not technically over there exists no patriotic reason why our American soldiers in North Russia should not have an equal chance" for a normal life after wartime.

The troops farther east in Siberia were not silent, either. On the morning of March 20, members of the 339th Infantry refused to pack their sleds and report to the front. They were influenced in part by anti-war letters circulated throughout the unit, along with what contemporary newspapers called "Bolshevik pamphlets" inviting troops to the class war.

Another anonymous soldier wrote that troops were being ordered to kill civilians. Illinois senator Medill McCord read his letter aloud on the House floor: "Do you know the things being done in Siberia to disgrace the name of the United States, to enslave this people, to butcher noncombatant men and women!"[27] The soldier claimed to have seen fellow soldiers kill pregnant women and unarmed men, "driven insane" by conditions in Russia and pushed by Russian general Aleksandr Kolchak. The entire Illinois congressional delegation led an unsuccessful resolution to forbid troop replacements in Russia.

This "clamor" and unrest among troops was cited as one reason the

Pentagon decided to completely withdraw forces from North Russia as soon as the snow melted. While the base on Archangel wasn't closed until 1924, whistleblowers helped turn the tide of public sentiment against the newest wave of war.

By then, Rodger Sherman Clark had been home for years, his "Polar Bear" days long behind him. Evan Thomas was in New Jersey, working as a union organizer beside Union Theological classmate Abraham J. Muste. W.E.B. Du Bois had moved uptown to join and support the artists' movement known as the Harlem Renaissance, whose members' works would include stories of the Great War's Black soldiers. That war's soldier-dissenters, now veterans, were just beginning to count the costs of their war—just in time for another to blaze across Europe, its dissent of another kind entirely.

CHAPTER SEVEN

1920 to 1945

Lewis Milestone, a squat man with a head shaped like an anvil, was too tired at first to notice the guy with the clipboard. Milestone was in the mood to celebrate: he had just finished his first-ever solo directing gig, a jewel-thief silent comedy called *Seven Sinners*. But the line for the speakeasy was long. Every man working for Jack Warner seemed crammed into this one corner of the backlot at 5800 Sunset Boulevard. As the line inched toward the door, Milestone's eyes wandered, until a smiling man stood before him, with a briefcase and a clipboard with sheets of signatures.

"What is this for?" Milestone asked.

The young man looked him over before he said, "Why, it's the Klan." His smile was as sunny as a Sunday afternoon.

Milestone kept his voice even. "You've got the wrong number. You don't want me, and I don't need you." He wondered if the man even knew that he was Jewish.

"What was that, Milly?" Milestone's colleague asked as the Klan booster moved away. "What did you say to him?"

Milestone looked behind him, at the man still getting signatures. "Wait till we leave here," he said softly. "When we get outside [away from the liquor line], I will tell you the facts of life."[1] Those facts, semi-obscured in Hollywood, were still the face of America after the Great War.

Milestone was one of 2.7 million Americans who had been part of that war, which had exposed those "facts of life" like a bright light held to a wound. More than 350,000 Black veterans had returned to a reinvigorated Klan and a summer of escalated anti-Black violence. Half a million were immigrants. Many were Jewish immigrants, like Milestone (born Lewis Milstein), or Catholic, demographics targeted equally by the Klan and both sides of a convulsing labor struggle.

Some of these former soldiers, having seen more of what was wrong with America, resolved to repair the damage. Over the next two decades, Milestone would become a high-profile dissenter by creating an iconic anti-war work in the new medium called cinema. That work's effects would ripple into the twenty-first century.

Milstein had lived in a mostly Jewish slum in New York's Lower East Side since arriving from Moldova in 1913. A 1917 notice from the U.S. military ordered him to report for duty uptown at Columbia University.[2] Issued a uniform and told to wait in a storeroom-turned-barracks, Milstein wilted. "Of smells there was a mixture of many disinfectants. I sat down on one of the cots and waited. I hadn't been that miserable and depressed since my first days in steerage."[3] After basic training in New Jersey, Milstein was ordered back to Columbia, to the top-secret U.S. School of Military Cinematography.

Milstein worked on training films in Washington, D.C., as assistant to Joseph von Sternberg. As the war wore on, he edited footage sent over by peers in France and Germany, some of it gruesome images of pieces of dead soldiers. He did not, in all honesty, wish he were there.

As the war ended, Milstein followed Signal Corps peers like Sternberg to Hollywood, changing his name to something less German-sounding. After five years writing screenplays and editing Rin Tin Tin movies, Milestone was noticed and promoted by millionaire mogul Howard Hughes, who introduced him to the Warner brothers.

Milestone's success was nowhere near typical for new veterans. Most of the "doughboys" had come home to a nation that expected them to return to the same jobs they had left, sometimes at lower wages, or as strikebreakers in anti-union battles. Those with injuries overwhelmed the agency set up to help them: from 1919 to 1921, "the Rehabilitation Division processed claims from 393,725 veterans for some form of vocational training. They found that two-thirds [almost 260,000] had a disability sufficient to warrant it." After the division's responsibilities were transferred to a newly established Veterans' Bureau, nearly ninety thousand additional vets sought help without the stigmatizing word "rehabilitation."[4]

Even without physical injuries, too many veterans were like Walter Waters, who seemed unable to leave the war behind. Waters' struggle began in 1916, when the Oregon native joined his state's National Guard, 146th Artillery. Long before the United States entered the European war, Waters' unit had taken part in a domestic military operation: they had guarded border camps at Nogales, Arizona, as fourteen thousand regular Army troops under General John Pershing drove into Mexico in pursuit of Pancho Villa. Waters' Guard unit deployed to Europe in 1918, joining the Army's 41st Division. His memoir does not say much about what his unit did there, its battles and steep losses at Saint-Mihiel and Château-Thierry, or about his work in France after the war, with the Allied occupation forces.[5] But Waters sharply recalls that in 1919, it was hard to get a job back home.

"Like many others of my age, I had no occupation or profession to resume," Waters writes. "Everything had to be commenced for the first time. . . . In the next few years I made numerous serious attempts to get going in some profitable business or position, as a garage mechanic, an automobile salesman, a farmhand, a bakery helper." When each failed, he reflected, "My inability to take root in fertile soil may have been due to the unsettling effects of the War on me." Like Civil War veterans a half-century earlier, Waters picked at his bad memories, trying to find a way forward.

News of such "unsettling effects" was already a national obsession. No sooner had most doughboys been welcomed home than newspapers blared headlines like these in the *New York Times*: "Shell Shocked Soldier Implicated in Shooting," "Seek Missing Veteran—Shell Shock Victim Wanders Far from Home," or "Shell Shocked Veteran Kills Self with Rifle." The articles asked about "proper facilities for the treatment of men who are not completely insane," next to stories about new veterans who had starved to death, despite the booming stock market and healthy peacetime economy.

Waters finally put down some tentative roots in Portland, Oregon, finding work at a cannery. Portland was an exciting place for many reasons, including a 1922 strike at the Port of Portland by the International Longshoremen's Association and Marine Transport Workers Union. Police responded by attacking picket lines, arresting five hundred, and rounding up anyone who might be with the International Workers of the World (IWW). Waters had a new name, Bill Kincaid, chosen to try to change his luck. For a while, it seemed that his bet had succeeded: he was employed, married, and had worked his way up to assistant superintendent. "I seemed to have escaped from the failure that had followed me in the past."

Much of the country seemed to be feeling the same way, "I'm Forever Blowing Bubbles" replacing "Over There" as America's number one song. Movie screens featured Charlie Chaplin's pratfalls, gangster tales with a heroic FBI, and lavish histories like *Nanook of the North* (with snow provided by Hollywood). The literary crowd was besotted with modernism, agog over a dirty Irish novel called *Ulysses* and *The Waste Land*, a poetic rant by an American self-exiled to Britain named Thomas Stearns (T.S.) Eliot.

From Oxford, Eliot had witnessed Europe's war and met its soldier-poets, Robert Graves and Wilfred Owen; he had also written about the war from overseas for *The Nation*, including a piece in which he described "Wounded men lying in the shell holes among the decaying corpses: helpless under the scorching sun and bitter nights, under repeated shelling."[6] But *The Waste Land* wrapped its truths in symbols and allusions, unlike the more direct approach of a pair of writers who had served in the war as ambulance drivers.

Harvard scion Edward Estlin Cummings had found himself subject to military justice twice. He had arrived at the Norton-Harjes Ambulance Corps in 1917 and had not made a secret of his anti-war views, leading to his arrest by the French military on suspicion of espionage. At the prison where he was detained, the *plantons*—a cross between orderlies and guards—were French soldiers who were ill or injured, serving while they healed. "As soon as they had recovered their health under these salubrious influences they were shipped back to do their bit for democracy, freedom, etc. in the trenches."[7] Cummings saw quasi-military discipline up close, in what he named the "hierarchy of fear." He saw prisoners disciplined with increasingly hostile forms of solitary confinement, for seemingly minor infractions: "Upon being sentenced to *cabinot*, whether for writing an intercepted letter, fighting, threatening a *planton*, or committing some minor offense for the nth time, a man took one blanket from his bed, carried it downstairs to the *cachot*, and disappeared therein for a night or many days and nights as the case might be."[8]

Upon Cummings' release and return to the United States, his draft board sent him back to service. Cummings reported to Camp Devens, Massachusetts, refusing his parents' efforts to get him an exemption. A writer-soldier, he told them, performs an essential role: "[He] keeps his eyes, ears, & above all his NOSE wide open, he watches while others merely execute orders."

Cummings also watched closely what happened to conscientious objectors. One was asked by his base commander, "What would you do if some German came through the window and raped your sister?"[9] That objector soon disappeared, likely sent to Fort Leavenworth to join the likes of Evan Thomas. Cummings had heard a lot about what some objectors went through, as shown in his 1922 poem "I sing of Olaf glad and big":

> *his wellbeloved colonel (trig*
> *westpointer most succinctly bred)*
> *took erring Olaf soon in hand;*
> *but—though an host of overjoyed*
> *noncoms(first knocking on the head*
> *him)do through icy waters roll*
> *that helplessness which others stroke*
> *with brushes recently employed*
> *anent this muddy toiletbowl,*
> *while kindred intellects evoke*
> *allegiance per blunt instruments—*

Cummings published the poem (as e.e. cummings) from Paris in the 1920s, where he was one of the so-called Lost Generation of American expat writers. Another former ambulance driver, Ernest Hemingway, published his wartime novel, *A Farewell to Arms*, in 1929, the same year an English translation emerged of the German bestseller *Im Westen nichts Neues* (literally, "Nothing New in the West") by war veteran Erich Maria Remarque.

Remarque's anti-war novel sparked riots in Germany, especially among the rising National Socialist (Nazi) Party. Under the title *All Quiet on the Western Front*, the English translation—stripped of some of its "'too robust' language and realistic war scenes"—was a best-seller.[10] Hollywood hired another young veteran to make *All Quiet* into a film that would chronicle the futility of war.

Lewis Milestone had kept the war close to his heart and to his work as a director. He had already earned one of the only "best comedy" Oscars ever awarded, for the silent comedy *Two Arabian Knights*, whose soldier-protagonists escape a German prison camp and dash around "Arabia." Milestone devoured *All Quiet*, which rang true to what he knew about the costs of war. He stayed up all night, story-boarding.

Milestone persuaded Universal to commit over a million dollars (about $15 million in 2019 dollars). He created a German war zone in Southern California so realistic that the Orange County health inspector wanted to halt the production. As lead, he hired a young hopeful named Lewis Ayres, who had just debuted in *The Kiss* beside Greta Garbo.

The set was an exciting place for Ayres. He especially admired the big man who controlled the explosions, who sat calmly at his massive switchboard as false mortars, shells, and muddy rain flowed at his command. "It was actually inspiring. Because you felt you were really there in that sense. . . . It did well up with an enormous cacophony of men shouting and screaming and firing, and these masses of artillery and all—and the lights, you know. . . . It was a very exciting scene for youngsters."[11]

Ayres also found the story a useful corrective to the images of Germany that had only grown stronger since the war, such as Army posters featuring images of Belgian babies pierced by German bayonets. "[The story] had so many things that were beautiful to it. Knowing that war from the point of view of the common man, so to speak, that his life and his hopes, his fears are the same."[12]

Ayres poured all that fear and excitement and empathy into his portrayal of Paul Baumer, who, after two years in the trenches, tells students back home, "We live in the trenches. And our bodies are earth. And our thoughts are clay. And we sleep and eat with death. And we're done for, because you can't live that way and keep anything inside you."

The *New York Times* called *All Quiet on the Western Front* "a spectacular achievement, a vocalized screen offering that is pulsating and harrowing, one in which the fighting flashes are photographed in an amazingly effective fashion."[13] The film went on to win the 1930 Academy Award for Best Picture, and a Best Director nod for Milestone. Producer Howard Hughes, who had given him his first big break, shot off a congratulatory telegram when he saw the film:

> SCENE IN THE SHELL HOLE GOT ME AND YOU KNOW I AM USUALLY HARD BOILED ABOUT THESE THINGS ALSO THE SCENE IN THE SCHOOL HOUSE WHERE LEW AYRES COMES BACK AND TELLS BOYS WHAT WAR IS REALLY LIKE WAS SUPERB AND I KNOW YOU ARE RESPONSIBLE FOR IT BECAUSE I SAW THIS BOY IN ONE OF GRETA GARBOS PICTURES AND HE WAS NOT VERY GOOD.[14]

Lewis Ayres had grown in the role and had managed to simulate the condition known then as "shell shock." In one scene, Paul is temporarily disabled by nightmares; another soldier cracks completely under the weight of his flashbacks. While soldier-poets like Siegfried Sassoon and Robert Graves kept such troubles front and center in Europe, Milestone was the first to show a mass audience in America something key to the worst thing about war: "You can't live that way and keep anything inside you."

The war's veterans, nearly three million strong, would soon be a stumbling, angry presence across both class and race lines; for instance, Walter Waters, who lost his cannery job shortly after the stock market crashed in 1929.

During months of unemployment, Waters and his wife drained their savings account. "Our savings vanished and the hope of work with them during the winter of 1931–1932. In the meantime, our personal belongings, one by one, found their way to the pawn shop."[15] By March 1932, Walters added, "We were not only penniless but had nothing left except a very scanty wardrobe. There were many days that winter when we experienced actual hunger."

While job-hunting, Walters discovered men like him—another "lost generation," rootless since the armistice. "I found that a sizable percentage of these men in Portland were, like myself, ex-service men. . . . Among these men there was profound discontent with [their current economic] conditions. There was a ravaging desire to change them but a complete and leaden ignorance of the way to do it. . . . These men did think and talk a great deal about the so-called Bonus."

Thus, Waters entered another ongoing national debate: whether former soldiers deserved a permanent pension or a lump sum, known as "adjusted compensation" or "the bonus." Veterans groups had long been split on the issue—the labor-oriented World War Veterans favored the bonus, while the anti-labor American Legion backed a proposal to pay it in government bonds.[16] When the stock market crashed in 1929, the promise of those bonds evaporated, and with it, the hopes of veterans who had not been able to find their way to prosperity.

Little of the veterans' discontent rendered them anti-war, especially with the news from Europe about the rise of Germany's Nazi Party. And the Espionage Act had dampened much of the progressive energy that had fueled resistance to World War I. But Waters was among those who turned his malaise into activism, helping organize a "Bonus Expeditionary Force" that in 1932 converged on Washington, D.C., 43,000 strong, for a "bonus march." One of their chants was more satiric than political, set to the tune of their war's last greatest hit: *Over there, over there/Tell the world to beware/'Cause the Yanks are starving, the Yanks are starving.*

They marched in groups of ten, of thirty, of several hundred. They marched from San Francisco, New Orleans, Poughkeepsie. Black and white veterans sometimes marched together. It was a march against invisibility, an escalating demand for recognition, as much as for a guaranteed pension. By the eve of the May 29 vote on a comprehensive package of veterans' assistance, there were four thousand veterans camped out in front of the White House, with an additional three thousand on the way. Welcomed by Anacostia Police Captain S.J. Marks,[17] the group published their newspaper, *The BEF News*, out of their fort "Camp Marks." The national organizing committee included the Workers Ex-Servicemen's League, a Communist group that echoed those at Fort Leavenworth nearly twenty years earlier.

Roy Wilkins wrote in the NAACP's *The Crisis* that Camp Marks was non-segregated: "There I found black toes and white toes sticking out side by side from a ramshackle town of pup tents, packing crates and tar-paper shacks. . . . For years, the U.S. Army had argued that General Jim Crow was its proper commander, but the Bonus marchers gave lie to the notion that Black and white soldiers—ex-soldiers in their case—couldn't live together."[18]

After six months, President Herbert Hoover ordered Colonel Douglas

MacArthur to move against the encampments, claiming they endangered public safety. MacArthur went further than his orders, ordering troops to evict the veterans and burn down their settlements throughout the region. Scores were injured, some badly, which helped doom the Hoover administration in that fall's election. When the next wave of bonus marchers got to Washington the following year (1933), the Roosevelt administration reserved spots in the Civilian Conservation Corps (CCC) for the veterans, asking states to establish camps for civic projects.

One such project was a new bridge between two of Florida's Upper Keys, Lower Matecumbe and Windley Key. Soon seven hundred veterans were encamped on the margins of Matecumbe's then-sleepy beach.

> Some of them were punch drunk and some of them were smart; some had been on the bum since the Argonne almost and some had lost their jobs the year before last Christmas; some had wives and some couldn't remember; some were good guys and others put their pay checks in the Postal Savings and then came over to cadge in on the drinks when better men were drunk; some liked to fight and others liked to walk around the town; and they were all what you get after a war.[19]

In nearby Islamorada, the closest thing to a town, children were told to stay away from the strange men.[20] Then came September 2, 1935, and the Labor Day Hurricane that took Key West by surprise.

The hurricane erased most of Matecumbe's trees and buildings; a train sent to rescue the veterans was crushed in its winds. The veterans were left alone. "Panicked men flailed blindly, their limbs tangling with those of others clawing just as wildly in return."[21] Ernest Hemingway, who now owned a home in Key West, was outraged, convinced that the train for the vets had been ordered too late. He got the leftist magazine *New Masses* to underwrite a reporting trip, and to publish the result, entitled "Who Murdered the Vets?"

The year 1935 was also marked by a student peace movement, whose members, drawing inspiration from the Oxford Pledge, declared: "We pledge not to support the government of the United States in any war it may conduct."[22]

In an April 11 Student Strike Against War, 175,000 students walked out on classes, many publicly signing the pledge. They devoured *WAR: No Profit, No Need* by Norman Thomas, whose brother Evan had been one of the most famous conscientious objectors of the previous war.[23] They also made a best-seller of *War Is a Racket* by Marine General Smedley Butler, who toured the country describing how U.S. wars were fought with the interests of the wealthy in mind. "I spent thirty-three years and four months in active military service as a member of this country's most agile military force, the Marine Corps. I served in all commissioned ranks from Second Lieutenant to Major-General. And during that period, I spent most of my time being a high class muscle-man for Big Business, for Wall Street and for the Bankers. In short, I was a racketeer, a gangster for capitalism."[24]

Advocates for conscientious objectors prepared for what would happen if war came. In November 1935, the historic peace churches—Mennonites, Brethren, and Friends (Quakers)—met in Kansas[25] to form what became the National Interreligious Board for Conscientious Objectors.[26] They began developing a proposal for how young men opposed to military service could still do "work of national importance," one that might sit well with the Roosevelt administration.

In 1936, General Butler voted for Norman Thomas for president, on the Socialist Party line; the two would become the public faces of the short-lived Keep America Out of War Congress (KAOWC), founded in 1938 to build on the European peace groups that pushed for total disarmament and international cooperation.[27] Unlike those groups, which contained enough war veterans to have held a Rally of Ex-Servicemen for Peace,[28] Butler was one of the only vets in Thomas' organization, which otherwise leaned for military credibility on Evan Thomas and Oswald Garrison Villard, grandson of William Lloyd Garrison and grand-nephew of the Union Army's George Garrison.

More veterans gravitated to the non-pacifist America First Committee, whose name (still a white supremacist favorite) came to be remembered for its most problematic members, most prominently aviator Charles Lindbergh, who joined General Stuart Wood, Far East Commander General Stanley Ebrick, and eight hundred thousand others.[29] Poet e.e. cummings was among the latter, along with Gore Vidal and John F. Kennedy, the thirty-fifth president commenting years later that "the people whose motto was 'America First' were correct and that we were just going to get, needlessly, entangled in what was basically a European war."[30] AFC joined with pacifist groups in urging a constitutional amendment that would require a national referendum before any war.[31]

The odds were still against anti-war forces of any stripe, with a Yale Divinity School professor (now famously) decrying the movement as fascism "called Americanism."[32] Even the mostly pacifist National Peace Congress broke apart in 1938 over whether to continue to support the amendment. Evan Thomas, World War I objector turned War Resisters League president, sighed, "[Anti-war Americans] are such a small group that we would kid ourselves if we think we are of any social importance."[33] The explicitly anti-war *All Quiet on the Western Front* was rereleased with a militarist spin.

The rerelease was timed to capitalize on the success of its star, Lew Ayres, in his new *Dr. Kildare* film series. In the near-decade since *All Quiet*, Ayres had become a matinee idol, married Ginger Rogers, and never forgotten his time as Paul Baumer. He even directed two movies with enlisted men as protagonists: *Leathernecks* and the Civil War drama *Hearts in Bondage*.

Although *All Quiet on the Western Front* was back in theaters, it was not the one Milestone and Ayres had loved. It had been cut to ninety minutes by request of the War Department, and now included a five-minute hectoring narration that recounted German history up to Hitler's rise. MGM then marketed the film with the slogan, *"At last! The UNCENSORED VERSION OF ALL QUIET ON THE WESTERN FRONT."*[34] The rerelease was a hit, though Milestone would later denounce the "brutal cutting, stupid censors and bigoted politicos" that had stripped his film of its most graphic details.

To one fan of *Western Front*, poet and reluctant law student William Kunstler, the war was both inevitable and personal: his family had welcomed refugees from Hitler's Germany, including the girl he wanted to marry. In late 1941, Kunstler reported to the Signal Corps post in Fort Monmouth, New Jersey, to become an Army cryptographer.[35] Newsreels burst with footage of Americans showing up to register for conscription, including movie stars and younger congressmen.

Military bases filled with new recruits, including seventeen-year-old Charles Evers, whose younger brother, Medgar, would soon follow. "With the war coming, Mama and Daddy didn't want me shot, but I liked the soldier's uniform, and I had to leave Mississippi."[36] Public opinion was firmly against anti-war efforts, whether the militarist AFC, pacifists like WRL, or left-wing groups carrying signs like "Roosevelt, Dewey and Hoover Are United for War." The *New York Times* applauded when an anti-war demonstration in Times Square was squelched by National Guard troops on horseback.[37] By the end of 1940, Congress passed America's first peacetime draft, the Selective Service and Training Act.

The Selective Service Act, crafted to address the concerns of both conscientious objectors and African Americans subject to the draft, created Civilian Public Service camps for the former and allowed the latter participation in more than menial positions. The NAACP, which in the previous war had fought the indignities suffered by Black soldiers, had secured an amendment that declared, "In the selection and training of men for service, there shall be no discrimination on account of race or color."[38] However, a secret agreement between FDR and NAACP president Walter White allowed for the establishment of separate-but-equal training camps and racially specific draft quotas, with White promising *sotto voce* that the organization would not test the contradictions between such segregation and that anti-discrimination amendment.[39] As 1941 proceeded, the NAACP wrangled with the War Department about the makeup of the new "colored units,"[40] while contending with the effect of escalating white resistance, including the March 1941 murder-lynching of Private Felix Hall at Fort Benning.[41]

The amendment's limitations sparked dissent to the left of the NAACP. A. Philip Randolph, editor of *The Messenger* and head of the powerful union Brotherhood of Sleeping Car Porters, started 1942 with a call for a Black-led march on Washington, D.C., to demand equality in the new defense establishment. "Negroes made the blunder of closing ranks and forgetting their grievances in the last war," Randolph told a rally, in a direct reference to W.E.B. Du Bois' 1918 editorial urging Blacks to serve now and fight for justice later. Chapters of the "March on Washington Movement" formed, swelled, and prepared for a July 1 march on the Capitol that would include one hundred thousand supporters. Finally, a week before the march, President Roosevelt issued the anti-discrimination Executive Order 8802: "In the selection and training of men for service, there shall be no discrimination on account of race or color."[42]

While Executive Order 8802 opened opportunities for Blacks in the defense

industry, it did not bar segregation in the military itself, thus producing conscientious objectors to Jim Crow, a handful of "absolutists" who refused to
comply with a draft that did not recognize them as equals. Winifred Lynn
explained to his Jamaica, New York, draft board that he understood the need
to fight Hitler, but would only do so for the Canadian military, rather than
comply with segregation.[43] Drafted anyway, Lynn filed a *habeas corpus* suit
against the War Department, but served throughout the war without his
objection's being legally recognized.[44]

That would not be the case for Lew Ayres. Ayres was studying philosophy,
having taken the interwar years to reflect on the revulsion against war he had
absorbed from *All Quiet*. He had joined the Red Cross and begun training
volunteers in Los Angeles in first aid.[45] After he began starring in the movie
series *Young Dr. Kildare*, he "became a one-man First Aid department to the
entire camp" at MGM, training thousands of crew members.[46] As the possibility of war increased, he tried to sort out his beliefs. "I read the Bible again.
I *tried to grope my way* to a better understanding, but I was still a long way
from the goal." Ayres also met quietly with his draft board. He knew what
he was going to do before the Japanese Army's "Hawaii Operation" destroyed
188 aircraft and shattered Schofield Barracks at Pearl Harbor, killing and
wounding more than five thousand servicemen.

On December 7, 1941, Ayres and his wife sat in their garden and listened
to the radio, glued to the reports from Hawaii. Friends kept stopping by, and
they swore at the radio as if it had done something other than report the
news. An older neighbor said, "Well, at least we are now one day closer to the
end of this war."[47]

Ayres knew that, in contrast to earlier wars, the mobilization process
included conscientious objectors. He knew about the Civilian Public Service
(CPS) camps coordinated by the interfaith National Religious Service Bureau
for Objectors,[48] wherein COs could do "work of national importance"—
logging or farming. The twelve thousand who did so were not required to
undergo military training or wear the uniform (and are thus mostly outside
the purview of this book). By the time of his induction medical checkup on
January 16, 1942, Ayres was asking the officers what his options were. "They
said no you may not make that choice, you have to go where we will put you,
and I said well then, I won't go at all."[49]

Nearly 37,000 conscientious objectors were processed by Selective Service by the war's end. The 150 newly established CPS camps were limited to religious objectors, and even some of those had to fight draft boards and boot camp authorities and courts to get in. At Fort MacArthur in San Pedro, a Mennonite reported that he was "kicked and my hair pulled by two privates—one colored and one white. . . . I was ordered to clean up the latrine and after refusing they dunked my head in the clothing washing basin."[50] Three thousand volunteered to work in mental hospitals.

Ayres' decision made headlines, in the face of popular passion for the war against the Nazis. His own fortunes, like Milestone's, would rise and fall in proportion to the level of public support for his decision. Ayres' CO status was as unprecedented in Hollywood as his public explanation of his position. Saying that the core basis of his objection was "the Christian creed of nonresistance to evil," Ayres added, "Today I stand convinced that as like attracts like, hate generates hate, murder incites revenge, so charity and forgiveness reflect their kind, and the world's brotherhood will be made manifest not through economic experiences but through man's awakening to the irresistible power of love."[51] In April 1942, Ayres arrived at Camp Cascade in Wyeth, Oregon, where he would do emergency first aid for the men pressed into service cutting timber. Fans chased Ayres' train as he made his way from Los Angeles to what the newspapers called "conchie camp."

The year 1942 was bringing many changes—including the first all-female military units, with some women officers. Chicago socialite Alice Bradley Davey (now best remembered under the pseudonym James Tiptree, Jr.) joined the initial Women's Auxiliary Army Corps (WAAC), which boasted 67,000 members. "More than 13,000 women applied for a few hundred positions," writes Davey's biographer. "Many of them were greeted at recruiting stations by crowds of jeering men and shouts of 'Are you one of them Wackies?'"[52] Davey loved the training, the "camaraderie of difficulty."[53]

Philip Berrigan, drafted from upstate New York, remembered that camaraderie very well. "I am nineteen years old and excited to be following my brothers into battle, anxious to slaughter infidels and . . . to charge pillboxes, blow up machine-gun nests, and fight hand-to-hand with my country's enemy."[54] However, Berrigan could not help noticing that the country's founding injustices were in play.

Berrigan had been stunned by Jim Crow at Fort Benning, where a 1941 lynching had happened nearly unnoticed. After sailing for Europe and noticing Black troops' substandard shipboard quarters, he found it hard to ignore how "black soldiers were treated with contempt [and] given the most menial jobs, scrubbing dishes, cleaning out latrines, shoes" and "forced to sleep in the suffocating bowels" of base housing.[55] Anti-Black violence was common at stateside bases from Norfolk to Nebraska. In 1942 alone, "race riots broke out in [bases in] New Orleans; Vallejo, California; Flagstaff, Arizona; Fort Dix, New Jersey; and the Air Force training school in Tuskegee."[56]

If 1942 felt brutal to Black troops and liberating to women like Alice Davey, it ended positively for Lew Ayres, whose persistent lobbying had paid off; his CO classification was switched to 1-A-O, which made him available for non-combatant military service. He was now in the Medical Corps of the U.S. Army's 45th Infantry Division, at Texas' Camp Barkley.

Unlike most of the 25,000-plus 1-A-O objectors, Ayres was neither a Jehovah's Witness nor a Seventh Day Adventist, whose forms of worship were laid out carefully in the DoD regulations. Witness and Adventist memoirs and oral histories abound, with tales of Ruff Sergeant declaring OF COURSE YOU WORK SATURDAYS, a protest, and Nice Captain honoring the objector's religious practices before the Christian soldier proves himself in battle (as seen in the 2016 film *Hacksaw Ridge*, based on the memoirs of Adventist CO Desmond Doss).

Ayres had no such schedule difficulties, only the stress of Camp Barkley's full hospitals. Survivors of the late-1941 Bataan Death March and the battle for Corregidor were "malnourished and dehydrated, steel still embedded inside many of them," recalled another Camp Barkley medic."[57] Others came from the Aleutian Islands and Guadalcanal, with Purple Hearts and searing wounds to prove it.

The year 1943 was an all-hands moment, drawing Brooklyn steelworker Howard Zinn into the Army Air Corps. Zinn, a union organizer, still remembered the violent suppression of an anti-war protest he had attended as a teenager. He remembered, *"Free speech? Try it and the police will be there with their horses, their clubs, their guns, to stop you."* This police repression was radicalizing for Zinn, whose future actions were shaped by the belief that "something fundamental was wrong in this country—not just the existence of poverty amidst great wealth, not just the horrible treatment of black people, but something rotten at the root."[58]

Still, Zinn was "eager to get into combat against the Nazis. I saw the war as a noble crusade against racial superiority, militarism, fanatic nationalism, expansionism."[59] Many saw the war as an extension of the struggle against fascism, especially after Russia joined the Allies in 1941: "There was lots of love for Russia in the air."[60] Zinn saw in both fights the same "uprooting of the old order, the introduction of a new kind of society—cooperative, peaceful, egalitarian."[61]

Zinn was also sensitive to the military's racial inequality. Like Philip Berrigan, he saw how badly Black troops were treated while traveling to Europe; as a lieutenant, he was able to use his power as a white non-commissioned officer when one of his sergeants demanded a segregated dining space: "You fellows are going overseas in the same war. Seems to me you shouldn't mind eating together. Sergeant, you'll have to sit there or just pass up this meal. I won't move either of you."[62]

Zinn was seeing just a glimpse of a larger issue. "The War Department regularly received reports on the low morale of the Negro soldier and accounts of black suicides, mental 'crack-ups,' desertions, and AWOLs," writes historian Harvard Sitkoff. "They trained in segregated base camps, mostly in the South, and found themselves barred or Jim-Crowed by the USO, service centers, theaters, and post exchange. . . . Blacks who protested were harassed and intimidated; those who persisted in their opposition were transferred, placed in the stockade, or dishonorably discharged."[63]

White soldiers who supported their Black colleagues could be disciplined as well. Sergeant Alton Levy, a white former labor organizer, was court-martialed for making "false and derogatory" statements about his command in Lincoln, Nebraska. "I did say the Negroes were mistreated. I did say only forty were allowed passes each night," Levy said at trial, before he was sentenced to hard labor for insubordination. "I did say that my training group, not the base, had about two hundred Negro soldiers. But here's the strange thing: Although these are allegedly false statements, at no time did the prosecution attempt to prove or establish that they were false statements."[64] And the Navy, which had not accepted Black seamen until 1942, welcomed them into a system designed to extinguish them.

Freddie Meeks, twenty-five, at first hoped that the Navy would offer something better than his hometown of Natchez, at the mouth of the Mississippi
River. While its city fathers kept trying to boost the port and recover its antebellum vigor, the reality of life for its African Americans was awful in 1940.
Natchez native Richard Wright described the town: "At night in the narrow alleys was the smell of burning hair coming from Negro beauty parlors
where black women tried to make their hair look like that of white people.
There was a persistently sour smell of earth around the backs of houses where
dishwater was thrown out of windows, for there was no plumbing. Over the
stench of the privies came the sweet scent of magnolias."[65]

When young Meeks boarded a bus in 1943 to go to basic training, he may
not have expected much better treatment at Michigan's Great Lakes Naval
Base. Still, he had never been anywhere like Great Lakes, a vast thirty-five-
year-old facility so far north you could see Canada. The Navy put the Black
trainees on separate grounds, housed, trained, and fed under the command
of white admirals and petty officers. Meeks expected one thing from the
Navy: a shipboard posting, so that he would join the upcoming assault on
Europe.

Instead, his unit was sent from Great Lakes to California's Port Chicago
(later known as Concord Naval Weapons Station, now Military Ocean Terminal Concord), a "dumpy lookin' place way back out there in the boon
docks. And you was kinda' disappointed to see such a little dumpy lookin'
place at that time, because I really wanted to go out on the ship. But they had
a lot of ammunition stored there though."[66]

Life for Black seamen at Port Chicago meant following orders from
white officers; in this case, loading munitions—live bombs, mines, and
ammunition—on the huge ships that pulled up the coast. "Well, you know
the white officers, they didn't have much to do with us no more than to
stand around and supervise and see that we load that ammunition." As Port
Chicago became the highest-traffic depot on the West Coast, those orders
came faster and faster, with some officers competing for whose units could
meet targets the fastest. The speed with which they were expected to work
increased the danger of their duty, compounded by the fact that the Black
seamen had never received training in how to handle munitions. Black units
waited for the training given white troops on ammunition handling to come

to their units. It never came. Each ship pulled away, headed to the Pacific, reminding the sailors that this was their mission.

That same fall, seventeen-year-old Medgar Evers graduated Army boot camp at Fort Benning. Evers became part of the same push to support the war. At first classified simply as "Laborer" at Fort Warren, Wyoming, Evers eventually shipped to Europe with the all-Black 657 Port Company as "cargo checker."[67] Evers was part of the Red Ball Express, a strategic corps charged with showing up in active theaters and transporting needed supplies for the invasions of Europe.[68] That included the French beach the Army had code-named Omaha.

Evers arrived in Normandy in the immediate aftermath of the May 1944 invasion. It was a harsh beginning: "On Omaha Beach, he saw lots of dead soldiers, and felt how awful it is to kill a man."[69] Evers went on to earn a Marksman Badge with Rifle Bar, the European–African–Middle Eastern Campaign Medal, and Bronze Stars for the Normandy and Northern France campaigns.[70] Evers never wrote about his wartime experiences; he did not mention the Red Ball Express after the war, when he faced Mississippians denying him the right to vote.

On July 17, just as Evers was leaving Normandy, an explosion at Port Chicago destroyed two ships moored there, flattening nearby homes and killing 350 people—300 of whom were Black seamen. Survivors had to clean up a disaster site strewn with the body parts of their comrades. Afterward, white officers at the scene were given a week's leave to process the trauma, but not Freddie Meeks, who had been hospitalized with minor injuries and night-mares, nor his peers. Some were still bandaged up a week later, when they were told it was time to start loading ammunition again.

This was too much for the 258 men ordered to do so. "We felt like we were getting a raw deal, because we was the one that was doing the dirty work. We were the ones fooling with the ammunition."[71] A month after the blast, Meeks and 257 other Black sailors refused orders to head to the docks and start loading again. Fifty of these, including Meeks, refused repeat exhorta-tions and threats, and were eventually tried for mutiny. "We didn't commit no mutiny," Meeks said. "We didn't take over no ship. We didn't take over a base. We had no weapons. We didn't even have a pen. We only refused to go back to work. Now how could that be mutiny?" Even with strong support from the NAACP (and representation from Thurgood Marshall), the court-martial only made national news when the men were convicted,[72] their story upstaged by the war's endgame in Europe and the continued threat of a land war with Japan.

That final year included relentless "saturation bombing" of German and Japanese cities; "In bombers named for girls, we burned/The cities we had learned about in school/Till our lives wore out."[73] In February 1945, that bombing included Dresden, where Chicago recruit Kurt Vonnegut was a prisoner of war; he would later call the bombing his "Armageddon." Philip Berrigan was part of the Battle of the Bulge, while William Kunstler met Lew Ayres in the Philippines during the naval battle of Leyte, a moment that would guide Kunstler for years. When the United States dropped an atomic bomb, none objected immediately, happy not to ponder a land war with Japan.

"War is far more horrible than I had ever imagined it," Lew Ayres told Hedda Hopper in his first postwar interview. "Maybe you don't know what a bombed city looks like . . . or kids [who] watch their parents being dumped into mass graves." Before long, Major Sheldon would write a lament wondering, "Do the butchers' blows still fall at Ravensbruck and Wounded Knee? Are the dead of Carthage and Hiroshima and Cuzco burning yet?"[74]

CHAPTER EIGHT

1946 to 1966

New York City, April 1946

Two young Army men walking into the museum stood out in the genteel crowd. Their pale-brown uniforms were crisp, as ironed as the armbands marked MP (for military police). They walked past groups of schoolchildren, quiet academics, women young and old showing off the season's new hats; for most, a trip to New York's Museum of Modern Art was special.

The officers headed straight to the INFORMATION desk, which was as polished as the marble floors in the seven-year-old building. Directed upstairs, they moved swiftly to the second-floor screening room. They were looking for the museum's copy of the new, still untitled film by John Huston, then on the schedule for the museum's Festival of Documentary Film.

A small crowd squeezed onto that room's folding chairs. Critics Archer Winston of the *New York Post* and James Agee of *The Nation* were in attendance at this months-early informal preview screening. The director, who had made this film for the Army Signal Corps, had been a giant of the cinema long before he had entered the Army. Ignoring the critics, the MPs walked directly to the back, speaking quietly to the projectionist. They departed carrying the film's four reels, before anyone had seen a frame of it.

Later that day, curator Iris Barry told the public that the museum was pulling several Army films due to "copyright restrictions (which) confine their showing to military personnel only." In addition to Huston's film, they seized the footage scheduled to precede it, *Army and Navy Screen Magazine*.[1]

That night, James Agee wrote a blistering response in *The Nation*, reporting that "a beautiful, terrible, valuable film by John Huston" had just been censored by the Army. "I don't know what is necessary to reverse this disgraceful decision," Agee closed, "but if dynamite is required, then dynamite is indicated."[2] MoMA's Barry did the next best thing and ran another of Huston's Army films, *San Pietro*—which had almost also been suppressed, accused of being "too anti-war." Huston had growled then that people should "take me out and shoot me" if he ever made a pro-war film.

John Huston had reported for duty shortly after Pearl Harbor, before he finished *The Maltese Falcon*. He'd left Humphrey Bogart tied to a chair, telling the studio, "Bogie will know how to get out." After a few training films, he had gone to Italy with the army's 36th Division, making what would be entitled *The Battle of San Pietro*. The filming was beyond stressful: Rey Scott, one of the cameramen, had snapped after months of bombardment. The film itself then faced blowback for its gruesome battles, its shots of soldiers' dead bodies being carried off the field. Afterward, Huston's heart did not quite leave the combat zone: "In Italy, when the guns stopped, you'd wake up and listen. [Back home] I was missing them in my sleep. I was suffering a mild form of anxiety neurosis."[3]

Huston was not alone: about half a million troops came home as psychiatric casualties. Hoping to persuade a nervous public that the war had not destroyed their sons, the War Department sent Huston to a Veterans Administration psychiatric hospital in Brentwood, Long Island. Huston's team shot thousands of feet of film, as he followed a dozen young men who entered the hospital paralyzed, or blind, or amnesiac. The process, he writes, was "almost like a religious experience." The resulting film is earnest. Young men learn to call their illnesses "psycho-neurotic anxiety disorders." Doctors assure them, and the camera, that "we're conducting an education campaign" to erase any stigma. But that campaign did not include the film Huston had titled *Let There Be Light*. "They wanted to maintain the 'warrior' myth, which said that our American soldiers went to war and came back all the stronger for the experience."

The truth was probably closer to what Huston's friend Ernest Hemingway had written in 1929: *The world breaks everyone and afterward many are strong at the broken places.* Huston, like many of those soldiers, was busy trying to find those broken places in himself and his nation.

So was Women's Army Corps major Alice Bradley Davey Sheldon, a former intelligence officer who in 1946 published a short story in the *New Yorker* with the ironic title "The Lucky Ones."[4] Sheldon did not write that story based on her high-powered intelligence work, like keeping details of D-Day plans secret: "Of course such a thing as an invasion involves such terrifically wide preparations, such as the guy who pastes the labels on the boxes of Spam, that it is a very interesting matter to afford military security to all the moves."[5] Her short story was instead based on her last year in Germany, de-Nazifying former German officers and helping manage the postwar's privations for internal refugees. She was also writing "the most interesting letters" to other new vets, Sheldon wrote her mother.

Sheldon had discovered the American Veterans Committee (AVC), a new group meant as a progressive alternative to the American Legion. Charles G. Bolté, a Dartmouth grad who had lost a leg in 1943 fighting with Britain's 8th Army, co-founded the AVC after hearing from hundreds of soldiers and new vets about what they wanted. "The fighting men have the strongest claim to peace, jobs, and freedom [but] are afraid they won't get them . . . and that the peace will be fumbled this time as it was the last time. They're afraid veterans will be selling apples again."[6]

Bolté was a colorful character, not against showing off his veteran cred in Manhattan's swanky venues. "He'd be at dinner and then suddenly raise his knife and sink it into his [wooden] leg, waiting for a reaction," recalled his Dartmouth peer Jerry Tallmer (then a reporter for the *New York Post*). Another night in a New York restaurant, the AVC head was approached by someone even more famous. "It's true! You do look like me," said Orson Welles.[7]

Sheldon had first discovered AVC in 1944, when she was working in the basement of the Pentagon. She hoped to draw more women into the group, since women had full membership in AVC (unlike the VFW and the Legion). She loved its mission statement, which started by calling for "adequate financial, medical, vocational and educational assistance for every veteran" and ended calling for the disarmament of Germany and the empowering of the new United Nations to "promote social and economic measures which will remove the causes of war."[8] AVC was the only veterans group with official standing at the San Francisco conference that created the new United Nations: photos of the unveiling included a smiling young man who resembled Orson Welles, carefully captioned "Charles G. Bolté, American Veterans Committee."

AVC's member list reads like a Rosetta Stone for postwar progressivism. In addition to Howard Zinn and William Kunstler, it boasted former Marine William Sloane Coffin, who upon his return in 1946 ran the Yale chapter. Both Medgar Evers and former chaplain Grant Reynolds, famous in Congress for his 1944 statement bemoaning the "plantation" conditions for Black soldiers, helped make AVC the first vets group completely free of segregation. Storytellers included John Huston, fellow Signal Corps vet William Wyler, the *New Yorker's* E.J. Kahn, and cartoonist Bill Mauldin. All knew that this young group was up against powerful conservative forces that preferred the well-fed VFW and American Legion.

AVC was determined to create an alternative, pushing for the creation of New Deal–style progressive policies.[9] The universities were filling with veterans warming to the AVC message. One veteran at Washington University remembered, "I'll tell you, at that time we were all imbued with a spirit that we had made the world safe for democracy and that we wanted to have an open society."[10] That included, most explicitly, racial justice: a group led by "Pfc. Clark Dennis" wrote for the *AVC Bulletin* about the expulsion of "Negroes" from a ship going home: "These boys, good American boys, had been told to pack their bags. . . . This is the most vicious and heartless discrimination that any of us have ever seen or heard of."[11] Urged by an official of the Veterans Administration to seek a job as a laborer, one South Carolina veteran answered, "I was a staff sergeant in the Army, traveled all over England [and] fourteen days in the English Channel. I wasn't going to push a wheel barrow."

AVC Bulletin, the organization's broadsheet, reported on "Christmas protests" at military bases all over the world: "191 of the leathernecks are members of Air Group 31, stationed in Yokosuka, Japan. . . . The entire group consists of enlisted men."[12] Newspapers blasted stories about the cables sent in January by 18,000 GIs in Germany and 6,000 in Japan; 4,000 GIs protesting in Manila; 1,500 in Rheims, and 15,000 at Hickman Air Force Base.

Even given the very real logistical issues involved in trying to move seven million people anywhere, the protests reflected the legitimate concerns of soldiers who had fought the Good War, but might not be prepared to become the cops of the world. Some wrote to Bolté, or Sheldon, or mused in the *AVC Bulletin* about what came next. One column entitled "The Veteran Is in a Poor Position to Avoid His Political Obligations" warned, "If the veteran doesn't speak for himself, others will speak for him, and he may someday hear his own interests attacked in his own name."

Bolté was a regular in Washington, D.C., his Orson Welles face and audible wooden leg a fixture on Capitol Hill. He testified in favor of the Seamen's War Service Bill, an expanded GI Bill of Rights, and the Murray Full-Employment-Bill, "which we endorse because unemployment is too dangerous a problem to be handled by the haphazard methods of the past." Peace was definitely on AVC's agenda: "All of us here grope for some solid means which would transfer the helm of the future into our hands, some device which would break for all time the rhythm of war," a corporal had written in a letter to Bolté. "[The new veteran] shall want to be an eager partner in the reconstruction, who has learned much, who can give much and is afraid of nothing."[13] In mid-1946, it looked like that "revolution in social consciousness" might actually be on deck. On June 3, the NAACP scored a victory at the U.S. Supreme Court, which declared in *Morgan v. Virginia* that segregation on interstate buses and trains was unconstitutional.

AVC's membership soared to one hundred thousand; Bolté brought in Douglas Fairbanks and other rich celebrities for a campaign to increase that number to a million.[14] Two weeks later, the press swarmed AVC's first big conference in Des Moines, Iowa. *Time* magazine quoted one young wife regretting having a convention that did not feature drinking and dinners, asking her vet husband, "Oh, why don't you just join the American Legion?"[15]

Even Superman supported the AVC. The producers of the nightly radio show *The Adventures of Superman*, which had recently pitted the Man of Steel against the Ku Klux Klan,[16] began its September 6, 1946, show with a crowd of returning GIs on the steps of a state capitol, "most of them battle-scarred veterans of the European and the Pacific campaigns."

AVC was hoping to shift the "American Way" further along the path blazed by FDR, and deploy that unity and shared sacrifice in the cause of fairness and justice. But a new "American Way" was coming, and its enemy was not injustice, but Communism.

After wartime ally Russia declared all of Eastern Europe as its own, talk
of "full employment" or "shared sacrifice" was stigmatized as too much like
Russia. The mid-term elections in November gave the Senate back to the
Republicans, including former Marine Joseph McCarthy.

One of McCarthy's first obsessions was quickly dissolving all federal control of business now that the wartime "emergency" was over—thus placing
the AVC in his crosshairs early. In January, when the Department of Commerce eliminated the Office of Price Administration, ending national rent
control, AVC complained to Congress, testifying that with the population
of renters exploding, the "operating income of landlords was at an all-time
peak," while new veterans were still without homes.[17]

AVC was already under suspicion for its flagrant anti-segregationism, talk
of full employment, and its plan for veterans to implement world peace. The
media asked whether the AVC was a communist front (perhaps because its
five New York City chapters also made up its "Left faction," including a
three-hundred-strong Brooklyn chapter named "Gung Ho" after the war cry
of the Chinese Communists).[18] Bolté emphasized that the overall direction of
the AVC was untainted by communism, to no avail: Mississippi representative John Rankin rammed through a resolution barring the AVC from testifying before the House Veterans Affairs Committee.

After Bolté stepped down as president of the group to become a Rhodes
Scholar, the organization kept fracturing, losing a third of its members.[19]
Most veterans were choosing the better-funded, less-controversial American
Legion and VFW. In both rhetoric and effectiveness, AVC began to dimin-
ish. Former servicemembers found other ways to create change.

John Huston turned the Maxwell Anderson project *Key Largo* into a troubled veteran's story; its Humphrey Bogart character recounts the Battle of San
Pietro. "We weren't making all the sacrifice of human effort and lives . . . to
return to the kind of a world we had after the last world war," Bogart's Army
officer tells a gangster, adding that his war was about "fighting to cleanse
the world of ancient evils. Ancient ills."[20] Huston was trying, like Bogart's
character, not to give in to cynicism and fear. That was not easy: 1947 was
full of both.

By 1948, FBI attention focused on another group of young veterans:
returning African American soldiers, who found themselves resisting Jim

Crow laws. This included Medgar Evers, who had come home remembering that Europeans had "treated him just like he was one of the people," his sister said later. "Not black or white."[21] Evers and his brother Charles had both returned believing their father, who had said that their service would make society "treat them with dignity. My children will be able to vote."[22] Young lieutenant Jack Robinson, later known by baseball fans as Jackie, was already a soldier-dissenter, court-martialed in 1944 for refusing to go to the back of an interstate bus. Robinson's arrest occurred two years before the U.S. Supreme Court's *Morgan* decision declared such segregation unconstitutional—and three years before Robinson first took the plate at Ebbets Field, the first Black player allowed to break Major League Baseball's color barrier.

The FBI was also tracking conscientious objector Bayard Rustin. Following a Quaker upbringing in the Philadelphia suburb of Chester, Rustin's pacifism had been triggered by two years at Wilberforce University. Like all students at the historically Black Wilberforce, Rustin trained in the school's mandatory ROTC program, until he stopped attending drill and lost his scholarship, repulsed by hundreds of hours of drill and command, rifle marksmanship, and "combat principles."[23] He moved to New York City, started attending City College, and became right-hand man to celebrated socialist/pacifist A.J. Muste.

Rustin had noted his CO plans on his October 1940 draft registration. His supporting materials for his Harlem draft board described his Quaker childhood: "I came to the firm and immovable conviction that war was wrong and opposed directly to the Christian ideal." He had skipped the government's Civilian Public Service (CPS) camps for more-direct refusal, cheered on by some who had already begun hunger strikes against segregation in Danbury, Connecticut, and Lewisburg, Pennsylvania. One of those "shock troops of pacifism" had written exultantly that prison had provided "the greatest and most worthwhile year of my life."[24]

Rustin had composed a very different letter to his draft board in February 1944. A.J. Muste's adopted son began by citing documents attesting to peace testimony since the 1920s, before he announced his true intentions—"conscription as well as war equally is inconsistent with the teachings of Jesus. I must resist conscription also." Rustin's statement named as inseparable war's killing and its racism: to believe otherwise was to think

that "racism can overcome racism, that evil can produce good, that men virtually in slavery can struggle for a freedom they are denied."

On March 9, 1944, Rustin entered the Federal Correctional Institution in
Ashland, Kentucky. Thus commenced two-plus years of organizing, prison
rebellions, and bureaucratic jousts between Rustin and a succession of outraged prison officials. And he did not really stop organizing: Muste visited regularly, and Rustin kept in close touch by mail with a civil rights group he had
midwifed, the Congress for Racial Equality (CORE). After the United States
dropped an atomic bomb on Hiroshima in 1945, Muste and Rustin (known
inside the Fellowship of Reconciliation as "Musty and Rusty") persuaded the
Justice Department to release Rustin from prison, promising that he would
swear off this dangerous race stuff and concentrate on nukes. But by 1946,
Rustin was also working with CORE, which soon commenced the "Journey
of Reconciliation," an interracial group riding interstate buses together.

Six days before Jackie Robinson debuted with the Dodgers, Rustin's group
launched from Washington, D.C., with two wartime conscientious objectors[25] happy to keep speaking truth to power by getting arrested regularly.[26]
Some of them were also joining Rustin's more pacifist work, which in 1947
mostly consisted of opposing the nuclear bomb and fighting to end draft registration. No one was being drafted for war, but FOR's Committee Against
Conscription still encouraged young pacifists to burn their draft cards (with
a polite note to Selective Service).

Rustin was also working with the NAACP's Committee Against Jim Crow
in Military Service and Training, demanding an end to military segregation.
This committee's co-chairs were labor leader A. Philip Randolph and former
AVC president Grant Reynolds. With Charles Bolté, Reynolds was working
on a book, *The Negro Veteran*. Rustin spent 1947 alternately getting arrested
for interracial bus-riding and lobbying hard on Capitol Hill, including testifying at congressional committees that were fine-tuning the new National
Security Act.

In September, when that act passed, Rustin was busy integrating the dining car on the Southern Railroad, refusing orders to move to a segregated car
on his way to Oxford, Tennessee. If he had left the train when it stopped in
Memphis, Rustin could have seen a skinny eighteen-year-old named Clarence Adams running down the street to an Army recruiting station.

September 11, 1947, was a little hotter than usual in Memphis, with temps hitting the 90s. Tempers were running high, and local police were knocking on doors. Clarence Adams had wanted nothing more than to be a boxer, ever since Joe Louis' last fight in 1938; the authorities knew he had gotten into some local scuffles of late. When they came after him, his father refused to open the door.

Adams did not want to know why police were looking for him: he just scooted. When he got to Front Street, in the older part of town, the Army recruiting center shone in the morning light, "and right then and there, on September 11, 1947, I enlisted." While his preliminary tests qualified him for the Air Force, he chose the Army, in which his uncles had served, even though they had also told him about discrimination. He chose Fort Dix, New Jersey, for basic training, which ended up teaching him that racism was not confined to the South. In January 1948, his unit arrived in Korea, where the United States was charged with "peacekeeping" in areas formerly occupied by Japan. The sub-zero temperatures froze his bones.

In June 1948, while Adams was coping with Korea's belated spring, Congress passed a new Selective Service Act. The new requirements included the first medical draft, to enable shorter tours for doctors; it did *not* mandate desegregated armed forces. While most of the Committee Against Jim Crow in Military Service and Training was outraged and said so, Bayard Rustin was almost glad to see military racism exposed more clearly. He and A. Philip Randolph formed a parallel group, the League for Nonviolent Civil Disobedience Against Military Segregation, with campaigns using the new tools of nonviolent direct action developed by Mahatma Gandhi in India. The League's protesters encircled the White House, carrying signs calling for an end to Jim Crow: Rustin hoped the campaign would spread to venues far beyond the military.

Rustin recruited volunteers in St. Louis, Minneapolis, LA, Philadelphia, Buffalo, Dayton and Chicago;[27] he secured pledges from hundreds of young men that they would refuse to register for the draft, and instructed that they also send a letter to the president, swearing not to do so "as long as racial discrimination and segregation exist there."[28] But after July 26, 1948, when President Harry Truman issued General Order 9981, ordering desegregation, most of the Committee fell over themselves in praise. Rustin was still arrested in September for blocking the entrance to New York's City Hall, in support of the few die-hards still refusing to register. The League was in tatters; Rustin booked a berth on the *Queen Mary* and headed to India for an international conference organized by Gandhi.

In July 1950, nineteen-year-old Clarence Adams was at Fort Lewis after a year in Asia, about to process out after serving in Korea on the Army's prior "peacekeeping" mission. Adams was looking forward to a career as a boxer, having won numerous matches on a base in Japan with an arm they called Greased Lightning. Instead, he wrote years later, "we heard over the PA system that President Truman had announced the outbreak of the Korean War and had ordered all soldiers with less than a year on their enlistment to be extended for twelve months." Thus was Adams a pioneer subject for the military policy that would later be named stop-loss.

That July speech by President Truman set the tone for the first of the century's two "hot" undeclared wars. After North Korean tanks poured over the (admittedly arbitrary) border between North and South Korea, Truman said, "This attack has made it clear, beyond all doubt, that the international Communist movement is willing to use armed invasion to conquer independent nations. An act of aggression such as this creates a very real danger to the security of all free nations." He was referring to the newborn People's Republic of China, a new player in the previously Soviet-run North Korea; he was also doubling down on the Truman Doctrine mandate to fight international communism at home and abroad.

Thus began three years of shadow-boxing with a high body count, between and among Korean armies backed by the United States, versus those backed by the Soviet Union and China. It would end in a semi-permanent standoff, one that extended to numerous continents and into civilian life.

At home, the Truman Doctrine meant even less tolerance for free expression, especially when it had anything at all to do with the military. "*A sickness* permeated the country," John Huston writes. "Nobody came to the defense of people being persecuted for personal beliefs."[29] A harsh "loyalty oaths" campaign was reaching its climax in mid-1950, especially in Hollywood. John Huston organized Directors Guild members to adopt a stance against such a requirement. Huston told Cecil DeMille that his faction were Signal Corps peers and "were in uniform when you were wrapping yourself in the flag." Then he went back to working on his last film for Warner Brothers, *The Red Badge of Courage.*

Based on the iconic Stephen Crane novel of the Civil War, *Red Badge* was a passion project for Huston and producer Gottfried Reinhardt (who had spent the war on training films like *K-Rations, How to Eat Them*). As lead they had hired the boyish Audie Murphy, whose childlike visage belied the fact that he was the war's most-decorated veteran. And as the lead's best friend they'd cast Signal Corps peer Bill Mauldin, the cartoonist who'd been in Italy with Huston in 1943.

Huston then crafted a loosely structured meditation on war and identity, a signature "dreamlike interrogation of power, delusion, and violence."[30] As shooting began, Huston took along a writer for the *New Yorker*, who also came to some of the Hollywood parties Huston hated. At his forty-fourth birthday party, held at the legendary Chasen's, "in the lapel of his dinner jacket, he wore the ribbon of the Legion of Merit, awarded to him for his work on Army Signal Corps films in the war."[31] As *Red Badge* filmed in Chico, he paid careful attention to unorthodox scenes in which young recruits laugh at veterans; when a platoon marches while softly singing "John Brown's body lies a-mouldering in the grave," and when a figure called the Tall Soldier dies before the protagonist's eyes. Huston called that last "the best scene in the movie."

But by mid-1950, Hollywood was busy drumming up support for war. At the White House's request, movie screens filled with anti-Communist movies: 1949's *The Red Menace* (1949), *I Married a Communist* (1950), and *I Was a Communist for the FBI* (1951) were just a few.[32] After previews highlighted *Red Badge*'s unorthodox form (and lack of a leading lady), Warner Brothers ordered a wholesale restructuring. Out went the Tall Soldier and veterans scenes; battle scenes were recut and compressed to form a story of triumph and victory. By then, Huston was in Africa shooting *The African Queen*, and he refused to see the new version.

All this was duly recorded by the FBI, which would call Huston in for a meeting in 1952 to ask about "misguided liberals" like Albert Einstein and "Commies" like Charlie Chaplin, who had been barred from re-entry to the United States the same year *Red Badge* was released. By then, the Hollywood blacklist was in full effect, Senator McCarthy had been re-elected, and resistance to the Korean War seemed almost inconceivable.

The FBI was also finally able to arrest W.E.B. Du Bois, after he organized a Peace Information Center that sent out "Peacegrams" ("One million signatures for the Stockholm disarmament petition!"). The FBI raided the center's office in February 1951, arresting Du Bois as a "foreign agent" under new national-security legislation.

Congress revised the Universal Military Training and Service Act, and over the next three years Selective Service would induct 1.3 million young men.[33] Over 1.5 million more volunteered, knowing that they were likely going to Korea anyway and wanting to choose how. Unlike in the previous war, no Civilian Public Service camps awaited those who could prove they were conscientious objectors, but that only made the process even lonelier for those who did. Most of the ten thousand men approved for alternative service, now known as I-W objectors, were Mennonites, Jehovah's Witnesses, and members of the Church of the Brethren; they took low-level hospital jobs or served overseas in church-run programs.

For young Staughton Lynd, the son of eminent sociologists (authors of the landmark 1923 study of the Midwest, *Middletown*), securing CO status was of itself a kind of dissent, one that laid the groundwork for more to come in future years.

After a Manhattan upbringing infused with his parents' socialist outlook, Lynd's stance was also shaped by some Quaker cousins and years attending the Ethical Culture School, whose 64th Street auditorium bore the maxim *Where men seek the highest is holy ground.* Like his father, he was something of a Marxist, joining the John Reed Club at Harvard University and falling in love with a lithe Radcliffe student who introduced herself by asking about the book *The Decline and Fall of British Capitalism.* She was also a Quaker, and the two were married in a Baltimore Friends Meeting in 1951.

Despite his Quaker affiliations, Lynd decided not to go for one of the I-W classifications, which felt too much like class privilege. He told the draft board that he'd rather follow the example of his cousin David Hartley, a conscientious objector who had been an ambulance driver during the previous war. At the draft board, Lynd brought his friend Walter Smalakis, a disfigured veteran of the 301st Infantry, to testify on his behalf. "You could still see the scars from his plastic surgery. I really think that's why they granted me I-A-O status."[34] Within the year, Lynd had completed basic training at Fort Dix and medic training at Camp Pickett, near Richmond, Virginia.

Camp Pickett, built in 1942 as the army upsized for war, had over three hundred buildings, including four movie theaters and a prisoner-of-war camp. Lynd reported to the Military Medical Replacement Training Center, which had been well-named during the war, when troops' life expectancy could be measured in seconds. Its low-rise buildings were not that dissimilar from some in New York. Most of the other trainees were Seventh Day Adventists, hoping to emulate Okinawa hero-medic Desmond Doss; there were only a few Mennonites, Church of the Brethren, and Quakers like Lynd.

The reason why became clear early on, as the medics-to-be were schooled on military triage: "Two stretchers come in, and one of the soldiers is gravely wounded. The other is less so. Who do you help first?" the instructor asked.

Lynd's hand shot up instantly: he had studied the Hippocratic Oath. But the instructor shook his head, saying that the top priority was the health of the *unit*, the health of the war. "At that moment, I realized I had made a horrible mistake," Lynd says, "thinking that being a medic meant I wouldn't violate my principles." He still completed the training, wondering what to do when the orders for Korea came.

Lynd likely knew that the picture did not look good, based on the ten thousand 1-A-O objectors who had deployed as medics from Pusan to Inchon. CO organizations had been busy addressing the pleas of deployed pacifists who "feel that we are being given definite combatant training, even though we are not obliged to bear arms. We are compelled to attend such classes . . . as squad tactics, minelaying, etc. Indeed, one of our objectors faces a special court martial next week because he refused to cover an infiltration course under 'mock battle conditions.'"[35]

Some waited until they were deployed, and ended up in the hospital: "After three weeks of horrible training, I had a nervous collapse and was taken to the United States Naval Hospital. . . . The first week at the hospital, I had another breakdown. After thirteen days of rest, I was released. The doctor diagnosed my case as a nervous condition resulting from emotional and religious feelings. . . . It was at this time that I told him I was a Conscientious Objector."[36] And they agonized even when their commands complied. "On the train from Inchon to Chunchon, I was ordered to take a weapon and stand guard on the train platform for an hour. I said to the Sarge that I could only do so without a weapon because of my religious beliefs. He agreed to this without an argument. . . . We may go up on the line shortly and I will be getting patrols. I will go but expect to do so unarmed."[37]

Despite Truman's executive order, the Army in Korea was still mostly segregated, until some massive losses in the early battles. The North Korean forces had "almost wiped us out," Clarence Adams writes. "We had so few men left, they had to use white and black soldiers together to keep up the fight." Nonetheless, command protocols remained unchanged: "The white officers in my unit did not associate with us except to give us orders."[38]

Adams also witnessed a flagrant violation of military strategy, as white infantry units retreated past his company, even though as light infantry they were supposed to provide cover for units with less agile weaponry. "So when it came time for us to go, we had no one to protect us . . . [we] were sitting ducks for Chinese mortar fire and machine guns." His Black regiment, Adams realized, "was being sacrificed to save white troops."

The narrative above is of November 25, 1950, just as U.S. forces had commenced a "Home-by-Christmas" offensive aimed at driving all Chinese troops from Korea. Adams' platoon had already lost half its men; the rest scattered and found themselves surrounded. Before surrendering, Adams emptied his weapon and threw it away. "If he's going to kill me, he's going to have to use his bullets."

Not only were the troops not home by Christmas, but the war was deepening, and would last three more years, most of them simultaneous with peace talks. In June 1951, just as advocates for conscientious objectors were sending case briefs to Secretary of Defense George Marshall, the first overture for peace talks was made by the Pentagon.[39] Soon, negotiations were taking place on the border between North and South Korea, mostly in the small village of Panmunjom.

Adams' unit had lost all but ten soldiers by the time of his capture in December 1950. While he and the others marched uphill in heavy snow, American bombers overhead were visiting napalm on the surrounding mountains and villages. "What really sickened me was when one of their napalm bombs hit a Korean hut. A woman with a baby on her back came running out of the house, engulfed by orange flames and thick black smoke. She and her baby burned to death before my very eyes." At this point, Adams adds, he exchanged looks with Richards, a fellow Black GI with whom he had been marching. "We both were thinking the same thing: If this guard shoots us, well, we deserve it because we should not be in Korea."

Adams survived the rest of the march, he believed, in part because as one of the famously "oppressed" he evoked more patience from his captors than did the white GIs. That did not stop horrific treatment in their first year at Pyoktong. When Chinese troops took over the camp, Adams agreed to communicate with them on behalf of the prisoners, securing better food, bedding, and amenities that made life in camp more bearable. As part of a faction self-titled "The Progressives," Adams helped mobilize prisoners to sign the Stockholm Appeal for Peace. In February 1953, Adams was among the prisoners co-signing an appeal to the U.N. General Assembly certifying that "we have been kept as comfortable as possible" and asking for an immediate end to hostilities.

In October 1951, the movie *The Red Badge of Courage* premiered in the United States; the *New York Times*, noting Huston's portrayal of battle from the inside, remarked on "the ragged and nondescript infantry, the marches, the battle lines, the din, the dust, the cavalry charges, the enemy surging out of the clouds of smoke, and the pitiful, wretched lines of the wounded reaching and stumbling toward the rear."[40] And the new Central Committee for Conscientious Objectors (my employer in the 1990s) published its very first *Handbook for Conscientious Objectors*, a set of legal guidelines that dissenters would carry for decades to come.

By the time the two sides signed an armistice in December 1953, two million civilians had died, along with forty thousand Americans. More than one hundred thousand U.S. troops had been wounded, 4,300 others granted conscientious objector status, and another forty thousand simply deserted (for all manner of reasons). Twenty-three "turncoats," including Adams, refused repatriation to the United States—not because they loved Communism but because they preferred the unknown of China or North Korea to Jim Crow. "The Chinese unbrainwashed me!" Adams told reporters. "The Negro had his mind brainwashed long before the Korea War. If he stayed in his place he was a good nigger."[41]

Impossible, said the media and the military: they must have had their minds scrubbed clean by Communist torturers. "Communist Brainwashing—Are We Prepared?" asked *The New Republic*.[42] When Adams told the press his reasons, his critique was dismissed by the white press as Communist propaganda, and Adams himself as "the average colored boy [who] faces up to the segregation and accepts it and goes on about his business." Adams' defection, it was assumed, must have been due to some personal weakness or deviancy.

By the time *The New Republic* was psychoanalyzing him in 1953, Adams was deciding to choose China as his new home. Over the next fourteen years, he would attend Chinese universities, start a family, and staff the Foreign Languages Press, editing translations to and from English at all levels. He also spoke with journalists from around the world. Among these was *Baltimore Afro-American* writer William Worthy, who then paved the way for a visit from W.E.B. Du Bois.

Adams had first read Du Bois in Camp 5, thrilled at the classic declaration that "the problem for 20th-century America is the problem of the color line;" he called the 1952 meeting "one unforgettable day." Du Bois' account of meeting the young veteran was equally chirpy, praising "the colored American prisoner of war who stayed in China rather than return to America and is happy with his wife and baby."[43]

Happy or not, Adams was also navigating his combat trauma on his own, with mixed results. "More than once have I jumped out of a deep sleep in the middle of a nightmare and taken a swing at anyone near me." Adams was not alone: during the war's initial phase, "military officials reported very high rates of neuropsychiatric casualties (250 per 1000 per year). In-country "forward psychiatry" reduced those numbers in later years.[44] Most returning vets did not seek treatment, of course; they were going home to an America where psychiatry still bore a stigma.

In 1952, Staughton Lynd was living in New Jersey, not far from family friend and World War II CO Dave Dellinger. Lynd was soon working for *Liberation Magazine*, founded by Bayard Rustin. The twenty-seven-year-old Lynd was "a junior sidekick to Dave Dellinger; I'd sit against the wall while Rustin, Dave, and A.J. Muste talked about their adventures."

Lynd was going back to school, no longer hampered by his Army discharge thanks to the Supreme Court. One of the others red-baited out of Fort Dix had taken the Army to court. "The Army told the Supreme Court, *Yeah, it was wrong, but there's nothing you can do about it*, which is always a bad thing to say to a judge. And so, the next thing I knew, we all had honorable discharges."[45] Now Lynd had access to the G.I. Bill, which helped when he was accepted at Columbia University; he moved into a Manhattan apartment not far from where he had grown up. It was 1954, and the civil rights movement was seizing on the Court's signature decision that year, *Brown v. Board of Education*. Rustin's stories at *Liberation* meetings were about Little Rock, Arkansas, and about the Reverend Martin Luther King, Jr.

Rustin first began to mentor King after December 1955, when a seasoned activist named Rosa Parks had publicly refused, in Montgomery, Alabama, to sit in the back of a bus.[46] That moment was noticed by Black soldiers as far away as China, where Clarence Adams exulted, and by a young Air Force recruit in Oakland, California, named Robert George Seale.

A hyperactive high school dropout, Seale believed so strongly in the promise of military desegregation that he kept going back to recruiting offices, even after being rejected by the Army for a foot injury. It was 1955, and change was in the air; Seale fought to get the U.S. Air Force to recognize he was not too injured to serve. In April he enlisted as a mechanic, then excelled in his basic and advanced training in Amarillo, Texas. When it was time to start his tour of duty, out of the spots available for mechanics he chose Ellsworth Air Force Base, in South Dakota.

The young Californian had no way of knowing that a Midwestern base could also feel Southern. Rapid City, the closest metropolitan area, had had a strong Ku Klux Klan klavern[47] and still regularly ejected African Americans from local hotels, bars, and laundromats. A special report to the U.S. Commission on Civil Rights assailed Rapid City's "serious deprivation of opportunity for non-white personnel."[48] A decade earlier in nearby Mayville, the population (whose ancestry was largely Norwegian) had treated Black airmen as an invasion force: "Emphasis is made by the police department and prominent citizens that Negro airmen are not wanted in the town, and neither are white airmen who choose to associate with Negroes."[49]

Seale knew nothing of this. "I'd heard about civil rights through the papers but was not focusing on it that much," he writes in his memoir *Steal the Time*. "I was personally more concerned about getting some sort of education."[50] Learn he did, mastering structural repair on high-performance aircraft, including the B-52. Seale also made some good friends, at least one of whom looked out for him when he had drunk too much, and organized a band, playing some gigs in downtown Rapid City after he bought some drums. Those drums, purchased while on leave in Oakland, were also expensive, $600 in 1956 dollars; even the payment plan was hard on his sergeant's salary.

In 1959, after he missed three payments, Seale's account was turned over to a collection agency, one owned by his (white) squadron commander, Rufus T. King. What followed, according to Seale, was a battle of wills, as over and over King threatened to jail Seale unless he paid up. Convinced that he was already set for the brig, Seale proceeded not to salute his squadron commander, telling himself "[King] thinks he's a white god or something." After a confrontation both physical and verbal—"I cussed out Colonel King for what he was . . . all the way down the streets. I had a whole big crowd of cats jiving and watching me cuss him out while they were taking me down in front of the barracks"—Seale was court-martialed, released with a bad-conduct discharge, and warned, "You're never going to be able to get a job after this, Seale."

Seale would prove them wrong, getting jobs with a number of Bay Area aerospace firms, including work on the early stages of the U.S. space program "doing electromagnetic field, black light, non-destruct testing . . . for all three stages of exhaust housing for the Gemini missile program." He also went to Merritt College, joining its Afro-American Students Association and becoming friends with a young firebrand named Huey Newton, who had just joined Sigma (the Black fraternity founded by Langston Hughes in 1914).

Seale and Newton were less interested in Langston Hughes or Bayard Rustin than in Malcolm X. Seale's memoir mentions neither, nor even Staughton Lynd, who had long been affiliated with the Student Nonviolent Coordinating Committee (SNCC). Lynd coordinated its Freedom Schools during the 1964 Freedom Summer in Mississippi, which Lynd called "the most important political experience of my life."

Seale and Newton knew all about Freedom Summer, including its casualties—one thousand arrests, eighty beatings, six murders, thirty-five shootings, and sixty-five bombed or burned-out buildings—and the concurrent humiliation of Black delegates by the Democratic Party. That December, Malcolm X called for Blacks to emulate African freedom fighters instead.

A few months later, Malcolm X was shot in Harlem, and Seale started fighting cops right there: "I got six loose red bricks from the garden. Every time I saw a paddy roll by in a car, I picked up one of the half-bricks, and threw it at the motherfuckers." Seale almost certainly remembered the day in 1966 that Rustin's protege, Stokely Carmichael, electrified SNCC by declaring: "We been saying 'freedom' for six years. What we are going to start saying now is 'Black Power.'"[51]

Staughton Lynd was welcome at SNCC even after white leadership was discouraged: Stokely's "I don't trust any whites" was followed quickly by, "I didn't mean Staughton!" Lynd stayed with the group throughout the voting-rights battle in Alabama, traveling to Selma in 1965. But on the train back up north, he read in the *New York Times* about a battle in the small Vietnamese city of Pleiku, where North Vietnamese troops had attacked the United States' Camp Holloway, drawing retaliation from forty-nine U.S. fighter-bombers. "Oh, so that's what I am now supposed to be doing: resisting what is happening in Vietnam," Lynd remembers thinking.[52] Lynd knew where to start, once he was finished marching from Selma to Montgomery with Martin Luther King.

As a new professor at Yale University, Lynd was also somewhat uniquely positioned—along with his friend Howard Zinn—to work directly with the anti-war movement already brewing on the nation's campuses. Lynd urged Bayard Rustin to work with him and to join a national anti-war march being planned by Students for a Democratic Society (SDS). But Rustin was reluctant to do so while the Voting Rights Act was still being debated, far more trusting of the Democratic Party than of the new anti-war coalition.

Rustin was also suspicious of SDS' welcoming Stalinist/Trotskyist groups into its coalition. "It's contrary to anything you ever taught me," Rustin told A.J. Muste, "You cannot have a vague slogan [and] bring in the Du Bois Club and the Communists and Progressive Labor." In the beginning of March, he met with SDS' Todd Gitlin. Dressed to the nines and in his trademark stentorian voice, the civil rights leader and executive secretary of the War Resisters League had an unusual message for the earnest young students. "He said we weren't being militant enough," Gitlin told me decades later. "We saw him representing the seamlessness of Gandhianism—and he was saying that with a week of sit-ins at Wall Street and the banks, we weren't risking enough."[53]

Rustin still was not offering to help organize a new anti-war campaign, clearly reluctant to lose whatever influence he possessed in Washington. He kept to the vision he had just published in *Commentary Magazine*, of going beyond protest, to a day when "a coalition of progressive forces . . . becomes the effective political majority in the United States."[54] To Lynd and the rest of *Liberation*, such deference to President Lyndon B. Johnson was exactly the opposite of speaking truth to power.

The *Liberation* circle's patience was exhausted when Rustin and Norman Thomas issued a statement demanding that SDS renounce any ties to "totalitarian" groups. "A.J. [Muste] was just aghast," Lynd remembers. Muste encouraged Lynd to write a response in *Liberation*; Lynd did, accusing Rustin of wanting a "coalition with the Marines."

The march went on, without Rustin, on April 17, drawing a then unprecedented 25,000 to the Capitol. Judy Collins performed, as did the "singing journalist," Phil Ochs, who sang his brand-new song about a universal soldier whose useless wars began in 1812.[55] "I even killed my brothers and so many others," Ochs' Civil War soldier says. "But I ain't marching anymore!" Ochs was neither a soldier nor a vet, though he had attended a military academy; his father, Jacob, a physician who had survived 1944's Battle of the Hürtgen Forest, had been one of the traumatized troops in the VA hospital filmed by John Huston in 1946. Lynd was familiar with Ochs, who had warned as early as 1964 in "Talking Vietnam Blues":

> *Well, training is the word we use,*
> *Nice word to have in case we lose.*
> *Training a million Vietnamese*
> *To fight for the wrong government and the American Way.*[56]

The day after the march, J. Edgar Hoover announced that "Communists [had] participated in the student march on Washington in April and were striving to start other demonstrations against United States foreign policy."[57] Staughton Lynd was certainly doing the latter, taking Gandhi's principles to a hyper-American, Beat extreme: "One can now envision a series of nonviolent protests which . . . might, if its insane foreign policy continues, culminate in the decision of hundreds of thousands of people to recognize the authority of alternative institutions of their own making."[58]

Meanwhile, young people were still being shipped to Vietnam. Some of them could hear, over Radio Hanoi, the voice of Clarence Adams from near-by China. "You are supposedly fighting for the freedom of the Vietnamese, but what kind of freedom do you have at home, sitting in the back of the bus, being barred from restaurants, stores and certain neighborhoods, and being denied the right to vote? . . . Go home and fight for equality in America."

Adams wrote later that "I knew that too many young blacks would be sent to a foreign country to be slaughtered. I wanted them to know what other young black Americans and I had been through in Korea." For his pains, Adams would be called by the Pentagon "the new Tokyo Rose," since the broadcast had migrated from China to Radio Hanoi. A year later, Adams would be in Washington, D.C., telling his story to the House Un-American Activities Committee.

Adams' return to the States in 1966 was sparked equally by homesickness and the changing climate in China, where authorities were insisting he go to a rural factory as part of the Cultural Revolution. He insisted on going home to Memphis with his Chinese wife and biracial children, trying to avoid the angry whites ready to punish the "traitor." (There he would remain until his death in 2007, his family's survival his last dissent.) In 1966, Adams told HUAC that soldiers like him had been too powerless to have value to the Chinese: "We just fought and took orders. Only the officers had any information to give." The Committee continued its discussion of expanded penalties for "assistance to enemies of U.S. in time of undeclared war."[59]

Not long after that, a Missouri member of HUAC, Richard Ichord, had a verbal sparring match with a young Indiana congressman named Andrew Jacobs, Jr. Ichord, who had spent World War II in the Navy Air Corps, knew Jacobs was both a Democrat and a peacenik; he also knew why. When asked by a reporter for the *Indianapolis Star* about whether there was a law against anti-war pickets, Jacobs had growled, "If there is, then I wasted my time crawling over half the mountains in Korea."[60] Thus, upon spying Jacobs at the House gym, Ichord hailed him, "Well, here comes a dove. . . . At least you're a fighting dove." Jacobs' reply coined a phrase continuously in use since: "I've thought it over and I've decided it's better to be a fighting dove than a chicken hawk."

A few weeks later, another one of the "fighting doves," Staughton Lynd, was in a Manhattan church, watching as a group of this war's resisters announced themselves to the world.

A photo of that day, June 30, 1966, is a snapshot of the peace movement Lynd was helping to build. Most prominent are three young men in Army uniforms: twenty-six-year-old Dennis Mora, who looks softened only by his slightly rumpled shirt, sits next to his Bronx High School of Science class-mate,[61] Stokely Standiford Churchill Carmichael, listed as a representative of the SNCC, not by name. Lynd's Kennedyesque profile is at the far right, at a long table in the 150-year-old New York Community Church. At the other end, his *Liberation* compatriot Dave Dellinger stands next to Carmichael; seated to their rear, the regal figure of eighty-one-year-old A.J. Muste. June 30, the day of this press conference, was seasonably hot and humid, their sweat almost palpable.

The letterhead of the "Fort Hood Three Defense Committee," co-chaired by Lynd and A.J. Muste, lists among its members and sponsors Dorothy Day, Noam Chomsky, and libertarian journalist Nat Hentoff. Peaceniks were effusive in support: "If I were a GI and saw a peace movement such as ours which opposes the war in Vietnam and supports those who refuse," wrote one committee member in an internal memo, "I would LOOK TO THEM TO PROTECT MY RIGHTS IN REFUSING TO GO. They can say to us that it is easy to say DON'T GO, BUT WE ARE NOT GOING TO JAIL, WE ARE NOT GOING TO BE PLACED IN THE BRIG."[62]

That day, Mora stood before the cameras and laid down a gauntlet that would be taken up by generals, presidents, and priests alike. "We are initi-ating today," Mora said, "an action in the courts to enjoin the Secretary of Defense and the Secretary of the Army from sending us to Vietnam. We intend to report as ordered to the Oakland Army Terminal, but under no circumstances will we board ship for Vietnam. We are prepared to face Court Martial if necessary."

Mora emphasized that the three, with their diverse backgrounds, could represent "a cross section of the Army and of America," and that many other soldiers felt as they did. "We have been in the army long enough to know that we are not the only G.I.'s who feel as we do. Large numbers of men in the service either do not understand this war or are against it."

The press conference had "an atmosphere of the revival meeting," wrote *New York Times* reporter Martin Arnold. Its call and response grew loud-er when James Johnson said staunchly, "The Negro in Vietnam is being called upon to defend freedom which in many parts of the country does not exist for him. Just as the Negroes are fighting for absolute freedom and self-determination in the United States, so is it with the Vietnamese in their struggle against the Americans."

Mora, Samas, and Johnson never made it to Oakland to make their declaration; they were seized and sent to Fort Dix, where the elderly Muste confronted prison officials while raising money for the young men's defense. Meanwhile, new veterans were cropping up at protests everywhere.

Fighting doves would be everything in the years to come—some active duty, some pious objectors like Lynd, and many, many combat vets geared up for one last fight.

CHAPTER NINE
1965 to 1980

"How MANY DO WE HAVE left? We haven't gotten to Monterey yet."

Susan Schnall looked at the pile of posters at her feet. "At least a hundred," she told the young man piloting the plane over Oak Knoll Naval Base, near Oakland, California.

Schnall looked younger than her twenty-five years, curly hair circling her face. She wore jeans and an Indian-cotton shirt, better for that day's heat than her Navy uniform. She felt glee at every stop, as they bombarded Northern California military bases with anti-war posters. "GIs and Veterans for Peace," huge letters above drawings of redwoods and soldier cartoons. "OCTOBER 12, 1968."

The one-engine plane had escorts: TV news choppers, a half-dozen local stations filming the helicopter's drops on Presidio Army Base, Yerba Buena Island, Treasure Island, and the deck of the *U.S.S. Enterprise*.

The TV stations knew it was her idea. "I had remembered when the United States Air Force was dropping flyers in Southern Vietnam. . . . I thought, if the U.S. can drop flyers on Vietnam, a country that was 6,000 miles away, why can't we drop flyers in the military bases here, and why can't we do this for Peace?"[1] As a member of the U.S. military, Schnall knew this campaign would cost her. At Monterey, they poured the last rolled-up flyers on the beaches below. This far south, with weather a little more like autumn, she wished she had a sweater. When they touched down near her home base, in Oakland, she began handing the posters to the gaggle of reporters. The journalists tried to out-shout one another: "Lieutenant—over here!"

No military police yet, but she knew that would come—especially after she marched wearing her full Navy dress uniform. "I saw General Westmoreland, in his uniform, testify before Congress in favor of the war. So I wore mine as I gave testimony against it."

On October 12, 1968, the first GI and Veterans March for Peace filled San Francisco's Market Street, snaking up the hill toward Castro Street. With three soldiers recruited by those posters, Susan Schnall marched in full uniform. Onlookers applauded. More than four hundred other soldiers and ten thousand civilians followed, many carrying American flags. A few others held a banner documenting U.S. war casualties: 28,286 killed, over 177,000 wounded. The U.S. war in Vietnam would last until 1975, seven more bloody years, and claim 55,000 troops along with millions of Vietnamese civilians and soldiers. As the casualties grew, soldiers—both active-duty uniformed personnel and veterans of America's wars past and present—helped lead an anti-war movement whose history still shouts down its successors.

By 1968, the United States had been an occupying force in Southeast Asia for eighteen years. Active warfare in Vietnam began in 1965, with naval assaults in the north and Operation Rolling Thunder, a lengthy, sustained bombing campaign that began on March 8, 1965. That same day, the Supreme Court announced a ruling that would fundamentally alter the course of the war.

U.S. v. Seeger ruled that agnostics, such as plaintiff Daniel Seeger, could declare themselves conscientious objectors (COs) if their anti-war beliefs had religion-like force.[2] Suddenly, far more young men could opt out of war than ever before. Hundreds of thousands of young men about to receive draft notices were entitled to tell authorities that they did not believe in war and qualified for alternative service. The Court put down a gentle land mine for the military, reducing the personnel available to fight during an escalating war. *U.S. v. Seeger* also opened the door for those already in uniform, if they could prove that their beliefs had been transformed by their time in the military. Servicemembers found an anti-war voice; their generation found a new vocabulary for dissent.

In 1965, hundreds of thousands of servicemembers shipped to Vietnam, up tenfold from the year before. That number was still far from an overwhelming percentage of its generation. Of the nearly 27 million eligible for the draft,[3] nearly 16 million were legally "deferred, exempted or disqualified," and about 600,000 of the rest dropped off the rolls or headed to Canada, classified thereafter as "evaders" (by demographers) or "resisters" (by peace activists). Of the nine million in uniform (8,720,000 enlisted; 2,215,000 drafted) during the era, only 550,000 were sent to Vietnam.

The class background of those deployed to Vietnam was not dissimilar from earlier wars. Eighty percent had no more than a high school education. A quarter came from families that were near destitute, while 55 percent were working class and 20 percent middle class. Ron Kovic enlisted in 1964 from a combination of patriotism, Marine-worship, and low job prospects: "One day that summer I quit my [supermarket-checker] job at the food store and went to the little red, white, and blue shack in Levittown. . . . I was going to leave on a train one morning and become a Marine."[4] William Perry, a Philadelphia boy with a police record, found in the Army the best alternative to prison. "All I knew was girls, and how to get the money to take them out properly," said Perry, who describes his 1965 self as a "second-story man" expert in petty theft. "Vietnam was my first real school."[5]

Perry and Kovic would soon join an anti-war movement that included Schnall, a handful of World War II veterans, and millions of others. Together, they would fight to end the war and change the world.

In 1965, Susan Schnall was in nursing school on a Navy nursing scholarship, despite the fact that she had always hated the idea of war. She had lost her own father before she could talk, when he became one of the many casualties of the Battle of Guadalcanal during World War II.[6] Schnall mostly knew her mother's sorrow and rage: "People don't understand the devastation that families go through in war," she said. "Every single one of [any war's] casualties had a context, a whole life."[7]

Schnall had wanted to be a nurse all her life. When Stanford University said yes, she accepted the Navy scholarship. "My rationalization was to undo the damage the United States was doing abroad. . . . These young kids were sent overseas and shot up; they needed good care, and that's what I was going to do." At her 1967 graduation, she wore a black armband. That year, the

Pentagon reported 232 Americans killed, 1,381 wounded, and four missing in action in Vietnam.

After wearing a peace sign around her neck at her Navy physical, Schnall endured a four-hour grilling from Naval Investigative Services. "It was pretty scary being in the military. They had control over your life and they made sure we knew it." Though an officer, she was immediately made aware that the doctors were not simply in charge: they were her superiors. One commented about her engagement: "If we wanted you to have a husband, we'd have issued you one." Those superiors were all temporary, limited to one-year tours by the "medical draft." She learned not to take them that seriously. "We were always training new doctors."

The result, she said years later, was a hospital run by women and corpsmen (enlisted medics). As casualties mounted, so did the pace at Oak Knoll Hospital. Another nurse, Margaret Butler, recounts her rough first day, when dozens of new casualties came into the Neurosurgery Intensive Care Unit: "As I wrote hurriedly, trying to assimilate all the information [about new patients], I suddenly went cold. My pen stopped. My colleague stopped her report when my tablet hit the floor. She was talking about my cousin, a Marine who I hadn't seen in two years. He now lay in a bed on the open ward with multiple shrapnel wounds of the head."[8]

Her fellow nurses and corpsmen kept Schnall sane, even through the hardest challenges. "I took care of one Marine, 19 years old—he told me about rounding up Vietnamese families and killing them. He kept saying how upset he was that he couldn't keep doing it." Schnall suddenly felt the limits of her own nurse's compassion. "I even brought in the Navy psychiatrist to ask—*why can't I do this?*"

Schnall was not the only person in uniform questioning his or her own involvement in the war. A few servicemembers were joining the local anti-war movement; Schnall talked to Pacifica Radio about that conflict between her military and medical values. By 1968, as the GI and Veterans March for Peace in San Francisco approached, a friend with a pilot's license helped Schnall rent a private plane, which she flew up and down Northern California.[9]

Todd Gitlin, then editor of the underground *San Francisco Express-Times*, remembers Schnall well. "She had such a presence, speaking to the crowd. Of course we all knew about the leaflets—and we thought it was fantastic!"

Thanks to Liberation News Service, underground papers around the country soon sported Schnall's image, with the headline: "First GI March Successful Despite Obstacles." Schnall herself was taken into custody and spent four months in the brig at the Oakland Navy Base. In her court-martial before a six-man panel, prosecutors used all that TV footage as evidence of "conduct unbecoming an officer."

When Schnall was convicted, on January 31, 1969, the news was reported by *The Bond*, a local paper meant for GIs: "On Jan. 31, The Navy court convicted her and, on February 3, sentenced her to 6 months at hard labor and a discharge. According to the Navy, however, she will not actually be jailed, but she will be dismissed from the service." Though this item was reprinted in other underground GI newspapers, it formed only a small box in the most popular one, *Vietnam GI*. Still, Schnall admired its editor, a former Army translator named Jeff Sharlet.

Sharlet had seen the war from both sides. He arrived in Saigon's Army Intelligence Division in early 1963, joining a very low-profile set of "advisors." Soon he was decoding and translating North Vietnamese radio messages at an airbase near Hue. The following summer, in 1964, Sharlet learned about the infamous Gulf of Tonkin incident, which sparked congressional escalation of the war; he soon learned about Pleiku, where in February 1965 Viet Cong troops attacked the United States' Camp Holloway. Soon enough, Sharlet was doing his own kind of intelligence gathering. "He spent long hours questioning ex-Foreign Legion men, who'd settled in Vietnam after the French left, peasants, ARVN officers, students, and even suspected VC agents. By the time he [left Vietnam] in July 1964, he'd put a lot of pieces together."[10]

In 1967, Sharlet started *Vietnam GI*, tired of being the one soldier at antiwar demonstrations. The paper was prized by Vietnam Veterans Against the War (VVAW), a new organization aimed at ending the war by any means necessary.

At first, the group's name had been just a few words on a banner, held by one of the protesters at a peace rally in Central Park's Sheep Meadow on April 17, 1967. As 600,000 people crammed into the park, TV cameras caught the Rev. Martin Luther King Jr. and Dr. Benjamin Spock, who would lead them on a march to the United Nations; they also caught the "burn-in," when a group of earnest suited men circled to burn their draft cards. The TV stations did not pay much mind to the hundred-plus contingent of World War I and II veterans, Veterans for Peace in Viet Nam, who marched to the U.N. right behind King and Spock, carrying flags and patriotic signs.

One of those older vets had handmade a "Viet Nam Vets Against the War" banner, hoping to attract younger veterans to their group. It worked: among those drawn to the banner was Jan Barry, whose 1963 tour in Vietnam as an enlisted infantryman had gotten him into West Point, before he resigned in 1964. Now, as everyone stood and prepared to march, Barry and four others held that homemade banner. They were startled to be hustled to the front of the line: "Vietnam veterans to the front!" Barry remembers feeling exposed as they marched, but also proud.

The new group soon found a home at 156 Fifth Avenue, the "Peace Pentagon." VVAW's tactics ranged from open protest to "zines" (home-produced magazines) to actual disobedience, putting sand in the gears of destruction. In the fall of 1967, they recruited Jeff Sharlet, who stopped by the office on his way to graduate school in Chicago. They talked about the new organization and how to expand it to include current GIs in the struggle. Civilian anti-war organizers had started "GI coffeehouses" in Texas and South Carolina, where soldiers could hang out, drink coffee, rap about politics and the war. But how could VVAW get the movement to reach all GIs, especially those in Vietnam?

Sharlet's answer was *Vietnam GI*, written entirely by soldiers and veterans. Not that the civilian-run GI papers weren't useful; The Bond, in Northern California, had covered the "Nine for Peace," nine soldiers who had publicly refused to deploy to Vietnam and holed up in a Haight-Ashbury church, and national TV soon showed the photogenic young men as they chained themselves together, raising their linked handcuffs to the world. But *Vietnam GI* was different.

Edited by Sharlet, Jan Barry, and other VVAW members, this new paper told the kind of stories you wouldn't see in *Stars & Stripes*, interviewing grizzled vets and on-base organizers. GIs shared gripes about their commands, informally and universally known as "The Brass." To cover its initial costs, Sharlet used the Woodrow Wilson Fellowship he had won at the University of Indiana. By January 1968, *Vietnam GI*'s first issue found its way to Vietnam APO boxes and stateside military bases coast to coast.

Sharlet's editorial perspective was clear: "This is the dirtiest war that Americans have ever fought in. Every day men fight—and some die—with nothing to show for it." He asked the soldiers reading it to contribute: "Some people say, 'We never should have gotten involved in the first place, but now that we're there we can't just pull out.' If you believe this, how do you think we can get out?"

Sharlet knew that he was inviting active-duty GIs to take on an enormous personal risk. The Uniform Code of Military Justice contains literally hundreds of infractions that are not crimes in civilian life. Any activity that looked like soldiers trying to establish a military union, illegal since the 1920s, was regarded as especially treasonous in time of war. But holding a single copy of any material is not illegal, and wasn't then, and the soldiers knew their rights. Letters poured in: "Your newspaper is UNREAL! Or rather all too real, that is as far as the lifers are concerned. It just hit here in Vung Tau. And when I say hit, be advised and assured that it did, in fact hit. The CO is running around . . . looking for all copies of your illustrious, filthy, dirty, lying, rotten, praise-worthy newspapers, that we enlisted men thrive on." Or, "Dear Sirs, I am serving against my will in this rotten hole. Please let me subscribe to your paper."

The VVAW team found ingenious ways to get the paper to the bases, sometimes reported afterward: "Remembering the GIs traditional starvation for reading material," wrote Specialist Jim Pidgeon of his visit to Fort Dix, "I just dug out a copy and began looking through it. A young recruit glanced at the title. 'Hey, pal. Could I see your paper when you're through with it?' 'Here, take it,' I answered. 'Got some more in my suitcase.' . . . In five minutes, twenty copies were in the hands of trainees." Asked by the sergeant on duty: 'Just one question. You one of these college peacenicks?' Pidgeon replied, 'No. In fact, I'm a Vietnam veteran. Care to see my separation papers, Sarge?' 'Never mind,' he answered and wobbled away quickly."[11] Dozens of veterans were making such drops all over the country.

It was a dark, chaotic time in both the war and the nation. The Tet Offensive began, a six-month series of battles across one hundred South Vietnamese cities and military installations. The offensive cost the lives of 1,536 U.S. troops, 45,000 North Vietnamese and Vietcong, and 2,788 members of the South Vietnamese Army, as well as countless civilians. On March 14, 1968, President Lyndon Johnson ordered the deployment of 43,500 additional troops, with plans to call up the reserves for more; two weeks later, he also told the country that he would not run for re-election.[12]

The next six months would also witness student takeovers of major universities, massive draft resistance (including WWII vet Philip Berrigan's most famous action, breaking into a Maryland draft board and burning the records), and the twin assassinations of Martin Luther King Jr. and Robert Kennedy. Inside the military, as troop levels in Vietnam rose so too did discontent, including a wave of racial consciousness among the lower-level enlisted Black and Hispanic troops. The wave of demonstrations and riots after King was killed on April 4, 1968, included soldiers; aboard the *U.S.S. Richmond*, Black troops aboard Navy ships wore black armbands and refused to work.[13] *Vietnam GI* was there to cover it all.

Papers like *Vietnam GI* offer a window into the evolution of the GI antiwar movement. From the first, almost decorous on-base protests at Fort Ord to the Nine for Peace, GI papers were the first stop for activists to learn about what had just boiled over. They covered the "stockade rebellions," where soldiers rioted at more than thirty military prisons around the globe. When Black soldiers at the massive Long Binh prison complex rioted in August 1968, Jeff Sharlet found sources to give him the inside scoop: the rebellion at "Camp LBJ," as it was called, was born of segregated conditions, alleged mistreatment, guards' racial slurs, and growing Black Power consciousness.

Long Binh highlighted the multiple kinds of resistance engaged in by Black personnel. "They said they were in Vietnam fighting a white man's war and that they were being made to fight their 'yellow brothers,'" remembered one former Marine Corps medic. "They would claim conscientious objector status and end up at Long Binh Jail," since refusal to fight "white men's wars" did not fit neatly into the CO regulations. Over those four days in 1968, a planned prison break turned into destruction, blamed by the authorities on marijuana and other drugs.

"One time the first sergeant was talking about these gooks or something," former supply sergeant Greg Payton remembers, "and it was like a light went off, it was a real revelation. [He] told me I was a smart nigger, that's just what he said." The second epiphany came after Payton first came to Long Binh: "I went to the stockade and it was all these black people . . . all these brothers. That blew my mind." The riot of August 19, Payton added, was hardly surprising. "Some guys got together and said they were going to have a riot in the stockade. . . . They broke the gate, broke the lock, let everybody out of maximum security, and started burning the hooches and what not."[14] The three-day riot, though amply covered by Sharlet's and other GI papers, received very little notice in U.S. media—partly because of events that week at the Democratic National Convention in Chicago, Illinois. Those events showed the power of dissident soldiers, though they also nearly wore out the Vietnam Veterans of America before the group passed its first anniversary.

Soldiers sparked the very first conflict of the 1968 DNC, days before the convention began. The city was locked down with more than twelve thousand Chicago police, bolstered by six thousand National Guard troops, but forty-three of those Guardsmen refused to join the enforcers. "When the First Armored Division began rolling into the convention town on Sunday, August 25, to report for duty, forty-three of its Mack members remained behind at Ft. Hood, Texas. The reason, according to their assistant commanding officer Colonel Joseph G. Carrowan, was that 'they felt they were carrying the white man's burden.'"[15]

Meanwhile, scores of Vietnam veterans were among the hundreds of thousands of activists arriving in the city, including Vietnam Veterans for Eugene McCarthy, most of whom were VVAW members. McCarthy had entered the race in late 1967 as "the anti-war candidate," won just enough primaries to guarantee him a spot at the convention, and replaced Robert F. Kennedy as liberals' aspirational candidate. However, McCarthy discouraged his veteran supporters from coming to Chicago. It was sure to be confrontational, especially given the huge police presence and the anarchic mix of protestors, including the Black Panthers, represented by Air Force veteran Bobby Seale. What no one expected—after McCarthy and his anti-war platform were defeated—was that hundreds would be beaten by police and tear-gassed on national TV.

VVAW volunteer John McTalbott showed up in a suit and tie, hoping to talk to delegates, but was tear-gassed with the rest. "Seeing those guys up above, looking at the troops and the cops, and knowing they were against me—for me this was as terrifying as anything in Vietnam."[16] With their energy sapped from the failure of McCarthy and a fair amount of PTSD triggered by Chicago, VVAW members went home and tried to regroup.

Meanwhile, the active-duty GI movement kept growing. Jeff Sharlet doubled down, issuing separate "Stateside Edition" and "Vietnam Edition" issues of *Vietnam GI* and getting them to a circulation of thirty thousand. He also kept getting scoops. A photographer leaked a photo that became a full page of the paper: a squad happily holding a severed head, its caption a challenge to the soldiers in the trenches to not "become a psycho like the lifer (E-6) in the picture who really digs this kind of shit. It's your choice." That image would appear on anti-war posters around the world, and still does in Saigon in the Museum of American War Crimes.

Sharlet published this photo in May 1968, a few months after civilians were murdered in the village of My Lai but a year before anyone would be held accountable. Not long after, Philadelphia soldier Bill Perry had a similar moment, which turned him into a radical committed to change.

When Sergeant Perry emerged from the tunnel on March 8, 1968, a toddler in his arms, the last thing he wanted to see was a photographer from Army Public Affairs. Perry's face still adorned the story in the *2-Star*: "Viet Mother Warns GI—And Dies."[17] By March 1968, the village of Song Be had been the site of fierce fighting for six months. In the airstrike on March 7, Perry and his first sergeant huddled in the tiny hutch of a Vietnamese woman, the local marijuana dealer, who had tipped them off that their platoon was about to be ambushed. "The ambush actually lasted about two or three minutes, and the platoon got pretty well shot up. For about five hours they called in artillery and air strikes and pretty well demolished the town of Song Be."[18]

A non-commissioned officer found Perry in the woman's home. "He automatically figured that we must be VC prisoners [under her capture] and he shot her up," Perry said. "Just like that—one minute she's there, the next minute her top half is GONE."[19] The Army turned Bill Perry from a grunt into a radical.

Worse than the accumulation of violence, he said, was that his command then ordered the soldiers to move on, out of the house, before making sure remaining civilians were out of danger. "I had to point my M-16 at the guy's throat before he let me go get the baby."

The following July, when Perry's platoon was in heavy combat, they found multiple dead GIs near Nui Ba Den, a mountain sacred in Vietnam. That discovery made some troops go a little berserk, he told a tribunal years later.

"They were very much into cutting patches and numbers on dead bodies in this particular incident." Perry would remember those bodies, and the GIs claiming their conquests, when he got home.

By February 1969, evacuations of wounded personnel were running at about three thousand a month. There were 537,120 soldiers, sailors, airmen, and Marines stationed somewhere in Vietnam. The more than 150 GI underground newspapers shared tips for how to undermine the war from within— work slowdowns, destroying office supplies, avoiding the enemy troops they had been charged with killing in search-and-destroy missions. Congressional hearings were held about all this quiet disobedience, which was becoming as much of a problem as active protests.

Jeff Sharlet, who had turned GI anti-war sentiments into a movement, was in Florida, being treated at the Veterans Administration for cancer. He was not the only Vietnam vet there with cancer; others had served, like Sharlet, in parts of Vietnam where the United States had dropped defoliant chemicals known as Agent Orange.[20] No one was yet connecting the two. When Sharlet died in June 1969, most GI papers reported simply, "We regret to announce the death of Jeff Sharlet, Founder and Editor of *Vietnam GI*."[21] His own paper gave it front-page coverage: "JEFF SHARLET DIES." Co-editor David Korematsu wrote therein that he had never stopped being an organizer: "At the end, he said he had many new ideas for our fight, but was just too exhausted to talk about them."

Sharlet's death hit the VVAW hard. It had not yet recovered from the Democratic Convention; the New York office had closed, the organization's paltry income barely enough to pay Jan Barry to answer the mail. Other veterans who had been part of the convention protests were still under grand jury investigation into that week's violence, six months spent considering charges against both the police and the protestors. Eight organizers were charged, including Bobby Seale, whose path to founding the Black Panthers had begun as an airman at Ellsworth Air Force Base. When the trial in Chicago began that fall, World War II vet William Kunstler, who had made a postwar career representing activists, stage-managed the complex defense of the Chicago Eight.

Seale, who rejected Kunstler and demanded his own lawyer, eventually saw his case severed from the rest, but not before creating some of the trial's most iconic moments—as when he was shackled and gagged after one too many courtroom outbursts. Thousands rioted in sympathy across the country, especially the young veterans who had begun turning up at the nation's colleges.

Bill Perry, then a student at Philadelphia's Temple University, led a team of young veterans who blocked Navy shipments after Seale's iconic moment: "Reservists respected us Viet Nam combat Vets, and they tipped off me & my anti-war Vets with great INTEL about a movement of 3 Tanks, from an Army Armory to the Naval Shipyard. My ambush squad, and our Pro-Black Panther troops captured 2 of the 3 Tanks, in the middle of Philly's Broad Street. . . . The timing of the early October movement of the Tanks dove tailed perfectly with the spectacle of a Black man denied his rights, as the whole world watched!"[22]

October 1969 was the Vietnam Moratorium, a series of protests that asked simply for a break in the violence. Former Marine William Sloane Coffin, now the chaplain at Yale University, was among the organizers: "We yearned for a revolution of imagination and compassion. We were convinced nonviolence was more revolutionary than violence."[23] The event was international, with observances in Europe and Asia.[24] The first of the two Moratorium events, on October 15, drew one hundred thousand to Central Park, with both vets and active-duty soldiers turning up at the simultaneous Moratorium rallies in cities across the country. In Central Park, *The New Yorker* watched as "a student nurse from Mount Sinai tried to present a handbill to a soldier who was wearing a green beret. He declined it, with a grin, but gave her a peace sign in return. [The] nurse stopped dead in her tracks. 'He did it,' she said incredulously. 'A Green Beret gave me the peace salute.'"[25] Afterward, Moratorium Committee organizers reached out to VVAW, which swung into action, placing a full-page ad in the *New York Times* proudly signed by 1,365 current GIs. On November 15, 1969, some of those same soldiers marched on Washington, D.C., along with a half-million others demanding an end to the violence.

The GI movement was taking action. December 1969's *Vietnam GI* exulted as medical personnel fasted on Thanksgiving, telling their command that there was little to be thankful for. The *New York Times*, a large number of other papers, and TV news reports carried news of the anti-war fast. Most accounts reported participation in the range of 150 or 200. The *Times* said that "out of the 141 soldiers of rank below specialist 5 serving with the 71st Medical Detachment . . . only eight appeared for dinner at the mess hall."

The AP quoted an Army nurse, Lieutenant Sharon Stanley: "A lot of these patients here don't believe in the cause for which they were fighting and received their wounds. What I don't like about this war is the fact that people of the United States had no say in starting it. We just sort of sneaked into it and suddenly we had 500,000 men fighting. The Vietnamese people don't care about the war and its outcome, so why should our boys keep losing their lives?"

The "John Turkey Movement" reported above spread to units all over Vietnam. The news energized the stateside movement; Susan Schnall cheered her fellow nurses as she traveled from one GI coffeehouse to another. And VVAW was turbocharged, membership rising.

Bill Perry remembers 1969 as a season of ceaseless action. It helped him fight the flashbacks that plagued him, the repeat glimpses of the woman being incinerated at Song Be, the mutilations at Nui Ba Den. Perry is now unsure if he'd heard by then about "Pinkville"—about a March 1968 slaughter in the village of My Lai. But neither he nor his fellow veterans were surprised when, in November 1969, major dailies and *LIFE* magazine burst forth with full-color photos of dead Vietnamese women and children.

The headline accompanying the photos from My Lai was telegraphic: "Lieutenant Accused of Murdering 109 Civilians." The story, by a freelancer named Seymour Hersh, ran first in the *Cleveland Plain Dealer*, before being picked up nationwide. "William L. Calley Jr., 26 years old, is a mild-mannered, boyish-looking Vietnam combat veteran with the nickname 'Rusty.' The Army is completing an investigation of charges that he deliberately murdered at least 109 Vietnamese civilians, in a search-and-destroy mission in March 1968 in a Viet Cong stronghold known as 'Pinkville.'"[26]

The article goes on to offer the formal charges—"premeditated murder by shooting them with a rifle"—before laying out its key question: "The Army calls it murder. Calley, his counsel and others associated with the incident describe it as a case of carrying out orders."

Hersh was in his own way a soldier-dissenter. He had run the base newspaper at Fort Riley before becoming a journalist in 1960, and after some years at Associated Press had been press secretary for Vietnam Vets for McCarthy.[27]

His 1969 scoops, filed with the alternative-media Dispatch News Service, were sparked by talking to Pentagon underlings—one of whom tipped him off about the 1969 investigation into Charlie Company's Lieutenant Calley.

When he got to Fort Benning, Hersh talked to Ron Ridenhour, a former Charlie Company sergeant who had learned about "Pinkville" and been horrified—especially learning that, amid the killing, the men had stopped for lunch: "There must've been a terrible God-awful racket, a horrifying sound, I'm sure. They couldn't eat, so they stood up, two of them and they walked over to the ditch and they divided up the survivors and they walked down the ditch, one on each side, finishing off all the survivors. . . . Pow, pow. Up and down the ditch once. When they returned to their food, the ditch was quiet."[28]

Ridenhour "gave me a company roster, and I began to find the kids." Hersh gained the confidence of enough of those "kids," including Calley, to write the first of a set of stories describing the day that Calley's platoon systematically shot more than three hundred women, children, and old men. He did not, at first, feature the massacre's initial whistleblowers—not Ridenhour, who had told the U.S. Congress; not Thomas Glenton, who had first tried the chain of command and been blown off by Major Colin Powell; not even Major Hugh Thompson, who had landed in-country and *ordered* an end to the killing in progress.

Instead, Hersh told the story with testimony of its participants—with color negatives of "Pinkville" photos, taken by former Army photographer Ernest Haeberle. In November, when the package arrived at the desk of the *Plain Dealer*, the story displaced the second walk on the moon. Those photographs made a moonwalk "routine" by comparison.

Some in Charlie Company expressed serious remorse. Paul Meadlo, whom Hersh interviewed over weeks in his hometown of Tierra Haute, Indiana, estimated 370 had died: "After the ditch, there were just some people in hootches," Meadlo said. "I knew there were some people down in one hootch, maybe two or three, so I just threw a hand grenade in."[29] He told CBS News that he still dreamed about Pinkville: "About the women and children in my sleep. Some days . . . some nights, I can't even sleep. I just lay there thinking about it."[30]

That willingness to talk openly about what he had done caused later scholars to explore Meadlo's "lawful disobedience" among those at My Lai. "Not only did he admit it, but he did so in a manner that was at times very candid. Doing so requires an extraordinary strength of character and personal resolve, traits strengthened with the passage of time and exposure to the friction between what he had done and what he believed down deep to be right."[31]

As the reporting steamrolled, Meadlo and some others were equally fearless at Calley's trial the following year, as well as during the subsequent investigation by General William R. Peers. Suddenly "My Lai" became a spur for discussions of war crimes in the media.

Half a world away, Fred Marchant, a twenty-three-year-old Marine, was taking in the photos from My Lai. Marchant, the adjutant general at Camp Schwab in Naha City, Okinawa, kept paging through the photos, over and over. *I am not a Nazi*, he said softly to himself. *I am not a Nazi.*[32]

When the war escalated in 1965, Marchant was living at home in Providence, Rhode Island. As Rolling Thunder began, his father, Air Force veteran Frederick Marchant, pounded on the wall at the news. Marchant Sr., who had spent World War II in a Hawaii motor pool, warned Fred—a community-college student hoping to transfer to Brown University—to keep his student deferment handy. "If you do get drafted, we'll make sure you get a desk job."

In 1968, Marchant was thrilled to receive orders for Vietnam after graduating from Brown. A poet, maybe he would tell the story of this war, as Homer did in Troy. And things began promisingly: at his first overseas stop in Okinawa, Marchant was promoted to adjutant general. "Here I am, 22 years old, and my commander's a Major! Part of my job is to read stateside newspapers and magazines! In a beautiful place." For a while, he thought idly that his "great job" might be "preparing me for a career in law enforcement," which like soldiering fit his working-class background.

Until those My Lai photos, which had Marchant "running counters in my mind, and thinking, *What have I done? What am I personally responsible for?*" When he heard out the window the *crack!* of a B-52 breaking the sound barrier, headed to Vietnam, it occurred to Marchant for the first time that even in Okinawa, "I was fundamentally part of taking other people's lives."

As a Catholic soldier, Marchant's first thought was, "OK, I'm going to Mass!" He went to the chaplain's office; Lt. Commander James Harris was known for being disgusted with the war, after twenty-seven months in Danang, where he had mentored multiple units of Seabees and Marines. Marchant ran into Father Harris' office, stacked with copies of the anti-war *National Catholic Reporter*. "I'm fucked, I gotta get a bad discharge," he moaned. As adjutant general, Marchant was familiar with the legal consequences. He feared the brig: "I'd seen prisoners, AWOL guys, minor drug busts."

In one of those copies of the *Reporter*, Marchant caught a mention of the Central Committee for Conscientious Objectors, a Philadelphia-based group established for those outside the peace churches.[33] "I'd thought that to be a CO required a purist peace position. Like you wouldn't kill a burglar or something." CCCO's reply was encouraging, suggesting mildly that the Navy's own regulations on the subject might be of help. Marchant found the Navy regulations on conscientious objection, "and my life changed."

Marchant then became one of a relatively small group of servicemembers discharged as conscientious objectors. Only seventeen thousand such discharges were approved during Vietnam, most of them after My Lai. In 1967, only 829 applications were made across all four services, but by 1971 the number of applicants had reached a peak of 4,381.[34] The process of doing so was intentionally difficult: the regulation that changed Marchant's life required (then as now) that a military psychiatrist, a chaplain, and an officer, appointed to investigate the matter, all decide that the soldier is deeply sincere in the beliefs described in an extensive application. The application asks the soldier to describe his beliefs, how they led to his opposition to war in any form, what made the beliefs *change* since taking the oath of enlistment.

Most did not get to the stage of even filling out the form. Thousands of enlisted men and women were harassed, disbelieved, and threatened for trying, especially African Americans. "One battalion commander was asked if he had any conscientious objectors in his unit. He said, 'Yes, I've HAD six: two are in jail and four are back on the line.'"[35] Marchant's experience in the months after My Lai was different. No one asked why he was delaying filling out the paperwork needed to get his long-sought Vietnam slot, or why he was reading books from the libraries at Kadena Army Base on the other side of Okinawa. "The base library was rich in peace literature," Marchant said. Philip Berrigan's work resurfaced, and "I remember reading a history of the Holocaust, about people who had stood up to the Nazis on a religious basis."

In the ninety-page application, Marchant described how his initial enthusiasm for battle had become a physical revulsion. He talked about his father, who still had a cough from cleaning the insides of the Enola Gay and had hated the idea of his son as a leatherneck—and added that he chose the Marines for the same reason his father feared them: "They always got sent to the worst places." The photos from My Lai, he said, broke in two his dream of being the war's Homer. "Such atrocities were not what I had signed up for. . . . Instead of being willing to countenance danger, etc., in order to convey the war in words, I began to realize that my participation enabled the very thing I deplored."

When Marchant told his fellow lieutenants what he was doing, "so many of them said to me, *I've thought of it!* They'd had many of the same doubts. . . . It's clear to me now that whatever My Lai meant to people, it delegitimized the whole Vietnam enterprise within the military." After the required psychiatric interviews, Marchant found even a war-hardened fellow like Camp Kinser's commander, Gen. Clyde Barrow, ready to hear what he had to say. "He knew me, and knew about me."

Barrow listened for four and a half hours. "It was a generous-hearted conversation," Marchant said years later. "He understood that I was a good provost martial having a crisis of conscience. I told him about how I had felt when I joined, and then I said I had realized it wasn't worth killing people to write about it!"

General Barrow asked many questions common to such interviews: "What if the Red Chinese came and raped your grandmother, would you kill then?" He asked if Marchant would have had the same objections in his father's war. "What about the Nazis?"

Prepared for these questions, the young lieutenant admitted that he did not know in 1970 what his beliefs would have been in, say, 1944. "But what I can say is this—that I'm not going to participate in war *now*, in my life."

In response, the general leaned back in his seat, the tension in the air ebbing. "The U.S. military itself is not dishonored in this war," Barrow said softly. "But it is hard." For the next two hours, Marchant said, Barrow told his war stories—from World War II and Korea as well as Vietnam. "He talked about how *every* death of a soldier hurt him personally."

While he waited for the decision from Washington, Marchant volunteered in the island's military prisons. The next time he saw Barrow was a month and a half later. "He was smiling," Marchant laughed. "And I had to think— this is good news. He couldn't be smiling if he'd screwed me!"

Marchant's CO discharge was approved in time for him to see his mother on her birthday, October 5, 1970. The new decade had started with less of a bang (or a revolution) than the whimper of unintended consequences.

While Marchant was undergoing his CO conversion, fellow Marine Paul Cox, a six-foot scion of Guthrie, Oklahoma, was on his second Vietnam tour. On April 15, 1970, he flew his helicopter over glittering rice fields, looking for a place to land.

Cox had enlisted at nineteen rather than be drafted; he spent his first tour doing desk work in Saigon because he had "some college," and re-upped rather than go back to the lumber mill. As the copter landed, he felt impossibly tall next to the diminutive women and old men who peered up from their tiny homes. Cox's squad went from house to house, each home made entirely of bamboo. Tiny altars at the entrances held tiny stones and small photographs. Out back: the family's chickens and ducks. But the Marines were here to remove these people from their homes.

They hustled out the villagers and placed them on trucks, shooing younger people away. Cox looked again at the grandpa he was waving out of the house. *Haven't I seen you before?* These people might already have been evacuated once and returned. They kept coming back from the resettlement camp thirty miles away. *This village is where their ancestors are buried.*

He asked the command what would become of this place. *It's a free-fire zone!* The houses were scheduled to be burned down, the people assumed to be Vietcong.

Over the next few months, Cox learned what that meant. *Any one of them could be ready to knife you, or have a bomb. They don't care if they live or die.* He started having trouble sleeping. This did not feel like freeing a people.

No one was ever, ever glad to see them. *Why should they be?* He found himself flinching every time he asked some old man, "Hey, papa san, any VC here?" knowing he'd hear, "Oh no, no VC here, no, no, not for many weeks." No nervous gesture, no half-smile. Then sometimes a booby trap would then explode, some mortar wrapped in a leaf or a trip-wire.

More dangerous were the days in the rice paddies, the fields overgrown with no one to tend them. All might be booby-trapped with stolen U.S. Army grenades tricked out in simple cups. Soon after Cox's arrival, the platoon lost twenty-six men in one day—all because of the inevitable stupid order to walk trails, to hack your way through country to find people *so we can blow them away or put them in a camp.* Then came the day they crossed Liberty Bridge.[36]

Liberty Bridge, from Danang to Hoi An, was a mud-caked mass of concrete that had replaced an older bridge destroyed two or three times. South Vietnamese scouts greeted them, warning of Vietcong nearby. They approached Go Noi Island—not really an island except when rain swelled the river around it. Close to two hundred Marines had died there the previous year, when the Viet Cong had attacked Danang.

Today's mission was to yet again empty Go Noi, long since declared a free-fire zone. Much of the island's vegetation was gone. The humidity weighed on Cox's skin like an invisible blanket. The platoon patrolled for four days, without much incident. On the fourth day, a booby trap exploded, and all else tumbled after.

One member of another squad found the trap, they all crowded around to see, and as they'd all learned, *It only takes one grenade.* The rest of the squad was either trying not to cry or slamming their fists in rage. By the time Cox arrived, the medevac had already come and gone. Only a lieutenant Cox already hated remained to tell what happened.

The next morning, the platoon's captain did something Cox found just as puzzling. That day, the squad who had suffered the most losses on the previous day would be "walking point" (i.e., first). Cox was too tired, too focused on keeping his own squad alive to protest.

His squad followed the still-enraged group, followed by the radioman and company commander. As they got to the other side of the ville, the commander called out: "Find out if there are any friendlies in the area."

The report back: "No." Before anyone in Cox's squad could even approach the village, he heard the distinctive *crack!* of the M-16—like a firefight but one-sided, all outgoing rounds, no other ordnance. The sound continued for about ten minutes.[37] Afterward, Cox led his team deeper into the area. He stopped at the first hut at the edge of the village and led his men purposefully into its low gloom.

The woman inside could be forty-five, sixty, or even thirty. She was dying silently, her intestines swirling down onto the ground. Cox thought he might have to be sick. He left the hut and turned the next corner, only to find much worse: groups of eight to twelve people, outside each group of huts, who had been rounded up and shot. *But this village does not have any military men.*

When both squads reunited, the captain looked around. "Everyone all right?" Receiving no answer, he called for volunteers to go back in and search the rest of the village. Thirty men jumped up, ten were chosen, their fatigue vanishing into their desire for revenge. For about forty-five minutes, the sound of shooting was a thick soundtrack for the dusky air.

When they returned, the men were in high spirits: *Oh yeah, we greased some gooks!* The captain picked up his radio; were these guys going to get in trouble? But then the captain congratulated the entire unit for a job well done. Time to move on now. The headlines back home about My Lai, all the talk of "no more war crimes," felt meaningless in this heat.

As Cox turned, his eardrums jumped: behind them, a B-52 was breaking the sound barrier. He was used to air strikes, but usually they preceded going in, to protect the troops; this is the first one he'd seen called in to finish off a village. Or, perhaps, to destroy the evidence: bodies shot dead without provocation.

At breakfast in Danang about a week later, Cox's squad was buttonholed by Naval Intelligence officers—fat lifers in civilian suits with sagging collars and matching chrome 38-caliber handguns. Someone had just reported to the South Vietnamese consulate that eighty-four civilians were killed that day, and these NCIS guys were here to put together a report.

The lieutenants passed out sheets of paper and newly sharpened pencils, saying briskly, "Tell us what you saw." Cox wrote slowly, carefully, what he saw. What he inferred, from the sounds and the situation, didn't get put on the page; it was only speculation, after all. What was left: *I saw a lot of bodies. And there wasn't a firefight.* And that was the last they would hear of what happened on that beleaguered island; the report would remain classified for forty years. What had happened inside him was none of their business.

The same day in April 1970 as that incident at Ga Noi, House hearings began in Washington about My Lai. By then, fourteen officers had been charged with having enabled illegal murders. At the end of the month, the United States invaded Cambodia, sparking demonstrations across the United

States and inspiring Ron Kovic to give his first public speech. Young vets who had gone back to college had stunned some and thrilled other students, who exulted, "The Vietnam vets are going crazy! The next morning we found out about the students getting killed at Kent State."[38] At Kent State University, young National Guard troops, called in for riot control, had ended up firing sixty-seven rounds out into the crowd, killing four students and injuring nine.

In the aftermath, VVAW chapters formed at Kent State and other universities, joining new waves of protest. One veteran wrote about Kent State, "It isn't enough to send us halfway around the world to die, I thought. It isn't enough to turn us loose on Asians. Now you are turning the soldiers loose on your own children. Now you are killing your own children in the streets of America."[39] Soon, Vietnam Veterans Against the War would unfurl its own witness to the war's deepest shame.

On September 7, 1970, a hundred Vietnam veterans formed a skirmish line at Valley Forge State Park, Pennsylvania. A four-day late-summer march had left their "boonie" caps as damp as in Vietnam. At the waiting rally in the other end of the park were two thousand civilian peace activists, a few newspapermen, and at least one FBI informant. Jane Fonda and Donald Sutherland called out, "What do you want?" and the crowd responded, "Peace! Now!"

After crossing the park the sweaty marchers assembled in formation, trying not to smile at the civilians cheering them. It had been an intense week, with no small amount of PTSD as these "advance patrols" re-enacted scenes from their time in Vietnam. In small towns along the way, some locals were horrified. In Bernardsville, New Jersey, one team dragged a twenty-seven-year-old woman while other vets placed a mock rifle at the young woman's throat, asking, "Where are the gooks, Mama-san?" Some in houses on the route told reporters the march was "disgusting," though one World War II vet said he agreed with the vets "whole-heartedly." A local twenty-two-year-old Vietnam vet added, "This war is a waste of men, and it's a good thing to show this to the public."[40] Now, these advance patrols were as ready as their civilian boosters to party.

John Kerry, VVAW's newest officer-member, was at the rally as the patrols walked in. A well-connected young ex-lieutenant from Massachusetts, Kerry had signed up for Operation RAW (Rapid American Withdrawal) only a few weeks earlier. He had not joined the vets in their four-day guerrilla theater from Morristown to Valley Forge.

At first, Lt. Kerry sat a few rows behind Jane Fonda, clean-shaven amid the bearded vets who surrounded the young actor. Then, he made a speech that caught the attention of the FBI, which added "one John Carry [sic]" to its watch list. Among Kerry's words that day: "We are here to say that it is not patriotism to ask Americans to die for a mistake and that it is not patriotic to allow a President to talk about not being the first President to lose a war and using us as pawns in that game."[41]

Kerry's membership was part of VVAW's post–My Lai growth spurt. By the time of Operation RAW, the group's rolls had grown from around five hundred to two thousand, with members in almost every state.

That number, like the war itself, mostly does not count women: the VVAW was a boys' club. When nurse Lynda van Devanter, a vet of the 71st Evac mass-casualty unit who had been part of the "John Turkey" protests, tried to join, she was told she did not "look like" a veteran and was turned away. "If we have women in the march, Nixon and the news reporters might think we're swelling the ranks with non-vets. . . . I'm sorry, but you can't be a member of our group."[42]

The fulcrum of VVAW's growth that year was the long-awaited trial of Lt. William Calley. In preparation, VVAW began to collect testimonies by the bucketful, looking for evidence that My Lai was anything but uncommon. A decorated battalion commander in Vietnam had just filed charges that some troops in his brigade had engaged in "transmission of electrical shock by means of a field telephone [and used on a Vietnamese girl] a water rag treatment which impaired breathing, hitting with sticks and boards, and beating of detainees with fists."[43] Some VVAW members participated in a Citizens Commission of Inquiry, co-created by Cleveland attorney Tod Ensign.

Ensign took depositions from former officers who had served in Vietnam, describing atrocities that Ensign linked to specific military policies: "search and destroy," "free-fire zones," "take no prisoners." These policies created an overall dark strategy, in which "search and destroy" missions were conducted without taking Vietcong prisoners, "disposing" of the enemy in other ways, and establishing "free-fire zones" such as Ga Noi or Pinkville.

The depositions outlined the results of these three core policies. Soldiers described "search and destroy" missions with no internal prisoner-of-war facilities; thus, a common question from commanders when they saw a prisoner was, *What is that gook doing here? Waste him!* "These were the policies dreamt up at Harvard and converted into military strategies in Washington," Ensign added. "When the vets heard Westmoreland say that My Lai was just a couple of bad apples, they couldn't believe it."[44] At one inquiry event in Buffalo, the audience was particularly moved and the mood militant: "We were giving them a chance to turn around what was being said about them, that these were war criminals and bad apples."

Organizers agreed that it was time for a bigger event, to ensure that Congress and the media received this information. Part of that discussion inside VVAW included GI ally Jane Fonda, who was working with Hollywood peers on a traveling show called *F.T.A.*, a set of black-comedy skits using some of those testimonies. She would take that show to U.S. military bases around the world. Fonda insisted that rather than New York or Washington, their national media event should be held in Detroit, the heart of working-class America.

To Ensign, the choice seemed absurd. "Whoever thought that TV cameras were gonna trek out to Detroit was really smoking something I kind of wanted." CCI instead held a "responsible" National Veterans Inquiry in December, a three-day event in Washington, D.C.'s Dupont Hotel. There, Daniel Notley of the 1st Marine Division described a massacre nearly identical to what had happened in My Lai, the only difference being a lower body count.[45] Americal Division lieutenant Michael Uhl testified, "Field telephones were regularly being used by his unit as electrical torture devices to question prisoners."

The Detroit event, called the Winter Soldier hearings, was held January 31 to February 2, 1971. It felt needed after the New Year as the military commenced Operation Dewey Canyon, an incursion into Laos and Cambodia. As the Nixon administration battled press inquiries about the incursion and the in-progress Calley trial, VVAW punched up the pressure with a full-page ad in the February 1971 issue of *Playboy*, picturing a coffin draped in an American flag: "In the last ten years, over 335,000 of our buddies have been killed or wounded in Vietnam. And more are being killed and wounded every day. We don't think it's worth it."

In February, nearly one thousand people crowded into rooms at a Howard Johnson, three hundred or so giving testimony over the event's three days. Acting as older statesmen of sorts were Lt. John Kerry and World War II bombardier Howard Zinn, each taking notes with a lawyer's intensity.

Footage from the event shows a characteristic mix of youth, openness, high spirits, and that intense quiet that comes from having seen the indescribable. The witness list included members of the infamous American Division and the 3rd Marine, Fred Marchant's outfit. And day after day, these very young men told horror stories of what had become normal in Vietnam.

Philadelphia's Bill Perry was there, ready to talk about what he'd seen. He was kind of amused by the Detroit choice, finding it "kind of sweet, and pretty typical. They thought auto workers would come and learn the TRUTH about the war." He most remembers looking forward to kicking back and partying: "They said, *Hey come and meet Barbarella.* How could you turn that down?"

That week, soldiers become veteran-activists, prizing combat experience more than ever. To counter the idea that they were lying, soldiers showed slides, lifted their discharge papers to cameras.

Scott Camil, whose cherubic face seemed embraced by his short beard, spoke softly as he described treatment of Vietnamese civilians.[46] After Camil's testimony, Bill Perry urged the room to explore "what causes people to act this way, and what we can do to combat [that]." The testimony horrified even some of the event's organizers. "It was jarring," John Kerry told the *New York Times* thirty-five years later. "We'd all heard the stories—just scuttlebutt. But not first-hand."[47]

As a means of reaching the public, however, Winter Soldier was a bust. The Detroit papers ran features every day, carefully copied and filed by the FBI. But CBS News refused to use the hours of film they had shot, and the "newspapers of record" (the *Times, Washington Post, Chicago Tribune*) ran scant items compared to their ample My Lai coverage. If My Lai had once thrown the moon landing off some newspaper front pages, NASA struck back during Winter Soldier: the news cycle featured Apollo 14's Alan Shepherd playing golf on the moon.

In New York, the VVAW leadership tried to fight off another 1968-like crash. John Kerry helped the winter soldiers out of their funk: "'I have a suggestion that we take all of this that we want to convey in a march on Washington.' And on his feet, he convinced this group of angry people to put their anger into a creative direction." Kerry was spending more of his time at the New York offices, mistrusted by some but unstoppable, with "one foot in the VVAW office, and the other in Wall Street," asking for support from wealthy donors.

While the VVAW spent March planning its Washington action, other soldiers and veterans were in the newspapers. On March 12, Marine Corps veteran and Pentagon wonk Daniel Ellsberg leaked the full text of the previously classified seven-thousand-page *United States–Vietnam Relations, 1945–1967*, later known as the "Pentagon Papers." On March 29, the verdicts came down from the My Lai trials, with Calley sentenced, but not the higher-ups on whom he had relied. On March 30, according to later-declassified documents, a confidential army directive ordered personnel to "intercept and confiscate personal mail containing anti-war and other dissident material sent to soldiers in Vietnam."[48] The reason for that last directive would soon be visible to the world, thanks to VVAW and its "Operation Dewey Canyon III," which lasted from April 17 to 23, 1971.

That week started with a media blitz: John Kerry on *Meet the Press* about Calley's conviction, calling the My Lai massacre similar to "what thousands of other soldiers have committed." Describing the Winter Soldier investigation, Kerry added his own testimony on national TV: "I took part in shootings in free-fire zones. I conducted harassment and interdiction fire. I used .50 caliber machine guns, which we were granted and ordered to use, which were our only weapon against people. I took part in search and destroy operations."[49] The sight of a clean-cut lieutenant speaking so directly, flanked by two nodding generals, put Kerry higher up on the commander-in-chief's enemies list: "Destroy the young demagogue before he becomes another Ralph Nader."[50]

While Kerry was on *Meet the Press*, carloads of vets were arriving in Washington, D.C., some with their own tents. By sundown, nine hundred had camped at West Potomac Park, not far from the Lincoln Memorial. By the end of the week, 1,500 were encamped on the Mall, then marching to Arlington National Cemetery and to Capitol Hill to present demands to legislators.

As veterans in wheelchairs entered the House building to lobby for withdrawal, Congress' fighting doves helped protect the vets from the sneers of the chicken hawks. Ron Dellums and George McGovern led "rogue" congressional hearings on war crimes, as hundreds of vets jammed into scheduled meetings with their own representatives. On Wednesday, the vets refused to stop sleeping right on the Mall, backed up by local law enforcement: neither D.C. cops, many of them veterans, nor National Guard troops followed orders to evict the encampment. "There will be no such operation!" went buzzing from tent to tent. Kerry, not camping with the rest, persuaded his friend and senator Edward Kennedy to come meet the team. "I remember sitting down talking to them, that night there for . . . a period of an hour or so," Kennedy said years later. He arranged for Kerry, Camil, and others to come to dinner at the house of Senator William Fulbright, an event largely remembered by participants for the contrast between the media star and the unwashed Camil.[51]

On April 22, two hundred vets filed into a Senate hearing room to hear Kerry give the Senate Foreign Relations Committee an expanded version of the speech they had heard at Operation RAW. Wearing all his ribbons and medals on full green fatigues, Kerry described the Winter Soldier testimonies: "We feel because of what threatens this country, not the reds, but the crimes which we are committing that threaten it, that we have to speak out." Then he posed a question that resonated with many outside the hearing: "How do you ask a man to be the last man to die in Vietnam? How do you ask a man to be the last man to die for a mistake?"

On April 24, Kerry was among the eight hundred veterans on the steps of the Capitol who threw back their medals, ribbons, war memorabilia. Those actions and Kerry's words have been quoted thousands of times by admirers and detractors, including when Kerry ran for president thirty years later.

A rarely seen book Kerry wrote about that week, *The New Soldier*, echoes the one with the same title published in 1945 by the defunct American Veterans Committee. Looking at its ample photos and Kerry's title essay, it's both hard and easy to understand why it was so often quoted to prove him a traitor. Its rhetoric evokes the same postwar optimism that drove lefty soldiers in 1945, when the previous book was a must-read. "The New Soldier has come back determined to make changes without making the world more unjust in the effort to make it just, [and] that there is greater dignity and power in human spirit than we have yet been willing to grant ourselves."

The week of protests thrilled the anti-war movement and scared the Pentagon. A few months later, Colonel Robert D. Heinl sounded an alarm in the *Armed Forces Journal.*[52] Heinl blamed stateside organizers and veterans' groups, noting fourteen anti-war GI organizations "operating openly" in Vietnam. Heinl's report also identified "at least six" anti-war veterans' groups, taking specific aim at Rep. Ronald Dellums, described as "running a different sort of military production," and welcoming the VVAW to Capitol Hill before and after Winter Soldier. Of the GI newspapers, Heinl was careful to find the most inflammatory among them—including an unnamed "West Coast sheet" that allegedly advised: "Don't desert. Go to Vietnam and kill your commanding officer."

As atypical as that last quote was, it tapped into an ongoing debate about the uses of nonviolence buzzing inside the active-duty GI movement. That still-growing movement was about to have its deepest impact.

At the end of 1971, Paul Cox was back at Camp Lejeune. After three weeks, Vietnam still laced his dreams, the spring firmly becoming North Carolina's patented hundred-degree summer, the heat mandating a slower pace than the adrenalin still in his system. All the Marines in the reception unit were similarly wired and sullen by turns, and the bunk was flooded with underground GI newspapers.

Why didn't he see these when he was in-country? No matter: the crew around him was now promising to help Cox start a new one. The base's first, *Head On*, had been launched in mid-1969, a few months before an on-base riot prompted congressional investigations of racism at Lejeune; its replacement, *On Korps*, had lasted only long enough for the arrest and/or transfer of the Marine officers who edited it. There was still lots to cover, between the all-Black Council of Concerned Marines and continued command retaliation, which ranged from "reaction forces" armed with tear gas to personnel action like that which had ended the former editor's career.

GI newspapers and soldier-activism had a famously dynamic relationship: reporting on the unrest unfurled more. Cox paged through a big, thick hippie lifestyle handbook to lists of anti-war groups, coffeehouses, and the U.S.

Serviceman's Fund. A fistful of Dexedrine in one hand and a pen in the other, he stayed up all night, writing letters to every single address. The next morning he drove north to Fayetteville, eighty-seven miles away, to the Haymarket Square Coffeehouse at the Fayetteville Quaker House.

The small building was relatively new, the previous coffeehouse having been torched two years earlier.[53] Its theater-cum-hangout space bustled; a few months earlier, Jane Fonda and Donald Sutherland had brought *F.T.A.* (Fuck/Free the Army!), a variety show not unlike *Laugh-In*, to the coffeehouse's small stage. Now shaggy guys cut pieces of cake and poured cups of coffee from a stained percolator, or sat around ramshackle tables with GIs. The latter were out of uniform, but easily recognized from the razor-cut heads, the weariness. Cox knew that look. Stacks of Fort Bragg's GI paper, *Bragg Briefs*, filled one of the tables.

The coffeehouse's contact, Sergeant Lee Sayer, was nearly as tall as Cox, his grin far wider. He told Cox that rich people all over the country would help, not just Hollywood types. The printer of *Bragg Briefs* could do Lejeune's, if Cox drove to Durham with the cash. First, of course, they had to go back and write something. They already had the name, *RAGE*. The first purchase Cox made after that meeting was a nice IBM Selectric with two type balls, the best he could afford.

Over the next eighteen months, Cox would ensure that the paper was complete, funny, and spread everywhere—including in town, where he would hand it out and make sure it was in the new radical bookstore, United We Stand, next to the Malcolm X books. Each copy of *RAGE* was a proud 11 x 17 broadsheet.

The team put it together in the barracks, and when each article had been retyped and every page laid out, Cox got into his little Volkswagen Beetle and peeled off for Durham, where the printer stayed up all night for *RAGE*. It was usually three o'clock in the morning when they got back to Lejeune, hundreds of papers stuffed into trunks and back seats.[54] Cox would make it through Lejeune's front gate without a problem: at three a.m., it was easy to get past the young, green military police. If one of them did wake up, Cox reached into the pile and threw a paper: "Read this!" At least once, he heard back the murmur, "Hey, far out!"

It usually took till five o'clock or so for the base to get wind and fill with military police, by which time Paul and his buddies had melted safely back into the crowd of anonymous Marines.

Still an Oklahoma boy, Cox kept his blond hair tight and his shoes shined, and he showed up to work every day. In mid-1972, the "early out" program came to the Marine Corps and was quickly offered to Cox. He was not there the following year, when Marines started meeting with the National Black Draft Counselors at that United We Stand bookstore, only to see the bookstore burned to the ground a few weeks later. *RAGE* covered that event, and continued through the end of the war, without him.

Cox crossed the country three times on a GI coffeehouse tour, then melted back into a job at the paper mill. From "super-busy" he became quite still—sleeping a lot, drinking too much, not saying the word "depressed." Then he found a home in the Bay Area, among its still-fervent anti-war and veterans communities.

Faces from Ga Noi, noises from firefights still spattered Cox's dreams, but that would be with him forever. But, for the first time in a long time, he could feel something that was not just rage.

That same year, VVAW's San Francisco chapter brought up the rear of the Veterans Day parade. One 101st Airborne vet remembers it fondly: "The cheers went up as we made the turn and headed down Polk to City Hall. . . . The media and onlookers went nuts. Shouts of "Right on" and "Stop the war" were heard all through the crowd. The brass sat down and looked at the floor."[55]

Still, fractures were showing. Factions vied over how to conduct their planned Last Patrol, a national campaign trip to Miami to confront both political conventions. The Republican National Convention had been moved there from San Diego due to the California movement's relentlessness: in San Diego, sailors on the aircraft carrier *U.S.S. Coral Sea* were agitating to prevent deployment, setting up petitions in shopping centers to demand the ship stay home. VVAW, which had in New York blockaded offices of the Committee to Re-Elect the President, gathered all its forces to descend on *both* conventions.

Leading the Southern California delegation was former Long Island Marine Ron Kovic. Surviving footage shows Kovic and others mobilizing their own brigade from coast to coast: "It is a historic event like the Bonus

March of thousands of veterans upon the Capitol in the thirties. And now it is we who are marching, the boys of the fifties."

As 1973 ended, many soldier-dissenters were moving on to other projects. Susan Schnall went to work for the New York City Health Department; back in school were vets Paul Cox and Fred Marchant, who was finally getting his doctorate. For Marchant, the war's end presented him with a sense of unfinished business: "The war was over, and I had not done a thing to stop it." In their separate cities, each cheered as the Nixon administration began to implode.

That administration, like the war, was melting away, leaving the reality underneath mostly unchanged. For the soldiers and vets left behind, it meant there was a lot of work ahead—and quite a bit, it seemed, of black comedy.

In early 1973, a long, contentious battle had resulted in a new name: VVAW/WSO, the WSO for "Winter Soldier Organization." The reconfigured organization was now open to civilians, some of whom considered themselves more "politically advanced;" they took it upon themselves to school the weary vets about the "correct" priorities. Many were active with a Maoist group called the "Revolutionary Union," which in 1974 instructed its Midwest "cadre" "to link up with veterans, [who are a] potential revolutionary force."[56]

A handful of VVAW leaders joined the RU, which started pushing a "militant" line in all its materials. A civilian volunteer named John Judge was astounded by the transition, though he did find some comic elements: "They came in with these handlebar mustaches and sideburns, like Stalin, and flannel work shirts, saying 'We only read Marx and Engels here.' I told them, 'Those books are 150 years old now.'" The leadership also expelled any members they deemed not "correct," including many who had been working triple time to help the new veterans get what they needed, from Newark to Napa, California.[57] As member rolls plunged, the VVAW's Washington demonstrations were explicitly aimed to "begin to realize our goal of linking the veterans' struggle with the overall anti-imperialist movement." Its new posters and newspapers, with headlines like VVAW BATTLES V.A. THUGS, astonished Judge. "Were they really advocating physical violence against medical personnel?"[58]

Eventually, with massive blowback from less "militant" members, the organization split, the more Leninist faction forming the new group

"VVAW-Anti-Imperialist." But the years of turmoil "destroyed the single most visionary and effective peace group in history," Judge told me years later. An organization once powerful enough to scare Nixon had become just another largely ineffective pressure group.

By the mid-1970s, most Vietnam soldier-dissenters had taken on a new, essential challenge: charting the damage the war had left behind on their bodies and minds. Conferences and symposia addressed what one California vet called "the different situations that the vets were now dealing with, seeing how the V.A., and the U.S. Government weren't." Chief among these was the damage caused by Agent Orange, the defoliant used by the United States in the Mekong Delta, the one that had killed Jeff Sharlet. Some in that fight carried its toxins in their bodies; others were medical professionals like Susan Schnall, who helped ensure that the VVAW's efforts did not forget the Vietnamese sufferers of the illness.

The war's psychological toll was this generation's version of "battle fatigue" or "soldiers' heart." Fred Marchant saw a glimpse of how to combat it when he met a clinical psychology student at Harvard working on the subject with Robert Jay Lifton. "He told me about Lifton's book about the war," Marchant said. "I was so grateful. I remember thinking—*this is the kind of complexity I want.*" Lifton and his colleague Chaim Shatan, who had both been at Winter Soldier, were the first to publish on what was then called "Post-Vietnam Syndrome."[59] It would take almost ten years before the psychiatric establishment finally added post-traumatic stress disorder as a clinical condition. Veteran-dissenters have borne witness and made that happen.

Ron Kovic started writing and could not stop. "Convinced that I was destined to die young, I struggled to leave something of meaning behind, to rise above the darkness and despair." For five months, *Born on the Fourth of July* poured out of him, and arrived with a flood of literature from Vietnam storytellers.

Tim O'Brien's memoir, *If I Die in a Combat Zone, Box Me Up and Ship Me Home*, was gingerly acclaimed by the *New York Times* as "a beautiful, painful book, arousing pity and fear for the daily realities of a modern disaster." Novelist Larry Heinemann, whose Army infantry unit had fought beside Tim O'Brien's Marines, offered in 1977's *Close Quarters a* searing, matter-of-fact description of life in-country.

In 1977, Ron Kovic met with young film director Oliver Stone, who had won a Bronze Star and a Purple Heart for his service not far from where Heinemann's platoon had sweated it out. After Vietnam, Stone had gone on to study with Martin Scorsese at NYU; his student film, *Last Year in Vietnam*, lasts a quiet, moody six minutes, with a new veteran (Stone cast himself) putting his medals and commendations in a box.

Kovic was not sure any director could film his story. He told Jane Fonda's screenwriter for *Coming Home*, "There's a whole society out there that just doesn't fit with the experience that this generation went through."[60] A decade later, Stone would film *Born on the Fourth of July*.

These storytellers were part of how Vietnam's soldier-dissenters shaped the next decade. All of them knew there was more work to do. What they did not know, quite yet, was that a president promising "morning in America" would try to erase it all, and that there would be more new soldiers forced to join them in fighting for change.

CHAPTER TEN

1980 to 1991

By SUNSET ON AUGUST 19, 1983, the Georgia heat had finally dropped below 90 degrees at Fort Benning. Most grunts from the 192nd Infantry's basic training units were tucked into their barracks; even the officers still on base were beginning to wind down. But then came the flood of Spanish streaming through the base's trees, lush magnolia, and towering oaks, as if from the darkened skies:

> I would like to make a special appeal to the members of the Army and specifically to the ranks of the National Guard, the police and the military. Brothers, each one of you is one of us. We are the same people. The peasants you kill are your own brothers and sisters. When you hear the voice of a man commanding you to kill, remember instead the voice of God—Thou Shalt Not Kill!

It took a while for MPs to find the boom box hidden near the top of one of the Georgia trees, held by a beefy forty-five-year-old man with tears of joy on his face.

Vietnam veteran Roy Bourgeois had gotten in with a borrowed dress uniform, coded "patriotic," masking the Berrigan-style priest he had become. Now he blasted the base with the voice of his friend Oscar Romero, the recently slain archbishop of El Salvador. "It was a sacred moment," Bourgeois later recalled. "Those soldiers coming out of the barracks, looking into the sky, not being able to see us, hearing the words of this prophet."[1]

Twenty years earlier, Bourgeois had joined the Navy to get out of his hometown of Lutcher, Louisiana, a lumber and sugar town thirty-five miles west of New Orleans. Taking his Navy chaplain's advice and joining the Maryknoll order upon exiting the Navy—"He said, 'They're the Marines of the church, they go to the worst places'"—Bourgeois had also joined VVAW, no longer the young hawk who had once tried to bar Dan Berrigan from speaking at his seminary.

Bourgeois went to El Salvador after fleeing the conditions at his first missionary posting in Bolivia: "It hurts me deeply to know that my country, the United States, is supplying military advisers and arms to a repressive dictatorship at war with its own people," he told reporters about El Salvador.[2] Bourgeois devised his first Benning action in the summer of 1983, after learning that five hundred Salvadoran troops had come to Fort Benning, Georgia, to receive "counter-insurgency training."[3] He moved to Georgia full-time a few years later.

By taking action against U.S. policy in Central America, Bourgeois joined fellow veterans turned activists. One was Vietnam veteran Brian Willson, who confronted U.S. arms deliveries to El Salvador and lost both legs as a result. At the decade's end, after a dramatic U.S. invasion of Panama, Willson returned to Central America to witness the damage done.

A new generation of soldier-dissenters arose from the new post-conscription military. Jeff Schutts hoped in 1981 that the Army would be an armed Peace Corps; instead he thrashed his way toward a CO discharge during the last days of the Cold War. Ellen Barfield, one of the first women in the new, post-Vietnam Army, was by decade's end arrested regularly at nuclear facilities. Both generations were soon conjoined in the new group Veterans for Peace, which has since reminded successive administrations of the costs of war.

Bourgeois' action took place ten years after the official end of the U.S. war in Vietnam, and three years into a new Republican administration that had promised to erase its memory. Most of the previous war's soldier-dissenters had moved on into their lives, hoping that soon, as John Kerry had envisioned in 1971, "We will be able to say 'Vietnam' and not mean a desert, not a filthy obscene memory, but mean instead where America finally turned, and where soldiers like us helped it in the turning."[4] Instead, a conflation of radical-right reaction yielded the election of movie actor Ronald Reagan, who defeated the relatively conservative Democrat elected in 1976, Navy veteran Jimmy Carter.

In 1980, the defense establishment was on a roll. Carter had secured generous budget increases for the Pentagon, as well as a substantial investment in its new secret weapon: the all-volunteer Army, one trained to serve U.S foreign policy goals like a newly sharpened blade.

The new all-volunteer force was made of human beings like Ellen Barfield, scion of a Texas military family. Barfield, one of the first to bite on the Pentagon's "Opportunities for Women!" ad campaign, would transform from one of the Army's best engineers to one of its most frequent civilian adversaries.

On May 19, 1980, Camp Humphreys, fifty-five miles south of Seoul, was suddenly on lockdown. Corporal Ellen Barfield did not learn why until years later. A garrison of two square miles, Humphreys boasted ships, helicopters, and aircraft from all four U.S. military branches, as well as units of the Korean Army. The base's command did not often encourage contact with Koreans: "We were given a flashcard with some simple phrases, for when we went shopping at 'the ville,' the little shop down the road," said then Corporal Barfield. "When I went off base I saw swarms of raggedly clad people—some begging, some prostituting themselves, many just working far too hard for far too little."[5]

Barfield grew up around the military, with a grandfather and three uncles who had served in the Air Force. Enlisting when her husband, Kurt, received his first deployment orders to Germany, she soon become a transport engineer at Landstuhl Air Force Base. "I actually wore the Army Corps of Engineers' castle on my shoulder!" With women a minority in the Army, Barfield tried to take the resulting hazards in stride, from the lack of a proper women's shower to male peers who seemingly could not keep their hands to themselves. Barfield liked her work, though she felt isolated; more liberal than her Army peers, she made sure to read *The Nation* in her scarce spare time.

Camp Humphreys was an English-speaking monolingual fortress; its busy troops were not encouraged to learn local news or politics, even as the Republic of Korea was seeing furious protests against the military dictatorship of

Chun Doo-Hwan. "We knew there had been an assassination, but that was it." Barfield learned much later what had happened on May 19: in the "Kwangju uprising," Korean Army soldiers had battled students and other protesters in hand-to-hand combat and riot gear, leaving 207 dead, 2,392 wounded, and 987 missing. If she had been called into action that May, Barfield said, "it wouldn't have been combat, it would have been killing civilians!"[6] She didn't need details to know that she was not going to be part of this anymore. When she returned to the United States toward late 1980, the November election suggested dissent was not going to be easy.

As Barfield finished out her tour and considered veterinary school, Roy Bourgeois returned to the United States after years of being chased out of Latin America by regimes he despised. In El Salvador, he had spent days with the guerrillas opposing its military government and causing alarm back home, until the Associated Press reported that the "missing priest" had turned up unharmed at the U.S. embassy.[7]

A patriot like his father and grandfather, Bourgeois had volunteered for shore duty in Vietnam and won a Purple Heart after a bomb struck his officers' barracks in Saigon. Vietnam had also been his crucible as a peacemaker. After he found the orphanages for Vietnamese children run by Canadian missionary Father Lucien Olivier, Bourgeois had a new mission and a new role model:[8] "From that point on, I found myself more involved with kids and less involved with fighting communism."[9]

It made some sense, then, that after Vietnam Bourgeois found a U.S. home with the Catholic Worker movement, at a house in Chicago led by fellow Maryknoll priest Peter C. Brien. They shared a rising concern about U.S. proxy wars in Central America, and were jolted into action after four American nuns were killed in El Salvador, just nine months after the assassination of radical priest Oscar Romero. Bourgeois also connected with what was left of Vietnam Veterans Against the War, which was starting to focus on Central America. Around the same time, Brian Willson was in Massachusetts, learning how to be a veteran.

After a year in Vietnam with the Air Force, Willson finished his law degree and spent years working on prison-reform issues, then was hired by a Massachusetts state senator to write a report on local prisons. In one of those prisons, he experienced his first flashback and broke down weeping, remembering the civilians he had seen killed.[10]

After that, Willson found a local Vietnam veterans' support group, something he had never thought he would need. "I went to that rap [therapy] group and I just wept. For the first time in twelve years I talked about the images of Vietnam. Many of my friends were shocked to learn that I was a Vietnam veteran. 'What? You're a Vietnam veteran? No!' I said, 'Yeah, I'm gonna face it now, and I'm gonna share it.'" That also meant, Willson said, learning more about American foreign policy and how to challenge it. In 1981, he took a leave of absence from his state job to enter treatment for what was becoming known as post-traumatic stress disorder.

Two signature events—the inaugural action of Philip Berrigan's Plowshares Movement and the launch of the Vietnam Veterans Memorial, planned for the Mall in Washington, D.C.—are both crucial to this period. Each threw down a gauntlet in a growing culture war, pitting those like Willson and Berrigan against an escalating, hyper-masculine backlash.

On September 9, 1980, the highway to King of Prussia, Pennsylvania, was quiet at 7 a.m., even with the steady stream of trucks headed to the mall-construction site a few miles away. The humidity had not yet abated nor the dew dried in Valley Forge National Park across the way—the same place where Washington's soldiers had spent the winter of 1780 freezing and starving, and where Vietnam veterans had once marched in the 1970 Operation Rapid American Withdrawal, smashing their rifles in front of Jane Fonda and the FBI. Two Vietnam veterans were present that September morning: John Schuchardt, who had resigned his Navy Reserve commission in 1965, and Neil de Mott, who had served in Vietnam with the Marine Corps and in Europe as an Army translator. Both followed Father Philip Berrigan to the entrance of the General Electric plant just miles from Washington's encampment.

None of the "Plowshares Eight" were looking for a quick response from President James Earl Carter. Some of them had recently camped out on Carter's lawn in Plains, Georgia, with a banner that read, "Nuclear weapons will massacre the innocent."[11] They knew that Carter, a former Navy submarine officer and governor of Georgia, had declared an "American Fighting Men's Day" to support Lt. William Calley, the My Lai defendant. And they knew he had already broken his few explicit promises to anti-war Democrats, eschewing amnesty for deserters and draft resisters still in hiding. Instead, draft "evaders" had received a pardon, deserters offered a lengthy discharge proceeding.[12]

Today's action in King of Prussia was a different confrontation. They had planned very carefully for this action, named from *Isaiah*: "They shall beat their swords into plowshares." Their "inside man," who had been a Navy engineer during World War II, had left doors strategically unlocked.[13]

Once the group was inside the gates, bear hugs from Father Carl Kabat and Sister Anne Montgomery distracted the guards. The rest stole past, "when hundreds of workers were filing past security gates to start the morning shift. . . . [T]o blend in with the employees, the activists manufactured false identification cards."[14] The Plowshares Eight carried vials of blood and hammers.

"Somehow it felt holy that we actually got into that room, because we didn't know where things were inside that building. We just kept walking into the test area and there they were: golden-colored warheads on a table."[15] And when they put their hammers to the Mark 12A nose cones, it sounded to some like church bells ringing.

After pouring blood on some of the documents nearby, the activists sat down and waited for the police. The subsequent arrest, trial, and appeals would take up the better part of the next ten years. Many would spend that decade in and out of prison on similar charges, along with a now international community devoted to aggressive non-violent resistance. After they were indicted in December 1980, Berrigan stood at the entrance to the plant, his banner proclaiming, "GENERAL ELECTRIC—THE CRIME IS HERE."[16]

John Lennon was dead. Ronald Reagan had been elected president. The country's conservative pushback now threatened to slow down or erase many of the changes wrought by Vietnam War priests, pranksters, and poets. "Morning in America" meant feeling good about being Number One in both military power and top personal incomes. Soldier-dissenters had new battles to wage, squinting from the klieg lights of this mass-produced morning.

From its first planning, the Vietnam Veterans Memorial both challenged and exemplified the reframing of the war's meaning. It was welcomed by the movie-actor president, who had said that the only thing wrong with the Vietnam War was that Johnson had not actively declared war for this "noble cause," this effort to keep "a small country newly free from colonial rule . . .

against a totalitarian neighbor bent on conquest."[17] The memorial itself, a black ribbon of marble that rose as the deaths it represents increased, illustrated the tension between that view and those who had fought so hard for change.

Even before its completion, tokens of remembrance appeared at the memorial's site on the Mall, first a Vietnam veteran's Purple Heart thrown into the wet cement of its foundation.[18] When the memorial was unveiled on Veterans Day 1982, the launch came amid a week-long "Salute to Vietnam Veterans," filling the Capitol with veterans of all political stripes, a long way perhaps from Operation Dewey Canyon III.[19]

Poet and Army vet W.D. Erhart wrote about the memorial's "silent wall of kids, this smell of rotting dreams," while Yusef Komunyakaa, Air Force veteran and author of the collection *Dien Cai Dau*, added "I go down the 58,022 names/half-expecting to find/my own in letters like smoke." In its first public week, "bearded veterans wearing old fatigue jackets and battle medals can be seen reaching toward the names of remembered dead warriors, running the fingers across the letters," wrote the *New York Times'* Francis Clines.

Marita Sturken, author of *Tangled Memories: The Vietnam War, the AIDS Epidemic, and the Politics of Remembering*, notes that the memorial "has played a significant role in the historization and rehistorization of the war, the center of a debate on precisely how wars should be remembered, and precisely who should be remembered in a war—those who died, those who participated, those who engineered it, or those who opposed it." The nation was debating that question with passion, as in the new film *Rambo*, released around the time of the memorial's opening.

Cynthia Enloe, the Boswell of militarism's gender spins, has described *Rambo*'s Vietnam-veteran hero as "a peculiarly post-Vietnam, pre–Gulf War type of American militarized male. . . . His message for American men who are pained by national humiliation and elite betrayal: don't go to veterans' therapy groups or march in peace parades; instead, engage in individualistic military adventurism that defies official hierarchies but restores a nation's "pride" in its military, and keep your emotional distance from women."[20] *Rambo* provided a "cleansing" of old wounds, and thus of "their primary cultural association with the loss of the war," in order "to confidently declare, in Rambo's words, that 'I do what I have to do to win, but somebody won't let us win.'"[21] The new jingoism did not itself help fill the ranks of the newish all-volunteer force, of course.

Military recruiters packaged enlistment to the "Me Generation"—the tail end of the Baby Boomers coming of age just before Gen X—as a consumer item with tangible benefits, emphasizing "job skills" and offering cash bonuses to high-scoring recruits. Symposia on "the new military" assumed that this professionalism would prevent the sort of internal dissent that had wracked the Vietnam War. Ads included little talk of combat (even for the Marines).

The result was a group of smart, resourceful young people, mostly from families with limited resources. They joined for any number of purposes: job training, college money, the opportunity to get out of a bad neighborhood, a military tradition in their families and communities. Most also joined for the chance to be involved in something serious, to become someone else beyond their usual patterns. Their response to military conditions, even in relative peacetime, created singular forms of dissent.

Jeff Schutts—hometown Byron, Illinois, population three thousand—joined Boston University's small Army ROTC in 1981. "There were only three of us," Schutts told me, "but we were also pretty radical. One was also president of our branch of the Committee in Solidarity with the People of El Salvador!"[22] Anti-Reagan activism was in the air, and not just on campuses. Ron Kovic told a crowd picketing one Los Angeles black-tie gala for Reagan: "Fourteen years ago, I got put in this wheel chair because of the same people who are in there tonight."[23] Even Bayard Rustin's old dream of an end to nuclear weapons gathered new steam.[24] Philip Berrigan, a year after his Plowshares arrest, told the *New York Times* that he saw a "reawakening" of protest akin to what had followed his Catonsville action.[25]

In 1982, after the movement coalesced around a nuclear "freeze," the president of Schutts' school, John Silber, said a freeze could create "such an imbalance [between the U.S. and the U.S.S.R. in conventional and nuclear arms] as to amount . . . to unilateral disarmament."[26] The freeze had already drawn a million people to New York's Central Park, with support from William Sloane Coffin, now pastor at Manhattan's Riverside Church and founder of its Disarmament Program. "For too long, disarmament has been the concern of the anti-establishment. It is time to make it the business of the establishment," Coffin sermonized.[27]

Similar words surrounded Schutts in his left-wing ROTC, with teach-ins and gatherings on Boston Common. He started doubting his compatibility with the military when he traveled around Europe during a year off from school, including places where "peace camps" boasted caricatures of his future commander-in-chief. But Schutts returned to BU and graduated a newly minted Army lieutenant. "I took the oath with a copy of *Faust* in my pocket," he remembered.

Soon deployed to a medical battalion at the Fifth General Hospital in Stuttgart, the twenty-three-year-old Schutts was placed in command of a group of much younger enlisted corpsmen. "They're 19 years old, they want to explore Europe, they're getting drunk like everyone else—it was like being a camp counselor in some ways." But then came Able Archer 83, a November 1983 NATO nuclear command-post exercise, with three million troops simulating a response to a Russian attack. Able Archer spurred protests across Europe—including at the gates of the U.S. European Command, near where Schutts was stationed. "If I didn't know what my job was really for before, [I did now]." The young officer felt trapped, with no visible way out.

In 1985, Schutts submitted an application for a conscientious-objector discharge, after a year of working on it.[28] He was too busy to notice that a Vietnam vet had scaled the fences of Fort Benning.

Roy Bourgeois' 1983 action at Fort Benning came after a cross-country tour, speaking about Central America to Congress, campuses, think-tanks, and churches, including Coffin's Riverside Church. When he learned about five hundred Salvadoran troops arriving at Fort Benning, Georgia, for the thirty-year-old School of the Americas, he moved down there full-time. *"Counterinsurgency,"* he thought. *"I know what they mean by the insurgents. They mean the poor!"*[29] He rented an apartment across from the base and began to organize and occasionally submit to arrest, in order to call attention to the issue.

Central America policy was becoming a hot-button issue in Washington: Pete McCloskey, a Korean War veteran, was concerned enough to send journalist (and friend of Ron Kovic) Richard Boyle down to investigate. Boyle learned about "death squads" run by soldiers trained by the U.S. government, led by Salvadoran colonel Roberto d'Aubisson—a proud graduate of the U.S. Army School of the Americas, and a good friend of then Vice President George H.W. Bush. "I saw the victims of death squads, dumped into

El Playon [nickname for a lava field traversed by a major highway]. I photographed the corpses of election workers, journalists, labor organizers and human rights leaders all tortured, castrated, eyes gouged out," said Boyle. Every morning, he and *Newsweek* photographer John Hoaglund "would get up and just count the bodies."[30] This was the environment Bourgeois refused to forget.

As Bourgeois' frequent arrests at Benning became a cause célèbre, he created an uncomfortable situation for Republican senator Robert Dole when the latter visited Nicaragua. Nicaraguan president Daniel Ortega was grinning as he challenged Dole, holding up a photograph: "Look, these are U.S. policemen, and they are repressing the rights of a Catholic priest. You have him in jail because he protested against U.S. policy in Central America. Is this your democracy?"[31]

While Bourgeois was being name-checked by the president of Nicaragua, a number of his fellow Vietnam veterans were preparing to act. Brian Willson was now a prominent veterans' advocate with the VA's Massachusetts Agent Orange office, and director of the Vietnam Veterans Outreach Center in Greenfield, Massachusetts. Like Bourgeois' decoding of "insurgents" as poor people, Willson recognized that "the use of the terms 'Communist' and 'Marxist-Leninist' were code words used to cover up murders of civilians seeking self-determination (democracy)." He hoped to recruit fellow veterans he had met through Vietnam Veterans of America, the group founded by VVAW's Bobby Muller.

Willson prepared a 1983 resolution that called for VVA to send unarmed observer teams to positions along the Nicaraguan borders with Costa Rica and Honduras, and into the war zones of El Salvador.[32] But VVA's members proved far too conservative, and torpedoed his hopes that a healing experience could be made of their horrific war.[33] In 1984, however, Willson helped elect to the Senate perhaps the most famous dissenting Vietnam veteran in America: John Kerry.

Willson had actually witnessed John Kerry's most (in)famous moment, in 1971: in law school after returning home from Vietnam, Willson had been both startled and empowered by Operation Dewey Canyon III.[34] Kerry's testimony then had made him cry: "My whole experience as a Vietnam veteran was validated in that speech," Willson told the *New York Times* years later.

Kerry was lieutenant governor of Massachusetts under Michael Duka-
kis, elected partly by mobilizing support from Nuclear Freeze supporters,
many of whom admired his anti-war credentials. When he decided to run for
Senate, Kerry tapped Vietnam veterans like Willson. His Democratic rival,
James Michael Shannon, thought that the electorate would never get over
Kerry's anti-war record, saying, "That dog won't hunt." The next day, "The
Doghunters were born," a Kerry aide said years later. "A band of Vietnam vets
who supported Kerry heard their own service demeaned and rallied almost
spontaneously."[35] The tireless energy of the Doghunters was largely credited
with ensuring Kerry's victory, and Brian Willson was among those asked to
join the new senator's first veterans advisory board.

Kerry soon joined his mentor Ted Kennedy as a strident voice on both
nuclear arms and Central America. Together, they tried to stem increasingly
open aid to anti-government "contras" in Nicaragua, recruited by the CIA
under a no-longer-secret Reagan executive order. The contras had been provided with $24 million and a "Freedom Fighters' Manual" with tips on civil
disobedience, sabotage, and how to make a Molotov cocktail. And when the
administration admitted it had used funds from arms sales to Iran for the
contras, Kerry put his own staff on the investigation. Though only a junior
U.S. senator, he was making headlines, tagged a "randy outsider" by *Newsweek* magazine.

Meanwhile, Willson decided to go to the epicenter of the contra war.
He called VVAW peer Scott Camil, now living in Florida. "We went on a
fact-finding mission down there," Camil told me. "Some people even asked
me to help them get supplies to the rebels, but I couldn't go that far. I was
married!"[36]

Among the ten veterans on the trip was Charlie Liteky, awarded the Congressional Medal of Honor in 1968. The trip to Nicaragua broke him, Liteky
wrote. "Women seated in a semicircle—white-shawled and black-dressed,
young and old—were holding photographs of mutilated male bodies, given
to them by the military as visual aids to help them identify their mysteriously
missing sons and husbands. Those horror stories . . . finally crashed through
the emotional defenses I had built around my psyche."[37] Willson was also
devastated: "[When] I witnessed the caravan of open caskets on horse-drawn
wagons carrying eleven dead civilians from those attacks, mostly women and

children, I mumbled under my breath, 'I have been here before. My money is still murdering people in my name for a big lie.'"

In 1986, as Congress was approving $93 million in military aid to Central America, Willson went to Washington, D.C., with two members of his delegation: former artillery sergeant George Mizo, who in the Tet Offensive had been the sole survivor of an assault that killed the rest of his platoon, and Liteky, who on July 30 stood at the Vietnam Veterans Memorial and became the first veteran ever to return the Medal of Honor. "I find it ironic," Liteky told reporters, "that conscience calls me to renounce the medal for the same basic reason that I received it—trying to save lives."[38]

That September, all three announced that they were holding a fast in front of the White House: they would refuse all food and live on water until they had not only changed Congress' mind but also saw a national anti-war "spiritual awakening."[39] Supporters began flooding Capitol Hill and the Mall, with a congressional resolution of respect and sympathy fasts from the likes of Dick Gregory and Martin Luther King III.

After thirty-five days, as Mizo and Liteky's health wavered, John Kerry, who had visited both men frequently, issued a public statement beseeching them to "end the hunger strike before you die." They held out until October 17. "Veterans Fast Against War, Nation Shrugs," sighed the *Los Angeles Times*. Willson returned to his idea of a veterans' peace brigade, known as Veterans Peace Action Teams.

Willson found likely recruits for those teams from an organization founded in his own New England: the new, ambitiously named Veterans for Peace, founded in Maine in mid-1985.

Veterans for Peace was formed to bring together veterans from multiple wars and struggles, the Berrigan-style turbulent priests, and the surging artists and writers. The group's Statement of Purpose incorporated the Nuclear Freeze movement that had absorbed much of their energy, mixed with the uncompromising resolve of the Berrigans: "We, having dutifully served our nation, do hereby affirm our greater responsibility to serve the cause of world peace by applying the concept of engaging conflict peacefully, without violence."

With such a broad mandate, members dispersed. Some made regular trips to Vietnam: Greg Payton, survivor of the 1969 Long Binh prison riot, began to work with and for the hundreds of Amerasian children, many of whom asked him hopefully, "Are you my father?" Paul Cox was among the many who toured local high schools the day after military recruiters. Susan Schnall enfolded VFP in work on behalf of Agent Orange sufferers in Vietnam as well as at home. And many were talking about Central America—if only because of another Vietnam veteran, who released two films in succession that seared 1986 in his grief and rage.

Oliver Stone, who had failed to get Hollywood's approval for Ron Kovic's *Born on the Fourth of July*, had nonetheless stayed close to Kovic, and to his journalist buddy Robert Boyle. Stone eventually scraped just enough cash together to film *Salvador*, a work of bold-colors agitprop that reenacts well-known atrocities: priests and nuns killed, sincere guerrilla fighters. "I had really been confused by the American press reports," Stone said years later. "I was quite shocked to see how black and white [the situation] really was." American lack of interest in the subject reminded him of the civilian world after Vietnam.

By the time *Salvador* hit theaters, Veterans for Peace was already in-country.

Brian Willson went down to Nicaragua in 1986, just as the Iran-contra scandal began to expose the Reagan administration's covert war against the Sandinistas. Willson's VFP delegation met not only with President Ortega, but also with imprisoned American pilot Eugene Hasenfus, whose contra supply plane had crashed in Costa Rica and who told his fellow Vietnam veteran that some of the supplies he had been carrying were skimmed from arms first designated for El Salvador. The delegation also met with Foreign Minister Miguel d'Escoto, a Maryknoll priest, who told Willson that the war was only heating up.

When he returned to the States, Willson moved to Santa Cruz, California, and mobilized a pacifist branch of the Veterans of Foreign Wars to begin organizing his new Veterans Peace Action Teams (VPAT). The first team, with nineteen veterans, came together relatively quickly and included Plowshares activist John Schuchardt, World War II vet Dr. John Isherwood, and Korean War chaplain Gary Campbell. The team traveled to the border with Honduras, passing destroyed cooperatives and spending the night in clinics filled with burn victims from contra bombs. Asked by a young mother why this was happening, "I couldn't explain why people paid by the United States were ambushing trucks taking campesinos to health clinics or the market." The vets walked seventy miles, through a valley under frequent attack, and returned home in April determined to keep the work going.

Back in California, in addition to recruiting fellow vets for similar "deployments," Willson investigated how best to change American policy. Instead of focusing on Washington, he found a pressure point far closer to home: Concord Naval Weapons Station (site of the WWII explosion that had led to the dissent and prosecution of the Port Chicago 50), which stored much of the nation's nuclear arsenal and smaller, just as lethal arms in three hundred fortified bunkers. Those smaller arms left CNWS only on trains destined for naval ships bound for various U.S. client states. Activists had held vigils at the station on and off for decades; Willson bolstered these protests with a VPAT and declared them Nuremberg Actions, after the World War II war crimes tribunals.

In Concord starting in June 1987, activists blocked trucks carrying weapons, thus slowing operations at the facility as they were arrested, and often violently harassed by the Highway Patrol. Then Willson and the rest of his VPAT decided to take the Nuremberg Actions a step further: to declare another Veterans Fast for Life action, and to sit directly *on* the tracks, forcing the train to stop.

Marines at the station that day, according to Willson, had told the veterans that there might be violence. Why the train did not stop, on September 1, 1987, has since been the subject of litigation and numerous investigations. Both the transport company and Contra Costa County blamed the FBI, which had warned that the train might be "hijacked" by "extremists" like Willson.

Willson last remembers sitting in lotus position on the tracks, bolstered by the voices of hundreds of supporters as the train approached. "The next thing I remember is hearing a male voice speaking into my right ear saying: 'You are in the John Muir Hospital in Walnut Creek and you were run over by the train.' It was several days later now and I remember thinking, *'You must be kidding. They wouldn't run over me.'*"

Willson learned that before EMTs arrived, his multiple wounds had been stanched by medic Gerry Condon, a former Green Beret; that one leg had been sheared off below the knee and the other smashed beyond recognition.

While he was still unconscious, undergoing a dozen surgeries, ten thousand supporters had massed at CNWS, including Daniel Ellsberg and Jesse Jackson. And his ordeal would propel even more people to take action in the years to come.[40]

Among those both stunned and mobilized by Willson's agony was Ellen Barfield, still in Texas and just tasting activism nearly a decade after the Army. Living not far from Amarillo's Pantex plant, the Department of Energy's primary assembly and disassembly facility for nuclear weapons, Barfield had become involved in Texas' Red River Peace Network—a loose coalition buying property to establish a "Peace Farm" a few miles away. Reading about Berrigan and Roy Bourgeois as she managed the farm, Barfield started identifying herself as a veteran activist for the first time.

She still remembers the day she saw the horrifying news about Willson on TV. Driving home, "I knew I could be harassed, ignored, even arrested—but what happened to Brian taught me that in some cases, our government will actually kill peace activists!"[41] The thought did not deter her.

In March 1988, Barfield joined an action at the Nevada Test Site. Arrested among two thousand others, including Daniel Ellsberg, she was also among the twenty re-arrested the next day for refusing to leave. Meanwhile, Willson's VPATs kept visiting Central America and operated an alternative supply line of humanitarian relief. Gerry Condon, the Green Beret who had helped save Willson's life in Concord, organized a Veterans Peace Convoy, a forty-one-vehicle amalgamation of trucks, school buses, and cars trying to deliver tons of medical supplies and food to Nicaragua.[42]

When the convoy was blocked at the U.S.–Mexico border, William Kunstler's Center for Constitutional Rights helped it fight back, securing a ruling that stated, "The President has no authority to regulate or prohibit, directly or indirectly, donations of articles which the donor intends to be used to relieve human suffering."[43] That judicial slap at Ronald Reagan was a salve for all the soldiers who were trying to prevent another Vietnam in Central America and beyond.

The year 1988 was *also* when Lt. Jeff Schutts finally persuaded his command to rule on his CO application, three years after he had first turned it in. They did so in pure disbelief that such a provision was encoded in the Army personnel regulations, Schutts told me. The officer assigned to investigate still grilled him hard, asking the now standard question, "Would you kill Hitler?" and offering "an Orwellian speech that basically said yeah, I was sincerely opposed to war, but I wasn't a conscientious objector."

While Schutts was trying to get his dissent taken seriously, and federal jails back home filled with vets throwing themselves at nuclear sites, Oliver Stone finally managed to make soldier-dissent the core of Tom Cruise's new movie.

Stone's Vietnam narrative, *Platoon*, was a challenge to the all-healed-now -we-can-go-fight zeitgeist of the Reagan/Bush years, especially after the militarist glee of *Top Gun* with Tom Cruise. Stone's combat sequences were shot in a 360-degree panorama to convey the anarchic, traumatizing nature of patrolling in the jungle. Critic Gene Siskel called the film a relief "after all these war-is-fun movies."[44]

Stone said he was also gratified by the reaction from many Vietnam veterans, who saw themselves in the grunt's-eye-view narrative. The media was there as three members of Stone's old platoon watched it for the first time. "I hope this movie blows *Rambo* right out of the water," one told the *Los Angeles Times* in February 1987.[45] And asked at the opening of *Platoon* why he had stayed away from explicit politics, Stone told reporters: "I did that before, in a movie they never made—called *Born on the Fourth of July*."

In 1988, Stone secured the big budget previously denied him and the very star, Tom Cruise, who had exemplified the opposite in *Top Gun*. This big-budget *Born on the Fourth* came just in time for President George H.W. Bush's invasion of Panama in December 1989, whose pattern from sanctions to military might set a template for what was to come, for decades afterward.

The Panama invasion stunned many Americans. Brian Willson was not among them. Still adjusting to his wheelchair, Willson was glad he had accepted an invitation to go down to Panama for a conference on Central America.[46] In his own research, Willson was already familiar with the conflict's historical roots, starting with the filibustering William Walker in 1856. The conference featured Central American scholars and policymakers and discussed U.S. intervention in the region. Participants drove past Howard Air Force Base, part of a U.S. military installation that had doubled in size in recent years. They didn't talk that much about Panama's President Manuel Noriega, a longtime CIA asset now declared Public Enemy Number One by his former patron.

A graduate of the School of the Americas, Noriega had been prized by the Reagan administration, first under the CIA of then director George H.W. Bush, more recently working with Colonel Oliver North to undermine leftists in El Salvador and Nicaragua. He had also become commander-in-chief of Panama's armed forces and seized control of his country's government. The campaign against him was also sparked by two sources usually allied with Willson: Senator John Kerry and journalist Seymour Hersh, who had found in that relationship ample quarry for stories in the *New York Times*, twenty years after breaking the My Lai story.

Those front-page *Times* stories now reported that the CIA's man in Panama was also trafficking in drugs, money-laundering operations, and front companies that sold arms to a promiscuous army of buyers. Kerry's committee included Noriega in its investigations of U.S. support of the contras, as well as Republicans still fuming about the Panama Canal.[47] But any anti-administration tilt to either was drowned out by the blare of an amped "war on drugs" and continued anti-terrorism campaigns.

The pattern for the December 19 invasion in some ways foreshadowed consequent U.S. military/media operations, from investigations to indictment to invasion.

For a full eighteen months, Noriega had been cast by Congress and the news media as a rogue "narcoterrorist" who had to be stopped. U.S. military maneuvers in the Canal Zone grew more active. In mid-1987, Noriega had declared the United States and Panama to be in a state of war. Finally, after Noriega ignored a U.S. deadline for his resignation and Panamanian military forces sparred with Marines, the invasion came: more than 24,000 U.S. airborne and ground troops, supported from the air by AC-130 Spectre gunships, Apache helicopters, and F-117A Stealth fighter-bombers, in an effort designed "to be done in one fell swoop in the middle of the night in order to reduce casualties on both sides."[48] Instead, the battle lasted three days.

Apache helicopters dropped incendiary devices on neighborhoods; Marines manned roadblocks and conducted house-to-house searches and detention of suspected "insurgents." Whole neighborhoods were in flames, leaving apartment blocks and office buildings reduced to grand-looking shells. When it was over, fifty Panamanian soldiers, sixty to seventy U.S. personnel, and two to four thousand Panamanian civilians were dead, with innumerable wounded on both sides.[49]

Bush told a news conference that the troops would not come home without achieving the overarching goal of capturing Noriega. When asked by a reporter, "Was it really worth it to send people to their death for this? To get Noriega?" the president answered, "Every human life is precious, and yet I have to answer, yes, it has been worth it."[50] Veteran-dissenters rose at those words, chilled by the echoes of Johnson after the Tet Offensive and Nixon's declaration of "peace with honor."

In addition to Willson, an "Ad Hoc Committee for Panama" published an open letter to President Bush in the *Bulletin of Atomic Scientists*. Decrying the "clearly illegal" invasion and demanding immediate troop withdrawal, the petition had some familiar signatures: the ubiquitous William Sloane Coffin, Oliver Stone, and George McGovern (the World War II Army vet who had failed to become president in 1972). Meanwhile, Paul Cox and Presidio Nine veteran Keith Mather geared up to expand the Veterans Speakers Alliance, to counter the military recruiters sure to capitalize on the glamorous "victory."

In Stuttgart, Jeff Schutts, still wondering if his command would ever act on his conscientious-objector application, swallowed hard against the postinvasion cheers all around him and tried to fight his own despair. He had spent nearly a year on his application, starting in 1985, working through the expatriate Military Counseling Network with George Mizo, the Vietnam vet who in 1986 fasted in front of the White House with Roy Bourgeois.

Schutts was seized by the same sense of possibility that had brought many Germans to pick at the Berlin Wall with their bare hands. The anticommunist rationale that had governed his work felt more useless than ever. Finally, his command signaled that the Army was changing in ways that would help him. Forces in Europe were being downsized, and his division suddenly had too many officers. "They kind of let me out through a side door," Schutts said. His rank was intact, the CO claim suddenly moot.

Schutts would soon find himself working for the Committee on Conscientious Objectors, trying to help the newest wave of recruits cope with the new world order. As the Cold War that had dominated military policymaking for thirty years ended, what remained was the system's determination to send young people overseas to die for mysterious goals.

CHAPTER ELEVEN
1990 to 2001

On September 26, 1995, San Francisco's September heat had finally broken, just in time for the arrival of General Colin Powell. Hundreds crowded the sidewalk in front of A Clean, Well-Lighted Place for Books, waiting for the man some hoped might soon be president. The line snaked past San Francisco's Opera House and spilled onto Van Ness Street, waiting for the general who had just won a war.

Daniel Fahey, a former Navy lieutenant, was not surprised by the crowd, nor by the number of TV cameras. This line was quiet, well dressed. Most carried umbrellas against the light rain.

The TV cameras stopped for one second, zooming in on a heavyset man with an umbrella as blue as his eyes and a controversial sign: "COLIN POWELL: A BLACK BIGOT." The cameras moved on: this was San Francisco, full of protests at the way the military treated gay soldiers.

Fahey was also here to protest, but not about that. Trying to keep a low profile, he shadowed a small group walking beside the line, some extending flyers headlined "NOT A HERO!" The flyer contained a list of quotes from Powell's new memoir, including a line about witnessing war crimes in Vietnam from a helicopter. The crowd ignored the protesters. "I live in Hayward and had to get up at 5 a.m. to get here," twenty-year-old Patrick Healy told the *San Francisco Examiner.* "I wanted to be here because I think Powell's a great man. And even though I'm an independent, I will vote for him."[1]

Sam Diener, a ponytailed young man holding out "NOT A HERO!" flyers, smiled as people refused them.[2] Fahey walked quietly beside him, hands empty. Powell had been revered both in Fahey's ROTC program at Notre Dame and aboard his ship, the *U.S.S. Arkansas* (CGN-41). But by the time he had shipped for the Gulf in 1991, Fahey was secretly on the other team, waiting for approval of his conscientious-objector discharge.

Now, four years later, Fahey worked for a social-service agency called Swords to Plowshares, founded by Vietnam veterans. He also served on the board of the group that had helped him get out, the forty-seven-year-old Central Committee for Conscientious Objectors (CCCO), whose staff had written the Powell flyer. But Fahey also knew that the last thing his city-funded agency wanted was to alienate America's most famous veteran.

Finally, the line snaked downstairs into the bookstore itself. The CCCO group shifted gears, toward Powell's press conference in a room a few floors above. Sam Diener grinned when a gray-haired man in a wheelchair arrived, yelling "He's a liar!" The crowd stepped back before the shout: "150,000 people. Dead. Does he tell you that?"

Diener turned to face the man, others following discreetly behind. "Mr. Kovic," he said softly. "It's so good to see you here."

Fahey was soon gone. His lunch hour was over, office hours loomed. No time to confront the man so recently *his* general.

In 1990, Fahey was a newly minted lieutenant in advanced training in the Persian Gulf. Student Aimee Allison was in turmoil midway through her undergraduate years at Stanford University on an ROTC scholarship, during which she had met war veterans during medic training at the local VA hospital. Georgia-born soldier Charles Sheehan Miles was deep in basic training at Fort Jackson, knowing in his bones that he would fight in the Gulf. Only Jeff Paterson, stationed at Kaneohe Marine Corps Air Base in Hawaii, knew he was already a dissenter.

The Cold War had retreated into history. Under President George H.W. Bush, the U.S. military had been radically downsized, its active-duty forces cut from 2.17 million to 1.43 million.[3] What remained, as planned by Defense Secretary Richard Cheney, was a new kind of military, a well-trained group of warriors ready to fight beside National Guard and Reserve troops, if more were needed. They would "ensure that reserve units—especially combat units—would be ready to deploy when called up."[4] This contingency was supposed to be rare.

This "new military" was built to mobilize without a fuss. A billion-dollar marketing campaign recruited them; new training programs matched their skills to the demands of military occupations. This system, declared leaders in the Pentagon, was almost guaranteed to prevent the sort of internal dissent that had wracked the war in Vietnam.

The Pentagon had underestimated those they were hiring.

When Jeff Paterson became a Marine in 1990, the Cold War was in its death throes. But the U.S. military was still conducting war games in Europe, feeding its proxies in Central America, and recruiting two million servicemembers, including Paterson, the only son of a working-class single mother in rural California.

When he graduated from high school, Paterson explained, "the only other real option was being a ranch hand. The Marine Corps seemed like a good alternative." Besides, he liked the "Marine Corps mystique—kind of in your face," like the punk music he was fond of.

The new artilleryman brought that same energy to his first posting in Okinawa, Japan, not minding that "the local population despised us." He also liked that they were a little scared of buff, pumped soldiers like him. But when his company started training for possible duty in Central America, in support of the Marines in Panama, Paterson went to the base library and started reading. He was glad to find *The People's History of the United States*, by dissenting veteran Howard Zinn. "I came to have more sympathy for [Central Americans] than the organization I was a part of." When his unit was relocated to Hawaii, Paterson enrolled in some night classes at the local community college. His term of enlistment was ending soon, and he loved Hawaii. Maybe he would stay there.

Instead of "outprocessing" from the military, Paterson found his term extended because of what was happening in the Gulf. Longtime U.S. ally Iraq had invaded and occupied its neighbor Kuwait, even after President George H.W. Bush warned Iraq's president, Saddam Hussein, to pull out his troops. The result was Operation Desert Shield, which by August 1990 included forty-eight U.S. Air Force F-15s, the battleships *U.S.S. Missouri* and *U.S.S. Wisconsin*, and aircraft carriers *U.S.S. Dwight D. Eisenhower* and *U.S.S. Independence*. Five hundred thousand troops were mobilized, forty-thousand-plus of them reservist and National Guard troops. Now Paterson was "stop-lossed," ordered to pack his go-bag for Kuwait.

Paterson's expertise in munitions would be invaluable, his first sergeant told the unit. "Paterson can blow the m**fing ragheads to kingdom come."[5] Paterson started asking around what he could do, at bars frequented by Marines. When he met some organizers from Refuse & Resist, an anti-war group funded by Vietnam Veterans Against the War,[6] one said simply, *Do what's right.* "For four years I had followed orders, done what I was told to do. But now, for the first time, I was being challenged to do what was right and that was something very new to me." As for his public refusal, he grinned: "It seemed like a good idea at the time."[7] Instead of reporting for regular duty, Paterson held a press conference in a supporter's office, which forced the issue: "The officers had a big meeting and they were saying that they needed to make an example out of me so other people won't have crazy ideas."[8]

Paterson went on a hunger strike, until the Marine Corps "volunteered" him for duty in Kuwait and his platoon leader ordered him onto the plane. He refused and was arrested on the tarmac, but his command decided to eschew a long, drawn-out court-martial and let him go with an easily pumped out "other than honorable" discharge.

Paterson made his way to San Francisco in February 1991, as Operation Desert Shield became the kinetic Desert Storm. He even knew the address of the CCCO.

During the fall of 1990, CCCO's small office on Sutter Street was loud with ringing telephones. Operation Desert Shield meant sudden deployment orders for weekend warriors and new training for active-duty troops. All over the country, reservists were wondering what to do. Some callers were even rethinking their brisk answer of "No!" to that question in their enlistment papers, "Are you a conscientious objector?" Among these was Lieutenant Daniel Fahey, a six-foot-two farm boy from upstate New York. Fahey had joined ROTC so that he could afford to go to Notre Dame. He believed that as a member of the U.S. military, he would spread freedom and democracy.

However, as he prepared to graduate in June 1990, Fahey was troubled as he learned about U.S. policy in Central America.

That summer's advanced training mid-buildup increased Fahey's doubts. "To my surprise, the anti-Soviet propaganda I'd been fed for the previous years was quickly replaced by anti-Arab and anti-Islam sentiment: the words *sand nigger* and *camelhead* entered daily discourse. Some officers joked openly about nuking the Middle East and turning it into a parking lot." Fahey was as repulsed by the racism as he was by learning to shoot nuclear missiles, joining his fellow officers in asking, "Was it about resisting aggression, or ensuring the uninterrupted flow of cheap oil to industrialized countries?"[9]

If Fahey had picked up the *Congressional Record*, he would have known that Vietnam veteran Senator John Kerry was asking, "Are we ready for another generation of amputees, paraplegics, burn victims, and whatever the new desert war term will be for combat fatigue?" But Fahey wasn't reading the *Congressional Record* quite yet, or thinking about a conscientious-objector discharge. He was aboard the *U.S.S. Arkansas*, preparing for deployment and training to use a cool new kind of intercontinental ballistic missile: "As I watched CNN's coverage of the cruise missiles exploding in Baghdad, a battle was raging inside me," Fahey wrote later, "between my obligation to the Navy and the obligation to my conscience, which was forcefully telling me that I could never fire a nuclear missile at anyone."[10]

Fahey's doubts seemed unshared by most in the country, where support for war was overwhelming. Department stores like Macy's featured floor-to-ceiling American flags; telephone poles were swathed in yellow ribbons, a symbol made popular during the Iran hostage period and now used along with "Support Our Troops" signs. On January 15, the night those first bombs were dropped, the *New York Daily News* headline was a succinct, "KICKIN' BUTT!"

The few anti-war protesters were mostly overmatched by the ribbons and flags—except in San Francisco, where hundreds marched down Market Street against the war. In a faint echo of that 1968 march led by uniformed Navy nurse Susan Schnall, Vietnam veterans led the 1991 march, including Keith Mather of the 1968 "Nine for Peace." Right behind them were younger vets like Jeff Paterson and Jeff Schutts, the latter now a full-time staffer at

CCCO. The night before, Schutts and Mather had been arrested in a blockade of the Federal Building.

For Schutts, the previous six months had been a blur. Three years after finally getting his conscientious-objector discharge, he had arrived in San Francisco, immediately joined Veterans for Peace, and stopped by CCCO just to check in. On staff, Schutts was now a support veteran for enlistees.

As Schutts answered calls and sat down with nervous new soldiers, one thing became clear: the draft may have officially ended, but it had been replaced with a poverty draft. One by one, the callers had seen enlistment as the only viable way to join the middle class. They would blurt out the same lines: "I did this for college . . . the only way out of (my town, neighborhood). . . to help when my mom died/dad lost his job/we lost our house."[11] Very few had signed up to kill whomever they were told, whatever the job description.

Few of the callers knew much about conscientious objection. They would soon learn that it was the hardest way to get out of the military while staying alive.

Aimee Allison only joined the U.S. Army Reserve once she had an acceptance letter from Stanford University in her hand. She knew that there were few African American women at Stanford, and few of either gender from the East Bay town of Antioch, California. Joining ROTC offered "the only place I knew of that promised I wouldn't be judged or limited by my race or gender." By contrast, a school counselor "suggested that I got in [to Stanford] because of my race," racism being one of the only consistent features of life in Antioch. "High school classmates would chant the n-word when our team played its biggest rival the next town over. And after winning a local Junior Miss competition, a first for a black contestant, I was excluded from the local news and town parade."[12] After Allison took the Armed Services Vocational Aptitude Battery (ASVAB) test, recruiters told her, "Congrats—you scored high enough to get the premier job. You can be a combat medic!"

It did not feel like a premier job. At Fort Jackson, South Carolina, Allison burst into tears when ordered to chant, "Blood makes the grass grow!" "The chaplain, the one they say you should go to with any issues? He was there that day—and he was laughing."[13] Allison did like the medic training, including going to the VA hospital in Palo Alto to learn how it was done. It was there, she told me, that the realities of war first hit:

I saw the quads and paraplegics who were veterans, whose lives were shattered by war. We couldn't wear our combat fatigues, because we might tip off their PTSD—it was obvious, here are men whose lives are destroyed. And where do they end up? An overcrowded underserved VA hospital! [I realized two things:] the result of war is just more devastation, and hmm, maybe I don't want to be a doctor![14]

That fall, Allison chose to major in African American history, and while reading Reverend Dr. Martin Luther King Jr. she found herself drawn to the teachings of Gandhi. In November 1990, when her unit was ordered to requalify on their M-16s, Allison started reading a book her father had given her, the CCCO's *Advice for Conscientious Objectors in the Armed Forces.*

Reading that same book on the East Coast was combat medic Colleen Gallagher, a young Long Islander from a military family. Gallagher had spent the mid-1980s with the Naval Reserve while attending Hofstra University; helped by siblings who had served, she had put her enlistment together very carefully. Like Allison, Gallagher found her military role fit less and less for the person she was becoming in college. "It wasn't 'till I was in that I realized that what you do in naval hospitals is fix people up so they can go back in." Gallagher also realized during this period that she was a lesbian, and knew about the DoD regulations proclaiming all homosexuality "incompatible with military service."

Gallagher also knew that this fact would not stop her deployment: "operational needs" had prompted a suspension of all discharges for homosexuality. "The Department of Defense," the *Oregonian* later noted, "in essence said that homosexuals were acceptable as wartime cannon fodder, but not as peacetime patriots."[15] But she didn't just want out; she wanted to establish that she wanted no part of war.

The War Resisters League was glad to help, connecting Gallagher with anti-war vets, counselors, and attorneys. "Suddenly I'm giving speeches at rallies, and [William] Kunstler is my lawyer!" When the Navy was slow to process Gallagher's application, Kunstler's associate, Ron Kuby, forced the issue. "Just go down to Philadelphia with the rest of your unit," Kuby told Gallagher. "Make them process you there."

Despite the city's Quaker origins, the nearly two-hundred-year-old Philadelphia Navy Yard seemed unprepared for a conscientious objector. "At Philadelphia Naval Hospital, they put shackles on me!" Gallagher also knew how to fight back, including when ordered to take an experimental vaccine, part of the Pentagon's effort to prepare against chemical weapons. "Let me go home," Gallagher told the doctors, "and I'll get all the shots I need."

The CO hearing was grueling, with a transcript running close to one hundred pages. Gallagher described how she had been able to solve problems without using physical force. "I talked about my work with retarded adults, some of whom were violent." It all ended with Gallagher's honorable discharge.

Dan Fahey achieved the same status while still on a submarine in the Gulf, managing while under water to complete his application, go through the interviews, and get the call of congratulations from his attorney. For Allison, the process took longer, her case ultimately ending up in the Army Court of Appeals before her honorable discharge in late 1992. And for some others, their discharge was denied because they had been too outspoken about this war, their objections deemed "too political."

Two of those denied were Marine reservists, also from California but without Allison's Stanford bona fides: nineteen-year-old Tahan Jones, who had not yet started college, and Erik Larsen of Cal State Hayward. Both Larsen and Jones refused deployment and went AWOL, and crossed the country giving anti-war speeches. Larsen later learned that "the Pentagon was briefed weekly on my whereabouts and activities."

As ever, the dissenters were a minority. Of all those ordered to take the vaccines and ship to the Gulf, 696,661 service members obeyed orders and prepared to kick some ass. A few then turned to dissent.

Growing up in the Atlanta suburb of Sandy Springs, Charles Sheehan Miles, an Abrams tank crew member with the 24th Infantry Division, had hoped to attend West Point. He joined the Army as war loomed, inspired first and foremost by his father, Richard, a decorated Marine proud of his Vietnam service. In August 1990, while Paterson and Jones were resisting deployment, Miles found himself flying to Saudi Arabia two days after Iraq invaded Kuwait, only weeks after graduating from basic training at Fort Jackson.

All fall, as Shield turned to Storm, Miles' resolve was strengthened by the

U.S. media's sophisticated pro-war coverage (partly funded by the government of Kuwait), some of which described atrocities allegedly being committed in Kuwait by Iraqi troops. He was especially haunted, Miles told me twenty years later, by harrowing testimony (later proved false) about looted hospitals in Kuwait City, babies taken out of incubators.[16] Long after that PR campaign had succeeded and the invasion had begun, Miles watched Iraqi bodies burn, after an Iraqi fuel truck exploded during a battle near the Rumayla oil fields:

> I saw a young man, about my age, crawling toward the road, begging for help. His legs had been blown off, and blood soaked the ground around him. Like the good, terrified soldier I was, I pointed my machine gun at him and screamed, "Don't move, motherfucker!"[17]

"I wasn't even human anymore," writes Miles. Even after leaving Iraq, in his dreams he could see the eyes of that teenage soldier. He also knew that the country's environment had suffered serious damage; when his 24th Infantry left Iraq in March 1991, he remembered, many buildings and facilities were still burning. "In the coastal area where we fought, a lot of the area was just smoke."[18] Within a year, Miles would apply for and receive his own conscientious-objector discharge.

When the short, puzzling ground war officially ended, Miles did not share in the national exhilaration. Troops were greeted by parades, newspapers sang that America had gotten over its "Vietnam syndrome," and military recruiting spiked. For Miles and many of his peers, however, the struggle had just begun.

Dan Fahey wondered if he had the "years of service" section wrong, as he looked at the young man on the other side of the desk.

The three words on the door of the San Francisco office, "Swords to Plowshares," might evoke Philip Berrigan and his ilk padlocking themselves to some nuclear missile. But in 1995, once you opened the door, it sounded more like a newsroom, with hushed voices floating above the bass of constantly thrumming copy machines and printers. All the noise felt appropriate for a San Francisco veterans' service agency, which mostly gave assistance with veterans' day-to-day health and financial issues. Some of their clients had served as early as World War I, though most were fifty-something Vietnam veterans. Fahey worked with them all, but only the newer vets were sent directly to his desk.

This guy looked as young as Fahey, and his DD214 discharge certificate confirmed it. But his coughing, dizziness, and aching bones sounded a lot like one of those Vietnam vets sickened by Agent Orange. Working at Swords, Fahey had become familiar with these Vietnam vets; some had also been diagnosed with Agent Orange–related illnesses. Fahey had learned to start by asking, "Do you know what you were exposed to?"

Now, Fahey recorded Gulf vets who reported mysterious health problems: nausea, loss of concentration, blurred vision, fatigue, lack of muscle control and coordination, irritable bowels, headaches, rashes.[19] They had already begun sharing possible causes—those vaccines, or crawling out of "hot" tanks that had been coated with depleted uranium, or the sarin gases rumored to have been contained in an ammunitions depot in the southeastern city of Khamisiyah, demolished by U.S. forces on March 10, 1991. Mostly, these vets knew they were sick, and that no one seemed to want to deal with it. Another support group for Gulf soldiers' families explained that "we started to get [calls saying,] 'This is not the guy that I sent to the war. This is not the same person. . . .' what do we do?" Told by military doctors that the symptoms were psychosomatic, they were noticing "cognitive/neurological functioning changes that began to surface when we hit Riyadh. This showed up in weird behavior that I now can attribute to behavior much like brain concussion cases. . . . This was not PTSD!"[20]

To Fahey, what was also maddeningly familiar from the Agent Orange–related fight was the DoD's unwillingness to confirm what, if anything, the Gulf vets might have been exposed to. Only dogged reporting by the *New York Times* made the Pentagon admit to any problem: "After admission by the Pentagon that sarin gas shells were present in some bunkers, it was revealed that the military knew of their presence prior to their destruction. While the CIA claims that it informed top DoD officials, the DoD denied any prior knowledge."[21]

If the sarin revelations were mostly about the past, the other possible culprit in what was becoming known as Gulf War Syndrome was depleted uranium (DU), now integral to U.S. warfighting technology. The Gulf War had barely ended when memos began to fly about whether public concern about DU would render its use "politically unacceptable."[22] Researchers' requests for information were routinely denied.

Fahey took the problem public. He worked with CCCO on articles for its magazine, *The Objector* (edited by this author), initiating one of the first public discussions of DU's prevalence and possible consequences. Then the tall, blond, photogenic Navy vet took it on the road, with appearances on *60 Minutes*, a *Vanity Fair* profile, and high-profile Capitol Hill meetings. Fahey met Charles Miles, who had helped organize Swords-like groups in Georgia and Massachusetts before convening a national Gulf War Resource Center.

Miles had heard such testimonies from his own 24th Infantry Battalion. A medic who had deployed with Miles' battalion to Iraq remembers: "The signs and symptoms . . . appeared quickly with countless troops vomiting and getting pale." The medic took the illness home with him, experiencing "joint pains, extreme itching that would have me shredding skin, and a feeling that resembled rubbing alcohol burning a cut in the bottom of my stomach."[23]

It took four years before that medic's illness was recognized by the Veterans Administration—and even then, he was given a disability rating for *undiagnosed illnesses*. At least now, that veteran reflected, his health issues were part of VA statistics, "which means I am on record as a casualty."

After he left Georgia for Massachusetts, Miles printed out pages of clippings and investigative reports and talked to his Vietnam-vet father about what was going on with local vets. His veterans-news internet mailing list had hundreds of messages a day. In 1994, "I read the Senate Banking Committee's report on Gulf War illnesses and found myself overcome with anger." Miles was enraged by Pentagon statements "that Iraq had no chemical weapons anywhere south of Baghdad during the 1991 Gulf War."

Miles "knew for a fact they were lying. Buried in my bags was a copy of my battalion's operations log from the 1991 ground war, including reports that scouts had discovered chemical weapons not far from the Rumayla Oil Fields during one of their missions." Turning that anger into action, Miles "created a fake letterhead on my computer and wrote letters to both Massachusetts senators announcing an 'organization' called Gulf War Veterans of

Massachusetts and asking for a meeting as soon as possible." That group did not exist yet, Miles concedes: "I didn't even actually know any other Gulf War veterans in Massachusetts (though I soon would). Gulf War Veterans of Massachusetts was a fiction I modeled on Gulf War Veterans of Georgia."[24]

These grassroots groups eventually worked together with the newly formed National Gulf War Resource Center, tapping all that grassroots energy to confront Washington. Miles became executive director of the national group, though the budget barely hit six figures and paid him only a stipend. To pay the rent, he found jobs running computer systems in D.C. Dan Fahey joined the new national group's board of directors. At the center's first national conference in 1995, Fahey and Miles were far from the only COs present.

Groups from the Red Cross to Physicians for Social Responsibility were putting out their own campaigns on DU: the issue was national. The resulting "coalition" had as many alternate versions of reality as disputes with the Pentagon: "Most of the veterans who suffer from Gulf War Syndrome are in most cases staunch nationalists who regard their illnesses as sacrificial wounds of war, while many anti-DU activists view Gulf War Syndrome as symbolic of the state's use of citizen/soldiers as experimental targets of imperialist ambition."[25]

That fall, Colin Powell, the war's "poster child" and possible presidential candidate, started his book tour for his autobiography, *An American Journey*. Miles was one of the first to confront Powell, at a book signing in Arlington, Virginia: "General, the Gulf vets are sick. You know that, don't you?"

Powell's book-signing grin froze, and he told the young veteran that the Pentagon was looking into it—"a politician's answer," Miles remembered. The next thing he knew, he was shouting, and security personnel were lifting him away. He just kept screaming, "People are dying. People I know!"

A similar scene in San Francisco took place less than a month later. Dan Fahey had had enough time to mobilize peers who might want to confront Powell on the broader issues of war and peace. He turned naturally to the Central Committee for Conscientious Objectors, and to the counselor who had helped him long-distance while he was still aboard that submarine.

The politics of celebrity crossed with some complex racial discourse had made opposing Powell problematic for pacifists. That anti-Powell flyer bore only the name "Coalition Against Bigotry and Violence," because CCCO had refused to allow the organization's name on a flyer assailing the most respected Black man in America.[26] "Can't we speak truth to power?" the board's only African American member had asked, and been voted down. Thus was formed the vaguely named "coalition," protesting alongside one gay man with a balloon and Ron Kovic.[27] Journalist Norman Solomon watched it unfold, as Kovic said, "You didn't tell the truth about the war in the Gulf, General" and was answered only by platitudes about "these young men and women" he had commanded.

"Beneath Powell's amplified voice," Solomon writes, Vietnam veteran Ron Kovic can be heard only in snippets: ". . . 150,000 people . . . the bombing . . ." Kovic's numbers came via Veterans for Peace (VFP), which had long been sending delegations to Iraq, trying to assess the damage done while providing clues to what was behind the new vets' health crises.

VFP hadn't waited till after the war to be heard, of course. Desert Shield, the warm-up, had roused members' voices coast to coast. Scott Camil, the babyface of Winter Soldier 1971, told reporters, "I am encouraging members of the American military not to participate in Operation Desert Shield," and said to reservists, "Your allegiance shouldn't be to the flag or politicians but to the Constitution this country was founded on."[28] Members were doing their best to help reservists make that decision. After the war began, some spoke at anti-war marches, while others prepared for a long slog. And after the unexpected "victory" in March, they paid close attention to reports of the damage done. In the shorter term, it gave some of the newest vets clues as to why they could not stop coughing.

Brian Willson compiled the immediate death toll: "*The New York Times* reported 100,000 Iraqi military killed, and 300,000 wounded. . . . Other estimates suggest 200,000 Iraqi soldiers killed (*London Times*, March 3, 1991), with many more maimed. Civilian dead directly from bombings and immediate after effects are in the 25,000 to 50,000 range." Initial reports from the United Nations used terms like 'near apocalyptic results,' 'relegated to a pre-industrial age,' and 'devastation,'" Willson wrote, quoting a U.N. assessment of the damage done to Iraq's infrastructure, including all electricity and even production of vaccines.

In the fall of 1992, VFP convened a nineteen-member delegation, including Willson, Ellen Barfield, and John Schuchardt, a member of the Plowshares

Eight. They toured bombed-out hospitals and destroyed factories and saw
the dual effects of the war and the punishing sanctions that followed. Most
overwhelming was the Ameriyah Shelter, opened in February to civilians,
that was then hit by U.S. bombs. Barfield wrote in *The Veteran*:

> The shelter was used as night quarters for women and children;
> the men stayed in their homes.
>
> Who was supposed to live, died. The shelter capacity was
> 2,000. . . . Estimates of the number killed vary. One of the men
> we talked to said they removed 700 to 800 bodies. Many were
> blown apart or vaporized in the intense heat though, so the body
> count is not enough. . . . I just stood and cried. The spirits of the
> dead lingered, and it was hard to dispel the horror.[29]

Elsewhere in Iraq, Barfield noted, the water system was broken. "The streets
of Baghdad had been flooded with sewage until late August. . . . [The bombers had] hit plants where chlorine, sulfate and other treatment chemicals were
made, destroyed power stations, and damaged water and sewage lines." More
delegations followed.

In December 1997, Barfield talked to the *Los Angeles Times* about a recent
VFP mission, including a delivery of $30,000 worth of antibiotics and medi-
cal and surgical supplies for hospitals in Baghdad, Basra, and Mosul.

"We saw lots of children suffering from cancer, and with little or no medi-
cines they are guaranteed to die," she said. "One child in particular had been
at the hospital for four months. His mother was a teacher. He was a Kurd, but
had learned Arabic in that time and the doctors were amazed. He was still in
good shape, but was going downhill."

When Barfield returned home on January 20, an immigration officer in
New York seized her passport. But that experience was for her perhaps more
encouraging than she would have expected. "The guy was really nice," she
recalled. "He said our intentions were probably good. His superior said, 'We
need a better world.'"[30]

As the decade ended, VFP became known for similar projects stemming
from multiple U.S. wars, from building a children's hospital in My Lai and
serving as election monitors in El Salvador to the Vietnam Friendship Vil-

lage, a community center west of Hanoi hoping to compensate in some small way for the effects of Agent Orange. The village, with its special housing for severely disabled children and family-style residences for orphans and housemothers, was the brainchild of George Mizo, who had first returned to Vietnam only two years after joining Brian Willson in a fast outside the White House. Helping launch the village was Jeff Schutts, grateful for Mizo's counseling in the 1980s and turning from his own military counseling to something more celebratory.

While the VFP pursued penance and the Iraq dissenters some form of justice, some witnessed the quiet escalation that would help return the Persian Gulf to the status of a war zone.

Dan Fahey could not believe what he was hearing. Had the U.S. ambassador to the United Nations just called the deaths of half a million children "worth it?"

Ambassador Madeleine Albright was speaking to CBS' *60 Minutes* about her three sometimes rocky years at the United Nations. Correspondent Lesley Stahl's eyes were huge as she shared footage of an Iraqi woman with a listless baby in her lap. "We have heard that a half million children have died," Stahl said. "I mean, that's more children than died in Hiroshima. And, you know, is the price worth it?" Albright's eyes dropped for a moment before she said, her throat full, "I think this is a very hard choice, but the price—we think the price is worth it." Yes, she had.

Stahl didn't question the sincerity of Albright's soulful assertion, which was of a piece with the Clinton administration's foreign-policy style, masking atrocities with publicized anguish. Despite Fahey's efforts of the past few years, Stahl did not ask Albright whether the infant in the footage had been exposed to DU. Both CBS and Albright had received the report Fahey's Military Toxics Project had released in January, "Radioactive Battlefields of the 1990s: The U.S. Army's Use of Depleted Uranium and Its Consequences for Human Health and the Environment."

In 1996, Fahey was working nearly full time on the issue, challenging the military's continued use of DU in the Balkans and other conflicts under the Clinton administration. Fahey thought that Albright's statement would make a searing opening for a documentary about the Pentagon and State Department's refusal to acknowledge the issue. When such a film was released years later, it featured Fahey saying what he and Charles Miles had wanted to ask Colin Powell: Given the numerous Pentagon studies from 1990 indicating DU's dangers, "You have to wonder why no warning was ever disseminated to any ground forces prior to the war, even just to say: 'Stay away from the vehicles that have been hit, don't go climbing onto the equipment afterwards.'"[31]

In general, most of the American public had moved on from Iraq. The war's most famous dissenting soldier was the white supremacist who cracked the decade in half: Timothy McVeigh, who had won a Bronze Star in the Gulf. The white-power movement he was following had been sparked by Vietnam veterans, who escalated the Rambo psychology into a domestic race war.[32] In April of 1995, McVeigh, accompanied by his former NCO Terry Nichols, drove a truck loaded with explosives into central Oklahoma City and blew up the Alfred P. Murrah Federal Building, killing 168 people, including 19 children. Press stories included contradictory statements on what he had seen and done, some musing about how an aspiring Green Beret had grown so full of rage against his government. For years to come, the concept of the "dissenting soldier" would evoke more the shaven-headed neo-Nazi McVeigh than the assured Fahey or the tireless Jeff Paterson.

Paterson, now in Oakland, was one of the few recent vets to speak out against President Bill Clinton's "soft" wars, excoriating the daily bombing of Iraq and even questioning Clinton's even more popular interventions in the Balkans. Historian Howard Zinn, from his tenured perch at Boston University, critiqued the soft militarism that had become chic after 1991, writing a few years later, "Our culture is in deep trouble when a film like *Saving Private Ryan* can pass by, like a military parade, with nothing but a shower of confetti and hurrahs for its color and grandeur." But most, like Kovic and Paterson, found themselves marginalized, their allies and funders the "usual suspects" who challenged the military during peacetime: pacifists and the sectarian left. Then the gender-dissenters took up the slack and destabilized the militaristic status quo.

Kathleen Gilberd, of the Military Law Task Force (MTLF), had been an anti-war activist since Vietnam, one well known for her tireless and brilliant advocacy for military personnel. Bridget Wilson, a former Navy captain and full-time attorney in San Diego, said that Gilberd's legal strategies had often "set the bar, especially during the AIDS crisis."[33] In 1992, Gilberd and

MLTF had initiated a lawsuit when the Pentagon instituted mandatory AIDS testing. Emphasizing the Task Force's mission to keep such information confidential, Gilberd told the Associated Press, "The rights of people in the military need to be protected against a system which is both institutionally and informally discriminatory."[34] More recently, MLTF had been the first to help gay personnel fighting discharge.

As gender wars unfurled in the military, Gilberd also became a national expert on dealing with women who reported sexual assault as well as discrimination. She had seen a now-landmark Veterans Administration study, in which nearly a third of all women veterans reported some level of abuse. Gilberd heard early about the June 1996 Army rape scandal at Aberdeen Proving Ground, when six brave young women in basic training spoke out against sexual abuse by drill sergeants. That spring, Drill Sergeant Delmar Simpson was convicted and sentenced to twenty-five years in prison for raping six female soldiers under his command, and a subsequent national Army hotline "recorded 1,288 complaints of abuse in its seven months in operation, 353 of which resulted in criminal investigations."[35]

These six young women knew that trainees were not "supposed" to complain about drill sergeants, but they also knew that they could. They had seen a 1995 made-for-television movie five years earlier, about sexual assault at the navy's Tailhook convention, whose victims had won lawsuits against the Tailhook Association and Hilton Hotels. After six thousand women had served in the Gulf, female trainees like those at Aberdeen were seen as essential by both sides, and their charges more likely to be taken seriously.

Thousands more women, of every rank and branch of service, told their stories to reporters and their members of Congress. Local VA hospitals started developing treatment programs for rape survivors. By 1998, these testimonies would spur a Department of Defense Task Force headed by General Evelyn Foote, another former WWII WAC who understood that sexual harassment and abuse had long been endemic.

Foote's participation in the debate placed the issue as one of "readiness," a move away from dissent that was welcomed by advocates pressing for the final lifting of all restrictions on women in combat. This argument, definitely not anti-war, took the discussion out of the hands of advocates like Gilberd. Similar arguments did the same for gay personnel, who over the decade secured victories in the courts and in the establishment of nonpartisan research and advocacy groups. Still, military gender issues would remain a trope of partisan politics.

Meanwhile, the U.S. military's main business continued, from new intervention in Kosovo to continued pressure on Iraq.

A "readiness" campaign in the press, not dissimilar to the pre–World War I "preparedness" movement, was advocated by the Project for a New American Century (PNAC), a think tank formed by military advisers to former President George H.W. Bush. In 1999, Congress passed, and President Clinton signed, an Iraq Liberation Act that aligned with PNAC's goals, and escalated bombing of Iraq resumed.

As the 1990s ended, Aimee Allison was busy starting a new nonprofit consulting business, Dan Fahey was en route to graduate school, and Charles Miles was beginning his war memoir *Prayer for Rumayla*. For a time, the only ones active on military issues were those involved with the G.I. Rights Hotline: the VVAW's Greg Payton still talked to soldiers on behalf of the War Resisters League, and Jeff Paterson still campaigned against sanctions on Iraq. None of them responded right away to the 2000 election, which handed the reins of power to PNAC signatories like Donald Rumsfeld and Dick Cheney.

On September 11, 2001, Charles Sheehan Miles was working a software job when he learned that a plane had hit the Pentagon. His first thought was, "Please, please don't let it be Arabs." The anti-Arab slurs he remembered from the war still echoed in his head.[36] Before Miles or anyone else could get an idea of what was going on, authorities were taking action against dissenting soldiers—starting with Philip Berrigan.

"On September 11, I watched appalled as the second tower of the World Trade Center came down," Berrigan told the *Progressive*. "The guards called me out, took me to the lieutenant's office, shackled and handcuffed me, and took me to solitary. . . . During my twelve days in segregation, no further daylight was provided. One lieutenant came to announce, 'No phone, no visitors!' The result? Limbo-incommunicado." Those additional measures were not for Berrigan's own safety: the prison's authorities spied trouble in the seventy-seven-year-old cleric, veteran of World War II and longtime protester against the war machine, who at the time was serving a thirty-month sentence for a Plowshares action.[37]

Berrigan's response would come soon enough; it would take a little more time for Miles and Dan Fahey to form Veterans for Common Sense. What they feared would come next, and would happen quickly: the war they had first been ordered to fight now seemed to metastasize into a near-permanent conflagration.

CHAPTER TWELVE

2001 to 2020

WHILE PHILIP BERRIGAN WAS LOCKED down on September 11, 2001, the next generation of soldier-dissenters was just waking up.

National Guard medic Margaret Stevens, based in New Jersey, started packing her go bag; she knew she was headed to Ground Zero as medical support. Diplomat's son Aidan Delgado learned about the day's terrorist attacks just after he had enlisted in the Army Reserves. Jennifer Hogg knew she needed to check in with her unit of the National Guard; she knew deployment would mean a tearful scene where soldiers all around her hugged their wives, while Hogg knew better than to do the same with her own (female) partner. Stephen Eagle Funk, living in Northern California's East Bay, was awakened by a call from his East Coast sister about "what's happening in New York," and thought briefly of his father, the Vietnam veteran his mother had escaped long ago.

Garett Reppenhagen, an Army sniper home on leave, watched the World Trade Center fall on TV and wondered what that meant for him. Fourteen-year-old Chelsea Manning, born in Oklahoma, with her own Navy-vet dad, learned about the attacks while in school in Wales, where she had moved with her mom. Brandon Bryant, in Missoula, Montana, saw the attacks on TV in his high school, in the shadow of their town's Army recruiting station. And ten-year-old Texan Reality Leigh Winner heard about it in her hyper-patriotic elementary school, then again in geopolitics lessons from her father.

That morning, Jonathan Wesley Hutto, a staffer at Amnesty International, had just returned from the World Conference Against Racism in Durban, South Africa. Hutto "was preparing a report back [from the conference] when BOOM, the entire agenda went up in smoke, literally."

A lot went up in smoke that day, whose memory has been evoked in the decades since to justify U.S. imperialism. That date—September 11, 2001—has been thrown in the faces of all the young Americans in this chapter, asking how they could dissent in its face.

These twenty-first-century soldier-dissenters emerged amid the nature of twenty-first-century warfare. The country's stealth empire swelled, its colonies replaced by "cooperative security locations" sprinkled with well-trained Special Forces personnel, while the military-industrial-intelligence complex enabled long-distance assassinations. Crucial was the ability to see, monitor, and kill human beings half a world away.

A generation raised on the internet, many conversant in the language of trauma, knew what to call the destruction of human bodies, its toll on warriors as well as targeted communities. They also felt the country's founding injustices, from racism to misogyny, pressing on their necks.

For Jennifer Hogg of Buffalo, New York, September 11, 2001, included her National Guard unit's being called up to serve at Ground Zero. Hogg had enlisted a year earlier, "when I was in high school [and] bought into the honor of the military." Adding to the post-attack stress, she remembers, was the military's mandate to stay closeted. As they prepared to deploy to Ground Zero, soldiers all around Hogg hugged their wives, said goodbye to their kids. "If I did not have the freedom to hug my girlfriend goodbye," she said years later, "then what freedom was I protecting? What freedom could we offer to the world if we treat it so restrictively based on who a person falls in love with?"[1] Margaret Stevens, a Black sergeant with the New Jersey National Guard, also questioned what her country was proposing. "I counted myself among the soldiers who questioned the goals, values and actions of the U.S. military even during times of so-called peace."[2] Those questions grew as the nation stayed on a war footing.

As Secretary of State Colin Powell made his case at the United Nations for war against Iraq, Gulf War vets warned in September 2002 that "the Bush presidents, father and son, have a poor record of truth-telling when it comes to war and the UN—that they often cheat when they can't win an argument on its merits."[3] Jennifer Hogg attended an anti-war rally organized by Veterans for Peace, which was now headed by former Marine Dave Cline, founder of the Fort Hood GI coffeehouse The Oleo Strut.

Recently retired from the U.S. Postal Service, Cline organized military families and reservists into this war's first Bring Them Home Now! campaign. "A lot of people in the military are looking at it like a job," he told reporters about the troops who had contacted him. "They're not supposed to be charging around the world, and the things that they were led to believe they're fighting for are falling apart." In New York, Cline welcomed to the stage a young Marine named Ghanim Khalil, who declared that he would resist all efforts to deploy him to Iraq.[4]

Jennifer Hogg was in the crowd that day, years after her service at Ground Zero. "We were going to invade Iraq. No matter how much I thought before that as a soldier I just do what I am told, I knew that there was something not right about this unfolding appetite for destruction. March 20, 2003, was the first day I took a stand against the war in Iraq and it was not even 24 hours old."[5] Hogg was not yet ready to openly dissent.

Across the country, Stephen Funk was about to become the war's first public active-duty conscientious objector.

Who are you? The question had always been under the surface for Native American/Irish/Chinese/Filipino-American Stephen Eagle Funk.[6] Raised mostly by his feminist Chinese grandmother and his grandfather/personal hero—the first nonwhite engineer at Boeing—he had a difficult relationship with his Vietnam-veteran father. What did that mean about him?

Funk knew he was smart, rather extravagantly so: he had burned through his years at the Nova School, an alternative high school where demonstrations counted as field trips and students sat in a circle to vote on school policies. He was accepted to thirteen colleges at the end of it. Such freedom felt a little like chaos, its foundation like an ocean.

When his first attempt at college unraveled, Funk moved to his sister's place in Northern California, hoping for eventual admission to the University of California. The liberal Bay Area was conflicted and confused by the new "war on terror;" military recruiting surged even at UC Berkeley's ROTC program. Sometimes Funk went to one of the area's anti-war marches, which felt more like social occasions.

A guy Funk's age, "Alex" (not his real name), began visiting Funk at his retail job, asking, "Do you like your job? How much do you like it? What do you want to do next?" Alex said he liked his job because of the product he was selling: the Marine Corps. Funk ignored him at first, but Alex kept coming back, talking about teamwork and leadership, and how if Funk joined the reserves, he only had to be there one weekend a month to qualify for tens of thousands of dollars' worth of scholarships.

Funk did not tell anyone he had signed up until two weeks before boot camp. His father, Paul, Vietnam veteran and an engineer in Washington State, was in the Bay Area on business that week.

In the reserves, he would earn some money for school, Funk told them all; besides, wouldn't he be helping his country in a time of need?

Paul Funk spoke softly, "There's a war going on now, you know."[7]

Funk explained that he would be able to help out if America were attacked again. Alex had explained that really, war would not be his job. That night, Funk slept better than he had in months.

Things were different when he arrived for basic training at Camp Pendleton, a spiral of U.S. bases in Southern California that hosted 40 percent of U.S. military personnel. At first, Funk focused on its terrain, part coastal, part chaparral, part hard desert. And on the obstacle course, the ropes training. Not so easy, with all the M-16s everywhere.

Soon enough, Funk's drill sergeant guessed that Funk was gay: "Hey! You! My limp-wristed recruit, do you plan on joining us?"[8] Within a few weeks, he was being investigated; if they caught him with another man, they could bring him up on charges. *I'll show them*, Funk thought. *Queer boys can be Marines, too.* His strength grew quickly; he excelled at target practice.

Still, it all made him want to throw up. TV news images of wars, military video games—none of it was anything like standing in 100-degree heat and being ordered to run and shoot an automatic weapon. It felt worse at Camp Lejeune, where he was sent for advanced training: the M-16 was nothing compared with the mobile 133-caliber Howitzer. An early snow made each of them glow. He felt frozen, as if he were already dead.

One night, Funk went to the base's internet café and searched: "military discharge morality violence." The term that popped up was kind of old-fashioned, something he had heard from his father. He wrote his sister an email: "I think I might be . . ." When he next went home on leave, she had set him up for a talk with a Gulf War conscientious objector.

It had been more than a decade since Aimee Allison's CO discharge. Now an Oakland management consultant, she put down her BlackBerry and looked across the café table at the young lance corporal, whose near-shaved head gave him the look of a wiry Buddha. Choosing her words carefully, Allison told him he didn't have to do this if he did not want to.

"What do you mean?"

"Stephen!" she said gently, "you're gay!"

Funk held out his hands helplessly, as if to say, *Well, duh.*

"You know you can get out more easily than this."

"I know," he said. "But I don't want to do it that way."

Allison sat back, feeling younger by association. Funk was twenty, as she had been back when she found herself throwing up during weapons training in Fort Jackson, South Carolina. If anyone had suggested back then that being female and Black meant she did not belong in the military, she would have shown what those pushup-hardened biceps could do. Now, she looked down at Funk's files and thought about the discharge she had fought for all the way to federal court in 1992.

"I can't just mention," Funk said with a careful smile, "that I've been at every anti-war demonstration?" They also did not have much time. The process was and is relatively uniform across all services, at its core a personal statement and evaluations by a psychiatrist, a chaplain, and an investigating officer.

The Marine Corps was also particularly hostile to conscientious objection after enlistment. And even Allison's Navy CO process had taken nearly a year, including testimonials and two appeals to the Court of Appeals for the Armed Forces. If Funk's unit were deployed overseas as rumored, he would have to complete the package overseas, alone in a war zone.

Allison had only recently joined the board of the Committee for Conscientious Objectors, supporting its branch of the GI Rights Hotline. The hotline was nearly overwhelmed: in January 2002 alone, there had been 3,582 calls, about 700 of them new objectors like Funk.[9] Many, if not most, hotline callers either sought non-CO discharges or had already taken the other time-honored route of functional dissent, AWOL/UA (absent without official leave/unauthorized absence). In the case of a reservist like Funk, the latter could mean failing to report for drill or, as Funk eventually chose, for activation for war.

On April 1, 2003, Funk was back at Camp Pendleton for a press conference. He distributed copies of his conscientious-objector application, in which he also came out of the closet. "I was appalled by the amount of hatred I found in the military," Funk wrote. "The military cultivates anti-gay sentiment among its enlisted. I also believe it perpetuates feelings of hatred against all that are different either culturally, ethnically or otherwise."

Then he turned himself in, forty-seven days after his unit had been activated to replace one headed to Iraq. The next eleven months would go by in a blaze of flashbulbs and a constant barrage of microphones. And while he expected nothing but torment from his reserve unit, Funk got an equal measure of bashful Marines coming up to him and saying, "I'm totally for the war, but I'm glad you're doing this, 'cause you represent a lot of us."

The Iraq invasion was otherwise rolling out as planned.[10] Deployed to Anbar Province, sniper Garett Reppenhagen noticed early that his unit had been told to shoot "farmers who went out at night to water their crops," since anyone not at home was judged an insurgent.[11] He was also sometimes ordered to shoot into "mobs" that included civilians. It all jibed too closely with the awful stuff he was reading in the book he had gotten before deployment at an "alternative" bookstore in his hometown.

Then based in Germany, Colorado native Reppenhagen had served in Kosovo, where he had "helped save Mother Teresa's church" and worked to implement the Geneva Conventions. Home on leave, he had stopped off at an alternative bookstore in Manitou Springs, whose owners loved the same neopunk music that he did. "I told the clerk, 'Hey, I'm a high school dropout, I'm in the Army and I'm probably going to Iraq,'" said Reppenhagen. "What do I need to read?"

The young woman behind the counter didn't miss a beat: she ran for Howard Zinn's *A People's History of the United States*. Zinn's 1980 volume, newly reissued in a new eight-hundred-page paperback, had already sold a million copies, beloved by many for its alternative tilt on America's history, despite critics (one called it "bad history, albeit gilded with virtuous intentions.")[12] The bookstore clerk was unknowingly bringing together two dissenting soldiers.

In Iraq, Reppenhagen heard echoes of the Howard Zinn book in his command's orders. Was "haji" the same as "gook?"

Aidan Delgado, the diplomat's son who had enlisted just before 9/11, was now a combat mechanic with the 320th Military Police. As blown away as Funk by the brutality of basic training, Delgado was studying Buddhism by the time he arrived in Iraq with the invasion. He was horrified by the behavior of some in his unit: "Guys in my unit, particularly the younger guys, would drive by in their Humvee and shatter bottles over the heads of Iraqi civilians passing by. They would keep a bunch of empty Coke bottles in the Humvee to break over people's heads."[13]

Delgado had already submitted a CO claim to his command when his company was assigned duty at Abu Ghraib Prison.[14] Now regarded by his command as a traitor, Delgado was assigned to a back office at the prison, where he could learn about the lives and families of the "hajis" he had been taught unsuccessfully to hate. His command had gone by the book on processing his CO application, starting the process without delay; this was not the case with countless other commands, even when the request was made by equally articulate and passionate soldiers.

By then Funk had been court-martialed for desertion, his six-month sentence feeling almost "restful" after all the fuss. By night, he and forty other COs put up parade tents for the base. At least he was finally among other misfits. War resisters were sort of at the top of the prison hierarchy, as another Iraq resister explained years later. "In civilian prison, bank robbers are at the top of the heap. In military prison, everyone has a story about being f**ked by the military—but us, we're the ones who f**ked the military!"[15] At least the media were gone, and Funk could get some reading done.

Just as Funk's military career was ending, another began. Howard University graduate Jonathan Wesley Hutto had been searching for the next challenge after working for both Amnesty International and the American Civil Liberties Union. Hutto first told the recruiter facing him in the coffee shop, "There's no way I'm joining Uncle Sam's Army." One of Hutto's proudest moments at Howard had been welcoming Black icon Kwame Ture, formerly Stokely Carmichael; one of his mentors at school had been part of the GI movement during Vietnam, just as Ture had supported the Fort Hood Three. But Hutto's career and life were now in flux, and he faced a student-loan debt of nearly $50,000. When the recruiter told him that the Navy would pay all his loans within five years, "I started listening harder."

After consulting with his mom and choosing his rate as photographer's mate, Jonathan enlisted in the United States Navy. On January 14, 2004, he set off for boot camp at Great Lakes, the now renamed facility that had housed the Port Chicago 50 a half-century earlier. He got through boot camp's first weeks by running a familiar hip-hop lyric through his head: "It's like a jungle, sometimes it makes me wonder how I keep from going under."[16] Also in his mind was an invocation from Kwame Ture, who had coined the phrase "Black Power."

Ture had told Hutto's Howard University class, "The more we struggle, the more we know; the more we know, the more we can do. Our people are going to need us to do it until we die. Therefore we prepare ourselves for eternal struggle." That had made sense to Hutto as a student from a working-class background, and he would repeat those words to himself throughout his time in the military: *The struggle is eternal.*

Hutto knew about the GI rebellion that had helped end the war in Vietnam and improved conditions for Black servicemembers, its stockade riots at Fort Dix in 1971 and Fort Lewis in 1972. He knew that even as it wound down, as U.S. troop levels declined in favor of bombings from aircraft carriers, the rebellion had continued in the U.S. Navy with a grassroots "Stop Our Ships" movement, organized by troops aboard the *U.S.S. Constellation* and the *U.S.S. Coral Sea.*

Hutto felt inspired to keep training, even when he saw a Confederate flag included among "the many flags we marched under as a division."[17] He was not the only one in quiet resistance; a few peers spoke of the Iraq War "as a conflict for profit involving companies such as Halliburton." But the poverty draft was real.[18] Hutto looked forward to his advanced training at Fort Meade, in photography and military information operations.

Hutto was targeted early at the Fort Meade "A-school" for racist harassment, taking a group to an anti-war march in Washington, D.C., just before graduation. The harassment continued right through his shipboard assignment on the *U.S.S. Theodore Roosevelt*, based in Norfolk, Virginia. After one disappointing hearing about the harassment, Hutto briefly left Norfolk, going UA (Navy for AWOL). Hutto returned only after his Vietnam-veteran mentor urged it, so he could fight from the inside. He eventually found kindred spirits in his ship's enlisted troops.

Garett Reppenhagen had long since settled in at Forward Operating Base Scunion, near Baquba. In early 2004, Reppenhagen and his friend Jeff Englehart did something unprecedented: they started a blog called *Fight to Survive*. They told what they thought of as the truest of stories. Its May 15, 2004, entry:

> The girls black swirling hair was matted down with blood and her skin was peppered with sores and cuts. One side of her face was red and bruised with her eye swollen shut. . . . "What happened?" asked Sgt Spoon through the translator. From a short conversation with the shaken man Spoon found out that while his daughter was sleeping, bombs from the sky hit his house. . . . Chalk up another success for our team. We invest a lot of money to kill people that are trying to help humanity, even help us as we try to destroy them. Now, with their backs to the wall, they fight us the only way they can to even the odds, with terrorism.[19]

By the time that blog went live, Reppenhagen's Iraq tour was about to end. He was already in touch with anti-war veterans back home. He returned to a country coming to terms with how the United States was fighting terrorism, including using practices normally called torture.

The U.S. media was now swamped with photos from Abu Ghraib. The abuse in the photographs horrified civilians, though it was no surprise to many in the military.

Starting in 2001, the Pentagon and CIA engaged in systematic mistreatment of Muslims tagged as "enemy combatants," held in military prisons both in the Middle East and in Guantanamo Bay, Cuba. The same technical revolution that had created the internet was used to track some of the oldest, low-tech atrocities of war: the computerized Detainee Information Management System (DIMS) documented some of the tactics used to extract information—sleep deprivation, humiliation (nudity, casual abuse of the Quran), and "enhanced interrogation" that sometimes included waterboarding, the torture technique first developed in the Philippines.[20]

Brandon Neely was deployed to Guantanamo Bay, Cuba, in January 2002, right after it was assigned to hold "enemy combatants" seized in Middle Eastern battlefields. Detainees were sometimes force-fed and worse: "The medic looked up one quick time and punched the detainee twice on the left side of his face with his right fist. The medic then just turned around and walked out of the cage like nothing happened. The detainee was then un-handcuffed from the cage and laid down on the cement in the cage. He was then hogtied. He laid in this position for a couple hours."[21]

The rationale for such tactics, Neely said, was that detainees at Guantanamo were "the worst of the worst." Under the same reasoning, similar tactics and worse were being used by troops with detainees in prisons overseas, including Iraq.[22] These "enhanced interrogation" techniques were developed by military psychologists who had reverse-engineered the SERE (Survival, Evasion, Resistance, and Escape) program, created to help troops who had been captured by the enemy. Front-line troops also improvised home-grown techniques to elicit the suffering of their "terrorist" detainees.[23]

Seymour Hersh, who broke the My Lai story a half-century before, knew some of what these soldiers carried. He commenced "frenetic reporting on Abu Ghraib"[24] after being tipped off that General Antonio Taguba had begun to investigate abuse at the prison. Starting with anyone associated with the military police companies based there, Hersh soon heard from a middle-aged military mom that her daughter "came back a different person—distraught, angry." She had brought home a DVD with "an extensive series of images of a naked Iraqi prisoner flinching in fear before two snarling dogs."[25]

Photos like those came into the hands of the Taguba committee, thanks to whistleblower Specialist Joseph Darby, who received a specific commendation in the committee's (classified) April report. Darby's name was then spoken on CNN, which forced him out of Iraq: "I had to raise hell to get out of the country."[26] Darby thus first defined the role of military whistleblower for the Iraq War.

Torture's legal infrastructure soon came to light, one devised after the fact. The scandal even roused John Kerry, who had been part of the near-unanimous vote to authorize the war in Iraq, unlike his vote more than ten years earlier. "It's not just the little person at the bottom who ought to pay the price of responsibility," Kerry told union members at a steamfitters' hall in Philadelphia. "Harry Truman had that sign on the desk and it said, 'The buck stops here.' The buck doesn't stop at the Pentagon. And in this case, it doesn't just stop with any military personnel."[27] By then, Kerry was speaking as a presidential candidate, and didn't dare mention any Winter Soldier ghosts the scandal might have roused for him.

To challenge President George W. Bush, whose whole re-election campaign was centered on his status as a "war president," Kerry's campaign had remodeled John Kerry as a war hero. At the Democratic National Convention, Kerry saluted the gathering: "Reporting for duty!" The makeover was fruitless: "Swift Boat Veterans for Truth" ads soon flooded the airwaves.[28]

Kerry was thus even more resistant to meeting his former VVAW allies in Veterans for Peace, who had scheduled their convention in Boston precisely to have that conversation.

Also disappointed was a new group co-founded by Stephen Funk, who had just finished his prison term at Camp Lejeune. His name was spoken by the four twenty-something vets in Boston's Faneuil Hall, in front of a bust of John Adams, as they announced the formation of Iraq Veterans Against War (IVAW).

All those assembled in Boston knew they were working against the popular conflation of the Iraq War with 9/11—the same mistake a few of them had made before enlisting. As angry as they were that Kerry refused to meet with them, they still watched, dumbfounded, as the Swift Boat campaign succeeded and Bush was re-elected, starting his second term with a "surge" that would add even more troops to the Iraq War.

Part of that "surge," Brandon Bryant joined the Air Force as an "imagery analyst" who would remotely operate drone aircraft, like "the guys that give James Bond all the information that he needs to get the mission done."[29] Both the training and the work meant eighteen-hour days at a remote airbase, where Bryant watched suspected militants and their families, and sometimes told the pilot sitting next to him where to drop a bomb.

By 2006, there was not much room, given the pace and the intensity of his schedule, for Bryant to pay attention to the casualty figures from Iraq and Afghanistan, let alone listen to anti-war types—whether it was Iraq Veterans Against the War or Cindy Sheehan, the Gold Star mother holding a protest vigil in Crawford, Texas, across from President Bush's summer home.

That summer, Sheehan addressed Veterans for Peace's annual conference in Dallas and invited members to join her at what she was calling "Peace House." Dozens accepted, including Garett Reppenhagen, newly back from

Iraq, driving the forty miles to Sheehan's encampment in a painted school bus. Reppenhagen told the media that had come to gawk, "Almost every day I was there, I saw something that made me hate the war. I saw dead children and women, injured Americans."[30]

Reppenhagen worked for the newly formed Veterans for America; he shared an office with Gulf War vet Steve Robinson and Bobby Muller, the wheelchair-bound Vietnam icon who had thrown away his medals with John Kerry in 1971 before founding Vietnam Veterans of America. They taught Reppenhagen how to navigate the halls of Congress and which members were veterans—like John Murtha, a Marine who had served in Vietnam but had never opposed that war. Murtha, who had represented his conservative Pennsylvania House district for more than thirty years, had supported the president since September 11, as noted and praised by Vice President Richard Cheney.[31]

On November 17, 2005, Murtha summoned the spirit of his mentor and fellow Irishman Thomas P. "Tip" O'Neill, who had told Lyndon Johnson that the Vietnam War had gone horribly wrong. Murtha spoke passionately and slowly, blinking back at the cameras as if daring them to tell him to stop. "The war in Iraq," he began, "is not going as advertised. It is a flawed policy wrapped in illusion." By the end of the speech, Murtha called the presence of coalition troops a source of the insurgency and emphasized: "We cannot allow promises we have made to our military families in terms of service benefits, in terms of their health care, to be negotiated away." Murtha took a breath, looking as weary as the soldiers he was describing.

The flashbulbs hadn't quite stopped before the partisan response began. As Murtha arrived at the House floor, an Ohio Republican handed him a message from "a Marine I know: 'Cowards cut and run, but Marines never do.'" It echoed the bile that had been directed at John Kerry for thirty years.

As 2005 ended, Murtha helped the House pass the Detainee Treatment Act, a spending-bill amendment that explicitly banned the use of torture by U.S. military personnel. Garett Reppenhagen had testified on that bill's behalf at a press conference alongside Charles Miles, founder of the Gulf War Resource Center.

The new year would bring an especially bloody year in Iraq. A wider variety of dissenting voices began going after the military's own original sins, which were also those of the nation.

On January 10, 2006, Jon Hutto could not believe what had just happened. The photo lab was not that small aboard the *U.S.S. Theodore Roosevelt*, a CVN-71 aircraft carrier. It was a home base of sorts, where Hutto had composed numerous stories for the ship's newspaper, *Rough Rider*. That day, Hutto, now an E-3 seaman, had stopped by to check out opportunities for a U.S. Navy–paid degree program in journalism. When a few petty officers came in, including a lead petty officer (LPO), he greeted them cheerfully.

The lead petty officer returned the greeting warmly enough—then, suddenly and with casual cruelty, he "pulled down a hangman's noose [from an overhead vent], right in front of me." Watch out, he added, for that African American petty officer elsewhere on the ship, who "could use a lynching." The responding laughter of the others rang in Hutto's ears.

The struggle is eternal. Hutto knew that to seek justice from his command, he needed to sound the alarm. The next six weeks would contain multiple investigations, a Captain's Mast (non-judicial punishment) of numerous petty officers, including the one with the noose, and an anonymous survey of enlisted personnel that reported a pattern of racism and sexist behavior by petty officers. When the perpetrator was sentenced to only a reduction in rank, Hutto turned to Congress, securing some help from civil rights icon Representative John Lewis. "My shop changed for the better," Hutto wrote. "New sailors coming in, women and sailors of color . . . do not face the intolerance we once faced."

Hutto also began to consider his options. He was proud of having brought these offenses to light, and of his journalistic work for the *Rough Rider*—especially during the previous summer, after Hurricane Katrina hit Louisiana, a piece for which he had interviewed shipmates from New Orleans. But now it might be time to challenge more than his immediate command.

Hurricane Katrina offered one possible next step for anti-war vets: the hurricane's landfall had trashed plans for a fifty-stop bus tour leaving Camp Casey, full of Veterans for Peace. Now, VFP focused instead on the inadequacy of federal help in the region, including the absence of local Guard and Reserve troops now deployed overseas.[32] Rescheduled for March 2006, just as Hutto's ship was pulling into port, the bus tour became a march from Mobile, Alabama, to New Orleans, the first to make newer vets its leading contingent.[33] Garett Reppenhagen spoke publicly about reading Howard

Zinn before deployment, how his initial rejection of the war had become total, and how his generation felt ready to change what it meant to be a veteran.[34]

The post-9/11 gung-ho spell felt broken; even politicians and entertainers were talking about the need for change. John Murtha, along with libertarian Minnesota governor Jesse Ventura, endorsed the new Operation Truth, soon to be renamed Iraq and Afghanistan Veterans of America. The 2006 landscape also included VoteVets, which couched its policy briefs in military-speak about metrics and missions, and the still-growing IVAW, which would soon have chapters in all fifty states.

That was the atmosphere in which Hutto began to read David Cortright's *Soldiers in Revolt*. Cortright's comprehensive summary of the Vietnam-era GI movement reminded Hutto that active-duty personnel could fight from the inside. After his ship pulled into Norfolk, Hutto persuaded Cortright to meet with about twenty servicemembers based there.

As the event began, Hutto huddled with Cortright and Liam Madden, a Marine Corps communication specialist who had served in Fallujah just as the United States was about to pulverize it. Over the next few days, clustered troops brainstormed what a twenty-first-century movement might look like. One flyer, sent by a former co-editor of Jeff Sharlet's *Vietnam GI*, included the note, "This newsletter is your personal property and cannot legally be confiscated from you. 'Possession of unauthorized material may not be prohibited.'[35] DoD Directive 1325.6 Section 3.5.1.2." That directive, "Guidelines for Handling Dissident and Protest Activities Among Members of the Armed Forces," issued a decade earlier, also declared that troops could participate in off-base demonstrations, although not in uniform; group organizing and petitioning were still proscribed.[36]

Hutto and Madden then met with the director of the Center on Conscience and War (formerly NISBCO), an attorney who spent her days with GI Rights Hotline calls. "How could they mobilize all the troops afraid to speak out publicly? The answer was in the Military Whistleblower Protection Act."[37] They chose the most twenty-first-century organizing mode then possible, an online campaign at AppealForRedress.org.

The text of the appeal, well-crafted with Cortright to protect servicemembers, read in full: "As a patriotic American proud to serve the nation in uniform, I respectfully urge my political leaders in Congress to support the prompt withdrawal of all American military forces and bases from Iraq. Staying in Iraq will not work and is not worth the price. It is time for U.S. troops to come home." Started in October, within weeks the appeal had six hundred signatories; it was soon a topic in the White House briefing room.

The appeal held a press conference on Martin Luther King Day 2007, a date chosen to highlight the neglect of Katrina communities and the billions wasted on the wars. "For Dr. King, the plight of African Americans in America was tied to the plight of the peasant in Vietnam."[38] By then, the signature count exceeded one thousand, and thirteen of the signatories had just recorded a segment of CBS' *60 Minutes*, emphasizing that most of their critics had never been in uniform.[39]

The next morning, Madden, Cortright, and supporters traveled to D.C. to deliver those thousand-plus appeals in person. After statements by Liam Madden and VFP's David Cline, the assembled vets streamed into the House and Senate offices to deliver their message. "I am here as a citizen," Army helicopter mechanic Magruder said into the microphone, ensuring that that word carried the appropriate weight. "I want the Congress to understand that as a citizen soldier that I have the right to [appeal] and speak out against an unjust war."[40]

Over the next few weeks, two civilian-organized anti-war marches on Washington featured Hutto, Madden, and Garett Reppenhagen, for whom IVAW activities were part of the job description. While not at 2003 levels, the marches drew a more-than-respectable half a million participants. As Hutto's story demonstrated, soldier-dissenters were starting to take on military racism and its sexism—not a moment too soon.

The military had reported 112 incidents of sexual assault and rape in Iraq and Afghanistan in 2004, not counting victims who did not report for fear of retaliation. Jennifer Hogg and fellow guardsman Margaret Stevens began meeting to brainstorm how to confront this scourge, including the deaths of female soldiers claimed as suicides. Hogg reported, "The current occupation of Iraq has left 97 women dead, the most so far of any American military intervention. Forty percent (39) of those are attributed to non-combat related injuries. Still uncounted in these numbers are suicides and murders that happen in the United States or on military bases post deployment."[41]

Before the year was out, Hogg and Stevens had founded the independent Service Women's Action Network (SWAN), which would garner far broader support than an anti-war group, although gender dissent was still a hard calling. "It was very radical in its beginning," said Stevens, later the author of flagship scholarship on Black radicalism.[42] "We would sit with maps of every US base in the *world*, making plans to *mobilize*. We were going to create a force that could make the whole operation stand *still*."[43] Joining them was Former Marine Corps Captain Anu Bhagwati, who would become one of the group's most visible organizers. The group also called out the racism often interwoven with sexual abuse.

But SWAN's board soon called for a narrowing of the group's mission so as to communicate better with supporters in Congress. It became a lobbying group, like the mainstream veterans' organizations whose commendable work included a new post-9/11 GI Bill and calling attention to the troops' complex health issues.[44] The American Medical Association published findings that one-third of all returning vets had some psychosocial disorder, often with accompanying disorders such as traumatic brain injury and substance abuse issues.[45] Talk-show host Phil Donahue finished his movie *Body of War*, featuring IVAW member Sergeant Tomas Young, a wheelchair user since a bullet left him paralyzed a week into his Iraq deployment.

Meanwhile, IVAW commenced a series of public protests often characterized as political theater, even when their intended audience was Congress. Perhaps most memorable now were two echoes of their VVAW mentor/predecessors: first, multiple repeats of that 1970 Operation Rapid American Withdrawal (RAW), then a Winter Soldier for a new millennium, since the star of the previous editions now chaired the Senate Foreign Relations Committee.

The street-theater Operation First Casualty ("The first casualty of war is truth!"), or OFC, premiered in Washington, D.C., in mid-2007. As in the 1970s' Operation RAW, its veteran-activists interacted with volunteer "civilians" through IVAW's urban-warrior techniques that mimicked the Iraq War itself.[46]

That Memorial Day, Garett Reppenhagen led its New York City sequel, intended to defamiliarize the cityscape by adding disorienting glimpses of war's realities.[47] To the tourists aboard the Lexington Avenue subway line, the uniformed young men may have seemed like a theatrical troupe, until the train approached Union Square and Reppenhagen shouted, "Move out!" Thus began the "military occupation" of Manhattan and Brooklyn.

At five locations soldiers "walked point," scoped in all four directions, and detained suspicious persons with hoods and handcuffs. The "suspects" were civilian volunteers, the "actions" went on for less than ten minutes each, and passers-by were given not summonses but postcards that said, "Scenes like this occur every day in Iraqi cities and towns, conducted by American soldiers and funded by your taxes."

IVAW's combat veterans had devised "scenarios" to illustrate the damage that troops, often exhausted and enraged, inflict on civilians they do not know or trust. And rather than wear just their military jackets and "covers" (hats) over civilian clothes, they decided participants would be in full uniform—for many, for the first time since being discharged from the military. That act, which flirts with violating the military's arcane and complex regulations, was in itself an act of protest.[48]

At Rockefeller Center, the platoon treated the famed skating rink as a detention center, according to a volunteer from Military Families Speak Out. "They lined us up against the wall . . . I started screaming out to the crowd nearby," she said. "Those people . . . did not know what the hell was going on. There were hundreds of them looking up with their mouths agape, frozen in their tracks."[49]

IVAW repeated OFC in a dozen other cities, including Chicago, San Francisco, Santa Monica, and both 2008 party convention cities, Denver and St. Paul. IVAW hoped to confront both nominees, "Out of Iraq and Into Afghanistan" Barack Obama and pro-war militarist (and torture survivor) John McCain. But the terms of the national debate on the wars were still being set by the previous era's most famous veterans.

Aidan Delgado, who had just published his memoir, *The Sutras of Abu Ghraib*, had been blowing the whistle every day since his CO discharge, traveling the country with a slide show of Abu Ghraib photos.[50] Eventually, Delgado gave his photo-filled disc to Army investigators. Delgado then said to his IVAW peers, "Winter Soldier Iraq. We have to do it." Now a student at the University of Florida in Gainesville, Delgado had met one of Gainesville's most venerable peaceniks: Scott Camil, whose bearded face still symbolized

Winter Soldier for many. The idea energized old VVAW hands from Camil to Dave Cline.

Cline, who despite lingering Agent Orange issues was always in motion, announced the new Winter Soldier at the fortieth-anniversary convention of Veterans for Peace. Cline died a few weeks later from complications of hepatitis-C (which he blamed on a blood transfusion at a VA hospital). The new Winter Soldier was dedicated to Cline by three generations of veterans.

As VVAW prepped for the event, one December gathering at a Brooklyn apartment brought in dozens of members. They had assembled at the behest of former VVAW president Barry Romo, who paced around the room, looking like a cross between Joseph Stalin and Yul Brynner. "These guys coming back now—they're so raw," Romo told the group. "They're gonna need everything we can give them."

They gave them Winter Soldier: Iraq and Afghanistan, a three-day event in College Park, Maryland, which included "Rules of Engagement" panels in which Reppenhagen talked about civilians in the crossfire. Separate panels on sexism, racism, and post-traumatic stress disorder emphasized the interrelationships. One medic described her own harassment and assault: "I dreaded every day when I went to work because this surgeon would catch me in the hallway and push me against the wall."[51] SWAN co-founder Margaret Stevens ensured the event's panel on military misogyny kept racism in clear view. Nonetheless, like the 1971 Detroit event for which it was named, Winter Soldier was mostly ignored by both the D.C.-based media and Congress—as was the smaller "Winter Soldier on the Hill" held six weeks later.

The summer of 2008 was an apotheosis for IVAW and the rest of the anti-war movement, as factions splintered at the prospect of ending eight years of Republican rule. After the last primary assured Obama's nomination, competing factions descended on the fall debates, resulting in clashes with mounted police before a debate on Long Island, after candidate Obama refused to meet with a group called Veterans Against War.

Obama's victory in the general election put a pin in the anti-war movement's bubble, including the still-fetal IVAW.[52] Studies have since noted that much of the anti-war movement's mass appeal was rooted more in hatred of Republicans than of war.[53] As 2008 ended, the next wave of soldier-dissenters was just beginning their military careers, in what would soon be known as "the military-internet complex."[54]

Brandon Bryant and Chelsea Manning had been tracked into intelligence soon after enlisting. Bryant had just transferred to Cannon Air Force Base, "the shittiest place in the world," he said, charged with hunting down targets for the Joint Special Operations Command. Manning, a young computer genius, was born in Oklahoma to a Welsh alcoholic mom and her husband the Navy intelligence analyst; she had enlisted in 2007 after surviving homelessness and bouncing from job to job from Oklahoma to Maryland.

Manning's five-foot two frame and slight build had brought on bullying from middle school to basic training, but her brilliance was obvious; rather than flunk Manning and discharge her, the Army chose to "recycle" the soldier to advanced training rather than lose that brain.

Online, Manning was following the national movement to end the mandatory-closet policy known as Don't Ask, Don't Tell (DADT). Given Obama's explicit promises to end DADT and support military women, organizations focused on gender-dissent were both plentiful and visible in early 2009.[55, 56]

Daniel K. Choi, who had spent his fifteen months in Iraq under DADT, came out on national TV to ensure Obama came through. Standing his full six feet, two inches, Choi told MSNBC in March 2009, "By saying three words to you today, 'I am gay'—those three words are a violation of title 10 of the U.S. code" that required servicemembers to be closeted.[57] The DADT repeal took most of the first two years of the Obama administration,[58] during which Choi was arrested twice for chaining himself to the White House fence with other vets.[59] The legal consequences of Choi's dissent would far outlive Don't Ask, Don't Tell. Chelsea Manning cheered for Choi from her Fort Drum computer.

Manning rose quickly as an intelligence analyst at Fort Drum. On her first deployment to Iraq that fall, Manning shared on Facebook photos of her promotion from private first class to specialist. She did not share what she was learning at Baghdad's Forward Operating Base Hammer, from the confidential Secret Internet Protocol Access Router Network (SIPR). What she learned and did inaugurated the next class of soldier-dissent, which mixed high- and low-tech and challenged President Obama's military-industrial-security complex.

Having promised less to end America's wars than to run them better, the Obama administration had staffed up with hundreds of "experts." The infrastructure first mandated by the 1947 National Security Act against the "Communist threat" was now a blend of newly named agencies and well-paid private contractors. By 2010, there were 1,271 government organizations and 1,931 private companies, working in approximately ten thousand locations across the United States on homeland security, counterterrorism, and intelligence.[60] "Although other leaders may have created more oppressive spying regimes, none has come close to constructing one of equivalent size, breadth, cost, and intrusiveness."[61] The Obama administration also continued the Pentagon's expansion overseas, replacing or supplementing U.S. bases on foreign soil with hundreds of smaller "lily-pads" that could house Special Forces, drone bases, or both.[62]

The administration had replaced the global war on terror with overseas contingency operations, with rhetoric that emphasized human rights and the "responsibility to protect." In fact, its foreign policy actions mostly continued those of the Bush administration. The administration changed virtually none of the Bush administration's CIA programs and operations, while escalating the number of targeted killings, including a six-fold increase in the number of covert drone strikes. Moreover, the administration approved the targeted killing of American citizens without judicial warrant, while working to stem challenges to other national security measures, "often claiming the state secrets privilege."[63]

This "smarter" foreign policy—more top-secret operations abroad, expanded surveillance, a vastly more powerful national security ecosystem—made dissent a far more complicated task, at least for those still in uniform.

Manning had had serious reservations about the Iraq War even before she deployed. She tried to brush them aside as she created "intelligence products": an "incident tracker" drew on the military's burgeoning list of "significant acts," or SigActs, which ranged from movements for a particular "insurgent" to battles fought, won, and lost to seemingly peaceful meetings of persons of interest. "I started working extensively with SigActs early after my arrival at Fort Drum. In the months preceding my upcoming deployment, I worked on creating a new version of the incident tracker and used SigActs to populate it." Tracking SigActs from both Afghanistan and Iraq, Manning was soon astonished and horrified at much of what she saw.

After the Army dispatched a unit to hunt down and kill attendees at a local meeting she was monitoring, Manning told a counselor, "I feel like a monster."[64] A few weeks later, Manning learned about the new media organization WikiLeaks—which had released thousands of pager messages from the morning of September 11, 2001, reports on Icelandic bank fraud, and questionable procedures at the U.S. prison in Guantanamo Bay.

All that activity also made WikiLeaks a keen area of interest to the U.S. Justice Department and agencies like it worldwide. The organization's founder, the Australian hacker Julian Assange, had become Public Enemy Number One. So would most soldier-dissenters from now on.

By mid-January 2010, when Manning finally went home on leave, the question of military whistleblowing was in the headlines. A whistleblower had just told military investigators about the 5th Stryker Brigade: "The platoon has a reputation. . . . They have had a lot of practice staging killings and getting away with it."[65] Photos later emerged from what journalists called the "kill team," photos whose release had been delayed by rules demanding silence from low-ranking soldiers.

Manning, who had earned commendations for how securely she backed up her data, in early 2010 downloaded SigActs onto a CD-ROM disc, labeling it "Lady Gaga." At her aunt's Maryland home, Manning began her leak, using the Wi-Fi of a nearby Starbucks. She made a call first, reaching a Metro reporter at the *Washington Post*, who didn't bite after she asked if he "would be interested in receiving information that would have enormous value to the American public." Manning also tried the *New York Times* with a similarly vague query, but she was scheduled to return to Iraq soon and was running out of time. Manning then turned to WikiLeaks, its protocols meant to protect anonymity. Her cover note would end up as a prime exhibit in her court-martial: "Items of historical significance of two wars. Iraq and Afghanistan Significant Activity, SigActs, between 0001 January 2004 and 2359 31 December 2009 extracts from CSV documents from Department of Defense and CDNE database. These items have already been sanitized of any source identifying information. . . . This is one of the most significant documents of our time, removing the fog of war and revealing the true nature of 21st century asymmetric warfare."

In April 2010, Manning also came out to her command as transgender.

She took a selfie of herself in a blond wig and sent it to Master Sergeant Paul Adkins, explaining, "This is my problem. . . . I've been trying very, very hard to get rid of it by placing myself in situations where it would be impossible. But it's not going away."

The data Manning transferred to WikiLeaks' anonymous cloud server included "detainee assessment briefs" from Guantanamo and the video that WikiLeaks would title *Collateral Murder*, showing Army helicopters targeting and killing civilians, including two Reuters journalists. Manning also confided in the well-known Adrian Lamo, who'd been prosecuted for hacking and had had a transgender partner, about both about her gender struggles and her identity as a whistleblower. He seemed the perfect listener for Manning's *cri de coeur*, "The CPU is not made for this motherboard!"

They talked for several weeks, Lamo promising Manning confidentiality, but Lamo contacted the FBI after hearing her describe some of the data she was sharing with "one certain Aussie." On May 27, 2010, investigators captured Manning at Forward Operating Base Hammer (Kuwait) and seized her computers, later transferring her to Marine Corps Base Quantico in Virginia. By then, the information the investigators wanted was being shown to the world.

Most in the military saw Manning as a traitor. That included the people in the darkened rooms in New Mexico where drone warfare was conducted, and Brandon Bryant had long since let his brain and conscience go on autopilot. "We spent so much time not talking about what we saw, and there [Manning] was spilling everything he knew!" At that point in mid-2010, Bryant had been working twelve-hour shifts for about four years, including a stint in Iraq at the war's bloodiest point. The crew rarely had a day off; when not actively firing, he would be "monitoring" a possible target through meetings, weddings, meals. He felt it in his body: after he watched a man bleed out after a drone shot him down, Bryant broke down weeping on the drive home.

He had pulled over, Bryant told journalist Matthew Power, and called his mother back in Missoula: "She just was like, 'Everything will be okay,' and I told her I killed someone, I killed people, and I don't feel good about it. And she's like, 'Good, that's how it should feel, you should never not feel that way.'" Bryant was preoccupied by the fact that his reenlistment date was approaching; most in his position were trying to dream up the best incentives they could think of to sign up for another tour. He had already heard a $100,000-plus signing bonus mentioned, but he was not sure he could go through with it. "So I was a little distracted," he wrote later, "as I stomped through the first two security doors of the bomb-proof, concrete block that was the 3rd Special Operations ROC [RPA Operations Center]." That day, Bryant was told to prepare to kill American citizen Anwar al-Awlaki, an imam followed by the terrorists they were targeting.

Bryant's account of that day is vivid and self-critical: "An idea formed in my head right then that I was going to be the one to kill [Anwar al-Awlaki]. I was going to place the missile on his sorry ass and be a killer of killers. As I picked up the papers from the printer I started to feel wrong about it. By the time I walked back to the computer to shut everything down my mind and body decided to go into full rebellion."[66]

Six months later, news broke of the killing of Osama Bin Laden by SEAL Team Six, lifting the veil from what the Obama administration had chosen to replace "boots on the ground" in America's wars. Special-operations teams, from SEALs to the Army Rangers, would empower the president's choice of who needed to be killed next, and operators like Bryant would seal the deal.

By then, Bryant was out of the military. As he left, the Air Force gave him a certificate noting the total number of people killed by his team over the past three years: 1,676. However, he wasn't ready to violate his top-secret clearance and talk about it, as Manning had so publicly done.

By early 2011, Manning's treatment at Quantico was garnering worldwide attention. Amnesty International called out as torture the months of solitary confinement, including a period when Manning was forced to sleep naked lest she use briefs to strangle herself (not a trivial matter, given her gender dysphoria). A now international support coalition, coordinated by Gulf War resister Jeff Paterson, organized buses to deliver supporters to the gates of Quantico. From one of the protests, the Pentagon Papers' Daniel Ellsberg told reporters that Manning "is me 35 years ago!"[67] Manning's treatment put a sharp spotlight on the way the treatment of whistleblowers had changed since Ellsberg's time.

The Obama administration was unafraid to use the 1917 Espionage Act that had once threatened Ellsberg. Whereas before 2009, a total of five persons had been charged under the act, the ensuing years would feature nearly double that many Espionage Act prosecutions, including the soldier at Quantico.

The Manning trial highlighted the Obama administration's crackdown on national-security whistleblowers. Whereas the Abu Ghraib whistleblowing of Joe Darby and Aidan Delgado had raised questions about the use of classified material, under Obama the number of actual arrests for such acts skyrocketed, a trend that accelerated after the president was re-elected in 2012. In an era of "information warfare," the national-security state claimed this crackdown as a matter of survival. For those hoping to expose military malfeasance, the stakes had rarely been higher.

The "Bradley Manning Support Network" had strengthened since its founding. For her Article 32 hearing, the network hired attorney David Coombs, a reserve lieutenant colonel with twelve years of active-duty and judicial experience. Fort Meade, the famously low-profile base near NSA headquarters, set up its own media center to handle the publicity from the court proceedings.

Fort Meade was broiling hot the first week of June 2013, when hundreds of activists gathered for Manning's sentencing hearing. Senior Airman Heather Linebaugh, a young Air Force vet who said she was there because "Manning gave me a voice," took the mike and began to speak. "I did the same intelligence analysis as Bradley Manning. I saw the horrors of war and the needless killing every day that I served. I saw the lies that we tell people every day," Linebaugh said, her skin glistening from the 95-degree heat.

Linebaugh later described her work at a base in far northern California, a tight space not unlike the Nevada room from which Brandon Bryant had executed drone strikes. She worked in concert with sensor operators like Bryant: "I watched everything live and told the sensor operator (SO) who to bomb. I was also the one who made film clips and sent them to the customer [i.e., the command]. I was the person who needed to give the OK to the SO and pilot." It was a job so stressful, Linebaugh added, that even before her term of service ended, she was being evaluated for post-traumatic stress disorder. "You watch people die every day—including Americans, soldiers you sort of know."

Just as stressful, Linebaugh told the crowd at Fort Meade, were "sloppy strikes" that led to unplanned deaths. "I saw what really happens in war, the unjustified killings. Because officers tell the enlisted, 'That's what you're ordered to do, shut the hell up and do your job.' . . . If we tried to talk about it, if we tried to tell someone else about it, we were told, 'It's okay, collateral damage happens. You just have to accept it.' We treat Manning as a criminal, when she really woke us up to something that happens every day." Linebaugh wrestled with information about which she was forbidden to speak.

Analysts at Linebaugh's base had shared the horrors they had seen, but only to one another. Her senior commanders were "pretty supportive" of her anguish, while others took any sign of distress as an insult to their hard-working, super-smart enlisted personnel. They warned that "if we spoke out about certain missions, definitely to the media, we would 'end up like Bradley Manning.'"

When she asked whether Manning had had the legal option of applying for conscientious-objector status, Linebaugh's sergeant exploded, "We're at war!" Her command warned all analysts in the room not to breathe a word of their concerns outside the bunker walls. That warning resonated throughout the base: "I saw quite a few posters going up, with an image of the typical soldier sitting in a jail cell in handcuffs."

In December 2012, *The Guardian* ran Linebaugh's blockbuster denunciation of the drone program. "I knew the names of some of the young soldiers I saw bleed to death on the side of a road. I watched dozens of military-aged males die in Afghanistan, in empty fields, along riversides, and some right outside the compound where their family was waiting for them to return home from the mosque." Brandon Bryant followed her op-ed with his own dissent, describing his most anguished moments to *Der Spiegel* in an interview entitled, "Did We Kill a Kid?"

Such international attention on the drone war generated pushback from the Obama administration. Former soldier-dissenter John Kerry, now secretary of state, claimed its right to kill from a distance: "Our actions are legal. We were attacked on 9/11. Within a week, the United States Congress overwhelmingly authorized the use of force. . . . Under domestic law and international law, the United States is at war with al Qaeda and the Taliban and their associated forces."[68] If that included the drone war, whistleblowers were also "enemy combatants" of sorts, deprived of the right to explain their actions to the public.

Manning was eventually charged with thirty-five counts, including a viola-tion of the Espionage Act. In the sentencing phase, she was finally allowed to make a statement on behalf of her plea of guilty for ten specific offenses, none of which was espionage. "I believed that if the general public, especially the American public, had access to [this] information . . . this could spark a domestic debate on the role of the military and our foreign policy in general as well as it related to Iraq and Afghanistan." Manning's statement, leaked and posted online, didn't alter Judge Denise Lind's decision to find her guilty of all but the espionage charge.

The day that the verdict was announced, Manning stated publicly that she was female, her chosen name Chelsea Elizabeth Manning. Manning's gender issues had been no secret to anyone looking for them: she had told Adrian Lamo, the hacker who had turned her over to the FBI, that what she feared most about arrest was having her image "as a boy" plastered everywhere. Now, as she prepared to serve her thirty-five-year sentence at Fort Leaven-worth, her lawyers filed requests that she receive hormone therapy and be allowed to serve out her sentence as a woman.

Most military gender dissent had been sanitized after the repeal of Don't Ask, Don't Tell; gay-rights advocates wrapped their cases in martial prose, as did women fighting to secure justice against perpetrators of sexual assault. Neither wing was much interested in Manning, except to wince that their political opponents were already using her case to oppose openly gay service members.

Manning thus brought together almost all the 21st-century threads this book has been watching. She used information-warfare techniques, her back-ups and algorithms, her cutting-edge internet hacks, to expose torture and asymmetric warfare, while Manning herself unfurled the misogyny and rac-ism at militarism's core, between her own gender-dissent and the leaks' expo-sure of U.S. treatment of local allies. Her role would outlast that of many others, as the Forever War became less about specific combat zones and more about making every spot on the globe a potential zone, where soldiers might deploy at a moment's notice.

In mid-2014, billboards began appearing with the face of Daniel Ellsberg, urging others to follow Manning in exposing lethal truths. Thus was launched ExposeFacts.org, founded by Ellsberg and Jesselyn Radack, a former State

Department attorney and a whistleblower herself.[69] Radack, who had suffered retaliation after leaking information about the abusive treatment of John Walker Lindh, the "American Taliban," had just been named one of America's top national-security thinkers by *Foreign Policy* magazine. Radack announced the new group in a press conference held with Ellsberg and two post-9/11 soldier-dissenters: Matthew Hoh spoke of his multiple Iraq and Afghanistan tours, and Colonel Ann Wright, who had served since Vietnam, resigned from the State Department rather than see that war's mistakes repeated. They had founded the new organization, they said, to encourage this class of "@War" soldiers to consider coming forward, and to guarantee that the next Chelsea Manning knew someone had her back. Events on the ground virtually ensured that there would be more.

When Stephen Funk took the stage at Judson Memorial Church, the IVAW gala was almost over, and no one knew what to expect. A few, though, were not surprised when the founder of "Make Drag, Not War" started to take off his clothes.[70]

Judson Memorial Church, built in 1890 as a Baptist enclave in Manhattan, had long been a crucible of social-change activism, supporting 1964's Freedom Summer and the premiere of Daniel Berrigan's play, *The Trial of the Catonsville Nine*, not to mention Andy Warhol's Factory collective, Kate Millett, and Yoko Ono (at one 1968 "happening," Ono's clothes were ripped to shreds in an anti-war gesture). In more recent years, it had often been home to events featuring soldier-dissenters from Howard Zinn to Funk himself, after his release from Camp Lejeune. And now came the tenth-anniversary gala for Iraq Veterans Against the War.

As slender, fit, and muscular as he had been at boot camp a decade before, Funk strutted easily to George Michael's "Freedom." He started peeling off the uniform, ultimately descending beneath the stage. A few measures later, Funk leapt to the stage in a full-length orange jumpsuit reminiscent of Guantanamo. Finally, one pull unlocked the whole costume, and Funk slithered out of it, his glittery G-string matching his nails, proudly dancing to Lady Gaga's "Do What U Want." When the music stopped, Funk turned slowly, revealing his "tattooed" back: I AM CHELSEA MANNING.

By September 2014, President Obama had just announced a new military

campaign against some old adversaries in Iraq. The Sunni militias once subdued by U.S. forces, now arising as the far-more-poisonous Islamic State in
Iraq and Syria (ISIS), had reclaimed many of the regions won most bloodily
in that war. In Operation Inherent Resolve, the Pentagon began to weave its
hundreds of overseas bases into what the *New York Times* called "an ISIS-
Foiling Network,"[71] while announcing a withdrawal agreement with the new
government of Afghanistan, one that would allow ten thousand troops to
remain in that country for up to ten years.[72] Thus, the gala's grimmest joke:
"Looks like we won't have to change [IVAW's] name." The event was dedicated to an IVAW member and Afghanistan vet who had committed suicide
a week earlier.

Before inviting co-founder Funk to the stage, the event highlighted The
Right to Heal, a trauma-awareness campaign run jointly with Iraqi NGOs,
and Project Recovery, now expanded beyond soldiers with PTSD to the full
spectrum of combat trauma (e.g., traumatic brain injury). The event did not
highlight the many other organizations and initiatives created by IVAW
members, whether Funk's Dialogues Against Militarism, co-founded with
Israeli veterans; Garett Reppenhagen's environmental Veterans Green Jobs,
or the Christian-pacifist Centurions Guild, founded by Logan Isaac.[73]

Over the next few years, Isaac, a former surfer who in 2007 had become a
CO mid–Iraq deployment, would publish the memoir *Reborn on the Fourth
of July* and go to divinity school. In his MDiv thesis at Duke University, Isaac
explored "moral injury"; i.e., the trauma induced by harming others.[74]

Originally coined in the 1980s by Dr. Jonathan Shay from his work with
Vietnam veterans, moral injury had taken on new resonance in the new
war, with some veterans hoping to broaden established guidelines for post-
traumatic stress disorder to include it. Following some signal clinical studies
documenting its prevalence, the Veterans Administration agreed and developed its own treatment protocols for moral injury.

What those Vietnam veterans found most wounding was being involved
in the deaths and mutilation of others; the newer vets were unflinching as
they accepted culpability. Brandon Bryant cited his moral injury as he told
journalists, "I mean, I swore an oath, you know? I swore to defend the Constitution against all enemies, foreign and domestic. And how do you feel if
you can't use 'I obeyed orders' as an excuse? It's 'I obeyed the Constitution,

regardless of lawful or unlawful orders.' [But] lawful orders follow the Constitution." Psychology professor Nancy Cooke, science director of the Cognitive Engineering Research Institute in Mesa, Arizona, said that working on drones can produce "cognitive tunneling," wherein deep focus on the work opens personnel up to more pain. Cooke's institute, with its focus on team dynamics, supports the Air Force's effort to ameliorate such stress. But most subsequent drone resisters tended to emphasize the trauma suffered by the countries targeted by the drone war.

As they joined forces with Pakistani villagers and European anti-drone activists, these dissenters challenged the whole premise of the new imperial superstructure: that a relatively few smart people could justly prosecute a war against terrorists continents away. They would continue that challenge for the final years of the Obama administration, even in America's film industry, which suddenly featured movies by soldier-dissenters all over the political spectrum.

The year 2016 bore two documentaries about the drone war. *DRONE* featured a buff and agonized Brandon Bryant. *National Bird* framed Heather Linebaugh's story, along with that of drone pilot Cian Westmoreland; Lisa Ling, whose moral injury from her work creating the system's algorithms led her to work with survivors in Pakistan; and Daniel Hale, who told the camera, "I expect to be arrested."

These were not the first films to contemplate the dilemmas of the drone war. Following the lead of Andrew Niccol's 2014 *Good Kill*, 2016's fictional portrayals included *Eye in the Sky* and *Drone*, all of them portraying drone operators as conflicted, honorable men who nonetheless kill on the commander-in-chief's signal. Michael Bay's *13 Hours in Benghazi* used testimony from Marines who had survived a 2012 terrorist attack in Libya to blame former Secretary of State Hillary Clinton, by then the Democratic nominee for president, for the deaths of their peers.[75] Clinton was already disliked by soldiers and veterans along the political spectrum, who worried about Clinton's role in the Obama administration's "smart" warfare. When Clinton lost that election on November 8, 2016, it meant that the administration's carefully honed tools would be handed over to a new president who explicitly celebrated what some called war crimes.

The Trump administration has intensified the previous administration's strategies, with airstrikes against targets from Syria to Afghanistan and a further intensified crackdown on leakers. Air Force linguist Reality Leigh Winner was one of its first casualties.

Though she never deployed overseas during her six years of active duty in the Air Force—with the 94th Intelligence Squadron, 707th Intelligence, Surveillance and Reconnaissance Wing—Winner's work supported lethal drone operations, often witnessing deaths in real time. Her experience echoes those of Brandon Bryant and Heather Linebaugh: "I think she and I could have been friends, back in the military," said Brandon Bryant. "[At my drone base] we had 'miracle-rooms,' where they were translating short and long wave transmissions. I might have worked with someone like her." Bryant added, "She seems the kind of person the Air Force should treasure: smart and honest."

According to Winner's friends and family, her signs of combat stress were tangible. Matt Boyle, who dated Winner in 2016 as her term of service was ending, said "it was in her demeanor," that the naturally bubbly jock whom he had met at a CrossFit class turned distant and stony. "It was definitely traumatizing. . . . You're watching people die. You have U.S. troops on the ground getting shot at, you miss something, a bomb goes off, and you get three people killed."[76] From Fort Gordon's Center of Cyber Excellence and her home base at Fort Meade, Maryland, Winner helped facilitate drone strikes using her four languages (Arabic, Pashto, and Dari, in addition to English) and her training at the Defense Language Institute in Monterey, California.

When such missions were at a fast clip, Boyle told me, "She would say things like 'After what happened at work this week I'm not ready to step away' or 'You don't understand, I'm on mission tomorrow, I can't make a mistake.' But Reality isn't the type of woman who says she was traumatized and need help. She's the type who would just double up and try harder."[77]

Winner had already decided that she was leaving the military. She told her mother, Billie Winner-Davis, that she wanted to work for a humanitarian organization, serving poor families like the ones she had seen long distance. Something different from what she had done for the Air Force: "producing 2,500 reports, aiding in 650 enemy captures, 600 enemies killed in action and identifying 900 high value targets."[78]

Winner kept in close touch with her biological father, Robert, a Texas psychologist. They shared anxieties about the upcoming election; Robert served as "my confidant, someone who believed in me, my anger, my heartbreak, my life-force. It was always us against the world." They whispered together about that "orange fascist" Donald Trump. Winner also vented on Twitter as "Sara Winner," following both WikiLeaks and Edward Snowden, both anathema to her colleagues at the National Security Agency. On November 9, Sara Winner tweeted, "Well then. People suck. #ElectionDay."

Winner was home in Texas when Robert Winner died, on December 21, 2016. "It was Christmastime and I had to go running to cry to hide it from the family."[79] Adding the invariably traumatic death of a parent to her ongoing combat trauma opened up the potential for what psychologists call "complicated grief," which can distort someone's affect and behavior for years.

After she left the military, Winner moved to Augusta, Georgia, to work for intelligence contractor Pluribus, International. The new job gave her access to a wide range of material, including a memo containing information about Russian attempts to hack U.S. voting machines, efforts since documented in Special Counsel Robert Mueller's lengthy investigation.

Pluribus was among the contractors trusted by the NSA to look at potential evidence in these investigations, though that evidence was not part of Winner's antiterrorism work there. It was, however, the source of the memo on Russian efforts to disrupt voting systems in the U.S. published by *The Intercept* in May 2017.

By then, Winner was familiar with the outlet, founded to report the findings of whistleblowers in the wake of leaks by Army vet and former NSA contractor Edward Snowden; *The Intercept* also often quoted Jesselyn Radack of ExposeFacts.org. Radack had represented Linebaugh and Bryant when they faced federal charges for speaking publicly about the drone program; she reached out to Winner's family in June 2017, after eleven FBI agents surrounded Winner's house, got her to talk about copying that memo and mailing it to *The Intercept*, and arrested her, leading to an indictment under the Espionage Act. "The government has a dozen laws they could have chosen to charge her with, such as 'Mishandling of classified information,'" Radack told me. "But the Espionage Act is just easier."

Brandon Bryant agreed. "They're trying to make an example of her to the other drone vets who might be close to deciding to do something different." Such deterrence was an explicit goal of Attorney General Jeff Sessions' Justice Department, whose prosecutors painted the Dari-speaking Winner as a probable terrorist.

Sessions, whose press reps had decades earlier lambasted the idea of international justice and the then newborn International Criminal Court,[80] was also looking for ways to re-imprison Chelsea Manning, whose sentence had been commuted by President Obama. Justice's habit of reclassifying publicly published information offered a tool to do so.

Manning had stepped rapidly into her new life after release, with a string of media appearances, a book contract, and a documentary-in-progress entitled *XYCHELSEA*. As the documentary would explicate in 2019, it wasn't that easy being the simultaneous heroine of the antimilitarism, transgender rights, and online-rights movements. At one stop, when asked her thoughts about Reality Winner or Edward Snowden, she winced. "Nothing to say about other cases. I can barely talk about my own." In stark contrast to her Fort Meade testimony about seeing her intelligence 'products' used to kill innocent people, Manning offered no details of her work in Iraq.[81]

Similar strictures affected Reality Winner's case as it moved through federal courts; the trial regularly included semi-private sessions open only to attorneys with the proper security clearances. After the court rejected multiple efforts to have her case dismissed because she had not been granted her Miranda rights,[82] the Winner family decided to accept a proposed plea bargain, in which Winner would serve sixty-three months at a medically oriented prison facility not far from her family's home.[83] Winner's sentence was announced on August 23, 2018, also the fifth anniversary of Chelsea Manning's sentencing.

Jeff Paterson's CouragetoResist.org, which had birthed the Manning Support Network, helped build a similar one for Winner. Veterans for Peace was not initially a member; when asked about Winner in January 2018, VFP's Ellen Barfield shrugged, pointing to the United States' well-documented record of election-meddling overseas. But chapter by chapter, dissenting veterans found common cause with Winner. By 2019, VFP was helping organize a national vigil to mark the anniversary of her arrest.

On June 3, 2019, Billie Winner-Davis held a vigil in front of the White

House, bolstered by dissenting-soldier supporters seasoned from the Manning fight. That week, Manning had just re-entered Alexandria Detention Center, a Virginia facility contracted to hold federal prisoners. Her crime was contempt of court, for refusing to talk to a grand jury—one convened to indict Julian Assange, that "certain Aussie" she had admitted leaking to in 2010.[84] On March 11, just as this book was going to press, Manning attempted suicide in prison; a day later, a federal judge ordered Manning's release, but the case against her refusal to testify remains unresolved.

As the decade approached its end, a broader range of voices was claiming the soldier-dissenter space, including two candidates for president. They did so as writers, musicians, and in an explosion of podcasts, a new form born for the tiny entertainment centers most Americans carry as a phone. Individual servicemembers kept the GI Rights Hotline busy, some going all the way to CO: the Center for Conscience and War, nearly one hundred years old, guided hundreds of conscientious objectors to successful discharge in the past decade, with fewer than fifty denials.[85] Others found their way through the work of lawyers and volunteers who had been at it for a half-century, like Kathleen Gilberd, now chair of a Military Law Task Force, or San Francisco's Steve Collier, who on a soldier-dissenter podcast told his former CO client, Rosa Del Duca, the story of Stephen Eagle Funk, the first Iraq War CO.[86] And Garett Reppenhagen, now Veterans for Peace's executive director, joined the climate action "Fire Drill Fridays," getting arrested in D.C. alongside longtime GI ally Jane Fonda.

These soldier-dissenters acted as the Trump administration threatened war with Venezuela and Iran, as well as an unprecedented deployment to the U.S.–Mexico border. Only the organizing of active-duty troops could stop the latter, Margaret Stevens wistfully told me. "If we could get hundreds of troops to do a literal *about-face* . . . ? That would be a sight to see." And Jon Hutto wrote that he had never stopped advocating such organizing, citing his university role model and Fort Hood Three sponsor: "The struggle is eternal."[87]

Mark Twain was right when he wrote that history doesn't repeat itself, but it rhymes. I hope these pages have noticed enough of our past's blank verse to be useful.

ACKNOWLEDGMENTS

THIS BOOK WAS BORN AT Columbia University, in Samuel Freedman's book seminar.

It was born in 1998 at the CCCO office in San Francisco.

It was born when I was eleven years old and had my mind gently blown reading a book by 1967 dissenting soldier Howard Levy.

It was born when, as a college junior, I wrote a play about draft resisters during Vietnam—borrowing its title, *Too Many Martyrs*, from the folk-singer Phil Ochs, just like the title of this book.

I was only six years old when Ochs sang "I Ain't Marchin' Anymore" at the 1968 Democratic Convention, but as a backwash boomer I felt drawn to his era, and identified more with that summer's protesters than you might expect. In sixth grade, I was handed a copy of Howard Levy's book *Going to Jail* because I had exhausted my school's library—that's how I learned that yes, my country had prisoners of conscience. I thought about them as I was writing that 1982 play with the Phil Ochs soundtrack, and twelve years later when I went to work for the Central Committee for Conscientious Objectors, finding in 1995 that part of the job was talking to soldiers who were calling the GI Rights Hotline.

I started saying that "if there's gonna be a revolution, it's going to happen because of anti-war veterans." I meant the ones on my volunteer team at

CCCO, mostly Vietnam veterans, and still hold this truth to be self-evident: fundamental, progressive change has been escorted into American life with such figures, half-ignored even as they're being lionized for other reasons.

After I moved East and became a journalist, I went looking for such figures—especially after September 11, 2001, which had swamped those phone lines I had left behind. And at Columbia University's Graduate School of Journalism, I told Sam Freedman that I wanted to write a book about the Hotline—its unlikely pairing of soldiers who called and the veterans, lawyers, and peace activists who answered. But Freedman challenged me to construct something different: "How about a history of soldiers who dissent?" Such a task took a lot longer, which is why this book has countless godfathers and godmothers.

For godmothers, I first think of Adria Quinones, who's had my back since seventh grade at Hunter High School, and who put in two years of unpaid volunteer time to help me deliver a super-clean manuscript to the other god-mother, Julie Enszer, my amazing editor at The New Press. Adria also helped me ensure the narrative was as intersectional as the reality it chronicles, while Julie gifted us with the term "foundational injustice" for what recovering-Catholic me had kept calling America's "original sins." I can't thank either of you enough for not giving up on this project, or on me. And I cannot forget the book's first editor, Naomi Schneider of the University of California Press, who first fell in love with the book proposal I wrote in Freedman's book semi-nar. Same for my actual mom, Victoria Lombardi, who inspires me every day. None of this would be possible without Sam Stoloff of the Frances Goldin Literary Agency, who sold the book *twice* and never stopped believing in it; or without the skilled fetal neurosurgery of Emily Albarillo, April Rondeau, and the rest of the New Press production team, whose partnership made seamless its actual birth and who recruited the best indexer in the business, the bril-liant Laurie Prendergast.

Sam Freedman is one of the book's top-level godfathers, but the other one is Joseph Solanto: my mom's older brother, who has mentored me for a half-century now, ever since Uncle Joe and Aunt Carol taught me why the Vietnam War was a bad idea. Joe, a middle-school principal who was inter-viewed by Sam Freedman long before I entered Columbia, has supported my journalism in multiple ways. A quiet "thanks" wave to Sam Diener, my companero at the Central Committee for Conscientious Objectors in the 1990s. The next level of godfathers/mothers includes far more names than I can fit here, but has to include Steve Morse, whose Vietnam-era GI organizing inspired the book's creation: I called him in December 2005 and told him "I'm writing a book about you!" Steve is now on the long honor roll of outtakes, with narratives that had to be cut as Julie and I made the book more focused and manageable. The godparent-list includes those who taught me, in two separate graduate-school programs, how to craft the hardest form in existence, narrative nonfiction. Thank you, Dale Maharidge, Fred Tuten, and Linsey Abrams for the craft lessons that made it all conceivable. A special thanks to the great Adam Hochschild, who at the 2006 Power of Narrative conference coached me on creating vivid historical characters, then telling me about his own days as a Vietnam-era dissenting reservist. Boundless gratitude to any of my classmates, from Hunter High through grad school, who put up with me; your voice whispers behind these pages.

I need to thank the many veterans who let me keep asking questions, sometimes over years, and organizations that let me embed with them: Veterans for Peace, About Face/Iraq Veterans Against War, and the support networks for Chelsea Manning and Reality Winner. Jonathan Welsey Hutto, who gave me this book's final invocation from Kwame Ture, also worked hard to help me recover from some unforced errors.

A book like this depends on libraries, of course, and I'm grateful for my visits to University of California's Bancroft Library; the Library of Congress' Manuscript Division; the Hoover Institution (where I first learned about the 1919 Polar Bears); the Massachusetts Historical Society; the Margaret Herrick Library in Beverly Hills, whose 1930 telegram from Howard Hughes to Lewis Milestone has been one of my touchstones; the Schomburg Center, which opened my eyes about Bayard Rustin's Committee Against Jim Crow in the Armed Services; and of course the Swarthmore Peace Collection, which had to put up with my less-than-dexterous fingers on some fragile archives.

I am also ceaselessly grateful for some broad financial support, starting with the Lynton Fellowship at Columbia and ending with the 125 members of my 2013 Kickstarter campaign, especially major donors Code Pink,

CouragetoResist.org, and Women'sVoicesForChange.org. In between, I received grants from the International Peace Research Association and the Northern Manhattan Arts Association—many thanks.

Last but emphatically not least: Rachel McGregor Rawlings, your brilliant partnership has been crucial to this book and my life. I can't imagine either without the girl I fell in love with on International Women's Day, nearly a quarter-century ago.

NOTES

Chapter One: 1754 to 1803

1. George Washington Papers, Series 3, Varick Transcripts, 1775–1785, Subseries 3A, Continental Congress, 1775–1783, Letterbook 3: Sept. 1, 1777–Aug. 31, 1778, https://www.loc.gov/item/90898036/.

2. Jacob Ritter and Joseph Fouke, *Memoirs of Jacob Ritter: A Faithful Minister in the Society of Friends* (Philadelphia: T.E. Chapman, 1844).

3. Ritter and Fouke, *Memoirs.*

4. Sarah Vowell, *Lafayette and These United States* (New York: Riverhead Books, 2015), 102.

5. James H. Kettner, "The Development of American Citizenship in the Revolutionary Era: The Idea of Volitional Allegiance," *American Journal of Legal History* 18, no. 3 (July 1974), 208–42.

6. Eric Slaughter, "Reading and Radicalization: Print, Politics and the American Revolution," *Early American Studies* 8, no. 1 (Winter 2010), 5–40.

7. James Madison, *The Debates in the Several State Conventions on the Adoption of the Federal Constitution, as Recommended by the General Convention at Philadelphia, in 1787* (New York: Burt Franklin, 1888), 379; *The Political Thought of Benjamin Franklin*, ed. Ralph Ketchum (Indianapolis: Hackett Publishing, 2003), 398.

8. One "most Horrible Mutiny," staged in 1763 by Massachusetts militiamen dispatched to Quebec, may have been little more than a genteel event of committees

presenting petitions. One private wrote in his diary of "Confusion," by which he meant argument and refusal, not violence: "And so now our time has come to an end according to enlistment, but we are not yet got home nor are like to. . . . The Regiment was ordered out for to hear what the Coll. had to say to them as our time was out and we all swore that we would do no more duty here so it was a day of much Confusion with the Regiment."

9. "[Our] Army was a proper Organiz'd Body and that they by the Several Governments from whom these Troops were rais'd were Executors in Trust which was not in their power to resign, and, even should they do it, it would End in a DISSOLUTION OF THE ARMY . . ." Quoted by Major General Winslow to Major General John Shirley, via Fred Anderson, "Why Did Colonial New Englanders Make Bad Soldiers? Contractual Principles and Military Conduct during the Seven Year's War," *William and Mary Quarterly, 3rd Ser.* 38, no. 3 (1981), 395–417. Anderson lists in an appendix no fewer than thirty such polite mutinies among the Massachusetts militiamen.

10. Letter to Armistead Mason, July 6, 1817, via James Fairfax McLaughlin, *Matthew Lyon, the Hampden of Congress* (Wynkoop Hallenbeck Crawford, 1900), 409.

11. McLaughlin, *Matthew Lyon*, 26.

12. McLaughlin, *Matthew Lyon*.

13. J. Kevin Graffanigno, "The Country My Soul Delighted In: The Onion River Land Company and the Vermont Frontier," *New England Quarterly* 65, no. 1 (Mar. 1992), 24–60.

14. "The soldiers considered themselves sacrificed to the merest of those persons who bought the crops for a trifle, and wanted to get our party there to eat them at the public expense."

15. *Pennsylvania Packet*, April 1779.

16. Joseph Plumb Martin, *Narrative of a Revolutionary War Soldier* (Dover Editions), 24.

17. John B.B. Trussell, Jr., *The Pennsylvania Line: Regimental Organization and Operations, 1775–1783* (Pennsylvania Historical and Museum Commission, 1977), 252.

18. Charles Patrick Neimeyer, "No Meat, No Soldier: Race, Class, and Ethnicity in the Continental Army," Ph.D. dissertation, Georgetown University, 1993. Much of my initial exploration on this topic was spurred by this exhaustive work by Neimeyer, who later turned this research into the iconic *America Goes to War: A Social History of the Continental Army.*

19. J. Reuben Sheeler, "The Negro on the Virginia Frontier," *Journal of Negro History* 43, no. 4 (Oct. 1958), 279–97.

20. Sidney Kaplan, "A Negro Veteran in Shays' Rebellion," *Journal of Negro History* 33, no. 2 (Apr. 1948), 123–29.

21. Trussell, *Pennsylvania Line*, 248.

22. Trussell, *Pennsylvania Line*.

23. If you do not want to dig through scholarly databases to learn more about these women, a good start would be Tracy Crow and Jerri Bell, *It's My Country Too: Women's Military Stories from the American Revolution to Afghanistan* (University of Nebraska Press, 2017).

24. Those cross-dressing women have since been claimed by some champions of gays in the military, though evidence of any "Boston marriages" (cohabiting women, presumed lesbian) among them is sparse. Popular LGBTQIA history items, such as "Gays in the Military Calendars," often also include Baron von Steuben, the Hessian general who trained Washington's troops, and the homoerotic stylings of the romantically omnivorous Alexander Hamilton. With evidence of active homosexuality so hard to find, it would take nearly two centuries for anyone in their position to even consider their right to be included in the Declaration's assertion of self-evident equality.

25. C.O. Parmenter, *History of Pelham, Massachusetts* (Amherst, MA: 1898), 391, via Mary Ann Nicholson and Elmer Smails, *The Family of Daniel Shays* (New England Historic Genealogical Society, 1987).

26. Maurer Maurer, "Military Justice Under General Washington," *Military Affairs* 1 (Spring 1964), 8–16, http://links.jstor.org/sici?sici=0026-3931%28196421 %2928%3A1%3C8%3AMJUGW%3E2.0.CO%3B2-3.

27. "A Narrative of the Conduct and Sufferings of Some Friends in Virginia, 1760," in Peter Brock, ed., *Liberty and Conscience: A Documentary History of the Experiences of Conscientious Objectors in America through the Civil War* (Oxford: Oxford University Press, 2000), 28.

28. Ritter and Fouke, *Memoirs*, 48.

29. Joseph Fanning Watson, *Annals of Philadelphia and Pennsylvania in the Olden Time* (Parry & McMillan, 1855), 300.

30. As early as 1763, colonists had chafed at British-agreed restrictions from crossing the Allegheny Mountains, defied by surveyor George Washington; the first act of the new Congress was the Northwest Ordinance opening up the assault on native lands west of the Alleghenies. Roxanne Dunbar-Ortiz in *Indigenous Peoples' History of the United States* and Gerald Horne in *The Apocalypse of Settler Colonialism* develop this at great length.

31. Stephen Butz, *The Shays Settlement: A Story of History and Archaeology* (History Press, 2015).

32. Unless otherwise cited, my narration of the mutiny hews closely to Carl Van Doren's *Mutiny in January* (Viking, 1943).

33. *Pennsylvania Packet.*

34. Land as currency was one of the enticing features of this new country, a bargaining chip used often. Few asked what had happened to the land's previous inhabitants.

35. Letter to Col. Frederick Bland, April 4, 1783.

36. Robert Gross, "A Yankee Rebellion? The Regulators, New England, and the New Nation," *The New England Quarterly* 82, no. 1 (Mar. 2009), 112–35.

37. There's little evidence that the "White Indians" made active allies of Native people, let alone discussed citizenship with them.

38. That earlier rebellion in North Carolina was sparked by a Quaker named Husband, who had urged his peers to "rouse all our Powers to act like free publick spirited Men" at the ballot box. The earlier group, known as "the Farmers," confronted local officials with their guns until the British Army subdued them. The name "Regulators," originating during the republican era two hundred years earlier, was meant to imply order in rebellion, a countervailing force against corrupt rule.

39. Gross, above, writes: "Concord, Massachusetts, enlisted one company of 64 volunteers under Captain Roger Brown to 'suppress the insurgency.' I was able to find the age of two-thirds of these men (43 out of 64). Their median age was twenty-two. Of the 40 men whose marital status could be determined, 85 percent were single. Six out of 10 were from Concord and adjoining towns; only a quarter stayed in Concord until they died. Few came from families long established on the land."

40. Shays recounted: "1. all men who are in favour of paper money & tender laws; those are more or less in every part of the State. 2. all the late insurgents & their abettors. In the three great western Counties [the insurgents] are very numerous. We have in the convention eighteen or twenty who were actually in Shay's army." To George Washington from James Madison, 3 February 1788." *Founders Online*, National Archives, last modified June 29, 2017, http://founders.archives.gov/documents /Washington/04-06-02-0069. [Original source: *The Papers of George Washington*, Confederation Series, vol. 6, *1 January 1788–23 September 1788*, ed. W.W. Abbot (Charlottesville: University Press of Virginia, 1997), 82–3.]

41. John Noble, *A few notes on the Shays Rebellion* (C. Hamilton Press, 1903), 35.

42. A. Gwynn Henderson and David Pollock: "[The village] served as an international native diplomatic center, a regional diplomatic center with Europeans, and a

trading center at the western end of the Pennsylvania traders' southern trade route. The lower Shawnee Town was at least twice as big as its predecessors and larger than most contemporary Indian settlements on Ohio. An array of nations, divisions, factions, and bands lived there, its inhabitants a mixture of indigenous peoples, Europeans, Africans, and the offspring of their unions. By January 1751, this multi-ethnic population is estimated to have been somewhere between twelve hundred and fifteen hundred people." Given this diversity, it is not surprising that the French characterized it as a "republic."

43. Daniel P. Barr, "A Monster So Brutal: Simon Girty and the Degenerative Myth of the American Frontier, 1783–1900," *Essays in History*, 40 (1998). Accessed at http://etext.virginia.edu/journals/EH/EH40/barr40.html#n2.3, first on 10/1/2007.

44. Consul Wilshire Butterfield, ed., *Washington-Crawford Letters* (Robert Clarke & Co., 1877), 66, via Consul Wilshire Butterfield, ed., *Washington-Irvine Correspondence* (Madison, WI: D. Atwood, 1882), 15–16.

45. Barr, "A Monster So Brutal."

Chapter Two: 1803 to 1844

1. William Apess, *A Son of the Forest: The Experience of William Apess, a Native of the Forest: Comprising a Notice of the Pequod Tribe of Indians* (self-published, 1829), accessed via GaleNet 2007.

2. John Underhill, *Nevves from America; or, A New and Experimentall Discoverie of New England: Containing, a True Relation of their War-like Proceedings these two year's last past, with a figure of the Indian fort, or Palizado* (London: I. D[awson] for Peter Cole, 1638), 84.

3. Apess, *Son of the Forest*, 93.

4. C. Edward Skeen, *Citizen Soldiers in the War of 1812* (University of Kentucky Press), 81.

5. Apess, *Son of the Forest*, 57.

6. Letter to William Duane, August 4, 1812, National Archives, accessed at https://founders.archives.gov/documents/Jefferson/03-05-02-.

7. Skeen, *Citizen Soldiers*, 81.

8. *Niles Weekly Register*, June 7, 1813.

9. Skeen, *Citizen Soldiers*, 10.

10. Skeen, *Citizen Soldiers*, 10.

11. Apess, *Son of the Forest*, 99.

12. John Wayles Eppes to Francis Eppes, September 30, 1814.

13. Robert Remini, *The Life of Andrew Jackson* (HarperPerennial, 2011), 33.

14. Remini, 55.

15. Quote via Amos Kendall, in Sean Michael O'Brien, *In Bitterness and Tears: Andrew Jackson's Destruction of the Creeks and the Seminoles* (Westport: Praeger/Greenwood, 2003), 86.

16. Skeen, *Citizen Soldiers*, 80.

17. Daniel Webster, House of Representatives, December 9, 1814.

18. Henry Ware and Samuel Worcester, *Memoirs of Noah Worcester* (James Monroe & Co., 1844).

19. Ware and Worcester, *Memoirs*.

20. William Apess, "An Indian's Looking-Glass for the White Man" (1833), via Barry O'Connell, ed., *On Our Own Ground: The Complete Writings of William Apess, a Pequot* (Amherst: University of Massachusetts Press, 1992)

21. Carl Edward Skeen, *Citizen Soldiers of the War of 1812* (University of Kentucky Press, 1999), 33.

22. Ethan Allen Hitchcock, *Fifty years in camp and field* (Putnam, 1909).

23. Stephen E. Ambrose, Andrew J. Goodpaster (Afterword), Dwight D. Eisenhower, *Duty, Honor, Country: A History of West Point* (Johns Hopkins University Press, 1999), 78.

24. Thayer to Armistad, November 30, 1818, via Ambrose et al., *Duty, Honor, Country*.

25. Wilson Fairfax to Nicholas Trist, December 18, 1818.

26. R. Ernest du Puy, "Mutiny at West Point," *American Heritage* 12, no. 1 (Nov. 1955), 22–27.

27. Poe came close to making it into this book; the best resource about his time in the military is William F. Hecker's *Private Perry and Mr. Poe: The West Point Poems, 1831* (Louisiana State University Press, 2009).

28. David Crockett to Charles Schulz, December 25, 1834, via the Gilder-Lehmann Institute of American History.

29. By a non-citizen, however.

30. Kim McQuaid, "William Apess, Pequot: An Indian Reformer in the Jackson Era," *New England Quarterly* 50, no. 4 (1977), 605–25.

31. The Black Panthers, 150 years later, could have borrowed that sentence intact.

32. Alexis de Tocqueville, *Democracy in America* (Modern Library, 2004), 391.

33. Letter to Henry Benson, March 3, 1833. That old soldier was William Ladd, a New York minister whose own regional group actually pre-dated Worcester's.

34. William Garrison, "A Noble Example," in *Genius of Universal Emancipation* (Baltimore, 1829), via Peter Brock, *Liberty and Conscience: A Documentary History of Conscientious Objectors through the Civil War* (Stanford University Press, 2002).

Chapter Three: 1845 to 1861

1. Rev. Ilsley, "An Affecting Scene," *Advocate of Peace and Universal Brotherhood*, January 1846, 66.

2. To John Farmer, June 6, 1837.

3. To John Farmer, June 6, 1837.

4. Charles Sumner, "The True Grandeur of Nations," July 4, 1845.

5. Rev. Ilsley, "An Affecting Scene," *Advocate of Peace and Universal Brotherhood*, January 1846, 66.

6. The term "Slave Power," used as early as the 1780s, had arisen more recently during the 1839 birth pangs of the Republican Party, in which Rep. Thomas Morris said, "Slave power is seeking to establish itself in every State, in defiance of the constitution and laws of the States within which it is prohibited In order to secure its power beyond the reach of the States." Speech in Reply to Speech of Henry Clay, February 9, 1839.

7. During his long post-presidential career as a congressman, Adams favored the term "slavocracy" as he ranted against the planters who controlled the House and Senate.

8. Marian H. Studley, "An 'August First' in 1844," *New England Quarterly* 16, no. 4 (December 1943), 567–77.

9. Henry David Thoreau, "On Civil Disobedience."

10. Frederick Douglass, "Slavery and America's Bastard Republicanism: An Address Delivered in Limerick, Ireland, on 10 November 1845," *The Frederick Douglass Speeches, 1841–1846*.

11. By contrast, Hitchcock's friend Stephen Austin, a fellow graduate of New England prep schools, had acquired his initial piece of Mexico the way Ethan Allen might have done—by buying it.

12. Houston had, ironically, both participated in Indian removal and, as an adopted member of the Cherokee Nation, testified to Congress against Texas speculators seizing Cherokee land; his newer role in creating Texas statehood bore the same chameleonic quality.

13. Ephraim Kirby Smith, *To Mexico with Scott: The Letters of Captain E. Kirby Smith to His Wife* (Harvard University Press, 1917).

14. Albert Lombard, *The High Private, with a Full And Exciting History of the New*

York Volunteers (1848). Lombard's history, which is short on details of the actual war, does have a whole chapter titled "INSUBORDINATION."

15. A successive First New York deployment a year later would proceed to San Francisco, taking part in the conquest of California. See Francis D. Clark, *The first regiment of New York volunteers, commanded by Col. Jonathan D. Stevenson, in the Mexican war. Names of the members of the regiment during its term of service in Upper and Lower California, 1847–1848, with a record of all known survivors on the 15th day of April 1882, and those known to have deceased, with other matters of interest pertaining to the organization and service of the regiment* (Published by GeoSea's Co.,1882, accessed via Project Gutenberg).

16. John Campbell to Alice Campbell, October 21, 1847, American Civil War Letters, Special Collections, University of Virginia, Charlottesville, VA.

17. Rosemary King, "Border Crossings in the Mexican-American War," *Bilingual Review* 25 (2000), 1, via Robert Fantina, *Desertion and the American Soldier* (Algora, 2006), 45.

18. Daniel Harvey Hill, *A Fighter from Way Back: The Mexican War Diary of Lt. Daniel Harvey Hill, 4th Artillery, USA* (University of Texas Press, 2002), 2.

19. Editorial, "The War with Mexico," *North Star* (Rochester, New York), January 21, 1848.

20. Kirby Smith, *To Mexico with Scott.*

21. Nicholas Trist to Virginia Randolph Trist.

22. Amy Greenberg, *A Wicked War: Polk, Clay, Lincoln, and the 1846 U.S. Invasion of Mexico* (Random House, 2012), 213.

23. Wallace Ohrt, *Defiant Peacemaker: Nicholas Trist in the Mexican War* (University of Texas Press, 1998).

24. Ohrt, *Defiant Peacemaker.*

25. Via Glenn W. Thrush, *Origins of the War with Mexico: The Polk-Stockton Intrigue* (University of Texas Press, 2014).

26. "We are in a strange situation—a conquering army on a hill overlooking an enemy's Capital, which is perfectly at our mercy, yet not permitted to enter it, and compelled to submit to all manner of insults from its corrupt inhabitants."

27. Ethan Allen Hitchcock, *Fifty Years in Camp and Field* (Putnam, 1909). "They knew that he had disapproved of the motives of the administration which began it and yet had been actively present in the battles which effected the conquest of the invaded country."

28. Angelina Grimke Weld, 1851, via John Demos, "The Anti-Slavery Movement and the Problem of Violence," *New England Quarterly* 37, no. 4 (December 1964), 501–26.

29. Hannah N. Geffert, "John Brown and His Black Allies: An Ignored Alliance," *Pennsylvania Magazine of History and Biography* 126, no. 4 (2002), 591–610

30. Frederick Douglass, *Life and Times of Frederick Douglass* (GC Wolfe, 1892), 337–42, via W.E.B. Du Bois, *John Brown* (Random House, 2010), 178.

31. Mary Ellen Snodgrass, *Civil Disobedience: An Encyclopedic History of Dissidence in the United States* (Routledge, 2013), 97.

32. "I recall well when Brown came to our cabin one night with thirteen slaves, men, women and children. He had run them away from Missouri. Brown left them with us. Father would always take in all the Negroes he could. Silas took the whole thirteen from our home eight miles to Mr. Grover's stone barn." Via "She Looks Back Seventy-five Years to the Founding of Lawrence," *Kansas City Star*, January 13, 1929, section C.

33. *Atlantic Monthly*, "Three Interviews with Old John Brown," 44: 266 (December 1879), 738–44.

34. *The Liberator*, March 20, 1857.

35. Via Roy Morris, *Ambrose Bierce: Alone in Bad Company* (Oxford University Press, 1998).

Chapter Four: 1859 to 1880

1. William Schouler, *A history of Massachusetts in the Civil War: Volume 1* (E.P. Dutton, 1868), 51.

2. James Beale, "A Famous War Song," *The Magazine of History with Notes and Queries* 12 (July–December 1910), 71–2)

3. Via Ta-Nehisi Coates in *The Atlantic*, Roger L. Ransom, "The Economics of the Civil War," EH.Net Encyclopedia, edited by Robert Whaples, August 24, 2001, http://eh.net/encyclopedia/the-economics-of-the-civil-war.

4. James MacPherson, *For Cause and Comrades: Why Men Fought in the Civil War* (Oxford University Press, 1997).

5. Roy Morris, *Ambrose Bierce: Alone in Bad Company* (Oxford University Press, 1999), 21.

6. "Prattle," *San Francisco Examiner*, May 1890.

7. Hitchcock had already lost his chance at a post in Hawaii or China due to the enmity of Secretary of War Jefferson Davis (another ex–West Point student).

8. Ambrose Bierce, "What I Saw of Shiloh," in *Tales of Soldiers and Civilians* (Putnam, 1898).

9. Via *Drum Beats: Walt Whitman's Civil War Boy Lovers*, Charley Shively, ed. (Gay Sunshine Press, 1989), 187–88.

10. "Here we have a splendid chance to study human nature, for we have all kinds of men in the Reg." . . .

11. The official records of the above Union and Confederate Armies, via the Web.

12. Bierce, "What I Saw of Shiloh."

13. Robertson's father, Judge William B. Robertson, published his son's letter in the local newspaper, *Sugar Planter*.

14. *The Autobiography of Jesse Macy* (Springfield, IL: C.C. Thomas, 1932), 36.

15. The Non-Resistance Society had actually closed its doors in 1849, and while Garrison kept writing about his own pacifism (including in his Brown elegy), most of his energies since then had been focused on resisting the Slave Power.

16. *The War of the Rebellion: A Compilation of the Official Records of the Union and Confederate Armies*, Series III, Volume III, page 14.

17. Charles Francis Adams, "An Address at the Opening of the Fenway Building of the Massachusetts Historical Society, April 13, 1899," *Historians and Historical Societies* 7 (Issues 1–10), 152.

18. S.E. Edmonds, *Nurse and Spy in the Union Army: Comprising the Adventures and Experiences of a Woman in Hospitals, Camps and Battle-Fields* (MS Williams, 1864).

19. CMSR for Mrs. S.M. Blaylock, Twenty-sixth North Carolina Infantry, War Department Collection of Confederate Records, RG 109, NA.

20. Kate Clifford Larson, *Bound for the Promised Land: Harriet Tubman, an American Hero* (Ballantine, 2009).

21. Reprinted in William McFeely, *Frederick Douglass* (W.W. Norton, 2017), 225.

22. That wish was far from universally shared. Ambrose Bierce, despite his firm abolitionism, turned down a commission with the 13th U.S. Colored Troops (USCT) because he feared "the darkies would not fight"—a decision he later regretted after watching the Black soldiers of the 13th slash their way through rebel defenses: "Better fighting was never done." In March 1864, the 10th Michigan Infantry refused to march behind the 1st Michigan Colored Infantry's band, and entire brigades refused to fight alongside "colored" troops. And some of the white officers commanding some USCT units chose to act like overseers—especially Col. August Benedict, the famously cruel officer who sparked a mutiny in December among Black sailors in the 4th Regiment Corps d'Afrique at Fort Jackson, near New Orleans.

23. *The Commonwealth*, Boston, 1, no. 45, July 10, 1863.

24. Diary 1864, via Jean McMahon Humez, *Harriet Tubman: The Life and the Life Stories* (University of Wisconsin Press, 2003), 63.

NOTES   265

25. Wilbert H. Luck, *Journey to Honey Hill* (Washington, D.C.: Wiluk Press, 1976).

26. Letter to *The Christian Recorder* from an anonymous 55th Sergeant, April 1864.

27. Pringle wrote in his inevitable memoir that "I wept, not so much from my own suffering as from sorrow that such things should be in our own country, where Justice and Freedom and Liberty of Conscience have been the annual boast of Fourth-of-July orators so many years."

28. *The Autobiography of Jesse Macy.*

29. Robert Fantina, *Desertion and the American Soldier* (Algora Publishing, 2007), 65.

30. Peter Levine, "Draft Evasion in the North during the Civil War, 1863–1865," *The Journal of American History* 67, no. 4 (Mar. 1981), 816–34.

31. Ivar Bernstein, *The New York City Draft Riots: Their Significance for American Society and Politics in the Age of the Civil War* (Oxford University Press, 1991).

32. "Letter to General Patton," *Clearfield Republican*, January 1863, via Robert F. Sandow, "Deserter Country: Civil War Opposition in the Mountains of Pennsylvania," Ph.D. dissertation, University of Michigan, 2003.

33. "—& I am half disposed to predict that after the war closes, we shall see bevies of star-straps, two or three of our own Major Generals, shot for treachery, & fully deserve their fate." Letter of April 27, 1864, endorsed by Whitman "for J P Kirkwood | 44 Union Square | New York City."

34. Reprinted in Warren Getler and Bob Brewer, *Shadow of the Sentinel: One Man's Quest to Find the Hidden Treasure of the Confederacy* (Simon and Schuster, 2003): "To interfere with the draft; encourage desertion; provide intelligence; smuggle supplies; assassinate US military and state government officials; and eventually generate fear about a general uprising."

35. United States War Department et al., *The War of the Rebellion: A compilation of the official records of the Union and Confederate Armies* (USG Printing Office, 1902).

36. Via Ella Lonn, *Disloyalty in the Confederacy* (UNC Press, 1934).

37. Lonn, *Disloyalty.*

38. Frederic Bancroft and William A. Dunning, "The Reminiscences of Carl Schurz, Vol. Three: With a Sketch of His Life and Public Services from 1863–1869" (New York: Doubleday, 1906), 69.

39. Mark Weitz, *More Damning than Slaughter; Desertion in the Confederate Army* (University of Nebraska Press, 2005), 112.

40. Eric Dean, *Shook Over Hell: Post-Traumatic Stress, Vietnam, and the Civil War* (Harvard University Press, 1997), 96.

41. Donald Lee Anderson and Godfrey Tryggve Anderson, "Nostalgia and Malingering in the Military during the Civil War," *Perspectives in Biology and Medicine* 28 (1984), 156–66.

42. Letter to Louisa Whitman, April 19, 1864, in Walt Whitman, *The Wound Dresser: A Series of Letters Written from the Hospitals in Washington During the War of the Rebellion* (1898).

43. Grant to Sherman, April 4, 1864, Library of Congress.

44. To demonstrate one day in Kentucky that those words did not represent cowardice, "I took the opportunity to march the entire length of the line bolt upright with vital organs exposed to the enemy's bullets." Foolish and dangerous, Macy acknowledged, but "it did tend to convince the men at the time that I was not a coward."

45. Macy, *The Autobiography of Jesse Macy*, 97.

46. Via Edwin Legrand Sabin, *Carson Days (1809–1868)* (New York: A. C. McClure & Co., 1914), 414.

47. Soule survived only until April 1865, when he was shot dead by a fellow Colorado veteran allied with the disgraced Chivington.

48. "The Battle of Honey Hill: A Federal Account of the Battle," *Philadelphia Weekly Tribune*, May 1864.

49. Phone interview with Prof. Ritchie Garrison, August 4, 2014.

50. On July 14, 1887. Also see *New York Times*, "THE COLOR LINE IN THE G.A.R.," December 2, 1891.

51. When efforts were made to address this in 1892, with the organization's head, John Palmer, the Louisiana branch dissolved its own charter rather than obey orders "that the colored posts in the Department of Louisiana shall be recognized by the posts composed of their white comrades."

52. Lewis Douglass to John McElroy, Library of Congress.

Chapter Five: 1880 to 1902

1. From catalog records of *The New National Era*, 1871–1877, Library of Congress.

2. *Cleveland Gazette*, May 13, 1898. Sourced via Catherine Reef, *African Americans in the Military* (New York: Facts on File, 2010).

3. "Lewis H. Douglass on Black Opposition to McKinley." First printed in

American Citizen (Kansas City), November 17, 1899. Reprinted in Foner, ed., *The Spanish–Cuban–American War and the Birth of American Imperialism*, vol. 2, 824–25.

4. Drew Faust, *The Republic of Suffering: Death and the American Civil War* (Vintage, 2008).

5. "Boston Honors Col. Shaw," *New York Times*, June 1, 1897.

6. Don Rickey, Jr., "The Enlisted Men of the Indian Wars," *Military Affairs* 23, no. 2 (summer 1959), 91–96.

7. Rickey, "Enlisted Men," 40.

8. Rickey, "Enlisted Men," 40.

9. Via Sherry L. Smith, *View from Officers' Row: Army Perceptions of Western Indians* (University of Arizona Press, 1991), 139.

10. William A. Dobak and Thomas D. Phillips, *The Black Regulars, 1866–1898* (University of Oklahoma Press, 2001), 85.

11. Smith, *The View from Officers' Row*, 103.

12. That general, William Hazen, arrived without his trusted Ambrose Bierce, the latter having refused the appointment when the transfer did not include a captaincy for him.

13. Including toward fellow literati: witness his page-long skewering of the visiting Oscar Wilde: "The ineffable dunce has nothing to say and says it—says it with a liberal embellishment of bad delivery, embroidering it with reasonless vulgarities of attitude, gesture and attire."

14. Edith Abbott, "The Civil War and the Crime Wave of 1865–70," *Social Service Review* 1, no. 2 (Jun. 1927), 212–34.

15. Franklin D. Jones, "Psychiatric Lessons of War," in F.D. Jones, L.R. Sparacino, V.L. Wilcox, and J.M. Rothberg, eds., *Textbook of Military Medicine* (Washington, DC: Borden Institute, 1995).

16. Among the many scholars who have charted the territory of Bierce's trauma, see Sharon Talley, *Ambrose Bierce's Dance of Death* (University of Tennessee Press, 2007).

17. Ambrose *Bierce*, "Prattle," *San Francisco Examiner, March 26, 1893*, 6. 17.

18. "FROM CUBA: Troublesome Negroes—Some Difficulties for the Future—News from the Seat of War," *New York Times*, March 23, 1872.

19. "SPANIARDS WITH REBELS: The Cuban War Is Being Waged with Desperation," *New York Times*, October 19, 1895.

20. Usefully summarized in John Byrne Cook, *Reporting the War: Freedom of the*

Press from the American Revolution to the War on Terrorism (New York: Macmillan, 2007).

21. Roy Morris, *Ambrose Bierce: Alone in Bad Company* (Oxford: Oxford University Press, 1998), 230.

22. Letter from Washington, May 13, 1899. Eli Lundy Huggins Collection, Bancroft Library.

23. Letter to Edward Holden, March 20, 1898. Quoted in Robert Hamburger, *Two Rooms: A Life of Erskine Scott Wood* (University of Nebraska Press, 2007), 118.

24. Record, 56 Cong., I Sess., 704–12, via https://www.mtholyoke.edu/acad/intrel /ajb72.htm.

25. Willard Gatewood, *Black Americans and the White Man's Burden, 1898–1903* (University of Illinois Press, 1975), 22–23.

26. "NEGROES SHOT LIKE DOGS: Many Wounded and Killed by New-Orleans Mobs," *New York Times*, March 10, 1895.

27. *Cleveland Gazette*, May 13, 1898. Sourced via Catherine Reef, *African Americans in the Military* (New York: Facts on File, 2010).

28. Lawrence Berkove, ed., *Skepticism and Dissent, Selected Journalism, 1898–1901, by Ambrose Bierce* (Ann Arbor: UMI Research Press, 1981).

29. "The Future Historian," 1902.

30. *Examiner*, July 31, 1898.

31. Sequence compiled in S.T. Joshi and David E. Schultz, eds., *A Sole Survivor: Bits of Autobiography by Ambrose Bierce* (University of Tennessee Press, 1999).

32. President McKinley had been blunt in his demands: "The cessation must be the whole archipelago or none. The latter is wholly inadmissible, and the former must therefore be required."

33. Leon Wolff, *Little Brown Brother: How the United States Purchased and Pacified the Philippine Islands at the Century's Turn* (History Book Club, 2005), 154–55.

34. Clay MacCauley, *A Day in Manila, the Noble City.*

35. Marion Wilcox, "The Filipinos' Vain Hope of Independence," *North American Review* 171, no. 526 (Sep. 1900), 333–47.

36. Clay MacCauley, *A Straightforward Tale.*

37. William Rhine Lander Stewart, ed., *The philanthropic work of Josephine Shaw Lowell: containing a biographical sketch of her life, together with a selection of her public papers and private letters, collected and arranged for publication* (New York: Macmillan, 1911), 477–8.

38. These also included the eminent Jane Addams and Mary Storer Mitchell.

39. Joan Waugh, *Unsentimental Reformer: The Life of Josephine Shaw Lowell* (Harvard University Press, 2010), 217. The WCTU had not yet derived its single-minded focus on the banning of alcohol.

40. Many thanks to journalist (and Marine) Carl Prine for help navigating the mass of scholarship on this tendency in military reporting and doctrines, including Douglas Porch's "No Bad Stories," *Naval War College Review* 55, no. 1 (Winter 2002), and Thomas Ricks' "The Nineteenth-Century Origins of Counterinsurgency Doctrine," *Journal of Strategic Studies* 33, no. 5 (2010), 727–58.

41. *San Francisco Call*, July 15, 1899. *Chronicling America: Historic American Newspapers*, Library of Congress, http://chroniclingamerica.loc.gov/lccn/sn85066387 /1899-07-15/ed-1/seq-1/.

42. *The Advocate of Peace*, CXI; *New York Times*, October 19, 1899.

43. "Chicago's Peace Jubilee," *New York Times*, October 17, 1899.

44. On that first day, Rabbi Emil Hirsch swooned: "We are proud that when War was declared, the nation was in the hands of a true American, one who loved peace." (Hirsch added that McKinley was "a worshipper of the Prince of Peace," perhaps the least Jewish statement made by anyone in the room.)

45. "THE JUBILEE PARADE: The President Reviews a Great Procession and Is Cheered By a Vast Crowd in Chicago," *New York Times*, October 20, 1898.

46. Erin Murphy, "Women's Anti-Imperialism, 'the White Man's Burden,' and the Philippine American War: Theorizing Masculinist Ambivalence in Protest." *Gender and Society* 23, No. 2 (April 2009), 244–270.

47. *Army and Navy Journal* 36 (November 11, 1899), via Michael C. Robinson; Frank N. Schubert, "David Fagen: An Afro-American Rebel in the Philippines, 1899–1901," *Pacific Historical Review* 44, no. 1 (Feb. 1975), 68.

48. Via Richard A. Kramer, "Race-Making and Colonial Violence in the U.S. Empire: The Philippine-American War as Race War," *Asia-Pacific Journal* 4, no. 6 (June 2006).

49. In the *Richmond Planet*'s special issue "Voices from the Philippines," December 30, 1899. Also in *The Booker T. Washington Papers: 1899–1900*, Booker T. Washington, Louis R. Harlan, Raymond Smock, eds. (University of Illinois Press, 1976), 695.

50. Ron Field and Richard Hook, *Buffalo Soldiers 1892–1918* (Osprey Publishing, 2005).

51. United States War Dept., "Report of Adjutant General, on Present Distribution of the Regular and Volunteer Forces," *Annual Report of the Secretary of War for the Year Ending June 1900* (Government Printing Office), p.7.

52. Field and Hook, *Buffalo Soldiers*, 20.

53. *San Francisco Examiner*, May 27, 1900.

54. Via Sherry L. Smith, *Reimagining Indians: Native Americans Through Anglo Eyes, 1880–1940* (Oxford University Press, 2002), 34.

55. "Imperialism vs. Democracy: An Address at Jefferson Birthday Dinner, Portland, Oregon, April 13, 1899," In *Pacific Monthly: A Magazine of Education and Progress* 2–3 (Pacific Monthly Pub. Co., 1899).

56. Erin L. Murphy, "Women's Anti-Imperialism, the White Man's Burden, and the Philippine-American War: Theorizing Masculinist Ambivalence in Protest," *Gender & Society* vol. 23 (2009), 244.

57. "Told Of 'Water Cure' Given to Filipinos: Witnesses Went Into Details Before Senate Committee on the Philippines," *New York Times*, April 15, 1902.

58. Paul Kramer, "The Water Cure." *The New Yorker*, February 25, 2008.

59. "SAW THE WATER CURE GIVEN: Edward J. Davis, a Volunteer from Massachusetts, Testifies Before a Senate Committee," *New York Times*, April 18, 1902, 3.

60. Richard E. Welch Jr., "American Atrocities in the Philippines: The Indictment and the Response," *Pacific Historical Review* 43, no. 2 (May 1974), 233–53.

61. *New York Herald*, October 15, 1900, via Andrew Jay Hoffman, *Inventing Mark Twain: The Lives of Samuel Langhorne Clemens* (William Morrow, 1997), cited in Helen Scott's "The Mark Twain they didn't teach us about in school," in *International Socialist Review* 10 (Winter 2000), 61–5.

Chapter Six: 1912 to 1919

1. Ronan McGreevy, "The sinking of the *Lusitania*," *Irish Times*, May 2, 2015.

2. See Chapter One, or Carl Van Doren's *Mutiny in January* (Viking, 1943).

3. W.E.B. Du Bois, "Mexico," *The Crisis* 8, no. 2 (June 1914).

4. Louisa Thomas, *Conscience: Two Soldiers, Two Pacifists, One Family—A Test of Will and Faith in World War I* (Penguin Random House, 2011).

5. W.E.B. Du Bois, "The African Roots of War," *Atlantic Monthly*, 115, no. 5 (May 1915), 707–14.

6. Editorial, *The Crisis* 10, no. 2, 3. "Whatever of brutality and inhumanity, of murder, lust and theft has happened since last summer is but counterpart of the same sort of happenings hidden in the wilderness and done against dark and helpless people by white harbingers of human culture."

7. Charles A. Fenton, "American Ambulance Drivers in France and Italy, 1914–1918," *American Quarterly* 3, no. 4 (Winter 1951), 326–43.

8. Gertrude Stein, *The Autobiography of Alice B. Toklas* (Random House, 1932).

9. Allan Nevins and Frank Ernest Hill, "Henry Ford and His Peace Ship," *American Heritage*, February 1958.

10. Interview, Frances Mygatt and Tracy Witherspoon, Columbia University Oral History Collection.

11. "Memorial Addresses Before the U.S. Senate on Behalf of Samuel A. Witherspoon," *Proceedings in the House Proceedings in the Senate, March 8, 1916–March 25, 1916* (Government Printing Office, 1917), 49, http://www.archive.org/stream /samuelawitherspo01unit/samuelawitherspo01unit_djvu.txt/.

12. Ellen LaMotte, "Heroes," *Atlantic Monthly*, August 1916, 208. The same magazine published the other articles mentioned here, all of which became *The Backwash of War*.

13. That "morale" charge, of course, has justified similar censorship from 1774 to 2018. Every edition of the book notes the bans, including the most recent reissue from Bloomsbury, which notes: "Her graphic and highly vivid studies of how modern weapons of war can truly wreck the human body and mind remain a potent reminder of the true costs of conflict. No wonder the American government banned *The Backwash of War* in 1918."

14. NAACP flyer 1916. Library of Congress, National Association for the Advancement of Colored People records, 1842–1999 (bulk 1919–1991).

15. "BRIEF PEACE NOTES," *Advocate of Peace (1894–1920)* 78, no. 8 (1916), 244–46, http://www.jstor.org/stable/20667586.

16. Shirley Millard, *I Saw Them Die: Diary and Recollections of Shirley Millard* (Harcourt Brace, 1936).

17. Jennifer Keene, *Doughboys: The Great War, and the Remaking of America* (Johns Hopkins University Press, 2001), 101.

18. James Jeffrey, "Remembering the Black Soldiers Executed After Houston's 1917 Race Riot," Public Radio International, February 1, 2018.

19. *Debs v. United States*, 1919.

20. Randolph's attitude toward Du Bois would shift over time, but in July 1918, *The Messenger* editorialized, "Within the last six years he has been Democratic, Socialist and Republican. His attitude toward the parties is the old, antiquated conception of swinging on to the one thought most likely to win [thus *The Crisis*' 1912 endorsement of Wilson]."

21. From a letter to Rep. Hubert Dent Jr. of the House Committee on Military Affairs.

22. Norman wrote with understated wryness, "I have been brought here because of my mother's deep concern for my brother Evan." Norman Thomas Papers, New York Public Library.

23. Appendix to *The Congressional Record*, 1919.

24. "MILITARY PRISONERS IN KANSAS MUTINY; Men at Fort Leavenworth Barracks Demand a General Amnesty Setting Them Free. ARMED SOLDIERS ON GUARD Forty-ninth Infantry Regiment is Called Out to Prevent Disorder—Prisoners Refuse to Work," *New York Times*, July 23, 1919.

25. Winthrop D. Lane, "The Strike at Fort Leavenworth," *Survey* 41 (February 19, 1919). All dialogue in this chapter is taken from Lane's piece, though the same issue contained Evan Thomas' essay).

26. Rodger Sherman Clark papers, Polar Bear Expedition Digital Collection, Bentley Historical Library, University of Michigan.

27. "LET LENIN ALONE, BORAH DEMANDS; Calls Blockade Against Red Russia More Cruel Than Late One Against Germany. WANTS TROOPS WITHDRAWN McCormick Presents to Senate Letter from a Soldier Charging Atrocities by Our Forces. Charges Anglo-Japanese Influence. Soldier's Charges of Atrocities," *New York Times*, September 6, 1918.

Chapter Seven: 1920 to 1945

1. Unpublished manuscript, tagged "Auto-Biography." Lewis Milestone Papers, Margaret Herrick Library, Beverly Hills.

2. He was nearly late to his own induction, since he'd hailed a taxi, like any New Yorker since the invention of the internal combustion engine.

3. Milestone manuscript.

4. Bernard Rotsker, *Providing for the Casualties of War: The American Experience Through World War II* (Rand Corporation, 2013).

5. When Waters arrived home at Fort Dix, New Jersey, in February 1919, a few of his peers from the 41st did not join him; they had been dispatched much, much farther east, to North Russia. Word of what some of them had done would dominate the newspapers, perhaps teaching Walters that dissent sometimes gets results.

6. The letter, dated June 8, 1917: "Sir—I enclose herewith an extract from a letter lately received from a young officer which I hope may interest some of your readers.

I may add that the officer in question entered the Army directly from a public school and began his service in the trenches before he was nineteen.—Yours &c.,

T. S. Eliot

18, Crawford Mansions, Crawford Street, W.1.

June 17th, 1917.

'June 8th, 1917

'Dear—, There is rather a good article in THE NATION this last week called "On Leave." You should read it. I have often heard it said that the curious thing about those who have been to the front is their complete indifference. They appear to be practically untouched by what they have seen and gone through, they talk about war in a callous and humorous way, they even joke about its horrors. The impression one has from them is that it is, on the whole, a dreary and unpleasant business, with its anxious moments and its bright moments, but not nearly such a hell as one really knows it to be.

'In the case of the vast majority, however, this is an attitude, a screen—I speak of educated thinking men—and it is not granted to many who have not shared the same experiences to see behind the screen. The reason for this, as the article points out, is the practical impossibility for the uninitiated to realize or imagine even dimly the actual conditions of war. And a man who has been through it and seen and taken part in the unspeakable tragedies that are the ordinary routine, feels that he has something, possesses something, which others can never possess.

'It is morally impossible for him to talk seriously of these things to people who cannot even approach comprehension. It is hideously exasperating to hear people talking the glib commonplaces about the war and distributing cheap sympathy to its victims.

'Perhaps you are tempted to give them a picture of a leprous earth, scattered with the swollen and blackening corpses of hundreds of young men. The appalling stench of rotting carrion, mingled with the sickening smell of exploded lyddite and ammonal. Mud like porridge, trenches like shallow and sloping cracks in the porridge—porridge that stinks in the sun. Swarms of flies and bluebottles clustering on pits of offal. Wounded men lying in the shell holes among the decaying corpses: helpless under the scorching sun and bitter nights, under repeated shelling. Men with bowels dropping out, lungs shot away, with blinded smashed faces, or limbs blown into space. Men screaming and gibbering. Wounded men laughing in agony on the barbed wire, until a friendly spout of liquid fire shrivels them up like a fly in a candle. But these are only words, and probably only convey a fraction of their meaning to their hearers. They shudder and it is forgotten.'"

7. Edward Estlin Cummings, *The Enormous Room* (London: Courier Dover Publications, 2002), 89.

8. Cummings, *The Enormous Room*, cont'd: "Before entering he was thoroughly searched and temporarily deprived of the contents of his pockets. The door was locked behind him and double and triple locked. . . . The third method employed to throw Fear into the minds of his captives lay, as I have said, in the sight of the Captor Himself. And this was by far the most efficient method."

9. Catherine Reed, *e.e. cummings: A Poet's Life* (Clarion Books, 2006), 43.

10. "Volume Expurgated on Book Club Advice," *New York Times*, May 31, 1929.

11. Charles Higham (interviewer), Film History Project, "Reminiscences of Lew Ayres," 1971, Oral History Archives, Columbia University.

12. Quoted in Lesley Coffin, *Hollywood's Conscientious Objector* (University of Mississippi Press, 2012).

13. Mordaunt Hall, "Review: ALL QUIET ON THE WESTERN FRONT: Young Germany Goes to War," *New York Times*, April 30, 1930.

14. Lewis Milestone Papers.

15. Walter Waters and William C. White, *B.E.F.: The Untold Story of the Bonus Army* (AMS Press, 1933), 18. All direct quotes from Waters are from this book.

16. Donald Lisio, "A Blunder Becomes Catastrophe: Hoover, the Legion, and the Bonus Army," *Wisconsin Magazine of History* 51, no. 1 (Autumn 1967), 37–50.

17. Lt. Col. Bryan Greenwald, "The Bonus March: A Forgotten Stain," *Military Review* 80 (March–April 2000), 92.

18. Via Paul Dixon and Thomas Allen, *The Bonus Army: An American Epic* (Walker & Co., 2006).

19. Ernest Hemingway, "Who Murdered the Vets? A First-hand report on the Florida Hurricane," *New Masses*, September 15, 1935.

20. Jenny Staletovich, "Revisiting the story of the lost soldiers of Florida's most powerful hurricane," *Miami Herald*, May 30, 2015.

21. Lee Standiford, *Last Train to Paradise: Henry Flagler and the Spectacular Rise and Fall of the Railroad that Crossed an Ocean* (Crossroads Press, 2003), 264.

22. Youth Committee for the Oxford Pledge, "Bulletin from the Youth Committee for the Oxford Pledge" (1938), CUNY Academic Works.

23. Lewis Milestone Papers.

24. Smedley Butler, *War Is a Racket* (Round Table Press, 1935).

25. "To consider their response, 79 representatives of the historic peace churches—Mennonites, Brethren and Friends (Quakers)—gathered in the City Auditorium on West Sixth Street in Newton, Kan., Oct. 31–Nov. 2, 1935. H.P.

Krehbiel, a leader in the General Conference Mennonite Church and founder of Mennonite Weekly Review, called the meeting." John Sharp, "Peace Churches Prepare for War," *Mennonite World Review*, October 26, 2015.

26. Now known as the Center for Conscience and War.

27. Guide to the Keep America Out of War Congress Records TAM.331 Tamiment Library/Robert F. Wagner Labor Archives, New York University.

28. Ron Rosenbaum, *Waking to Danger: Americans and Nazi Germany, 1933–1941* (Prager, 2010).

29. Rosenbaum, *Waking to Danger*.

30. Ruth Sarles, *A Story of America First: The Men and Women Who Opposed Military Intervention in World War II* (Greenwood Press, 2003).

31. H.J. Res. 167, 74th Congress, and H.J. Res. 89 and H.J. Res. 158, 74th Congress; Ralph M. Goldman, *"The Advisory Referendum in America," Public Opinion Quarterly 14, no. 2 (Summer 1950), 303–15.*

32. "When and if fascism comes to America it will not be labelled 'made in Germany'; it will not be marked with a swastika; it will not even be called fascism; it will be called, of course, 'Americanism.'" "DISGUISED FASCISM SEEN AS A MENACE: Prof. Luccock Warns That It Will Be Seen as 'Americanism,'" *New York Times*, September 12, 1938.

33. In Evan Welling Thomas, *The Radical "No": The Correspondence and Writings of Evan Thomas on War*, Charles Chatfield, ed. (Garland Publishing, 1974), 15.

34. Andrew Kelly, *All Quiet on the Western Front: The Story of a Film* (London: Tauris, 2002), 154.

35. David J. Langum, *William M. Kunstler: The Most Hated Lawyer in America* (NYU Press, 1999), 34.

36. Charles Evers, *Have No Fear* (Wiley, 1997), 47.

37. "Anti-War Rally Held in Times Square," *New York Times*, May 22, 1940.

38. Selective Training and Service Act of 1940, 50 U.S.C.A.A. Appendix, § 304(a), quoted in 140 F.2d 397, 398.

39. Melissa A. Geddis, "Segregation IS Discrimination: A Case Study of *Lynn v. Downer* and African American Resistance to Racialized Military Service in the Second World War," Master's thesis, Rutgers University, May 2015.

40. Michael G. Long, *Marshalling Justice: The Early Civil Rights Letters of Thurgood Marshall* (HarperCollins, 2011).

41. Alexa Mills, "A Lynching Kept out of Sight: Pvt Felix Hall Died in the Only Known Murder of Its Kind on a U.S. Military Base. How Hard Did the Government Try to Find His Killer?" *Washington Post*, September 8, 2016.

42. Selective Training and Service Act of 1940, 50 U.S.C.A.A. Appendix, § 304(a), quoted in 140 F.2d 397, 398.

43. "Gentlemen: I am in receipt of my draft-reclassification notice. Please be informed that I am ready to serve in any unit of the armed forces of my country which is not segregated by race. Unless I am assured that I can serve in a mixed regiment and that I will not be compelled to serve in a unit undemocratically selected as a Negro group, I will refuse to report for induction." Via Nancy and Dwight MacDonald, "The War's Greatest Scandal!: The Story of Jim Crow in Uniform," A. Philip Randolph Papers, Library of Congress Manuscript Division, Washington D.C., Box 18; Vis Geddis, "Segregation Is Discrimination," *Chicago Defender*, December 5, 1942, 7, 13.

44. "COURT BACKS SPLIT IN DRAFT OF RACES: 2 To 1 Decision of U.S. Appeals Tribunal Backs Separate Quotas for Induction," February 4, 1944. *Lynn v. Downer* is still seen as a stealth chip in the foundation of *Brown v. Board of Education*.

45. Higham and Ayres, "Reminiscences." Via Lesley Coffin, *Lew Ayres: Hollywood's Conscientious Objector* (University Press of Mississippi, 2012), 203.

46. William Bakewell, *Hollywood Be Thy Name: Random Recollections of a Movie Veteran from Silents to Talkies to TV* (Scarecrow Press), 133. Via Coffin, *Lew Ayres: Hollywood's Conscientious Objector*.

47. George James, "Noted and Not-So-Noted Relive Pearl Harbor Day," *New York Times*, December 6, 1988.

48. Judith Ehrlich and Rick Tejada, *The Good War and Those Who Refused to Fight It* (Paradigm Productions/Independent Television Service, 2000).

49. "I said I don't mind working with the army because you do have a tremendous problem with the Hitler situation, I can't deny these things, but I said as far as I'm concerned I couldn't kill, and I couldn't go into the army even on your side unless I did what I considered to be constructive work." Via Ehrlich and Tejada, *The Good War*.

50. Testimony via Swarthmore College Peace Collection.

51. "HAPPY TO BE C.O., AYRES EXPLAINS," *New York Times* (1857–Current file), April 1, 1942, 23.

52. Julie Phillips and James Tiptree Jr., *The Double Life of Alice B. Sheldon* (St. Martin's Press, 2006).

53. Leisa D. Meyer, *Creating G. I. Jane: Sexuality and Power in the Women's Army Corps During World War II* (Columbia University Press, 1998), 158.

54. Philip Berrigan, *Fighting the Lamb's War* (Monroe, ME: Common Courage Press, 1996), 13.

55. Columbia University Oral History Collection.

56. Harvard Sitkoff, "Racial Militancy and Interracial Violence in the Second World War," *Journal of American History* 58, no. 3 (December 1971), 669.

57. Tony Cantu, "Joe S. Jasso," U.S. Latino and Latina World War II Oral History Project, University of Texas.

58. Via David D. Joyce, *Howard Zinn: An American Vision* (Prometheus Books, 2003).

59. Howard Zinn, *You Can't Be Neutral on a Moving Train: A Personal History of Our Times* (Beacon Press, 2002), 73.

60. Clancy Sigal, phone interview, 2007.

61. Zinn, *You Can't Be Neutral.*

62. Martin Duberman, *Howard Zinn: A Life on the Left* (New Press, 2012).

63. Harvard Sitkoff, *Toward Freedom Land: The Long Struggle for Racial Equality in America* (University of Kentucky Press, 2010), 71.

64. Reva Craine, "The Case of Sgt. Alton Levy," *Labor Action*, 7, no. 42 (October 18, 1943), 4.

65. Richard Wright, "What Jim Crow Feels Like," *TRUE Magazine*, May 1946.

66. Don Collison, prod., "The Port Chicago 50: An Oral History," KCRW-FM, January 1, 1995. *American Workers* (radio series), Public Radio International.

67. From a transcription of Evers' DD214 later made public by Col. Eugene Tarr, Army Records Center, in June 1963.

68. Evers later told his wife about being part of the Express, which she recalls in her memoir *Watch Me Fly* (Little, Brown, 1999). At its height, the Red Ball transported 410,000 tons of materiel over seven hundred miles, the longest one-way traffic artery in the world. Via Charles R. Schrader, ed., *United States Army Logistics, 1775–1992, Volume 2* (U.S. Army Center of Military History, 1997), 532.

69. Charles Evers and Andrew Szanton, *Have No Fear* (John Wiley, 1997), 47.

70. Memo from Eugene Tarr, U.S. Army Records Center, June 14, 1963.

71. "The Port Chicago 50," KCRW.

72. "50 GET MUTINY TERMS: Sentences of Negroes in Navy Range From 8 to 15 Years," *New York Times*, November 19, 1944.

73. Randall Jarrell, "Losses," in *Losses* (Harcourt Brace, 1948).

74. James Tiptree Jr., "Her Smoke Rose Up Forever," in Barry Malzberg, ed., *Final Stage; The Ultimate Science Fiction Anthology* (Charterhouse Books, 1974).

Chapter Eight: 1946 to 1966

1. Press release, "Change in Museum of Modern Art Film Schedule," April 1946. Also Anon., "Copyright Restrictions Halt Army Pic Showings," *The Film Daily* (April–June 1946), 3.

2. *The Nation*, May 11, 1946.

3. John Huston, *An Open Book* (Da Capo Press, 1994), 65.

4. Alice Sheldon, "The Lucky Ones," *The New Yorker*, November 14, 1946, 104. The title is an ironic assessment of those German civilians who were not at that moment starving to death.

5. Julie Phillips and James Tiptree Jr., *The Double Life of Alice B. Sheldon* (St. Martin's, 2015), 141.

6. Charles G. Bolté, *The New Veteran* (Pocket Books, 1945).

7. Jerry Tallmer, personal conversation, October 2007.

8. Bolté, *The New Veteran*.

9. Quoting an unnamed prosperous Chicago executive, Bolté described the challenge in his 1945 book *The New Veteran*: "All my business friends are counting on the American Legion to Americanize the American youth. You know what they mean by Americanizing the youth—fix 'em up so they don't bother us with any ideas. Don't let 'em jar us out of our fur-lined foxholes into the real world, where things are changing," 45.

10. Interview of Todd Oldham with Corrine Edwards, November 11, 2004. Oral History Archives American Culture Studies, Washington University.

11. *AVC Bulletin*, February 1946, 5.

12. *AVC Bulletin*, March 1946.

13. "Citizens First," *Time*, XLVII (June 24, 1946), 28. Via Robert L. Tyler, "The American Veterans Committee: Out of a Hot War and Into the Cold," *American Quarterly* 18, no. 3 (Autumn 1966), 424.

14. "AVC BEGINS DRIVE TO ENLIST 1 MILLION," *New York Times*, June 7, 1946, 27.

15. "Citizens First," *Time*.

16. Wendy Wall, *Inventing the "American Way": The Politics of Consensus from the New Deal to the Civil Rights Movement* (Oxford University Press, 2008), 164–5.

17. *AVC Bulletin*, February 1947. AVC's Chet Patterson testified about this to Congress in February.

18. The chapter included former bombardier Howard Zinn, though he'd long

since stopped flirting with the Communist Party. Via Howard Zinn, personal interview with Ambre Ivol, Sorbonne Ph.D. student, April 11, 2007. Quoted in Ivol, "Of generational confusion and conceptual overlapping: Remapping the history of US public intellectuals through the life and work of Howard Zinn," paper delivered at Historians Against the War conference, April 11–13, 2008; Tyler, "American Veterans Committee," 427.

19. *New York Times*, November 26, 1948, 48. Via Tyler, "American Veterans Committee," 434.

20. *Key Largo*. Directed by John Huston (script by John Huston and Richard Brooks, based on a play by Maxwell Anderson), Los Angeles, 1948.

21. Adam Nossiter, *Of Long Memory: Mississippi and the Murder of Medgar Evers* (Da Capo Press, 2002), 74.

22. Nossiter, *Of Long Memory*, 74.

23. John D'Emilio, *Lost Prophet: The Life and Times of Bayard Rustin* (Simon and Schuster, 2003), 22.

24. Quotes from Muste and that CO, John McCartney, via D'Emilio, *Lost Prophet*.

25. These objectors included George Houser, who'd corresponded frequently with Rustin when both were in prison during the war years, and CORE co-founder James Farmer.

26. Rustin's coinage of "Speak truth to power" is usually attributed to September 1963, after the March on Washington. But those are the principles that animated Rustin's work as early as the Journey of Reconciliation.

27. D'Emilio, *Lost Prophet*, 154.

28. Memo, "Rustin and George Houser to Potential Resisters," July 7, 1948. In *I Must Resist: Bayard Rustin's Life in Letters* (City Lights Books, 2012).

29. John Huston, *Open Book* (Da Capo Press, 1994), 1.

30. Stephen Cooper, *Perspective on John Huston* (B.K. Hall, 1994). Found via Guerric de Bona, "Masculinity on the Front: John Huston's *The Red Badge of Courage* Revisited," *Cinema Journal* 42, no. 2 (Winter 2003), 57–80.

31. Lillian Ross, "No. 1512, Part 1," *New Yorker*, May 24, 1952. "'Well!' he said, looking oppressed, and slightly alien to the overflowing intimacy that was advancing toward him."

32. From Mari Jo Buhle, Paul Buhle, and Dan Georgakas, eds., *Encyclopedia of the American Left* (University of Illinois Press, 1992). "A labor leader modeled on Harry Bridges was the main villain in *I Married a Communist*, Hawaiian Communists were exposed by a two-fisted John Wayne in Big Jim McClain, and Communist defense

efforts for a Mexican American were depicted as insincere political and mercenary opportunism in *Trial*."

33. Selective Service Induction Statistics from World War I to the End of the Draft (1973).

34. Telephone interview, September 9, 2016.

35. NSBRO Directors Minutes, June 4, 1952, addendum d, pp. 1, 2, 3, in the Center on Conscience and War Records (DG 025), Part II, Series A, Box 1, Swarthmore College Peace Collection.

36. NSBRO Directors Minutes, June 4, 1952.

37. Center on Conscience and War, et al., "Timeline of Advocacy Efforts to Obtain Military Conscientious Objector Discharges, 1949–1960," *Civilian Public Service Story*, http://civilianpublicservice.org/storycontinues/hotline/advocacy.

38. Clarence Adams and Delia Adams, *An American Dream: The Life of an African American Soldier and POW Who Spent Twelve Years in Communist China* (University of Massachusetts Press, 2007).

39. NSBRO Consultative Council Minutes, January 29, 1951, addendum b, page 2, in the Center on Conscience and War Records (DG 025), Part II, Series A, Box 1, Swarthmore College Peace Collection.

40. Bosley Crowther, "THE SCREEN IN REVIEW; 'Red Badge of Courage' Based on Stephen Crane's Novel, at Trans-Lux 52d St.," *New York Times*, October 19, 1951.

41. *Chicago Tribune*, May 27, 1966.

42. "Communist Brainwashing—Are We Prepared?" *New Republic*, June 8, 1953, 5–6.

43. Keisha Brown, "Blackness in Exile: W.E.B. Du Bois' Role in the Formation of Representations of Blackness as Conceptualized by the Chinese Communist Party (CCP)," *Phylon (1960–)* 53, no. 2 (Winter 2016), 20–33.

44. Hans Pols, Stephanie Oak, et al., "War & Military Mental Health: The US Psychiatric Response in the 20th Century," *American Journal of Public Health* 97, no. 12 (December 2007), 2132–42.

45. Democracy Now, "Legendary Historian, Attorney & Peace Activist Staughton Lynd on War Resisters, the Peace Movement and the 1993 Lucasville Prison Uprising," October 20, 2006.

46. Including careful consideration and training at the Highlander Center in Tennessee.

47. Charles Rambow, "The Ku Klux Klan in the 1920s: A Concentration in the Black Hills," South Dakota State Historical Society, 1973.

48. United States Commission on Civil Rights, South Dakota Advisory Committee, "Negro Airmen in a Northern Community: Discrimination in Rapid City, South Dakota"(Government Printing Office, March 1963).

49. The President's Committee on Civil Rights, *To Secure These Rights* (New York, 1947), 162–3. Via Alan L. Graupman, *The Air Force Integrates, 1945–1963* (Office of Air Force History, 1985).

50. Bobby Seale, *Seize the Time: The Story of the Black Panther Party and Huey P. Newton* (Black Classic Press, 1966), 62.

51. Stokely Carmichael, Speech at University of California, Berkeley, October 29, 1966. Accessed via AmericanRadioWorks.publicradio.org.

52. Staughton Lynd and Alice Lynd, *Stepping Stones: Memoir of a Life Together* (Rowman & Littlefield, 2009), 77.

53. Telephone interview with Gitlin, February 11, 2009.

54. "From Protest to Politics: The Future of the Civil Rights Movement," *Commentary*, February 1965.

55. Richie Unterberger, "Liner Note for *All The News That's Fit to Sing*," 2000, for a CD reissue from Collector's Choice Music of that 1964 album.

56. Phil Ochs, "Talking Vietnam Blues," *All the News That's Fit to Sing* (Hannibal Records, 1964).

57. "RED ROLE IN PROTEST CHARGED BY HOOVER," *New York Times*, June 2, 1965, 52.

58. Staughton Lynd, "The New Radicals and Participatory Democracy," *Dissent* (Summer 1965).

59. Hearing August 5, 1966, House Un-American Activities Committee.

60. Andrew Jacobs, Jr, *1600 Killers: A Wake-Up Call for Congress* (New Century Publishing, 1999), 61.

61. That detail via another classmate, Dennis Fiorillo, via Google Chat, August 2015.

62. Reprinted in Jerry Lembcke, *The Spitting Image: Myth, Memory, and the Legacy of Vietnam* (NYU Press, 2000), 35.

Chapter Nine: 1965 to 1980

1. Alexa Gagosz, "MIT Professor Noam Chomsky, Vietnam resistors tell their stories," *Suffolk Journal*, April 15, 2010.

2. *United States v. Seeger*, 380 U.S. 163 (1965).

3. Lawrence Baskir and William Strauss, *Chance and Circumstance: The Draft, the War, and the Vietnam Generation* (Random House, 1978).

4. Ron Kovic, *Born on the Fourth of July* (McGraw-Hill, 1976), 83.

5. Personal interview, Philadelphia, January 30, 2009.

6. In William Short and Willa Seidenberg, *A Matter of Conscience: GI Resistance During the Vietnam War* (Addison Gallery of Art, 1992).

7. Telephone interview, January 6, 2009.

8. Margaret Butler, who served 1967–1969, in *Memories of Navy Nursing: The Vietnam Era* (Maryanne Gallagher Ibach, ed.). Material developed for the Vietnam Women's Memorial, Washington, DC.

9. "The military used all of the [TV] footage at my court martial—evidence I really was guilty," Short and Seidenberg, *Matter of Conscience*.

10. "You Want a Real War Hero?" *Vietnam GI*, August 1969.

11. *Vietnam GI*, August 1968.

12. Leslie Gelb et al., "U.S. Ground Strategy and Force Deployments, 1965–1968," Volume Four, Pentagon Papers.

13. Richard Moser, *The New Winter Soldiers: GI and Veteran Dissent During the Vietnam Era* (Rutgers University Press, 1996), 82.

14. Short and Seidenberg, *Matter of Conscience*.

15. *The Ally* (Berkeley), August 19, 1968.

16. Andrew Hunt, *The Turning: A History of Vietnam Veterans Against the War* (NYU Press, 1990), 30.

17. Jack Hurst, "Viet Mother Warns GI—And Dies," *2-Star*.

18. William Perry, Testimony, Winter Soldier Hearings, February 1971.

19. Interview, January 30, 2009.

20. From 1962 to 1971, the United States dumped nineteen million gallons of herbicides over Vietnam, destroying nearly five million acres of countryside as part of its defoliation campaign to deny enemy combatants protective cover.

21. *The Old Mole*, June 20–July 3, 1969, 2.

22. Bill Perry, Facebook photo caption, September 7, 2015.

23. William Sloane Coffin, *Once to Every Man: A Memoir* (Atheneum, 1977).

24. The Moratorium event in England was at a safe-house for deserters run by an American World War II veteran named Clancy Sigal, at Number 56 Queen Anne Street. In Europe, "there was a feeling that the Vietnam war was somehow a fascist war, and that anything to help American soldiers resist that war was good," Sigal told me. The overcrowded apartment was "a wonderful mix of AWOL soldiers, their girlfriends, and some lost souls," he wrote years later for the *London Review of Books*. "Simply put, my new job was to smuggle American deserters in and out of the United Kingdom, help arrange false papers, find safe houses in the UK, 'babysit' our less stable 'packages' (AWOLs in transit), personally accompany those too shaky to travel alone." By the end of 1968, the project had evolved "a classically English accommodation with the various secret services who kept tabs on us at one time or another."

25. Elizabeth Kolbert et al., "Moratorium," *The New Yorker*, October 25, 1969, 54.

26. Seymour Hersh, "Lieutenant Accused of Murdering 109 Civilians," *St. Louis Post-Dispatch,* November 13, 1969, A1.

27. "I got to like [McCarthy] a lot. . . . He opposed the war, and he said as much," Saul Landau, "Seymour Hersh," *The Progressive*, May 1998.

28. Testimony at the court martial of William Calley, 1971. Accessed via the University of Missouri: http://law2.umkc.edu/faculty/projects/ftrials/mylai/Myl_hero .html#RON.

29. Seymour Hersh, "Ex-GI Tells of Killing Civilians at Pinkville."

30. *New York Times* interview with Meadlo, via Arkansas Tech University, is available at https://faculty.atu.edu/cbrucker/Amst2003/Texts/MyLai.pdf.

31. Rives M. Duncan, "What Went Right at My Lai: An Analysis of the Roles of 'Habitus' and Character in Lawful Disobedience," Ph.D. dissertation, Religion, Temple University, 1997, 185 pp, DA 9813493.

32. Interview, Boston, March 2007.

33. Decades later, CCCO was the author's employer from 1995 to 2000.

34. Charles C. Moskos and John Whiteclay Chambers, *The New Conscientious Objection: From Sacred to Secular Resistance* (Oxford University Press US, 1993), 43.

35. "GI Justice in Vietnam: An interview with the Lawyers Military Defense Committee," *Yale Review of Law and Social Action* 2, no. 1 (1972), Article 3, http:// digitalcommons.law.yale.edu/yrlsa/vol2/iss1/3.

36. Unless otherwise cited, Cox's story here from interviews in California in 2006.

37. A young girl named Ho Thi An, who watched terrified that day, described it thirty years later to journalist Nick Turse: "'There were three of us standing at the entrance to the bunker, me and two old women—my neighbor and my grandmother,' she told me. The three had just scrambled out of their earthen bomb shelter when

an American took aim and shot the two elderly women, one after the other. . . . She later emerged to find that a total of fifteen villagers had been killed in Le Bac that day. All civilians."

38. Moser, *The New Winter Soldiers*, 107.

39. Quoted in Jean-Jacques Maurier, ed., *The Last Time I Dreamed About the War: Essays on the Life and Writing of W.D. Ehrhart* (McFarland, 2014).

40. Stephen Pogust, "G.I. March Is 'Disgusting' to N.J. Town," *Philadelphia Inquirer*, September 4, 1970.

41. Via Gerald Nicosia, "Veteran in Conflict," *LA Times*, May 23, 2004.

42. Van Devanter, *Home Before Morning: The Story of an Army Nurse in Vietnam* (University of Massachusetts Press), 231.

43. Sam Roberts, "Anthony B. Herbert, Decorated War Hero Turned Army Whistleblower, Dies at 84," *New York Times*, February 25, 2015.

44. Telephone interview, February 2009.

45. "ANTI WAR GROUP HEARS OF 'CRIMES,'" *New York Times*, December 2, 1970, 15.

46. Winter Soldier Testimony, read into Cong. Record: "[soldiers] stabbed her in both breasts, spread-eagled her and shoved an E-tool up her vagina, an entrenching tool, and she was still asking for water."

47. David Halbfinger, "Kerry's Antiwar Past Is a Delicate Issue in His Campaign," *New York Times*, April 24, 2004.

48. Via Vietnam Full Disclosure, https://www.vietnamfulldisclosure.org/about -this-site.

49. Michael Kranish, Brian C. Mooney, and Nina Easton, *John F. Kerry: The Complete Biography by the Boston Globe Reporters Who Know Him Best* (Public Affairs, 2004), 120–21. Nixon aides expressed "exasperation that more wasn't being done to undermine Kerry and the other VVAW organizers."

50. Michael Kranish et al., "With Antiwar Role, High Visibility," *Boston Globe*, June 16. 2003.

51. "A thousand drug addicts camping out," Bill Perry chuckled when asked what that week was like. "Honestly, there were maybe 200 guys really driving it politically—and a lot of them were drama queens, if you know what I mean. The rest of us . . ." Perry may have been at least partially right in his assessment, at least if the veterans' drug use were anywhere near that of the troops they had been. Even something as relatively gentle as marijuana might spread a haze over memories of the camp veterans set up on the Mall, cheered by sympathetic legislators from Bella

Abzug to George McGovern and Edward Kennedy.

52. Robert D. Heinl, "The Collapse of the Armed Forces," *Armed Force Journal,* June 7, 1971.

53. For more on that predecessor, see Adolph Reed, "Fayettenam: 1969 Tales from a G.I. Coffeehouse." Originally published in *The Objector* (CCCO, edited by this author) in 1996, now included in *Class Notes: Posing as Politics and Other Thoughts on the American Scene* (New Press, 2000).

54. One favorite cover was also a poster: a cartoon of a huge thermometer, with numbers like a church fund drive: 10,000 to, at the top, 110,000. But the numbers were rising from a tank, with the slogan below: "DONATE A SON TODAY—GO VIETNAM!!" The paper the crew ended up with was full of as many four-letter words as they could stuff into sixteen pages—full of what it said it was: *rage.*

55. Steve Hasna, "VVAW History: San Francisco Vets Day Parade 1972," *The Veteran* (VVAW mag, spring 1997).

56. Memo, July 1974, VVAW FBI Files, Swarthmore College Peace Collection.

57. Steve Hassna to Gerald Nicosia.

58. In-person interview, August 7, 2009.

59. *The Veteran.* That Arkansas VVAW member turned FBI informant who'd sparked the Gainesville trial was forgiven in later years because of his illness; he even had pasted to the wall of his office: "PVS Kills."

60. Ron Kovic, interview by Waldo Salt, November 8, 1974, transcript, Waldo Salt Papers, Research Library, University of California Los Angeles. Via Jerry Lembcke, "From Oral History to Movie Script: The Vietnam Veteran Interviews for 'Coming Home,'" *Oral History Review*, 26, no. 2 (Summer–Autumn, 1999), 76.

Chapter Ten: 1980 to 1991

1. James Hodge and Linda Cooper, *Disturbing the Peace: Father Roy Bourgeois and the Movement to Close the School of the Americas* (Orbis Books, 1995), 12.

2. AP via the *New York Times*, "Missing Priest Turns Up at Embassy in Salvador," May 7, 1981.

3. Linda Cooper and James Hodge, "SOA Watch Marks 25th Year of Speaking Out Against 'School of Assassins,'" *National Catholic Reporter*, November 10, 2014.

4. John F. Kerry, "Vietnam Veterans Against the War, Speech Before the U.S. Senate Committee on Foreign Relations," April 22, 1971.

5. "Why Was I a Soldier? Why am I a Peace Activist?" In Margaret Knapke, ed., *From Warrior to Resisters: US Veterans on Terrorism* (FXBear Publishing, 2005).

6. Interview, Washington DC, 2009.

7. "Missing Priest Turns Up in El Salvador," *New York Times*, May 3, 1981.

8. Mark Masse, *Inspired to Serve: Today's Faith Activists* (Indiana University Press, 2004), 88.

9. Wayne Partridge, "Profile of SOA Watch Founder, the Rev. Roy Bourgeois," *Columbus Ledger-Enquirer*, November 13, 1997.

10. "The guards were beating on a prisoner in the walkway in front of the cells, and I had a flashback to that village in Vietnam. I saw that mother's face. I thought, 'My God, we're still killing people, right here. It's happening right in front of my eyes in Massachusetts," Brian Willson, *On Third World Legs* (Charles Kerr Publishing, 1992).

11. "Berrigan and 6 Others Sentenced for Protests Near Carter's House," *New York Times*, January 11, 1977, A16.

12. Keith Mather of the Presidio Nine was among those who angrily refused the latter, choosing the yellow "D" sheet over what felt like a second draft.

13. Bob Smith, "In Memoriam: William Stuart-Whistler, 1926–2004," September 2004 newsletter, Delaware County Pledge of Resistance.

14. Sharon Erickson Nepstad, *Religion and Resistance in the Plowshares Movement* (Cambridge University Press, 2008), 32.

15. Nepstad, *Plowshares*.

16. Philip Berrigan, *Fighting the Lamb's War* (Monroe, ME: Common Courage Press, 1996), 13.

17. *Washington Post*, August 19, 1980. Via Betty Glad, "Black-and-White Thinking: Ronald Reagan's Approach to Foreign Policy," *Political Psychology* 4, no. 1 (March 1983), 33–76.

18. Notes for *A Personal Legacy: Objects Left at the Vietnam Veterans Memorial*, a joint exhibition of the National Museum of American History, Smithsonian Institution, and National Park Service/Department of the Interior, 1995.

19. Not that the four-year campaign to create a memorial had been easy, or its result uncontroversial: the design, won in juried competition by young architecture student Maya Lin, was also a gentle anti-war statement, with all the names of the dead on simple black granite panels, instead of brave human figures. Newspapers asked, "Is this a memorial to the dead, or to all Vietnam vets?" West Point infantry instructor Tom Carhardt began lobbying against the wall's "black gash of shame."

One of the critics was James Webb, a former platoon commander who'd become a staffer for the House Veterans Affairs Committee and board member of the Vietnam Veterans Memorial Foundation. Then on track to become assistant secretary of defense, Webb led the push for a new, separately commissioned statue of three soldiers mid-battle by Frederick Hart, one of the artists who'd helped build the National Cathedral. Hart's statement: "I see the Wall as a kind of ocean, a sea of sacrifice that is overwhelming and nearly incomprehensible in its sweep of names."

20. Cynthia Enloe, *The Morning After: Sexual Politics at the End of the Cold War* (University of California Press, 1993), 74.

21. Enloe, *Morning After*.

22. Telephone interview, May 2006.

23. Like most demonstrations before and since Vietnam, the LA rally included contingents from the ACLU, the Young Communist League, the Revolutionary Communist Party (formerly the RU That Ate VVAW), and the Worker's World Party, with newish color provided by Greenpeace and the openly gay Radical Faeries. "Protesters: Throw Reagan to Wolves," United Press International, *Spokane Chronicle*, May 26, 1982.

24. The Committee for a Sane Nuclear Policy (SANE), the long moribund group with whom Rustin had once protested French nuclear testing, revived under Vietnam-era veteran David Cortright. Cortright, *Soldiers in Revolt: The American Military Today* (Anchor Books, 1975), 249.

25. William Robbins, "Berrigans See a Reawakening for Antiwar Activists; Expecting a Sentence Movement Gaining Strength Network Around Country First-Strike Weapon Baltimore, Catonsville Raids," *New York Times*, December 13, 1980, A8.

26. Rushworth Kidder, "The Nuclear Issue: It Depends on How You View the World," *Christian Science Monitor*, November 12, 1982.

27. William Sloane Coffin, *The Collected Sermons of William Sloane Coffin—The Riverside Years, Vol. 1* (Louisville, KY: Westminster John Knox Press, 2008), 91.

28. Schutts may have learned the phrase "conscientious objector" during the 1980 imposition of draft registration, but certainly had not heard while in ROTC that people were still achieving discharge as COs—two years before, 136 army, 175 navy, 38 Marine Corps, and 100 air force personnel had done so—or that case law had emerged for active-duty CO discharges of volunteers, given a new "crystallization" of anti-war beliefs. It would take some time for Schutts to even ask, but when he learned that he could apply, his joy was as heartfelt as that of Fred Marchant seventeen years earlier.

29. Christa Hillstrom, "'War Is Not Peace': Father Roy Bourgeois," *YES Magazine*, April 8, 2011.

30. Telephone interview, May 2009.

31. Nicaraguan TV clip in "Father Roy: Inside the School of Assassins," 1997 (Robert Richter for P.O.V.). Transcript from "Dole-Ortega Exchange: A Lesson in Sovereignty," *Envio* (FSLN magazine), September 1987.

32. S. Brian Willson, "History of the Idea of the Veterans Peace Action Teams," Brianwillson.com.

33. "[Veterans] had put our lives on the line for lies and special interests, killing because our government commanded us to. Now we needed to seriously consider risking our lives through non-violent resistance for the truths prompted by our own conscience. It was my belief that such actions would help veterans in their healing, by serving as atonement and reconciliation for the killing we participated in in our pasts."

34. S. Brian Willson and Daniel Ellsberg, *Blood on the Tracks: The Life and Times of S. Brian Willson* (PM Press, 2011).

35. Dan Payne, "How Kerry Wins," Salon.com, April 13, 2004.

36. Telephone interview, summer 2007.

37. Charles Liteky, "Resisting the War Against the Poor," in *From Warriors to Resisters*, Knapke, ed., 18.

38. "Protester Renounces War Medal," *Charlotte Observer*, July 30, 1986.

39. George Mizo told the press, "Those of us who have seen firsthand that horror called war know how fragile life is, and how precious life is, and know that war is not the answer but part of the problem."

40. Most of the facts and figures in this paragraph are drawn from Willson's memoir *Blood on the Tracks* (PM Press, 2012).

41. Telephone interview, summer 2015.

42. Fawn Mrazo, "Peace Convoy Stopped at Border," *Philadelphia Inquirer*, June 16. 1988.

43. Lisa Bekin, "Judge Rebuffs U.S. for Blocking Convoy of Aid to Nicaragua," *New York Times*, October 1, 1988.

44. Gene Siskel, "FLICK OF THE WEEK: *Platoon* Shows the Real Vietnam," *Chicago Tribune*, January 3, 1987.

45. Jay Sharburtt, "Reunion: Men of a Real Platoon," *Los Angeles Times*, February 7, 1987.

46. Brian Willson, *Z Magazine*.

47. Frederick Kempe, *Divorcing the Dictator: America's Bungled Affair with Noriega* (New York: Putnam, 1990), 178.

48. Jane G. Schaller, Paul Wise, and Gregg Bloche, "OPERATION JUST CAUSE: The Human Cost of Military Action" (report, Physicians for Human Rights, 1991), 5.

49. Project Censored 1990, "What Really Happened in Panama Was a Different Story."

50. Andrew Rosenthal, "Fighting in Panama: Overview; U.S. TROOPS PRESS THEIR HUNT FOR NORIEGA; LOOTING IS WIDESPREAD IN PANAMA'S CAPITAL," *New York Times*, December 22, 1986, A16.

Chapter Eleven: 1990 to 2001

1. Julian Guthrie, "Fans line Up for Colin Powell at S.F. Bookstore," *San Francisco Examiner*, September 26, 1995.

2. Full disclosure: this narrative is from personal memory, supplemented by news clips and interviews with Fahey, now a professor of African Studies, and my old friend Sam Diener, then a core staff member of the Central Committee for Conscientious Objectors (CCCO) in San Francisco. I was one of those passing out those flyers, and had in fact helped Sam write it, having been hired by CCCO a few months earlier. CCCO's board of directors then decided not to endorse protesting Powell, given his popularity among people of color (though our only Black board member, Tamara Jenkins, wanted to do it, urging the board to "speak truth to power"). So, Sam, Dan, and I made up that ad hoc "Coalition Against Bigotry and Violence." I sometimes jokingly tell people I'm personally responsible for Powell's deciding not to run for president, because when we got into the press conference, one of the people I'd handed the flyer to was a beautifully dressed woman whom I realized later was his wife.

3. U.S. General Accounting Office, *Military Personnel: High Aggregate Personnel Levels Maintained Throughout Drawdown* (Report to the Chairman, Committee on National Security, Subcommittee on Military Personnel, House of Representatives, June 1995), 11.

4. GAO, *Military Personnel*, 36.

5. Quoted by author Robert Fantina in *Desertion and the American Soldier, 1776–2006* (New York: Algora Publishing, 2006).

6. Or, rather, a splinter of VVAW formed by its remaining Maoist "anti-imperialist" wing. Given my own inquiry into such groups' soldier outreach through history, I pressed Paterson on this when we talked in Oakland in 2006, but he said no one else was doing similar outreach in Hawaii. "No one else even seemed interested," he said.

7. Personal conversation, 2006, Oakland, California.

8. "Gulf War Resister Jeff Paterson: Up Against the Machine," Q&A, *Revolutionary Worker* #1087, January 21, 2001, posted at http://rwor.org.

9. Dan Fahey, "The 2 to 7 Watch," in Maxine Hong Kingston, ed., *Veterans of War, Veterans of Peace* (Honolulu: Koa Books, 2006), 95.

10. Fahey, "The 2 to 7 Watch," 96.

11. Or at least they did between 1995 and 2000, when I was answering the GI Rights Hotline. (I went from Communications to GI Advocacy Coordinator, and by 2000 was supervising a team of volunteer counselors.)

12. Aimee Allison, "You May Face Discrimination," in Elizabeth Weill-Greenberg, ed., *Ten Excellent Reasons Not to Join the Military* (New Press, 2006).

13. Interview, January 1998, first published as Q&A interview in *The Objector*, Spring 1998, 10.

14. Interview, January 1998.

15. La Tricia Ransom and Mary Ann Humphrey, "Pentagon's Own Reports Refute Military's Stand on Gays," *The Oregonian*, January 27, 1993.

16. Joshua Holland, "The First Iraq War Was Also Sold to the Public Based on a Pack of Lies," BillMoyers.com, August 2014. Also see Tom Regan, "When Contemplating War, Beware of Babies in Incubators," *Christian Science Monitor*, September 6, 2002.

17. Charles Sheehan Miles, "Swift Boat Atrocities and Why War Always Sucks," CommonDreams.org, August 30, 2004.

18. Phone interview, fall 2015.

19. Stephen Zavestoski, Phil Brown, Meadow Linder, Sabrina McCormick, and Brian Mayer, "Science, Policy, Activism, and War: Defining the Health of Gulf War Veterans," *Science, Technology, & Human Values* 27, no. 2 (spring 2002), 171–205.

20. An army nurse who had been at Khamisiyah reported: "I can tell you now that the symptoms of Gulf War illness began to appear when we hit Riyadh and then as we moved forward thru [*sic*] [King Khalid Military City] to our forward location. We just were not fully aware of what the symptoms were representing at the time. . . . When you are in a desert environment and you are at war your job and duty comes first." Nichols, 2007 testimony, available online at http://veterans.house .gov/hearings.

21. Zavestoski et al., "Defining the Health of Gulf War Veterans," 189.

22. M.V. Ziehmn, memo to Studies and Analysis Branch, Los Alamos National Laboratory, Subject: "The Effectiveness of Depleted Uranium Penetrators," March 1, 1991; LTC Gregory K. Lyle, US Army, memorandum to Director, U.S. Defense

Nuclear Agency, "Item of Interest: Depleted Uranium (DU) Ammunition," March 1991. Via Dan Fahey, "Depleted Legitimacy: The U.S. Study of Gulf War Veterans Exposed to Depleted Uranium," Presentation at National Gulf War Resource Center Conference, Atlanta, Georgia, May 4, 2002.

23. Dennis Kyne, quoted in Vietnam Veterans Against the War, *From Vietnam to Iraq: The Veteran Healthcare Crisis* (2005).

24. Charles Sheehan Miles, "Introduction," in *Saving the World on Thirty Dollars a Day: An Activist's Guide to Starting, Organizing and Running a Non-Profit Organization* (Cincinnatus Press, 2014).

25. Janice Harper, "Toxic Wars and Bodies Exposed: A Political Ecology of Health Analysis of Gulf War Syndrome," Paper at the Environmental Politics Colloquium, University of California–Berkeley, September 26, 2008. "The explanatory models of Gulf War Syndrome incorporate [the American] flag in contrasting ways, whether as a symbol of democracy through which sufferers seek and expect equal access to health care resources, or as a symbol of imperialist disregard for those who are exposed to the toxic weapons of conquest."

26. The group's spokespeople already spent much of their time contending with reporters and advocates who saw in the military an important bright spot for young people of color.

27. Norman Solomon, "Slick Torch," *Guernica, A Magazine of Art and Politics*, October 2007.

28. Mike Oliver, "New Fight for Peace for Vietnam Veteran," *Orlando Sentinel*, December 11, 1990.

29. Ellen Barfield, "The Losers After War, Part Two," *Oklahoma Peace Strategy News*, December–January 1991–92, 15.

30. Barfield quotes here are from Richard O'Mara: "She gives peace a chance. Volunteer: In her own quiet way, Ellen Barfield is trying to make the world a more humane place to live. She does it by helping the people of Iraq." *Baltimore Sun*, February 16, 1998. Soon, Barfield and other Veterans for Peace would also convene a specific VFP task force on water in Iraq, which as I write still maintains an Iraq Water Project.

31. Testimony in film *Hidden Wars of Desert Storm* (2000), by Gerard Ungerman and Audrey Brophy.

32. See Kathleen Belew, *Bring the War Home: The White Power Movement and Paramilitary America* (Harvard University Press, 2019).

33. Interview, San Diego, June 2006.

34. Genevieve Anton, "Military Chooses to Battle AIDS with Regulations / Some

Say Rules Are Too Harsh," *Colorado Springs Gazette*, June 21, 1992, A1.

35. Jackie Spinner, "The New Drill Sergeant: No More Cussing, No More Abuse," *Washington Post Magazine*, August 24, 1997. Accessed at http://www.washingtonpost.com/wp-srv/local/longterm/library/aberdeen/main.htm.

36. Telephone interview, August 2016.

37. Anne-Marie Cusac, "You're in the Hole: A Crackdown on Dissident Prisoners," *Progressive*, December 2001.

Chapter Twelve: 2001 to 2020

1. Hogg said this to numerous journalists and was quoted in outlets from *The Advocate* to *Women's Voices for Change* (which employed this author at the time).

2. Dee Knight, "Iraq Vets Call for Winter Soldier Investigation," *Workers World*, January 17, 2008.

3. Veterans for Common Sense op-ed, "Sounds Fishy, Mr. President," October 28, 2002.

4. Todd Ensign, "Army Reservist Ghanim Khalil, Announces that He'll Refuse to Deploy," *Citizen Soldier* (newsletter), February 2003.

5. Jennifer Hogg, "March 20," in Lovella Callica, ed., *Warrior Writers: Move, Shoot and Communicate: A Collection of Antiwar Writing* (Iraq Veterans Against the War, 2007).

6. Funk also has a ceremonial Native name meaning "he who stands for horses." His Anglo first name is that of a dead soldier-uncle.

7. Personal interview, January 2006. All of the Funk quotes are from that interview, conducted in San Francisco, California.

8. Interview, January 2006, San Francisco.

9. GI Rights Network data, via Center on Conscience and War.

10. The press, swept up in what a former *Newsweek* editor later called "war fever" as it embedded its reporters with military units and broadcast the initial "shock and awe" bombing campaign, had given less-than-full scrutiny to the December 2002 claims about Iraqi weapons programs made at the UN by Secretary of State Colin Powell. One of *Newsweek*'s top reporters, Michael Isikoff, "was getting some cautionary signals from the CIA, which we did not pursue the way we should have," said the editor (himself ironically the grand-nephew of World War I resister Evan Thomas).

11. Interview, January 2007.

12. Michael Kazin, "Howard Zinn's History Lessons," *Dissent*, October 2004.

13. Bob Herbert, "From 'Gook' to Raghead," *New York Times*, May 2, 2005.

14. Not the "hard site" of later scandal, but the thousands of prisoners living in filthy tents outside it.

15. Camilo Mejia, personal interview, Philadelphia, January 2011.

16. Jonathan Wesley Hutto, *Anti-War Soldier: How to Dissent Within the Ranks of the Military* (Nation Books, 2008), 18.

17. Hutto, *Anti-War Soldier*, 22.

18. "Knowing the situation does not end the economic compulsion to join," Hutto, *Anti-War Soldier*.

19. Post reprinted in the message board for democraticunderground.com, November 5.

20. United States Senate Intelligence Committee, *Study of the Central Intelligence Agency's Detention and Interrogation Program*, S. Report 113-288, December 9, 2014.

21. Brandon Neely, Testimony to the Center for the Study of Human Rights in the Americas, University of California at Davis, February 2009.

22. Joshua Phillips, *None of Us Were Like This Before: American Soldiers and Torture* (Penguin, 2010).

23. Phillips, *None of Us Were Like This Before*.

24. A sneak reference to Tim O'Brien's landmark book, *The Things They Carried*, about Vietnam soldiers in an equally questionable war.

25. Seymour Hersh, "The Unknown Unknowns of the Abu Ghraib Scandal," *Guardian UK*, May 5, 2005. Hersh's source "told me that a family member, a young woman, was among those members of the 320th Military Police Battalion, to which the 372nd was attached, who had returned to the U.S. in March 2004."

26. Phillips, *None of Us Were Like This Before*, 119.

27. Jodi Wilgoren, "Citing Prison Abuse and Iraq 'Failures,' Kerry Demands That Rumsfeld Step Down," *New York Times*, August 26, 2004.

28. The group was composed of conservative operatives led by John O'Neill, who'd first been tasked with destroying Kerry by Nixon himself—determined to puncture that war-hero image.

29. Matthew Power, "Confessions of a Drone Warrior," *Gentleman's Quarterly*, October 23, 2013, via https://www.gq.com/story/drone-uav-pilot-assassination.

30. Michael Hedges, "Anti-war Protesters Go After Bush at Home," *Houston Chronicle*, August 7, 2005.

31. Ken Rudin, "Long-time War Hawk, Murtha Is an Angry Dove," National Public Radio, November 18, 2005.

32. "A Brief History of Veterans for Peace," accessed at https://www .veteransforpeace.org/files/5313/3373/6024/vfp_history.pdf.

33. Nan Levinson, *War Is Not a Game: The New Antiwar Soldiers and the Movement They Built* (Rutgers University Press, 2014), 108.

34. Christian Parenti, "When G. I. Joe Says No," *The Nation*, April 24, 2006.

35. Tom Barton, *GI SPECIAL* (e-newsletter), 4J28B, October 28, 2006. Barton, a civilian, was Jeff Sharlet's partner in producing *Vietnam GI* until Sharlet's death, and in 2006 founded the Military Project, whose activists leaflet Reserve units before drill.

36. Marjorie Cohn and Kathleen Gilberd, *Rules of Disengagement: The Politics and Honor of Military Dissent* (New York University Press, 2009), 79.

37. Interview, Washington, DC, February 2007.

38. Hutto, *Anti-War Soldier*.

39. "GIs Petition Congress to End Iraq War: More Than 1,000 Military Personnel Sign Petition Urging Withdrawal,"*60 Minutes*, February 22, 2006.

40. Voice of America, "Congressional Democrats Look Forward to Votes on Iraq War Resolutions," November 1, 2007.

41. Jennifer Hogg, "Military Women: Ready to Rock the Boat," WomensMediaCenter.com, July 18, 2008.

42. Margaret Stevens, *Red International and Black Caribbean: Communists in New York City, Mexico and the West Indies, 1919–1939* (Pluto Press, 2018).

43. Telephone interview, July 30, 2019.

44. These included a scandal at Walter Reed Army Hospital's Building 18, where active-duty soldiers went for outpatient treatment, assembled in formation, and "lived amid mice, mold and mismanagement." Via Michael Weisskopf, "The Two Worlds of Walter Reed," *Time*, February 23, 2007.

45. Karen Seal et al., "Bringing the War Back Home: Mental Health Disorders Among US Veterans Returning From Iraq and Afghanistan," *Journal of the American Medical Association*, March 12, 2007.

46. Dora Apel, *War Culture and the Contest of Images* (Rutgers University Press, 2012), 79.

47. Performance-studies scholars have gone deep with this analysis, including Cami Rowe's book *The Politics of Protest and US Foreign Policy: Performative Construction of the War on Terror* (Routledge, 2013) and Erica Caldwell's 2012 Indiana

University thesis, "Bringing the War Home: Rhetoric of Space and Place in Operation First Casualty."

48. As stylized in form as OFC was, there were concrete consequences. Appeal co-founder Liam Madden was informed on June 25 that he was being dropped from his obligatory Individual Ready Reserve training with an Other-than-Honorable discharge. Why? He'd worn a partial uniform at protests, and had said at one peace rally that "The war in Iraq is, by Nuremberg standards, a war crime and a war of aggression" and "the president has betrayed U.S. service members by committing them to a war crime." The charging memo, with the added charge of "making disloyal statements," seemed to allege even though Madden was a civilian, military free-speech limits still applied.

49. Chris Lombardi, "Iraq Vets Make Memorial Day Maneuvers in NYC," *Chelsea Now*, June 1–7, 2007, 4. (Yeah, I snuck work for the book into my day gig.) Full disclosure: Brower was also speaking on behalf of World Can't Wait, a front organization for the Revolutionary Communist Party, descended from the group that helped destroy VVAW in the 1970s.

50. "There are pictures of children who were wounded and barely clinging to life, and some who appeared to be dead. There was a close-up of a soldier who was holding someone's severed leg. There were photos of Iraqis with the deathlike state of shock, stunned by the fact that something previously unimaginable had just happened to them. There were photos of GIs happily posing with the bodies of dead Iraqis." Bob Herbert, "Lifting the Censor's Veil on the Shame in Iraq," *New York Times*, May 5, 2005.

51. Transcript excerpted in Aaron Glantz, *Winter Soldier, Iraq and Afghanistan: Eyewitness Accounts of the Occupations* (Haymarket, 2009).

52. "It was just hard, the money drying up," then president Liam Madden told a documentarian years later.

53. Fabio Rojas and Michael Heaney, "The Partisan Dynamics of Contention: Demobilization of the Antiwar Movement in the United States, 2007–2009," *Mobilization: An International Journal* 16, no. 1 (spring 2011), 45–64.

54. Shane Harris, *@WAR: The Rise of the Military-Internet Complex* (Houghton Mifflin, 2014).

55. SWAN's Jenn Hogg testified at an unprecedented House hearing on female veterans' affairs, telling lawmakers and generals alike about healthcare inequities and military sexual trauma, and found congressional allies to introduce bills such as the 2010 "Sexual Trauma Response, Oversight and Good Governance Act." Anna Mulrine, "Unseen Foe for Troops: Sexual Assault in US Military," *Christian Science Monitor*, April 29, 2011.

56. Anu Bhagwati, now SWAN's executive director, avoided the anti-war vets she'd joined at Camp Casey, joining a centrist "Voices of Honor" tour that pressed to honor gays who were also good militarists with an immediate end to DADT. Human Rights Campaign, "Anuradha Bhagwati," July 31, 2009. "Speaking as part of the Voices of Honor tour to build support for the repeal of the Don't Ask, Don't Tell policy, Anuradha Bhagwati—a former Marine Corps officer and executive director of Service Women's Action Network—speaks out against the military's ban on gay servicemembers."

57. DADT, Choi added, "goes against every single thing that we were taught at West Point with our honor code, [which] says that a cadet will not lie, cheat, steal . . ." Neither the first nor last to cite his own military honor code to explain his dissent, Choi became the public face of the movement for DADT repeals—even more than the officers suing to remain in, like flight nurse Major Margaret Witt, who'd been cut after an eighteen-year career, just short of retirement.

58. The White House refused to act without legislative cover, incensing David Mixner, friend of the late Leonard Matlovich. "Listen, the president can issue a stop-loss order today." As Mixner told me in 2009, "Say we're fighting two wars, we need all our people, all discharges for homosexuality suspended until further notice. He's commander-in-chief: he could keep them from being dismissed today."

59. The first time, almost a year to the day after coming out on national TV, Choi stood silently in his desert camouflage uniform while a GetEqual colleague tweeted, "Memo to Lt Choi, et al: Obama doesn't really care about you. move along & be patient—he may have use for you in 2012."

60. Dana Priest and William Arkin, "A Hidden World, Growing Beyond Control," *Washington Post*, July 19, 2010.

61. "From 22,300 miles in space, where seven Advanced Orion crafts now orbit; to a 1-million-square-foot building in the Utah desert that stores data intercepted from personal phones, emails, and social media accounts; to taps along the millions of miles of undersea cables that encircle the Earth like yarn, U.S. surveillance expanded exponentially after Obama's inauguration on Jan. 20, 2009," James Bamford, "Every Move You Make," *Foreign Policy*, September 7, 2016.

62. Catherine Lutz, "Obama's Empire: An Unprecedented Network of Military Bases That Is Still Expanding," *Foreign Policy in Focus*, July 30, 2009.

63. Michael J. Glennon, "National Security and Double Government," 5 *Harvard National Security Journal* 1 (2014).

64. The counselor later told *New York Magazine*, "Ultimately, some guy loosely connected to the group got killed. . . . [Manning] was very, very distressed." Steve Fishman, "Bradley Manning's Army of One," *New York Magazine*, July 11, 2011.

65. Mark Boal, "The Kill Team: How U.S. Soldiers in Afghanistan Murdered Innocent Civilians," *Rolling Stone*, March 27, 2011.

66. Unpublished manuscript 2012, shared by Bryant in 2016.

67. Darryl Fears, "Protesters Arrested at Quantico as Rally for Alleged WikiLeaks Source Turns Tense," *Washington Post*, March 21, 2011.

68. "John Kerry Defends Drone Strikes," *Agence France Press*, June 1, 2013.

69. Deidre Fulton, "New Billboards in DC Encourage Whistleblowers to Come Forward," *Common Dreams*, July 9, 2014.

70. Stephen Funk, "Make Drag, Not War!" *Huffington Post*, November 11, 2011.

71. Mark Mazzetti and Eric Schmitt, "Pentagon Seeks to Knit Foreign Bases into Isis-Foiling Network," *New York Times*, December 10, 2015.

72. Spencer Ackerman, "New Afghanistan Pact Means America's Longest War Will Last Until at Least 2024," *Guardian UK*, September 30, 2014.

73. Neither did the event include the year's solidarity with Black Lives Matter, in a campaign Veterans for Peace called "Safe Abroad, Safe at Home," spearheaded by Margaret Stevens.

74. Logan Mehl-Laituri (Isaac's former name), "What Terrible Wisdom, What Awful Power to Unmake: Surveying Moments of Moral Identity During War," MDiv thesis, July 2013.

75. Steve Rose, "Fighting Dirty: Could Michael Bay's Benghazi Movie Take Down Hillary Clinton?" *Guardian UK*, January 27, 2016.

76. Kerry Howley, "The World's 'Biggest Terrorist' Has a Pikachu Bedspread," *New York Magazine*, December 25, 2017.

77. Interview via Facebook Messenger, March 2018.

78. On her way out, Winner was awarded a fulsome commendation: "Airman Winner provided over 1,900 hours of enemy intelligence exploitation and assisted in geolocating 120 enemy combatants during 734 airborne sorties (air missions). . . . She facilitated 816 intelligence missions, 3,236 time-sensitive reports, and removing more than 100 enemies from the battlefield. Furthermore, while deployed to support Combatant Command Airman Winner was appointed as the lead deployment language analyst, producing 2,500 reports, aiding in 650 enemy captures, 600 enemies killed in action and identifying 900 high value targets."

79. Howley, "The World's 'Biggest Terrorist.'"

80. That was to me, who asked about the International Criminal Court for Women's Enews in September 2000.

81. This author met Manning at one such appearance, at the University of

Pennsylvania. I even blogged about it: Chris Lombardi, "The day I Finally Met Chelsea Manning," https://aintmarching.net/2017/12/01/the-day-i-finally-met-chelsea -manning.

82. R. Robin McDonald, "Reality Winner's Lawyers Say FBI Interrogation Was Unconstitutional," *National Law Reporter*, February 28, 2018.

83. Dave Phillips, "Reality Winner, Former NSA Translator, Gets More Than 5 Years for Leak of Russian Hacking Report," *New York Times*, August 23, 2018.

84. Nearly a decade after Manning's leak, Assange and WikiLeaks were no longer the progressive darlings they'd been under the Bush and Obama administrations. Assange spent most of that decade being sheltered by the Ecuadorian embassy, resisting sexual-assault charges in Sweden; meanwhile, WikiLeaks had since published leaks from the Democratic National Committee, abetted by Russian intelligence and praised by candidate Trump, who said on TV, "I love WikiLeaks!" An indictment of Assange in the United States, drawn up under Obama but rejected under First Amendment grounds, had been issued under Trump, focused solely on Manning's 2010 leaks. A grand jury was convened, which called Manning as one of its first witnesses. Manning was already skeptical of the grand-jury process, which long had been used to demand confidential information from privacy experts and alternative-media outlets. She also did not know how much of that information was now classified. By refusing to testify, Manning was enacting her beliefs every day.

85. Email from CCW director Maria Santelli, July 26, 2019. Prior to Santelli's hire in 2012, the center did not keep statistics on their case results.

86. Rosa Del Duca, "Steve Collier," *Breaking Cadence* podcast, November 2018.

87. Jonathan Wesley Hutto, "To Fight Imperialism, Organize Soldiers and Veterans," *Democratic Left*, June 24, 2019. Full disclosure; I guest-edited that issue of the Democratic Socialists of America's quarterly, and asked Hutto (whom I met in 2007) to be a contributor.